MISCELLANEOUS ESSAYS AND ADDRESSES

MISCELLANEOUS
ESSAYS AND ADDRESSES

BY

HENRY SIDGWICK

London
MACMILLAN AND CO., Limited
NEW YORK: THE MACMILLAN COMPANY
1904
KRAUS REPRINT CO.
New York
1968

L.C. Catalog Card Number 5-7890

KRAUS REPRINT CO.
A U.S. Division of Kraus-Thomson Organization Limited

Printed in U.S.A.

PREFATORY NOTE

HENRY SIDGWICK had long intended to collect together essays and addresses written by him at different times; and some essays on ethical subjects he had published under the title of *Practical Ethics* in the "Ethical Library" series (Swan Sonnenschein and Co.) in 1898. The volume now published contains miscellaneous essays on other subjects. Several of them were specified by the author during the last few weeks of his life as suitable for such a collection, though with some hesitation in one or two cases. After due consideration, all the papers that he named have been included; and we have added a few others, which seemed likely to be of interest to the general reader. We have not included any of the papers published in *Mind*; some of them will appear more appropriately along with some hitherto unpublished philosophical lectures in a volume which is being edited by Professor James Ward.

It will be seen that the papers fall mostly into three divisions, according as they deal with literature, economics and sociology, or education; and it seemed best to arrange them, within the limits of each division, in chronological order. The only exceptions are the essay on *Bentham and Benthamism*, which we have placed between the literary and economic groups, and the essay on *Alexis de Tocqueville*, which has been printed at the end of the volume as a supplement. This paper was written when the author was twenty-three, and, not being among those specified by him, could hardly find a place among the maturer essays which compose the rest of the book; but it seemed of sufficient interest not to be omitted altogether.

With the exception of the two papers on Shakespeare, all those in the volume have been published before—most of them in Reviews and Magazines, *The Scope and Method of Economic Science* and *The Pursuit of Culture as an Ideal* separately, and *The Theory of a Classical Education* in a volume of essays. Thanks are due to Publishers and Editors for their kind consent to republication.

ELEANOR MILDRED SIDGWICK.
ARTHUR SIDGWICK.

CONTENTS

		PAGE
1.	ECCE HOMO (*Westminster Review*, July 1866)	1
2.	THE PROPHET OF CULTURE (*Macmillan's Magazine*, August 1867)	40
3.	THE POEMS AND PROSE REMAINS OF ARTHUR HUGH CLOUGH (*Westminster Review*, October 1869)	59
4.	SHAKESPEARE'S METHODS, WITH SPECIAL REFERENCE TO *JULIUS CÆSAR* AND *CORIOLANUS*	91
5.	SHAKESPEARE AND THE ROMANTIC DRAMA, WITH SPECIAL REFERENCE TO *MACBETH*	120
6.	BENTHAM AND BENTHAMISM IN POLITICS AND ETHICS (*Fortnightly Review*, May 1877)	135
7.	THE SCOPE AND METHOD OF ECONOMIC SCIENCE. An Address given as President of the Economic Science and Statistics Section of the British Association in 1885	170
8.	ECONOMIC SOCIALISM (*Contemporary Review*, November 1886)	200
9.	POLITICAL PROPHECY AND SOCIOLOGY (*National Review*, December 1894)	216
10.	THE ECONOMIC LESSONS OF SOCIALISM (*Economic Journal*, September 1895)	235
11.	THE RELATION OF ETHICS TO SOCIOLOGY (*International Journal of Ethics*, October 1899)	249
12.	THE THEORY OF CLASSICAL EDUCATION. (From *Essays on a Liberal Education*, edited by F. W. Farrar. Macmillan and Co., 1867)	270
13.	IDLE FELLOWSHIPS (*Contemporary Review*, April 1876)	320
14.	A LECTURE AGAINST LECTURING (*New Review*, May 1890)	340
15.	THE PURSUIT OF CULTURE AS AN IDEAL. A Lecture delivered to the students of the University College of Wales, Aberystwith, in October 1897	352

SUPPLEMENT

ALEXIS DE TOCQUEVILLE (*Macmillan's Magazine*, November 1861)   361

ERRATA

Page 64, line 11 from foot, *for* "but the term was somewhat indefinite" *read* "but the term is somewhat indefinite."

For footnote to page 168, end of first paragraph, see page 374.

I

ECCE HOMO [1]

(Westminster Review, July 1866)

FEW persons who have read through *Ecce Homo* will be prepared to deny, whatever faults they may find with its methods and conclusions, that it possesses very remarkable positive merits. As the present article will unavoidably be made up chiefly of censure and criticism, we wish at the outset to give most warm and sincere praise to the originality of the conception, the vigour of its execution, the sympathetic intensity with which the writer has grasped the chief points in the character and work of Jesus, the flowing and fervid eloquence with which he has impressed them on his readers. His conceptions are, of course, partly old, partly new; whatever we may think of the latter element, we willingly admit that he has made us feel the old as if it were new. It requires genius to produce this effect: and genius of a certain kind our author possesses. His book will probably have a most beneficial operation, especially among the persons whose impression will be that the author has preached them a series of good sermons, and meanwhile contrived somehow to set Christianity upon a basis impregnable to the assaults of modern criticism and science.

---

[1] *Ecce Homo: a Survey of the Life and Works of Jesus Christ.* 8vo. 4th edition. London: Macmillan. 1866.

[This book, now known to be by J. R. Seeley, was published anonymously, as was this article on it; but Sidgwick and Seeley were friends, and by the time the review was published each was aware of what the other had written, and they had already been in correspondence about the book.—ED.]

At the same time the author might fairly complain if we treated his book as belonging to the class which, as a literary cynic has said, tend to edification rather than instruction. It claims to be much more: it is clearly the result of a good deal of general reading and reflection; and eminent and cultivated persons have spoken of it as if it were likely to have a permanent influence on the thought of students. As we have a strong conviction that it is not calculated to produce this effect, it seems desirable that we should support this conviction by a close examination of its principal features.

The first thing that will surprise a student who has taken up the book is the total absence of any introductory discussion of the evidence on which the historical portion of the book is intended to be based. Considering that we derive our knowledge of the facts from a limited number of documents, handed down to us from an obscure period, and containing matter which in any other history we should regard as legendary: considering that in consequence these documents have been subjected for many years to an elaborate, minute, and searching investigation: that hundreds of scholars have spent their lives in canvassing such questions as the date of their composition, their authorship, the conscious objects or unconscious tendency of each author, his means of information, and his fidelity to fact, the probability of their being compiled or translated from previous works in whole or part, or of their having undergone revisions since the original publication, the contradictions elicited by careful examination of each or close comparison of them together, the methods of reconciling these contradictions or deciding between conflicting evidence, and many other similar points,—it might seem natural that the author of such a work as this should carefully explain to his readers his plan and principles for settling or avoiding these important preliminary questions. But by a *bizarre* arrangement of his matter, the author defers all discussion of this subject till he has reached his fifth chapter, entitled " Christ's Credentials." In this chapter he gives us, still fragmentarily and incidentally, his notions of historical criticism; and as we get nothing further from him on this important topic, it is desirable to examine the chapter somewhat closely.

He begins by saying, that, in his previous chapters, he "has not entered into controvertible matter": the inaccuracy of this statement, even as tested by his own definition of "controvertible matter," we pass by for the present, being eager to come to that definition. "We have not," he continues, "rested upon single passages, nor drawn upon the fourth gospel." Uncontrovertible matter, therefore, seems to be whatever the synoptic gospels have in common. If this were all that had been evolved, after the trouble spent in examining the relation between the three first gospels, it would be a somewhat meagre and jejune result; but let that pass. It is clear that, whatever else the synoptic gospels have in common, they all contain a number of miraculous stories. We hasten, therefore, to see what he will say of miracles; and what he does say of them is so extraordinary, that, for fear of misrepresenting him, we must quote the whole passage, referring at the same time to page 10, where similar views are indicated.

It will be thought by some that in asserting miracles to have been actually wrought by Christ we go beyond what the evidence, perhaps beyond what any possible evidence, is able to sustain. Waiving then for the present the question whether miracles were actually wrought, we may state a fact which is fully capable of being established by ordinary evidence, and which is actually established by evidence as ample as any historical fact whatever—the fact, namely, that Christ *professed* to work miracles. We may go further, and assert with confidence that Christ was believed by his followers really to work miracles, and that it was mainly on this account that they conceded to him the pre-eminent dignity and authority which he claimed. The accounts we have of these miracles may be exaggerated; it is possible that in some special cases stories have been related which have no foundation whatever; but, on the whole, miracles play so important a part in Christ's scheme that any theory which would represent them as due entirely to the imagination of his followers or of a later age destroys the credibility of the documents not partially but wholly, and leaves Christ a personage as mythical as Hercules. Now the present treatise aims to show that the Christ of the Gospels is not mythical, by showing that the character those biographies portray is in all its large features strikingly consistent, and at the same time so peculiar as to be altogether beyond the reach of invention both by individual genius and still more by what is called the 'consciousness of an age.' Now if the character depicted in the Gospels is in the main real and historical, they must be generally trustworthy, and, if so, the responsibility of miracles is fixed on Christ. In this case the reality of the miracles themselves depends in a great degree on the opinion we form of Christ's veracity, and this opinion must arise gradually from the careful examination of his whole life. For our present purpose, which is to investigate the plan which Christ formed and the way in which he executed it, it matters nothing whether the miracles were real or imaginary; in either case, being believed to be real, they had the same effect. Provisionally, therefore, we may speak of them as real.

Now every line of this seems to us to show ignorance or misapprehension of the question at issue, as at present understood by the most intelligent advocates on either side of the controversy. He states the dilemma as it was stated in the eighteenth century, but as we never expected to see it stated again, except in the official rhetoric of the less educated clergy. "Christ professed to work miracles; therefore, either he did work them, and was possessed of supernatural power, or he did not work them and was unveracious." Now German criticism for many years past has always started with the negation of both alternatives, and with the two assumptions which our author declares to be irreconcilable. The student who treats the gospel narratives historically—in using the word, we intend no *petitio principii*, but simply to express in a word, "according to the method applied everywhere else in history"— does not regard the reality of miracles as a question of more or less evidence, to be decided by presumptions with regard to the veracity of witnesses. If by miracle is meant a violation, or—if the word be invidious—transcendence of the laws of nature, or—if the phrase be ambiguous— the uniformities of our physical experience, he rejects the notion absolutely. If he admits one miracle, he is no longer competent, as historian, to say how many more he will admit, and whether any are to be repudiated; the theologian has to decide from principles peculiar to himself how much fictitious matter an inspired writer may be allowed to insert, and how much interference is consistent with the Divine wisdom. On the other hand, it is regarded as equally certain—though the certainty is of a different kind—that Jesus was not a wilful deceiver.[1] The whole constructive work of the critical school is based on the attempt to show that what our author assumes to be impossible may be done, that we can distinguish between history and legend in the biography of Jesus, without supposing him to have "professed to work miracles," unless we call phenomena not contrary to the analogy of experience by that name. Such are the cures of the so-called demoniacs and of persons afflicted with certain other diseases—those, namely, in which the influence of the nervous system may be believed to be occasionally very great. No one thinks of denying that, as far as these go, Jesus did and was believed to do what appeared to him and to others "mighty works." But it is a very different thing to assume that he was believed by himself and others to possess "boundless supernatural power." This theory and all that the author has based upon it[2] must be regarded as decidedly controvertible matter. To speak of miracles "provisionally as real" is the one thing that no one will do. The question of their reality stands at the threshold of the subject, and can by no device be conjured away.

We see then that the critical school will hardly admit that all that the synoptic gospels have in common may be relied upon as certain. It will be fairly urged that the rejection of miracles proper—as we may call what is inexplicable in accordance with the known laws of experience

[1] The partial acquiescence in deception, attributed to him by M. Renan, has found, we believe, no more favour in Germany than in England.

[2] Among other statements we are told that the Pharisees conceived Jesus to be capable of boundless mischief. The truth is, they conceived him to be a successful exorcist: no unique phenomenon, as is proved by Matt. xii. 24-27, to which our author refers. Cf. also Acts xix. 13-16.

—involves such destructive effects, that we require certain methods of reconstruction before we can deal with the documents at all. The phenomena the student has now before him are not miracles but the records of miracles, legends, myths, semi-legends, semi-myths, or whatever else he may call them. He has to account for them; and whether he treats them rationalistically, or semi-rationalistically, or on the principle of Mythus, or on the principle of "Tendenz," or by some process intermediary between, or compounded of these, whatever method he uses will necessarily affect his view of the rest of the gospel narratives. He must treat these latter as a whole: he cannot explain the composition of a part of them without, at the same time, determining the degree of authenticity possessed by the rest. It is very possible that he may come to the conclusion that certain other statements "common to the synoptic gospels" are not to be relied on. Thus, again, the question of miracles stands at the threshold of the subject in a way that seems never to have occurred to our author. It is possible that he may have good reasons for relying on the particular portions of the narrative which he has quoted and referred to; but if he writes for persons who "provisionally" reject miracles—and he seems to do so—he is bound to give these reasons. This self-confident construction, this arbitrary settlement, without vouchsafing an argument, of questions that have been long and elaborately discussed, would have been put forth in Germany by no man of equal ability with our author, not even by Ewald. The first chapter will afford an excellent illustration of what we have been saying. In it we have an account of the relation between Jesus and John the Baptist, in which the author clearly thinks that he has exercised a sober criticism of his authorities, and that his results are scarcely "controvertible." Indeed, he afterwards goes so far as to suggest an explanation of the marvels recorded as following the baptism, which is conceived after the crass rationalism of the school of Paulus. The account is as follows:—

The Baptist addressed all who came to him in the same stern tone of authority. Young and old gathered round him, and among them must have been many whom he had known in earlier life, and some to whom he had been taught to look up with humility and respect. But in his capacity of prophet he made no distinction. All alike he exhorted to repentance ; all alike he found courage to baptize. In a single case, however, his confidence failed him. There appeared among the candidates a young man of nearly his own age, who was related to his family. We must suppose that he had had personal intercourse with Christ before ; for though one of our authorities represents John as saying that he knew him not except by the supernatural sign that pointed him out at his baptism, yet we must interpret this as meaning only that he did not before know him for his successor. For it appears that before the appearance of the sign John had addressed Christ with expressions of reverence, and had declared himself unfit to baptize him. After this meeting we are told that on several occasions he pointed out Christ as the hope of the nation, as destined to develop the work he himself had begun into something far more memorable, and as so greatly superior to himself, that, to repeat his emphatic words, he was not worthy to untie his shoe.

He proceeds to say that John described the "character" of Jesus by calling him the Lamb of God. This last statement, as it rests on an unusual interpretation of a passage in the fourth gospel, even our author can hardly regard as more than a plausible conjecture. As regards the passage we have quoted, the relationship between Jesus and John rests on the authority of the third gospel only ; John's declaration of his unfitness, etc., rests on the authority of the first gospel only—the several occasions are to be inferred from none of the synoptics ; the "emphatic words," though no doubt applied by the early Christians to Jesus, do not appear to have been said of him personally, but rather of the unknown Messiah, whose forerunner John conceived himself to be. All that we learn from the synoptics of the subsequent relations of Jesus and John implies anything rather than a recognition of the former by the latter as Messiah.

This is a sample of the author's carelessness even in

applying his own principles. At the same time he entirely ignores the view held, not merely by Strauss and the mythicists, but by scholars who differ as widely from this school as Schenkel does, viz. that Jesus was never recognised by John as Messiah. The arguments that support these views are these. The supernatural circumstances recorded as attending the baptism show that fact has here been at least to some extent modified by legend. What is afterwards told us of John, that he continued at the head of a school distinct from that of Jesus, and in certain points strikingly opposed to it, that towards the end of his life, as though struck for the first time with the possibility of Jesus being the expected Messiah, he sent to inquire into his claims, that he was not convinced of their validity (for if he had been we should have heard of it, nor would Jesus have spoken of him as less than the least in the kingdom of heaven),—all seems irreconcilable with the protestations and revelations at the baptism, even when the supernatural element in these has been carefully extracted. Again, tradition had a peculiar incentive to colour the facts of this baptism. It was difficult to explain why Jesus should have undergone this baptism of repentance at all, in accordance with the traditional view of his person and attributes. Therefore, it is urged, in a later development of the tradition, which has found its way into one only of the synoptic gospels, John is represented as feeling and expressing the difficulty, and Jesus as removing it.[1] In the fourth gospel the difficulty seems no longer felt, while the development of tradition has gone much further. This theory is naturally ignored by the orthodox, but it ought to have been at least noticed by a writer who treats his authorities with the freedom of our author.

In the next chapter, on the Temptation, we find the following critical principle enunciated:—

[1] If this suspicion is once admitted, the reply of Jesus will be seen to contain a very inadequate answer to the difficulty. The baptism had a particular symbolic meaning; it implied past sin, present repentance, and preparation for the expected Messiah: it could hardly come under the head of duties incumbent upon the Messiah as well as all other men ($\pi \acute{\alpha} \sigma \alpha \nu\ \delta \iota \kappa \alpha \iota o \sigma \acute{\upsilon} \nu \eta \nu$).

The account of the temptation, from whatever source derived, has a very striking internal consistency, a certain inimitable probability of improbability, if the expression may be allowed. That popular imagination which gives birth to rumours and then believes them, is not generally capable of great or sublime or well-sustained efforts.

Wunderthätige Bilder sind meist nur schlechte Gemälde.

The popular imagination is fertile and tenacious, but not very powerful or profound. Christ in the wilderness was a subject upon which the imagination would very readily work, but at the same time far too great a subject for it to work upon successfully; we should expect strange stories to be told of his adventures in such a solitude, but we should also expect the stories to be very childish.

It is curious that the writer should not see that if this principle can determine anything, it can decide everything. The miraculous stories of the New Testament, with hardly an exception, and the majority of the miraculous stories of the Old Testament, whatever else they are, are certainly not "childish." What, for instance, can be more "sublime and well-sustained" than that most incredible of Hebrew legends—the account of the ascent of Elijah? What imagination could be more "powerful and profound" than that which produced the story of the transfiguration? The tales of the apocryphal gospels *are* for the most part childish, and this has been fairly urged on the orthodox side as an argument for plenary inspiration. But if we reject this subjective and æsthetic criterion as decisive of the whole question, we cannot trust it in any particular case, nor profess to tell legend from fact by mere literary discrimination. We pass by, then, our author's theory of the Temptation as one among many plausible conjectures, with this objectionable peculiarity, that it is based on the supposed consciousness by Jesus of (apparently unbounded) supernatural powers. If this consciousness be supposed veracious, it must be left to the theologian to realise and explain; if a delusion, it is one which the historian will find no sufficient ground for attributing to Jesus.

The rest of the first part of the book is taken up with an account of the external side of Jesus' work: the position he took up, as distinguished from the doctrine he preached. We find throughout the same apparent ignorance of the views of the most eminent critics, the same careless or arbitrary application of the writer's own principles. Along with these we find much clear and vivid insight into human nature and the larger facts of classical and Hebrew history—much artistic grouping and felicitous expression of familiar truths, and some that are less familiar. But as a historical essay we must rank the result very low, as it contains none of the distinctions and limitations, none of the *nuances* of colouring, so important to a historical picture, which long-continued, free, and careful study of the gospels has gradually brought out. His fundamental notion is that Christ represented himself as king; that he "laid claim to the royal title;" that he "calls himself habitually king;" and that in this capacity he proceeded to form a society, pronounce judgments, issue laws. He never even alludes to the fact, which strikes the least intelligent reader of the gospels, that Jesus, while he continually proclaimed "the kingdom of Heaven," never once applied to himself the title of king. Even the view of traditional orthodoxy is more faithful to the facts, in this respect, than our author's. Every popular preacher tells us that Jesus, from his humility, chose for himself the title of "Son of Man." It has been the subject of much controversy, and must be regarded as still undecided, what associations precisely would be called up by this phrase in the minds of the contemporaries of Jesus—whether those which it would derive from Ezekiel and other passages of the Old Testament, or those which the authors of Daniel and the Book of Enoch attach to it. But that it would not be generally understood as equivalent to Messiah seems clear, among many passages, from Matt. xvi. 13-17. Here Jesus asks, "Whom do men say that I, the Son of Man, am?" and regards as a divine revelation Peter's reply, "Thou art the Christ." To one who takes the synoptic gospels by themselves, nothing can seem plainer than that Jesus did not declare himself to his disciples as Messiah, at any rate till some time after his appearance as a preacher, and that he took pains to prevent a belief in his Messiahship from spreading among the people. He is represented as rebuking the demons who did homage to him. From some passages we should infer that he tried to conceal his healing powers, and imposed, with this object, strict silence upon those whom he cured.[1] In proclaiming, therefore, the kingdom of God, he would seem by no means to proclaim himself as king; but simply to take up and echo, in a different strain, the teaching of John. All the passages to which our author refers, in support of the opposite theory, he colours more or less wrongly. Jesus claims "power on earth to forgive sins;" but he does so expressly as "Son of Man." Now "Son of Man" can only be made to mean "king" indirectly, as meaning Messiah, and this meaning, as we have seen, did not clearly attach to the phrase. Again, our author tells us that Jesus was asked whether tribute-money ought to be paid, as a "way of sifting his monarchical claims." The more usual—and surely more probable—explanation is that the question was put to him not as king but as Rabbi. It was selected by his adversaries to bring him into a disagreeable dilemma, from the known difficulty of reconciling religious duty (as it was conceived) with political expediency. Again, "Christ continued to speak of himself as king with such consistency and clearness that those who were nearest his person . . . quarrelled for places and dignities under him." It would be truer to say that he gradually led—without any *distinct* claim on his own part—his disciples to regard him as Messiah, which in their minds meant—*inter alia*—king. If he had ever spoken of himself as Messiah or king the chroniclers would certainly have told us. No doubt at the close of his career, on his last entry into Jerusalem, "he pointedly refused" to silence "those who hailed him as Son of David." But it seems hasty to infer from this that "he clung firmly to the title of king, and attached great importance to it." Our author states that

---

[1] Sometimes with singular vehemence. Cf. Mark i. 43, ἐμβριμησάμενος.

"the Jews procured his execution because . . . they could not forgive him for claiming royalty and at the same time rejecting the use of physical force . . . They did not object to the king, they did not object to the philosopher; but they objected to the king in the garb of a philosopher." Here the writer is partly indulging a vigorous imagination, partly relying on the fourth gospel alone. According to the synoptics, it was not "the Jews" generally who procured his execution, but their religious leaders;[1] and they did so not primarily because he was king or philosopher, but because he was a religious innovator, who threatened to pull down the temple. No doubt the mob deserted and mocked their fallen favourite; but this desertion was not the cause, but the effect, of his apparent fall. If he could not save himself, and come down from the cross, he was no king for them. It is certainly possible to hold very various opinions with respect to the gradual progress or unveiling of the claims of Jesus, from his first announcement of the kingdom of heaven to the σὺ λέγεις with which he replies to Pilate—a phrase which, though not proclamatory, is not evasive. There is no doubt that he ultimately claimed, and was understood to claim, to be Messiah; but when, how far, how clearly, did he make the claim? The question has many difficulties, and every one who forms a definite theory must depend much on conjecture. But as our author does not even recognise that there is this gradual progress or unveiling, it would take us too far from his book to discuss the question any further.

It follows that we cannot attach much value to his remarks on what he calls "Christ's Royalty." So long as Jesus was not looked upon as king, but simply as holding the keys of the kingdom of heaven, he would be to his disciples more what John was,—a teacher laying down precepts, rather than a king issuing ordinances. The people would regard him as a leader of a school or sect, differing from the Pharisees, Sadducees, or Essenes, as each of these

[1] Their mortal hostility is represented as being of ancient date. Cf. Mark iii. 6.

sects differed from the other; but like them all, basing itself on the law of Moses, and superadding its peculiar tenets. It is true that his hearers contrasted his bold free handling of morality with the anxious servility of the learned commentators. But it does not therefore follow that they regarded him as a rival of Moses or representative of Jehovah. Here again, in endeavouring to form an exact idea of the relations of the teaching of Jesus to the written or even to the oral law, we come upon difficulties to which our author scarcely alludes, and which he does not in the least help us to solve. These relations appear either progressive or inconsistent, as far as the indications in the synoptic gospels can be trusted. At one time Jesus avers that he is not come to destroy the law, that one jot or tittle shall in no wise pass from it, that no one shall break one of these least commandments without heavy penalties; at another time he compares the existing institutions, apparently, to old wine-skins and old raiment, and asserts that "the Son of Man is Lord of the Sabbath." And in his remarks on what "was said by them of old time," though he for the most part supplements the Mosaic law, he also distinctly condemns maxims that are to be found in it (so Matt. v. 38, 43, and reff.). Again, he tells his disciples to observe and do whatsoever the Scribes and Pharisees bid them observe, even, it would seem, to tithing mint and anise and cummin, for they, the Scribes and Pharisees (not Jesus himself, observe), sit in Moses' seat. Elsewhere he says that they make the word of God of none effect by their traditions, and attacks particular traditions with indignant vehemence: he also says that they bind upon men burdens grievous to be borne. These apparent contradictions are variously explained: sometimes by subtle interpretations of particular passages, sometimes by referring conflicting precepts to different periods of Jesus' career, sometimes by assuming that one or other of our present gospels has been the work of at least two hands (for instance, the combination of a "universalist" and a "particularist" in Matthew's gospel is a theory held by some Germans). We do not object to our author that he disagrees with any or all of the existing views on the subject, but that he does not seem aware that it is necessary for him to have a view at all. So of the limits to which Christ confined his preaching: at one time he sends his disciples to the lost sheep of the house of Israel, and forbids them to go among the Samaritans; he can hardly be brought to heal a Syrophœnician, and compares the race to dogs; elsewhere he indicates in parables, and once expressly declares, that the kingdom will be taken from the Jews and given to another nation. These contrasts admit of a similar variety of explanation: the author of *Ecce Homo* does not notice them. The consequence of all this is that the many good things he has to say about Christ's legislation are useless to the accurate reader in their present form, because the framework in which they are placed is so carelessly and clumsily constructed out of unsupported assumptions. When we find, for example, a writer stating that Jesus regarded baptism as an indispensable rite of initiation into his kingdom, supporting his statements on an external and political interpretation of the interview with Nicodemus, quite alien to the spiritualism of the fourth gospel, and getting over the awkward fact that Jesus is never represented in the synoptic gospels as baptizing, by means of the assumption that he regards John's baptism as sufficient,—we have an uneasy feeling that even what we admire in him may prove unsound when closely tested. We are obliged to take to pieces his vigorous rhetoric and rearrange it for ourselves, which is a great drawback to the thorough enjoyment of it.

The author says, in his preface, that he has reconsidered the whole subject from the beginning, traced the biography of Jesus from point to point, and accepted "those conclusions about him . . . which the facts themselves, critically weighed, appear to warrant." We willingly believe him quite sincere in this assertion, but we could not select more appropriate words to describe what, in our opinion, he has omitted to do. At least we find it hard to understand how a man who has gone through this process should then write

—" no important change took place in Christ's mode of thinking, speaking, or acting; at least the evidence before us does not enable us to trace any such change," without supporting this opinion by arguments. There is no more fruitful source of error in history than the determination to find the tree in the seed, and to attribute to the originators of important social changes detailed foresight as to the shape those changes were to assume. To this vulgar prejudice our author seems to have yielded without the least attempt at resistance or self-justification. Because Christianity was ultimately preached as a universal religion, he assumes that Jesus must have intended from the first to found a worldwide society, and totally ignores, as we have seen, the scattered indications of a more limited conception to be found in the gospels, and the fact that even after his death his disciples preached for some time only to Jews and proselytes. Because the effort to impose upon all members of the Christian Society, become universal, the obligations of the Mosaic law was abandoned after a struggle (which many critical historians consider to have been long and bitter): because, as the expectation of Christ's speedy advent grew faint, and his expectant Church began to organise itself for long life without a Head, the moral teaching of Jesus assumed more and more to his followers the character of a code of laws—it is inferred that he deliberately proposed to himself to supersede the Mosaic law by a new one promulgated on his own authority, no explanation being even suggested of the passages in which he expressly asserts the contrary. Because Jesus was perpetually and consistently exalted after his death by his followers, we are told that he perpetually and consistently exalts himself: because Christians felt that their intensest religious ardours, and their most powerful moral impulses, sprang from and were bound up in their personal devotion to their Master, our author tells us that " Christ claims to be a perpetual attractive power . . . to humanity struggling with its passions and its destiny he says, Cling to me, cling ever closer to me," and represents Jesus as intending this passion for himself to be the root and first principle of all morality in the Church. It is true that he might justify himself abundantly from the fourth gospel for this colouring. But here as elsewhere he quotes the language of the fourth gospel, and then adds that the expressions of the synoptics "give substantially the same meaning." This makes it difficult for us to believe that his acquaintance with the critical school can be very profound; for he seems to know that certain persons reject the fourth gospel, and yet not to know that the marked difference between it and the synoptics, with respect to this "self-exaltation," is one of the reasons which induces them to do so. We do not mean here, or generally, that our author's view is entirely wrong, but that it is wrongly coloured. If he would rewrite the passages in which it is expressed in conformity with the conclusions of criticism, he might still use a good deal of his present eloquence. No doubt the Jesus of the synoptics shows a remarkable contrast of humility of temper with consciousness of pre-eminence; but the precise combination of humility and self-exaltation which our author paints can only be obtained by forcibly mixing the colours of the fourth gospel with those of the three first. In the synoptics Jesus for some time consistently abstains from exalting himself; he occasionally refers to his example as a means of influencing his followers, but not more markedly than another revered teacher might do; and though, where he speaks openly of his Messiahship, he assumes obedience and reverence to be due to him, and regards the refusal to pay them as a grievous sin, yet he does not make this duty towards himself prominent in his inculcation of moral precepts. The author refers to the institution of the Lord's Supper to support his view; but it fails to do so until interpreted in the fourth gospel, and here we have another instance of his singular style of criticism. He speaks of St. John's discourse, "which we may quote without distrust, as it is so manifestly confirmed by the accounts given by the other Evangelists of the institution of the Supper." Now no critic that we are aware of, who 'distrusts' this gospel at all, excepts from his distrust the discourse referred to: the question among such critics is whether we are to regard it (with Strauss and Schenkel) as intended to give the spiritual counterpart and substitute for the too carnal institution of the Supper,[1] or merely a later spiritual interpretation of it. There is exactly the same question with regard to the discourse with Nicodemus, in the third chapter of this gospel, which, as we have seen, our author takes and interprets in a fashion entirely his own. There are good reasons for rejecting the fourth gospel as an accurate narrative; there are good reasons for accepting it as such; there may be good reasons for accepting part, and rejecting part, but our author certainly does not put them forward. At the same time the most suspicious critic would hardly deny that there may be an element of truth in this gospel very valuable, as supplementing the other three, and that it is in itself not improbable that Jesus recognised the importance of the singular personal influence that he exercised over other men, and even foresaw that it would continue and increase after his death; but that he intended a passionate devotion to himself to be the mainspring and motive-power of morality in his followers, we certainly should not infer from our authorities reasonably estimated.

We have next to consider what is, according to our author, the chief principle and supreme rule in the morality taught by Jesus—the trunk, or stem, springing from the passion which he regards as the root. This he develops at great length in what is, perhaps, the most striking and effective portion of his work; we can hardly hope to do justice to it in a scanty summary, but we may avoid any serious misrepresentation. Christ, he says, placed the happiness of man in a political constitution. He did not consider, as certain philosophies had done, each individual as an independent being, but as a member of a society. The great duty he requires from all who enter the kingdom of God is

[1] It is certainly singular, and tends to support this view, that there is no mention of the institution of the Supper in the fourth gospel; but this question, which is connected with the much discussed Passover controversy, we must pass by.

a disinterested sacrifice of self to the interests of the whole society. This sacrifice is to be made without a view to the ultimate interest of the individual: indeed, to be complete it demands of a man what he cannot do with a view to his ultimate interest, that he should love his enemies. He "issued from the Mount an edict of comprehension," asserting the unity of the human race, their equality before God, and fraternity under God's fatherhood. He made morality universal, thus *giving* to men what a philosopher or two had *claimed* for them but coldly and ineffectually. But for the better execution of this edict, instead of giving detailed laws to his society, he tried to evoke the law-making faculty in each member of it. Philosophers had tried the same thing, but they had wrongly regarded reason as the law-making faculty; Christ saw that passion could be only controlled by passion, and therefore his law-making faculty is a passionate, enthusiastic philanthropy, or, in our author's fine phrase, the enthusiasm of humanity. This enthusiastic condition of mind is what is meant by the πνεῦμα Ἅγιον of which we hear so much in the early Church. More closely examined it is discovered to be a love not of the race, nor of each individual, but of man as man, or of humanity in each individual. Thus Christ, for the first time, placed the love of man distinctly in the list of virtues. Morality had previously been negative; he discovered Positive Morality—a new continent in the moral globe.

Now if this had been put before us in a sermon as a spirited general sketch of what Christianity has been to the world—of the moral idea that it has generated among mankind—we should not have been disposed to find fault with it. But the biographer of Jesus, if he would be loyal to historic truth, must forget all about the subsequent development of Christianity, and endeavour to see Jesus as he appeared to his Jewish contemporaries. We hoped from our author's preface that he might have done this; but we feel that he has not, and that in consequence his portrait wants fidelity in details. We feel continually as we read—'This is what has been felt since Jesus, and what would not have been felt had it not been for Jesus; but it is not precisely what Jesus taught.' Here and there we feel that if Jesus planted, Jean Jacques and Comte have watered.

If we cannot assert that any virtue may not be found at least in germ in the teaching of Jesus, we may still show that our author has brought into prominence the wrong points in that teaching, and mingled with it alien conceptions. In the first place it seems to us an overstatement to say that Christ placed the happiness of man in a political constitution, and did not consider him as an independent being. Isolation and self-sufficiency were marked features of the ideals that reigned in Greece during the post-Aristotelian period, and the ideal of Jesus may so far be contrasted with these. But the writer makes it too nearly akin to Benthamism. It seems to us truer to say that Jesus taught philanthropy more from the point of view of the individual than from that of society. His disciples were to do good to their enemies, to do good expecting no return, to give freely, to lend to those who could not pay; but, as our author himself admits, to each precept is attached a reason which comes home directly to the individual. This reason sometimes appeals to self-love —their reward should be great, they should receive again full measure, pressed down and running over : sometimes to a nobler sentiment—it was more blessed to give than to receive, they would be children of the Highest, they would be like God in His grand impartial effusion of benefits. All this is not what we call philanthropy in its essence, though it leads to the same results; much less is it the enthusiasm of humanity. Our author asks—" Can a man love his enemies with a view to his own interest ? " This is a difficulty to be felt by a more introspective age than that to which Jesus preached : it was at any rate not felt by the author of the third gospel.[1] But we are told that Christ " quoted a sentence from the book of Deuteronomy, in which devoted love to God and man is solemnly enjoined

[1] Cf. Luke vi. 35.

upon the Israelite," and declared "an ardent, passionate, or devoted state of mind to be the root of virtue." By the "sentence from the book of Deuteronomy" our author means two sentences, one from Deuteronomy and the other from Leviticus; the latter, which alone speaks of love to man, runs simply—"Thou shalt love thy neighbour as thyself." He has imported into this, in his mind, the ardour and passion that belong to the former sentence; this sentence expresses simply a calm, though very lofty ideal of equity: we do not love ourselves with passion or enthusiasm. Again, the injunction to the young man to sell his goods and give them to the poor was surely given, not primarily for the sake of the poor, but for the sake of the young man himself: it was a test, not of philanthropy, but of faith. We must repeat, we are only arguing about the comparative prominence of the two points. It seems to us that Jesus would have reversed Paul's estimate of πίστις and ἀγάπη; he valued love highly, but he speaks more of faith. What he chiefly inculcates is not enthusiasm, or if enthusiasm, not that of passionate affection; it is a calmer, and, some may think, a far grander sentiment, faith in virtue, in the ideal of which philanthropy is only a part—the readiness to sacrifice all, not for humanity, but for the good cause, for the right. In so far as the writer speaks of the state of feeling in the early Church among the followers of Jesus after his departure, his remarks seem to us far more correctly coloured. An "enthusiastic" or elevated "condition of mind" is no unfair modernisation, from one point of view, of the "outpouring of the Holy Spirit;" of that outpouring, love was one of the chief and most striking fruits. The word ἀγάπη, which is only found twice in the synoptic gospels, occurs more than a hundred times in the other books of the New Testament, in various passages of description, exhortation, prayer, and thanksgiving, culminating in the sublime encomium of Paul.

In what we have said we have left out as far as possible the strictly religious element in the teaching of

Jesus. We have done so because our author has done so, and because we do not join with many of his critics in condemning his treatment in this respect. He thereby confines himself to a part only of the work of Jesus, and his book is so far one-sided; but it is a part that can fairly be discussed by itself, and if this had been his only one-sidedness we do not think it would have been strongly felt. But it has led him into a further error which we must notice; it has led him to neglect the great difference between Jewish and ethnic morality, and consequently somewhat to misrepresent the relation of Jesus to the one and the other. Jewish morality was always suffused with the glow of religious feeling which makes the morality of most philosophers seem cold in comparison: the Greek moralised with his eyes turned inward, the Jew with his eyes turned toward the God of his fathers. To say that Jesus, in preaching positive morality, discovered a new continent in the moral globe, is strangely unfair both to Jews and Gentiles; but among the Jews morality was not only positive: it was even enthusiastic, towards each and all of the chosen people of God. Ethnic patriotism was a feeling directed chiefly toward the State; but Jewish patriotism, burning more brightly amid the ruins of national existence, flowed into the channels of individual sympathy and tenderness. When Jesus spoke to his disciples of other Jews as their brethren, he used no new and unfamiliar word. He does not find it necessary to inculcate almsgiving; he only attempts to purify it from the alloy of vanity and ostentation—a purification which it doubtless much needed, as we fear it somewhat needs still. Many a Tobit, no doubt, had given his bread to the hungry and his garments to the naked, had bitterly afflicted himself for the calamities of his suffering brethren, before Jesus shed on the virtues of philanthropy and tenderness the peculiar light of his sublime idealism. Here again, the old account of Christianity, which represents it as internalising and universalising what had before been too external and too limited, seems much truer than the antithesis which our author superadds between "positive" and "negative."

But in this work of Christianity what precise portion is the historian to attribute to Jesus? We have already hinted at some of the difficulties which hang about this question; and we approach the solution of it, we must premise, with a diffidence very unlike our author's confident certainty. We have to form our judgment upon slender evidence, examined in the doubtful light of historic analogy. Our author, in all the second part of his book, writes with a consistent determination to find his ideal of morality completely developed in Jesus. He unfolds a carefully considered utopia, or scheme of human progress, for which Jesus' words are made to supply from time to time texts or mottoes. Sometimes he strays considerably from his text, *e.g.* Christ is supposed to have said that the enthusiasm of humanity was the source of virtue: the best method of producing this enthusiasm is discovered to be family affection: therefore family affection must be encouraged in obedience to Jesus;—we feel that we have got a long way from "He that hateth not his father and his mother." Every student of morality is aware of the facility with which all the virtues may be deduced from each one, and no one who has realised the fertility, breadth, and originality of the moral conceptions of Jesus, can doubt that any ideal we are likely to form may be built upon a careful selection of his words. But the historian's hard duty is not to exaggerate, however strong the temptation to do so may be. It is only to hasty hero-worshippers that this will appear equivalent to *nil admirari;* the historically cultivated mind will feel that a portrait requires light and shade to give it the requisite reality, and that the more it gains in reality the more profound is the admiration that it excites. The defect of Renan's *Vie de Jésus* was not its historical fidelity but its want of that quality. It was not in so far as he had realised the manner in which the idea of Jesus was conditioned by the circumstances of time and place and the laws of human development, but in so far as he had failed to do so, that his work proved inefficacious to stir the feelings of Englishmen. We felt that he had looked at his subject through Parisian spectacles; and taken up too ostentatiously the position of a spectator—a great artistic error in a historian. His most orthodox assailants in England felt for the most part that their strength lay in showing not that the Jesus of Renan was a mere man and ought to have been more, but that he was not the right man.

The truth seems to be that in the simple and grand conception that Jesus formed of man's position and value in the universe, all the subsequent development of Christianity is implicitly contained: but that the evolution of this conception was gradual, and was not completed at his death. The one thing important to Jesus in man was a principle so general that faith, love, and moral energy seem only different sides of it. It was the ultimate coincidence, or rather, if we may use a Coleridgian word, *indifference* of religion and morality. It was "the single eye," the *rightness,* of a man's heart before God. It was faith in the conflict with baser and narrower impulses, love when it became emotion, moral energy as it took effect on the will. It was that which living in a man filled his whole body with a light, purified him completely, so that nothing external could defile him. This principle led to various results. In the first place (and in this respect the teaching of Jesus left nothing to be supplied) it intensified or deepened all moral obligations. This inner light could not produce right outward acts, except through the medium of right inward impulses. Moreover, the man who had it could acquiesce in no compromises, but must aim at perfection. The second consequence of the principle ought to have been, and is in Christianity as at present understood, that the degree in which a man possesses this inner rightness of heart fixes his rank in the kingdom of God at any time. Birth, wealth, worldly position, even intellectual culture (though it may enable one man to do more good than another), even past good works (if the spirit in which they were done is growing faint), are insignificant as claims in comparison with this. But, as actually preached by Jesus, this principle seems (if we take our authorities as they stand) to have assumed a paradoxical and one-sided shape. He gives not equality but superiority to those in poverty and bodily wretchedness. This shape, it is to be observed (by this time we need hardly say that the author of *Ecce Homo* seems not to have observed it), is especially paradoxical and one-sided in one of our three authorities. In all of them we find the saying that it is easier for a camel to go through the eye of a needle than for a rich man to enter the kingdom of heaven. In the first gospel we have the impossibility of serving God and mammon insisted upon, and in connection with this all careful provision for material wants discouraged. But it is only in Luke that we find a blessing pronounced on the poor and a woe on the rich:[1] it is only in Luke that we find applied to wealth the passionate phrase "unrighteous mammon," which, taken in connection with the parable that precedes, suggests the idea that there is something unholy in wealth, that it ought to be got rid of, while it is possible in getting rid of it to utilise it. These passages have been frequently understood as having only that point of paradox which a new truth requires in order to force its way into the world. But the phrases in Luke seem too strong to be explained in this way, and almost amount to a slight distortion of view. This may be referred to more than one reason, issuing naturally from the conception of Jesus combined with his circumstances. M. Renan is not perhaps entirely wrong in attributing the passages that discourage providence to the exuberance of simple faith in a Galilean peasant, ignorant of the complicated arrangements of society. But this hardly reaches the height of the character. We rather refer them to his severe uncompromising absoluteness of idealism, that requires careful tempering to be made practical.[2] Again (and this our author

[1] The question with regard to the two recensions of the "Beatitudes" as they are called seems to be this:—have we in the first gospel a softening down and spiritualising of the original teaching, or in Luke an Ebionitish exaggeration of it? It is difficult but important to decide.

[2] Compare his utterance with respect to purity, Matt. v. 27-30. Here, however, we would gladly think that the first gospel has, by a dangerous mistake, brought vv. 29, 30, into a wrong connection. Cf. Mark ix. 43-47.

finely describes), Jesus with his intense apprehension of what constitutes true human worth, would feel a peculiar horror at the hard insolent selfishness that often accompanies wealth; most men with character enough to break through the comfortable acquiescence of conventional ethics have felt this in some degree. Again, his estimate of human worth, together with faith in Divine equity, might seem to point to a hereafter, when the positions of rich and poor should be reversed. This is suggested by the parable of Lazarus,[1] taken together with the beatitudes in the same gospel. Besides, the practical experience of Jesus would lead him to take the worst view of the rich. His converts were found among the poor and lowly, who were at the same time intellectually babes. The rich would be to a great extent also the wise and prudent; property and education would combine in hindering them from joining the train of an unauthorised and vagabond master. These reasons may account for a partiality that requires to be accounted for in a teacher in whom all have recognised a rare ethical balance, and a singular freedom from asceticism.

Thirdly, when conscience was thus turned inward, and morality made to depend on the state of the heart, it was a necessary consequence that the ceremonial law must fall. This elaborate system of minute observances was needless, and if needless it was burdensome. But this deduction was only partially made by Jesus; to complete it was reserved for one only second to Jesus among the benefactors of mankind—for Saul of Tarsus. How far Jesus actually went it is hard to say. Where the account given by our authorities is as here *primâ facie* fluctuating and confused, the modes of reconciliation or explanation naturally vary. Perhaps we may say that he rejected anything in the written or oral law that seemed to him immoral or imperfectly moral, that among things indifferent he disregarded or attacked particular traditions that he felt to be specially vexatious or trivial, but in general contented himself with "exceeding the righteous-

[1] It is to be observed that the common view that the rich man is punished for *neglecting* Lazarus is at variance with Abraham's reply, and can hardly be deduced solely from the ἐπιθυμῶν χορτασθῆναι in verse 21 (Luke xvi. 19-31).

ness of the Scribes and Pharisees," superadding to the traditional external obligations his strict requisition of rightness and purity of heart. Still his murmur of burdens grievous to be borne foreshadows—but only foreshadows—a time when the handwriting of ordinances should be completely blotted out.

Fourthly, if man's position in the universe, or, more religiously, in the sight of God, depends upon his rightness of heart, it followed that the kingdom of God was opened to all of Adam's seed. But, here again, it is to Paul we owe the complete declaration that Christ has put on one level circumcision and uncircumcision, Greek, Jew, barbarian, Scythian, bond and free. Did the idea of Jesus reach to this? Perhaps hardly in the earlier part of his career, before his claims seemed finally rejected by the leaders of his people, when he felt himself limited in his work to the lost sheep of the house of Israel, when he forbade his disciples to evangelise the Samaritans, when he spoke of Syrophœnicians as dogs. Yet, even then, his conception seems not so much limited as not extended; circumstances have not extended it. He yields to a proof of faith in the Syrophœnician woman. Perhaps, toward the close of his life, amid forebodings of his coming doom, there rose in his mind a clear foresight that his kingdom would be of Gentiles —can we say that it would be universal? At any rate, we find no distinct expression of this in the synoptic gospels; and the historian must very doubtfully accept the discourses of the fourth, even where they most accord with the image he has formed to himself of Jesus.

We have sketched this outline in contrast with our author's, to show exactly to what degree we can admit that the "edict from the Mount" gave to mankind the universality of rights which a few philosophers had ineffectually claimed for them. We should like to say a word about these philosophers. In our author's treatment of them he, very needlessly, exceeds the limits of fair advocacy. He seems, indeed, to regard himself as holding a brief against philosophers in general. In one passage (p. 100) he draws a fancy portrait of the "philosophic good man." This is, perhaps, just within the limits of fair advocacy; that is to say, it is a spirited and instructive caricature. A philosopher might draw a fancy portrait of the religious enthusiast, equally fair, equally instructive, and equally one-sided. In truth, enthusiasm and reason are supplementary; neither can dispense with the other; and it is for the interest of the human race that each should keep a jealous watch on the other. But in one respect the past philosopher is at a great disadvantage, as compared with the past prophet, and has more claim on the tenderness of the historian. The philosopher introduces his new truth to the world enclosed in a system; when humanity has extracted and assimilated the kernel, the empty husk is found with the philosopher's name inscribed on it; the prophet hurls his new truth out in the form of a paradox, the point of which is ever after found useful. This applies peculiarly to Stoicism; we associate the term with salient extravagances; the most valuable part of the system that flourished under the name is so familiar, so axiomatic to us, that we do not value it. There is no fear that men will fall into the error of putting Stoicism for quantity of effect, or intrinsic excellence on a par with Christianity. The Porch was one entrance into the Church; and the panegyrist of Jesus ought to treat Stoicism with the tender and scrupulous fairness due to a forerunner superseded, and a rival outshone. One repeated unfairness in our author's treatment of the philosopher springs from a misconception which is strange in one who has evidently read his Plato. He speaks of "reason" as if it meant only logic; as if its supremacy kept the man entirely cold; as if it were impossible to feel ardour and enthusiasm for abstractions. "He who refrains from gratifying a wish on some ground of reason, at the same time feels the wish as strongly as if he gratified it." In an earlier passage he asks the philosopher triumphantly, "Where is the logical dilemma that can make a knave honest?" Now we admit that one of the great philosophical blots of Stoicism was the confusion it made between distinct mental faculties, elaborative, intuitive, emotional, volitional, so that a Stoic might commit the absurdity of trying, by a logical dilemma, to make a knave honest. But how was the Stoic himself made and kept honest, and pure, and self-sacrificing? Not by his logic, but by the enthusiasm that he felt when he contemplated the true law, the right reason, the wisdom that became dearer to him than any pleasure, the idea of good that rose up in and absorbed his soul, casting into shade the *prima naturæ*, the lawful objects of the earlier natural impulses. "It is one of the most remarkable features," we are told, "of Christ's moral teaching, that he does not command us to regulate or control our unlawful desires, but pronounces it unlawful to have such desires at all." Whether this is a thoroughly sound treatment of ethics we are not now inquiring; but it describes accurately Stoic theory, and Stoic practice. That an ordinary man, one of the masses, intellectually speaking, could only get his unlawful desires destroyed by means of a feeling of personal devotion, we are not prepared to dispute; and hence the effect of Christianity was incomparably greater in extent than that of any philosophy could have been. But to deny this efficacy to those *incredibiles ardores* that the inner vision of truth and wisdom excited in a few, is worse than a mere historical error: it implies a psychological deficiency.

In a way partly similar, partly different, our author tries to depreciate the tenet as held by the Stoics of human brotherhood, the universality of moral obligation. He does not deny that it was held by them in all completeness. He knows that Cicero's Stoic says, "Each one of us is a part of the world, hence we must prefer the common advantage to our own; the universe is the common city of gods and men": that Seneca writes, "We are members of a vast body; we are naturally kinsmen; there is *communio juris* among us all; live for another if you would live for yourself": that Marcus Aurelius writes (expressing in a scholastic form what may even be called the enthusiasm of humanity), "Unless you regard yourself as a member of the human society, you do not yet love men from the heart;

doing good does not give you a completed joy; you do it simply as a thing fit to do, not as doing good to yourself." Yet he seems unable to do hearty justice to philosophers. He says of the tenet: "It had become a commonplace of Stoic philosophy" (hinting it was confined to the lecture-room), "but to work it into the hearts and consciences of men required a higher power." Yes, "of men," but of what men? Not of Stoics, but of the mass of mankind, who never were and never could become Stoics. That a tenet may change the face of society, it must be accepted in some sort by the numerical majority. If Christians had remained as few in number as Stoics, the "edict" of Jesus would have had as much and as little effect as the "claim" of Zeno. True, the insincere Stoic was undoubtedly less controlled by his profession than the insincere Christian. The force of public opinion on him was smaller. There is just this element of truth in what our author means to say; but it is precisely what he has not expressed. Into the hearts and consciences of sincere Stoics the tenet was worked, probably as much as it has since been into the hearts and consciences of sincere Christians — that is, generally, in a very limited and unsatisfactory degree. To what Christian monarch can we point who more than Marcus Aurelius made this sublime principle his inspiration and his restraint, the subject of his meditations and the guide of his life?

We must now turn to our author's detailed account of the subordinate principles or laws (as he calls them) into which the teaching of Jesus branched. We find continual repetition of the same misplaced colouring, and the same mistaken ingenuity. When he gets hold of a vague popular misconception, he exaggerates it, he refines it, he elaborates it, he systematises it; he generally does anything but correct it. But we find him very refreshing to read; his style is so free from cant, haziness, self-consciousness, sickly sweetness, turgid rhetoric; his treatment so bold, independent, distinct, coherent. Indeed, the whole plan is too coherent. He is not content to find in Jesus a rare balance of moral intuitions; he insists on attributing to him an articulate system of ethics; consequently he is constantly suggesting for him, without any evidence, ideas, feelings, reflections alien to his age and inconsistent with the simple directness of the prophetic character. For instance, he points out the "apparent inconsistency" between the absolute purity and severity of the moral ideal of Jesus, and his readiness to sympathise with sinners. He then shows how the inconsistency is overcome by the conception of the "law of mercy." We should rather say that the inconsistency was never felt, and therefore not overcome. The one virtue seemed as natural, sprang as spontaneously as the other.

We have already discussed our author's "provisional" assumption of a right to speak of the miracles as real. This assumption is much used or abused in his chapter on Positive Morality. He works up into a more definite and imposing form the popular notion that Jesus was a wonderful example of practical philanthropy. He tells us we might have thought it more appropriate to Jesus to instruct more and give less time to the relief of physical evils; but no, he thought otherwise: "his biography may be summed up in the words 'he went about doing good'; his wise words were secondary to his beneficial deeds; the latter were not introductory to the former, but the former grew occasionally and, as it were, accidentally out of the latter." Now the perfect unselfishness of Jesus, and his tenderness for his fellow-men, affords the foundation for the popular notion; but the pointed form which is given to it in the passage we have quoted seems in direct conflict with our authorities. Even if we assume that the number of cases recorded is not exaggerated (an assumption which on purely historic grounds we shall find it difficult to admit), there is nothing which we should infer with more certainty from the gospels than that Jesus regarded teaching and preaching as his primary function. He is always represented as taking the initiative in this. He comes into Galilee preaching; he enters into the synagogue and teaches; he goes into the next towns that he may preach;

we read always, "he began to teach" by the seaside, in the synagogue, elsewhere; the multitude came unto him, and he teaches them as is his wont. But he exercises his gift of healing only when appealed to; the people throng round him and press him to exercise it; they "bring unto him" diseased persons, and he heals them; lepers and others fall in his way and entreat him; he heals all, but with occasional reluctance, with repeated efforts to keep his possession of the gift as secret as possible. It was the spiritually sick that he came to seek and to save; there is no evidence of any *eagerness* on his part to relieve ordinary physical evils.

In one of his two chapters on the "Law of Mercy," our author describes two repentances—that of Zacchæus, the rich receiver of taxes, and the well-known story of the woman who was a sinner. The passage is in his best style; the colouring is not overdone, the contrast and the observations to which it gives rise are as just and appropriate as they are fresh and striking. With this illustration he connects an excellent account of "the three stages in the progress of the treatment of crime: the stage of barbarous insensibility, the stage of law or justice, and that of mercy or humanity." This last stage, he tells us, was reached by the morality of Jesus. Law, to keep up a proper sensibility for the injured, has to be cruel to the injurer. But the mercy of Jesus overcomes the emotional difficulty, achieves the emotional feat, of sympathising with and loving the injurer, while at the same time hating the sin and pitying the sufferer far more than law. Therefore, it is a positive duty of Christ's followers to attempt the restoration of the criminal classes. Practical men may plausibly urge that the enterprise is hopeless; but Christ, says our author, rising into one of his loftiest strains of eloquence, knew of no limits to enthusiasm—

He laid it as a duty upon the Church to reclaim the lost, because he did not think it utopian to suppose that the Church might be not in its best members only, but through its whole body, inspired by that ardour of humanity that can charm away the bad passions of the wildest heart, and open to the savage and the outlaw lurking in moral wildernesses an entrancing view of the holy and tranquil order that broods over the streets and palaces of the city of God.

We willingly lend our hearts to this preaching. This is true Christianity : " the Article of Conversion is the true *Articulus stantis aut cadentis Ecclesiæ.*" But when we close the book the question forces itself upon us—What was it that Jesus actually did in this direction ? The attentive reader of the two chapters we refer to will discover a distinct and palpable *seam* running through them, where the exposition of the duty is sewn on to the account of the example. The question is how to deal with the criminal classes, the enemies of their kind, outlaws, injurers of society, who fall under the ban of law and justice. " Therefore," says our author, " Christ went among "—whom ? thieves and murderers ?—no, " publicans and sinners." There is surely a great difference between the two classes. The publicans were not enemies of society, but a sordid and repulsive part of its organisation; instruments that law used and despised, not objects against which it was directed. Mr. Plumptre[1] compares them with Roman Catholic excisemen in Ireland. " Sinners " is a vague term, but it is clear that the persons described by it were vicious as distinct from criminal, liable to social ostracism, not legal punishment. Suppose a man, then, in the habit of dining with excisemen and prostitutes, with a view to their moral improvement. He would show, perhaps, more heroism, certainly more originality, than a man who went as a city missionary among the criminal classes of London; but it would be only in a very general sense that we could say that the one man followed the example of the other. Again, there is no evidence that Jesus sought out publicans and harlots, and endeavoured to pierce through the hardened shell of vicious habit that encased their hearts. Some of them thronged among the crowd to hear him, and he did not repel them; similarly they had gone to John to be

[1] Smith's *Dictionary of the Bible.*

baptised, and he had baptised them. Those with whom he associated had, we may believe, already shown signs of repentance; his preaching had already stirred in them the impulse toward goodness. All honour to the tender insight that could discern and cherish this impulse when others saw only the mould of life and circumstance in which the character was assumed to have hardened! All honour to the magnanimity that in this work could brave the condemnation of the pious, the censure of those whose censure was felt heaviest![1] But the particular duty which our author sets before us of sympathising with and converting the hardened outlaw, while we sympathise with, and exact justice for, his victim, Jesus does not, from the evidence before us, appear to have actually undertaken. This emotional problem we have to attempt; let us solve it as it can be solved in the spirit of Christianity; but let us not strain history till it cracks in a morbid anxiety to make the emotional stimulus afforded by Christ's personal example as great as possible.[2]

But Jesus did not manifest only pity and tenderness, conspicuous as these qualities were in him: he also showed anger and resentment. Our author, therefore, to complete his work has to explain the Law of Resentment. We looked forward with some interest to this explanation, as we foresaw the difficulty in which he would be placed, and considered that his mode of dealing with that difficulty would be an excellent test of his qualities as a historian. For the objects of the resentment of Jesus were the religious teachers of his nation—a nation appointed by Providence to be the religious teachers of mankind. These are the only persons against whom he inveighs with bitter vehemence; for whose virtues he has no praise,[3] for whose faults he

[1] In choosing a publican for a disciple, Jesus would go further still. But, although the publicans were as a class rapacious and unjust, there was nothing incompatible, whatever bigots might think, in tax-gathering and virtue.
[2] A good instance of this straining is seen where our author endeavours to bring prostitutes under the head of "injurers," by describing them as "the tempters who waylaid the chastity of men." We hear the fact cracking.
[3] We ought to notice as an exception that he once said of one of them "that he was not far from the kingdom of God." This incident confirms us in the view we subsequently express.

has no excuse. Now the religious teachers of a people, whatever may be their defects and shortcomings (and we shall hardly be suspected of a disposition to underrate them), are not usually those against whom an impartial moralist concentrates his invective. Here, therefore, the example seems to require careful interpretation. The ordinary commentator, who is not troubled by any considerations of historic analogy, finds no difficulty at all. In reading Matt. xxiii. and the parallel passages in Luke, he conceives an idea of the Pharisees and scribes made to suit these passages. He willingly believes that they were hypocritical and rapacious, serpents and vipers, making long prayers to devour widows' substance, whose proselytes were children of hell, whose carefully purified vessels were full of extortion and excess. For purposes of edification this answers very well; every one feels that against so odious a combination of vices no invectives can be too vehement, too scathing. If it is pointed out to the commentator that Jesus elsewhere seems to speak of these persons as the whole who needed not a physician, the righteous whom he was not come to call to repentance: elsewhere as possessing a righteousness of their own, though below the standard of his lofty requirements,—he simply replies that these were different Pharisees and different scribes. The author of *Ecce Homo* is at once too genuinely honest and too widely cultivated to rest content with this. He finds it necessary to represent the Pharisees as a historian, using all the sources of evidence within his reach, may reasonably conceive them to have existed; and to realise the relations of Jesus towards them as a whole, in accordance with such representation. Only on this basis can he conscientiously expound the example and develop the Law of Resentment. Let us see what the result is.

In the first place, from his consistent determination not to treat the career of Jesus as in any respect progressive, he ignores what is the only true key to these relations. He cannot trace their gradual embitterment, arising out of the ever increasing clearness of the irreconcilable antagonism between the insulted bigots and the daring innovator, from the outset of Jesus' ministry, when he simply left the "righteous" on one side as having no immediate call to deal with them, to that period near its close, when, foreseeing and almost courting the inevitable doom, he poured out in those well-known charges the concentrated energy of his indignation. Still he quite appreciates the comparative historic value of the earlier and later utterances. Of the worst charges he says (we could not expect him to say more), "We have not the evidence before us which might enable us to verify these accusations." He sees that the point of the antagonism between the "one learned profession" and Jesus was, that the former were "legalists," that they asserted "the paramount necessity of particular rules." They "believed that the old method by which their ancestors had arrived at a knowledge of the requirements of duty— namely, divine inspiration—was no longer available, and that nothing therefore remained but carefully to collect the results at which their ancestors had arrived by this method, to adopt these results as rules, and to observe them punctiliously." He says that it may be urged that such men, however mistaken, did "in some cases the best they could, that they were serious and made others serious." But Jesus, he finds, "made no allowance" for them. How is this to be explained? How is our indignation against these sincere but mistaken bigots to be sufficiently stimulated? It appears that after all they were impostors of a very subtle sort. "*Their good deeds . . . did not proceed from the motives from which such deeds naturally spring, and from which the public suppose them to spring.*" When they tithed their property they were impostors, because they made people think they did so from "ardent feelings," whereas their real motive was "respect for a traditional rule." When they searched the Scriptures, they were impostors, because they pretended to be possessed with the spirit of what they read without really being so. Thus, because they followed "motives which did not actuate them, but which they supposed ought to actuate them," he thinks it right to say of them that they were "destitute of convictions"; "winning the reverence of the multitude by false pretences"; "actors in everything"; "their whole life a play."

Now we cannot conceive the true analysis of bigotry and legalism more blurred and confused than it is by this ingenious rhetoric—a rhetoric all the more dangerous because it is, as the author proceeds to show, of so universal application. Religious conservatives in all ages are men who cling to the letter without comprehending the spirit—who inherit the results of an enthusiasm whose counterpart in the present they misunderstand and dislike. But to say that, because they are destitute of enthusiasm, they are " destitute of convictions," that " their zeal for truth is feigned," because their view of truth is narrow, that " they love the past only because they hate the present," to charge them with wilful fraud as pretenders to an ardour and enthusiasm that they have not, to describe their virtues as being no virtues at all, because they are mixed with conventionality and triviality,—would be the blindest advocacy, or the most unscrupulous special pleading. In the secular strife between the old and the new, upon which human progress depends, our good wishes are entirely with the innovators. Nor have we a word of condemnation for the champions of this grand cause, if in the fiery heat of battle they strike somewhat merciless and sweeping blows. It is by such strokes that great victories have generally been won. Still the most terrible fury in assault may be combined with a just recognition of the merits of adversaries, a generous sympathy with whatever in them is or might have been virtue; and in our ideal we conceive these qualities combined. Such magnanimity we, in common with the whole Christian world, have read in the close of our Master's life, as told by Luke.[1] The end has come; the people, whose eyes he

[1] Here for the last time, our author quotes the fourth gospel to support his most infelicitous interpretation of the third. It is the only support he has. The reply to the high-priest is no "menace"; it is simply a calm assertion. His address to the women expresses mere sadness; most generous sadness: it is his people's deserved doom that grieves him: he would avert it if it were possible: hence the "forgive them." No one, we think, who read the account in Luke by itself, would take the words otherwise. We attribute the sentence he quotes from John xix. 11 to the indignation of a disciple.

has been vainly endeavouring to open, have made their choice; they have identified themselves with their traditional leaders; his work is closed, his strife is over, and with it the bitterness of the strife has melted into pure sadness, into all-embracing forgiveness. But our author reads the passage otherwise. It was only the Roman soldiers he forgave. Having hated in the world his enemies, the legalists, he hated them unto the end. In his dying moments he pointedly excepted them from pardon; thus giving his followers a most solemn intimation, that "the enthusiasm of humanity," though it destroys "a great deal of hatred . . . creates as much more," that the new commandment he gave unto them did not exclude bitterness, irreconcilable hostility, intolerant anger, vindictive enmity.

Here, then, is what the enthusiasm of humanity comes to; here is the last fashion of the Imitatio Christi. We are to love the whole human race, except our religious adversaries; we are to cherish the ideal of man in every man, only not in a legalist. We are to have an inexhaustible sympathy with those who are trying in every way to do wrong; nothing but enmity for those who are trying in a mistaken way to do right. We are not to burn any one, we are told, on the whole; we might burn the wrong man; but the spirit of *auto-da-fé* is thoroughly Christian; some one ought to be burnt if we could only tell who. Perhaps much of this is conscious paradox, meant to be taken *cum grano;* but we fear the writer may carry his readers—that he has carried himself—dangerously far. Other men have felt the profoundest pity for the Jewish nation, whose passionate patriotism and imperishable faith have passed through so fearful a doom of blood and fire to haunt the world as a spectral anachronism for ever; our author assures us, with the calm truculence of a thoroughgoing enthusiast—

Almost all the genuine worth and virtue of the nation was gathered into the Christian Church; what remained without was perversity and prejudice, ignorance of the time, ignorance of the truth—that mass of fierce infatuation which was burnt up in the flames which consumed the temple or shared the fall of of the Antichrist Barcochebah.

This thoroughly exemplifies the Law of Resentment; this is the "irreconcilable hostility" of the religious partisan. We disown the authority of this law; we decline to follow this example. We have not so learned Christ; it is not thus we would be filled with his spirit. Let the author of *Ecce Homo*, and those who think with him, look well to what they are doing. They would willingly deliver men from bondage to the letter of an ordinance; let them not bind upon us servile conformity to the pattern of a life. Neither the one nor the other is compatible with the true liberty of the spirit. For the spirit of moral heroes does not only live after them; it grows, it deepens, it enlarges after them. It transcends the limits of their earthly development; it overleaps the barriers that circumstance had fixed; it shakes off the bonds that action had imposed; it is measured not by what it did, but by what it might have done and will yet do. So we imitate our other patterns and examples in the essence, not the limitations, of their virtues; so we must imitate our great pattern and example, the great originator and source of our morality. True, the Christian has to combine anger with love, resentment with sympathy; but he is not to suppress the latter towards a special class of men, because he regards them as the counterpart of the antagonists of Jesus. Nay, this is the peculiar lesson that enthusiasts have to learn, if progress is ever to be peaceful: to recognise and love the virtues that may thrive wonderfully under the most besotted adherence to the most narrow and contemptible notions. In Jesus the limitation of sympathy arose from inevitable partiality of view; circumstances had sundered him too widely from the orthodox party; it was necessary that he should fight them to the death. We may imagine how differently he might have spoken of them if he could only have seen their best side instead of their worst. Surely he who could discern and cherish the sparks of love, the germs of devotion, the yearnings after virtue in the hearts of publicans and sinners, would have seen the glowing zeal, the anxious obedience, the earnest self-denial, the sublime aspiration, that lingered in and leavened that mass of paltriness and bigotry and error. He would have learnt of long prayers offered up not to cover spoliation, of teachers who bore, as far as men could bear, the burdens they laid on others, of proselytes of whom Pharisaic effort had not made children of hell, but who were soon to pour in eager throngs through the opened gates of the city of God. He might even have personally known one, then an eager pupil of the great pillar of legalism, the young Pharisee who more than any of his own followers was to inherit his spirit and complete his work, and strike the final and triumphant blow for the law of liberty and love.

Our limits compel us to stop. To develop and support fully on all the points on which we differ from our author our divergent view, would require a book as long as his own——nay, perhaps longer, as we should find it expedient to use more argument for each assertion. His method we think radically wrong; his conclusions only roughly and partially right. But we would not part from him in this tone. The one thing in which we agree with him outweighs all the rest. We desire as sincerely as he does that the influence of Jesus on the modern world should increase and not decrease. That his book will tend to produce this effect on the majority of readers we can hardly doubt; that such will be its operation on the minds even of students we think most probable. We cannot possibly have sound history without uncompromising criticism and perpetual controversy; but it is good to be reminded from time to time to drop the glass of criticism, and let the dust-clouds of controversy settle. Many students who cannot patiently lend their minds to our author's teaching may be stimulated by it to do as he has done: may be led to contemplate in the best outline that each for himself can frame, with unwonted clearness of vision and unwonted force of sympathy, the features of a conception, a life, a character which the world might reverence more wisely, but can never love too well.

II

THE PROPHET OF CULTURE

(*Macmillan's Magazine*, August 1867)

THE movement against anonymous writing, in which this journal some years ago took a part, has received, I think, an undeniable accession of strength from the development (then unexpected) of Mr. Matthew Arnold. Some persons who sympathised on the whole with that movement yet felt that the case was balanced, and that if it succeeded we should have sacrified something that we could not sacrifice without regret. One felt the evils that "irresponsible reviewers" were continually inflicting on the progress of thought and society: and yet one felt that, in form and expression, anonymous writing tended to be good writing. The buoyant confidence of youth was invigorated and yet sobered by having to sustain the *prestige* of a well-earned reputation; while the practised weapon of age, relieved from the restraints of responsibility, was wielded with almost the elasticity of youth. It was thought we should miss the freedom, the boldness, the reckless vivacity with which one talented writer after another had discharged his missiles from behind the common shield of a coterie of unknown extent, or at least half veiled by a pseudonym. It was thought that periodical literature would gain in carefulness, in earnestness, in sincerity, in real moral influence: but that possibly it might become just a trifle dull. We did not foresee that the dashing insolences of "we-dom" that we should lose would be more than compensated by the delicate impertinences of egotism that we should gain. We did not imagine the new and exquisite literary enjoyment that would be created when a man of genius and ripe thought, perhaps even elevated by a position of academic dignity, should deliver profound truths and subtle observations with all the dogmatic authority and self-confidence of a prophet: at the same time titillating the public by something like the airs and graces, the playful affectations of a favourite comedian. We did not, in short, foresee a Matthew Arnold: and I think it must be allowed that our apprehensions have been much removed, and our cause much strengthened, by this new phenomenon.

I have called Mr. Arnold the prophet of culture: I will not call him an "elegant Jeremiah," because he seems to have been a little annoyed (he who is never annoyed) by that phrase of the *Daily Telegraph.* " Jeremiah ! " he exclaims, "the very Hebrew prophet whose style I admire the least." I confess I thought the phrase tolerably felicitous for a Philistine, from whom one would not expect any very subtle discrimination of the differentiæ of prophets. Nor can I quite determine which Hebrew prophet Mr. Arnold does most resemble. But it is certainly hard to compare him to Jeremiah, for Jeremiah is our type of the lugubrious; whereas there is nothing more striking than the imperturbable cheerfulness with which Mr. Arnold seems to sustain himself on the fragment of culture that is left him, amid the deluge of Philistinism that he sees submerging our age and country. A prophet however, I gather, Mr. Arnold does not object to be called; as such I wish to consider and weigh him; and thus I am led to examine the lecture with which he has closed his connexion with Oxford,—the most full, distinct, and complete of the various utterances in which he has set forth the Gospel of Culture.

As it will clearly appear in the course of this article, how highly I admire Mr. Arnold as a writer, I may say at once, without reserve or qualification, that this utterance has disappointed me very much. It is not even so good in style as former essays; it has more of the mannerism of repeating his own phrases, which, though very effective up to a certain point, may be carried too far. But this is a small point: and Mr. Arnold's style, when most faulty, is very charming. My complaint is that, though there is much in it beautifully and subtly said, and many fine glimpses of great truths, it is, as a whole, ambitious, vague, and perverse. It seems to me over-ambitious, because it treats of the most profound and difficult problems of individual and social life with an airy dogmatism that ignores their depth and difficulty. And though dogmatic, Mr. Arnold is yet vague; because when he employs indefinite terms he does not attempt to limit their indefiniteness, but rather avails himself of it. Thus he speaks of the relation of culture and religion, and sums it up by saying, that the idea of culture is destined to "transform and govern" the idea of religion. Now I do not wish to be pedantic; and I think that we may discuss culture and religion, and feel that we are talking about the same social and intellectual facts, without attempting any rigorous definition of our terms. But there is one indefiniteness that ought to be avoided. When we speak of culture and religion in common conversation, we sometimes refer to an ideal state of things and sometimes to an actual. But if we are appraising, weighing, as it were, these two, one with the other, it is necessary to know whether it is the ideal or the actual that we are weighing. When I say ideal, I do not mean something that is not realised at all by individuals at present, but something not realised sufficiently to be much called to mind by the term denoting the general social fact. I think it clear that Mr. Arnold, when he speaks of culture, is speaking sometimes of an ideal, sometimes of an actual culture, and does not always know which. He describes it in one page as "a study of perfection, moving by the force, not merely or primarily of the scientific passion for pure knowledge, but of the moral and social passion for doing good." A study of this vast aim, moving with the impetus of this double passion, is something that does, I hope, exist among us, but to a limited extent; it is hardly that which has got itself stamped and recognised as culture. And Mr. Arnold afterwards admits as much. For we might have thought, from the words I have quoted, that we had in culture, thus possessed by the passion of doing good, a mighty social power, continually tending to make "reason and the will of God prevail." But we find that this power only acts in fine weather. "It needs times of faith and ardour to flourish in." Exactly; it is not itself a spring and source of faith and ardour. Culture "believes" in making reason and the will of God prevail, and will even "endeavour" to make them prevail, but it must be under very favourable circumstances. This is rather a languid form of the passion of doing good; and we feel that we have passed from the ideal culture, towards which Mr. Arnold aspires, to the actual culture in which he lives and moves.

Mr. Arnold afterwards explains to us a little further how much of the passion for doing good culture involves, and how it involves it. "Men are all members of one great whole, and the sympathy which is in human nature will not allow one member to be indifferent to the rest, or to have a perfect welfare independent of the rest. . . . The individual is obliged, under pain of being stunted and enfeebled in his own development if he disobeys, to carry others along with him in his march towards perfection." These phrases are true of culture as we know it. In using them Mr. Arnold assumes implicitly what, perhaps, should have been expressly avowed—that the study of perfection, as it forms itself in members of the human race, is naturally and primarily a study of the individual's perfection, and only incidentally and secondarily a study of the general perfection of humanity. It is so incidentally and secondarily for the two reasons Mr. Arnold gives, one internal and the other external: first, because it finds sympathy as one element of the human nature that it desires harmoniously to develop; and secondly, because the development of one individual is bound up by the laws of the universe with the development of at least some other individuals. Still the root of culture, when examined ethically, is found to be a refined eudæmonism: in it the social impulse springs out of and re-enters into the self-regarding, which remains predominant. That is, I think, the way in which the love of culture is generally developed: an exquisite pleasure is experienced in refined states of thought and feeling, and a desire for this pleasure is generated, which may amount to a passion, and lead to the utmost intellectual and moral effort. Mr. Arnold may, perhaps, urge (and I would allow it true in certain cases) that the direct impulse towards perfection, whether realised in a man's self or in the world around, may inspire and impassion some minds, without any consideration of the enjoyment connected with it. In any case, it must be admitted that the impulse toward perfection in a man of culture is not practically limited to himself, but tends to expand in infinitely increasing circles. It is the wish of culture, taking ever wider and wider sweeps, to carry the whole race, the whole universe, harmoniously towards perfection.

And, if it were possible that all men, under all circumstances, should feel what some men, in some fortunate spheres, may truly feel—that there is no conflict, no antagonism, between the full development of the individual and the progress of the world—I should be loth to hint at any jar or discord in this harmonious movement. But this paradisaical state of culture is rare. We dwell in it a little space, and then it vanishes into the ideal. Life shows us the conflict and the discord: on one side are the claims of harmonious self-development, on the other the cries of struggling humanity: we have hitherto let our sympathies expand along with our other refined instincts, but now they threaten to sweep us into regions from which those refined instincts shrink. Not that harmonious self-development calls on us to *crush* our sympathies; it asks only that they should be a little repressed, a little kept under: we may become (as Mr. Arnold delicately words it) philanthropists "tempered by renouncement." There is much useful and important work to be done, which may be done harmoniously: still we cannot honestly say that this seems to us the most useful, the most important work, or what in the interests of the world is most pressingly entreated and demanded. This latter, if done at all, must be done as self-sacrifice, not as self-development. And so we are brought face to face with the most momentous and profound problem of ethics.

It is at this point, I think, that the relation of culture and religion is clearly tested and defined. Culture (if I have understood and analysed it rightly) inevitably takes one course. It recognises with a sigh the limits of self-development, and its first enthusiasm becomes "tempered by renouncement." Religion, of which the essence is self-sacrifice, inevitably takes the other course. We see this daily realised in practice : we see those we know and love, we see the *élite* of humanity in history and literature, coming to this question, and after a struggle answering it : going, if they are strong clear souls, some one way and some the other; if they are irresolute, vacillating and "moving in a strange diagonal" between the two. It is because he ignores this antagonism, which seems to me so clear and undeniable if stated without the needless and perilous exaggerations which preachers have used about it, that I have called Mr. Arnold perverse. A philosopher[1] with whom he is more familiar than I am speaks, I think, of " the reconciliation of antagonisms " as the essential feature of the most important steps in the progress of humanity. I seem to see profound truth in this conception, and perhaps Mr. Arnold has intended to realise it. But, in order to reconcile antagonisms, it is needful to probe them to the bottom ; whereas Mr. Arnold skims over them with a lightly-won tranquillity that irritates instead of soothing.

Of course we are all continually trying to reconcile this and other antagonisms, and many persuade themselves that they have found a reconciliation. The religious man tells himself that in obeying the instinct of self-sacrifice he has chosen true culture, and the man of culture tells himself that by seeking self-development he is really taking the best course to "make reason and the will of God prevail." But I do not think either is quite convinced. I think each dimly feels that it is necessary for the world that the other

[1] Hegel.

line of life should be chosen by some, and each and all look forward with yearning to a time when circumstances shall have become kinder and more pliable to our desires, and when the complex impulses of humanity that we share shall have been chastened and purified into something more easy to harmonise. And sometimes the human race seems to the eye of enthusiasm so very near this consummation: it seems that if just a few simple things were done it would reach it. But these simple things prove mountains of difficulty; and the end is far off. I remember saying to a friend once—a man of deep culture—that his was a "fair-weather theory of life." He answered with much earnestness, "We mean it to be fair weather henceforth." And I hope the skies are growing clearer every century; but meanwhile there is much storm and darkness yet, and we want—the world wants— all the self-sacrifice that religion can stimulate. Culture diffuses "sweetness and light"; I do not undervalue these blessings: but religion gives fire and strength, and the world wants fire and strength even more than sweetness and light. Mr. Arnold feels this when he says that culture must "borrow a devout energy" from religion; but devout energy, as Dr. Newman somewhere says, is not to be borrowed. At the same time, I trust that the ideal of culture and the ideal of religion will continually approach one another: that culture will keep developing its sympathy, and gain in fire and strength; that religion will teach that unnecessary self-sacrifice is folly, and that whatever tends to make life harsh and gloomy cometh of evil. And if we may allow that the progress of culture is clearly in this direction, surely we may say the same of religion. Indeed the exegetic artifices by which the Hellenic view of life is introduced and allowed a place in Christian preaching would sometimes be almost ludicrous, if they were not touching, and if they were not, on the whole, such a sign of a hopeful progress: of progress not as yet, perhaps, very great or very satisfactory, but still very distinct. I wish Mr. Arnold had recognised this. I do not think he would then have said that culture would transform and absorb religion, any more than that religion would transform and absorb culture. To me the ultimate and ideal relation of culture and religion is imaged like the union of the golden and silver sides of the famous shield —each leading to the same "orbed perfection" of actions and results, but shining with a diverse splendour in the light of its different principle.

Into the difficulties of this question I have barely entered; but I hope I have shown the inadequacy of Mr. Arnold's treatment of it. I think we shall be more persuaded of this inadequacy when we have considered how he conceives of actual religion in the various forms in which it exists among us. He has but one distinct thing to say of them,—that they subdue the obvious faults of our animality. They form a sort of spiritual police: that is all. He says nothing of the emotional side of religion; of the infinite and infinitely varied vent which it gives, in its various forms, for the deepest fountains of feeling. He says nothing of its intellectual side: of the indefinite but inevitable questions about the world and human destiny into which the eternal metaphysical problems form themselves in minds of rudimentary development; questions needing confident answers—nay, imperatively demanding, it seems, from age to age, different answers: of the actual facts of psychological experience, so strangely mixed up with, and expressed in, the mere conventional "jargon" of religion (which he characterises with appropriate contempt)—how the moral growth of men and nations, while profoundly influenced and controlled by the formulæ of traditional religions, is yet obedient to laws of its own, and in its turn reacts upon and modifies these formulæ: of all this Mr. Arnold does not give a hint. He may say that he is not treating of religions, but of culture. But it may be replied that he is treating of the relation of culture to religions; and that a man ought not to touch cursorily upon such a question, much less to dogmatise placidly upon it, without showing us that he has mastered the elements of the problem.

I may, perhaps, illustrate my meaning by referring to

another essayist—one of the very few whom I consider superior to Mr. Arnold—one who is as strongly attached to culture as Mr. Arnold himself, and perhaps more passionately,—M. Renan. It will be seen that I am not going to quote a partisan. From "my countryman's" judgment of our Protestant organisations I appeal boldly to a Frenchman and an infidel. Let any one turn to M. Renan's delicate, tender, sympathetic studies of religious phenomena—I do not refer to the *Vie de Jésus*, but to a much superior work, the *Essais d'Histoire religieuse*,—he will feel, I think, how coarse, shallow, unappreciative, is Mr. Arnold's summing up, "they conquer the more obvious faults of our animality." To take one special point. When Mr. Arnold is harping on the "dissidence of Dissent," I recall the little phrase which M. Renan throws at the magnificent fabric of Bossuet's attack upon Protestantism. "En France," he says, "on ne comprend pas qu'on se divise pour si peu de chose." M. Renan knows that ever since the reviving intellect of Europe was turned upon theology, religious dissidence and variation has meant religious life and force. Mr. Arnold, of course, can find texts inculcating unity: how should unity not be included in the ideal of a religion claiming to be universal? But Mr. Arnold, as a cultivated man, has read the New Testament records with the light of German erudition, and knows how much unity was attained by the Church in its fresh and fervent youth. Still, unity is a part of the ideal even of the religion that came not to send peace, but a sword: let us be grateful to any one who keeps that in view, who keeps reminding us of that. But it may be done without sneers. Mr. Arnold might know (if he would only study them a little more closely and tenderly) the passionate longing for unity that may be cherished within small dissident organisations. I am not defending them. I am not saying a word for separatism against multitudinism. But those who feel that worship ought to be the true expression of the convictions on which it is based, and out of which it grows, and that in the present fragmentary state of truth it is supremely difficult to reconcile unity of worship with sincerity of conviction—those who know that the struggle to realise in combination the ideals of truth and peace in many minds reaches the pitch of agony—will hardly think that Mr. Arnold's taunt is the less cruel because it is pointed with a text.

I wish it to be distinctly understood that it is as judged by his own rules and principles that I venture to condemn Mr. Arnold's treatment of our actual religions. He has said that culture in its most limited phase is curiosity; and I quite sympathise in his effort to vindicate for this word the more exalted meaning that the French give to it. Even of the ideal culture he considers curiosity (if I understand him rightly) to be the most essential, though not the noblest, element. Well, then, I complain that in regard to some of the most important elements of social life he has so little curiosity; and therefore so thin and superficial an appreciation of them. I do not mean that every cultivated man ought to have formed for himself a theory of religion. "Non omnia possumus omnes," and a man must, to some extent, select the subjects that suit his special faculties. But every man of deep culture ought to have a conception of the importance and intricacy of the religious problem, a sense of the kind and amount of study that is required for it, a tact to discriminate worthy and unworthy treatment of it, an instinct which, if he has to touch on it, will guide him round the lacunæ of apprehension that the limits of his nature and leisure have rendered inevitable. Now this cultivated tact, sense, instinct (Mr. Arnold could express my meaning for me much more felicitously than I can for myself), he seems to me altogether to want on this topic. He seems to me (if so humble a simile may be pardoned) to judge of religious organisations as a dog judges of human beings, chiefly by the scent. One admires in either case the exquisite development of the organ, but feels that the use of it for this particular object implies a curious, an almost ludicrous, limitation of sympathy. When these popular religions are brought before Mr. Arnold, he is content to detect their strong odours of Philistinism and vulgarity; he will not stoop down and look into them; he is not sufficiently interested in their dynamical importance; he does not care to penetrate the secret of their fire and strength, and learn the sources and effects of these; much less does he consider how sweetness and light may be added without any loss of fire and strength.

This limitation of view in Mr. Arnold seems to me the more extraordinary, when I compare it with the fervent language he uses with respect to what is called, *par excellence*, the Oxford movement. He even half associates himself with the movement—or rather he half associates the movement with himself.

It was directed, he rightly says, against " Liberalism as Dr. Newman saw it." What was this? "It was," he explains, " the great middle class Liberalism, which had for the cardinal points of its belief the Reform Bill of 1832 and local self-government in politics; in the social sphere free trade, unrestricted competition, and the making of large industrial fortunes; in the religious sphere the dissidence of Dissent and the Protestantism of the Protestant religion." Liberalism to Dr Newman may have meant something of all this; but what (as I infer from the *Apologia*) it more especially meant to him was a much more intelligent force than all these, which Mr. Arnold omits: and *pour cause;* for it was precisely that view of the functions of religion and its place in the social organism in which Mr. Arnold seems at least complacently to acquiesce. Liberalism, Dr. Newman thought—and it seems to me true of one phase or side of Liberalism—wished to extend just the languid patronage to religion that Mr. Arnold does. What priesthoods were good for in the eyes of Liberalism were the functions, as I have said, of spiritual police; and that is all Mr. Arnold thinks they are good for at present; and even in the future (unless I misunderstand him), if we want more, he would have us come to culture. But Dr. Newman knew that even the existing religions, far as they fell below his ideal, were good for much more than this; this view of them seemed to him not only shallow and untrue, but perilous, deadly, soul-destroying; and inasmuch as it commended itself to intellectual men, and was an intelligent force, he fought against it, not, I think, with much sweetness or light, but with a blind, eager, glowing asperity which, tempered always by humility and candour, was and is very impressive. Dr. Newman fought for a point of view which it required culture to appreciate, and therefore he fought in some sense with culture; but he did not fight for culture, and to conceive him combating side by side with Mr. Matthew Arnold is almost comical.

I think, then, that without saying more about religion, Mr. Arnold might have said truer things about it; and I think also that without saying less about culture—we have a strong need of all he can say to recommend it—he might have shown that he was alive to one or two of its besetting faults. And some notice of these might have strengthened his case; for he might have shown that the faults of culture really arise from lack of culture; and that more culture, deeper and truer culture, removes them. I have ventured to hint this in speaking of Mr. Arnold's tone about religion. What I dislike in it seems to me, when examined, to be exactly what he calls Philistinism; just as when he commences his last lecture before a great university by referring to his petty literary squabbles, he seems to me guilty of what he calls "provincialism." And so, again, the attitude that culture often assumes towards enthusiasm in general seems to spring from narrowness, from imperfection of culture. The fostering care of culture, and a soft application of sweetness and light, might do so much for enthusiasm—enthusiasm does so much want it. Enthusiasm is often a turbid issue of smoke and sparks. Culture might refine this to a steady glow. It is melancholy when, instead, it takes to pouring cold water on it. The worst result is not the natural hissing and sputtering that ensues, though that cannot be pleasing to culture or to anything else, but the waste of power that is the inevitable consequence.

It is wrong to exaggerate the antagonism between enthusiasm and culture; because, in the first place, culture has an enthusiasm of its own, by virtue of which indeed, as Mr. Arnold contemplates, it is presently to transcend and absorb religion. But at present this enthusiasm, so far from being adequate to this, is hardly sufficient—is often insufficient—to prevent culture degenerating into dilettantism. In the second place, culture has an appreciation of enthusiasm (with the source of which it has nothing to do), when that enthusiasm is beautiful and picturesque, or thrilling and sublime, as it often is. But the enthusiasm must be very picturesque, very sublime; upon some completed excellence of form culture will rigorously insist. May it not be that culture is short-sighted and pedantic in the rigour of these demands, and thus really defeats its own ends, just as it is often liable to do by purely artistic pedantry and conventionality? If it had larger and healthier sympathies, it might see beauty in the stage of becoming (if I may use a German phrase), in much rough and violent work at which it now shudders. In pure art culture is always erring on the side of antiquity—much more in its sympathy with the actual life of men and society. In some of the most beautiful lines he has written, Owen Meredith expresses a truth that deserves to be set in beautiful language :

>   I know that all acted time
> By that which succeeds it is ever received
> As calmer, completer, and more sublime,
> Only because it is finished ; because
> We only behold the thing it achieved,
> We behold not the thing that it was.
> For while it stands whole and immutable
> In the marble of memory, how can we tell
> What the men that have hewn at the block may have been ?
> Their passion is merged in its passionlessness ;
> Their strife in its stillness closed for ever ;
> Their change upon change in its changelessness ;
> In its final achievement their feverish endeavour.

Passion, strife, feverish endeavour—surely in the midst of these have been produced not only the rough blocks with which the common world builds, but the jewels with which culture is adorned. Culture the other day thought Mr. Garrison a very prosy and uninteresting person, and did not see why so much fuss should be made about him; but I should not be surprised if in a hundred years or so he were found to be poetical and picturesque.

And I will go farther, and plead for interests duller and vulgarer than any fanaticism.

If any culture really has what Mr. Arnold in his finest mood calls its noblest element, the passion for propagating itself, for making itself prevail, then let it learn "to call nothing common or unclean." It can only propagate itself by shedding the light of its sympathy liberally; by learning to love common people and common things, to feel common interests. Make people feel that their own poor life is ever so little beautiful and poetical; then they will begin to turn and seek after the treasures of beauty and poetry outside and above it. Pictorial culture is a little vexed at the success of Mr. Frith's pictures, at the thousands of pounds he gets, and the thousands of people that crowd to see them. Now I do not myself admire Mr. Frith's pictures; but I think he diffuses culture more than some of his acid critics, and I should like to think that he got twice as many pounds and spectators. If any one of these grows eagerly fond of a picture of Mr. Frith's, then, it seems to me, the infinite path of culture is open to him; I do not see why he should not go on till he can conscientiously praise the works of Pietro Perugino. But leaving Mr. Frith (and other painters and novelists that might be ranked with him), let us consider a much greater man, Macaulay. Culture has turned up its nose a little at our latest English classic, and would, I think, have done so more, but that it is touched and awed by his wonderful devotion to literature. But Macaulay, though he loved literature, loved also common people and common things, and therefore he can make the common people who live among common things love literature. How Philistinish it is of him to be stirred to eloquence by the thought of "the opulent and enlightened states of Italy, the vast and magnificent cities, the ports, the arsenals, the villas, the museums, the libraries, the marts filled with every article of comfort and luxury, the factories swarming with artisans, the Apennines covered with rich cultivation up to their very summits, the Po wafting the harvest of Lombardy to the granaries of Venice, and carrying back the silks of Bengal and the furs of Siberia to the palaces of Milan." But the Philistine's heart is opened by these images; through his heart a way is found to his taste; he learns how delightful a melodious current of stirring words may be; and then, when Macaulay asks him to mourn for "the wit and the learning and the genius" of Florence, he does not refuse faintly to mourn; and so Philistinism and culture kiss each other.

Again, when our greatest living poet "dips into the future," what does he see?

> The heavens fill with commerce, argosies of magic sails,
> Pilots of the purple twilight, dropping down with costly bales.

Why, it might be the vision of a young general merchant. I doubt whether anything similar could be found in a French or German poet (I might except Victor Hugo to prove the rule): he would not feel the image poetical, and perhaps if he did, would not dare to say so. The Germans have in their way immense honesty and breadth of sympathy, and I like them for it. I like to be made to sympathise with their middle-class enthusiasm for domestic life and bread-and-butter. Let us be bold, and make them sympathise with our middle-class affection for commerce and bustle.

Ah, I wish I could believe that Mr. Arnold was describing the ideal and not the actual, when he dwells on the educational, the missionary, function of culture, and says that its greatest passion is for making sweetness and light prevail. For I think we might soon be agreed as to how they may be made to prevail. Religions have been propagated by the sword: but culture cannot be propagated by the sword, nor by the pen sharpened and wielded like an offensive weapon. Culture, like all spiritual gifts, can only be propagated by enthusiasm: and by enthusiasm that has got rid of asperity, that has become sympathetic; that has got rid of Pharisaism, and become humble. I suppose Mr. Arnold would hardly deny that in the attitude in which he shows himself, contemplating the wealthy Philistine through his eyeglass, he has at least a superficial resemblance to a Pharisee. Let us not be too hard on Pharisaism of any kind. It is better that religion should be self-asserting than that it should be crushed and stifled by rampant worldliness; and where the worship of wealth is predominant it is perhaps a necessary antagonism that intellect should be self-asserting. But I cannot see that intellectual Pharisaism is any less injurious to true culture than religious Pharisaism to true worship; and when a poet keeps congratulating himself that he is not a Philistine, and pointing out (even exaggerating) all the differences between himself and a Philistine, I ask myself, Where is the sweetness of culture? For the moment it seems to have turned sour.

Perhaps what is most disappointing in our culture is its want of appreciation of the "sap of progress," the creative and active element of things. We all remember the profound epigram of Agassiz, that the world in dealing with a new truth passes through three stages: it first says that it is not true, then that it is contrary to religion, and finally, that we knew it before. Culture is raised above the first two stages, but it is apt to disport itself complacently in the third. "Culture," we are told, "is always assigning to the system-maker and his system a smaller share in the bent of human destiny than their friends like." Quite so: a most useful function: but culture does this with so much zest that it is continually overdoing it. The system-maker may be compared to a man who sees that mankind want a house built. He erects a scaffolding with much unassisted labour, and begins to build. The scaffolding is often unnecessarily large and clumsy, and the system-maker is apt to keep it up much longer than it is needed. Culture looks at the unsightly structure with contempt, and from time to time kicks over some useless piece of timber. The house, however, gets built, is seen to be serviceable, and culture is soon found benevolently diffusing sweetness and light through the apartments. For culture perceives the need of houses; and is even ready to say in its royal way, 'Let suitable mansions be prepared; only without this eternal hammering, these obtrusive stones and timber.' We must not forget, however, that construction and destruction are treated with equal impartiality. When a miserable fanatic has knocked down some social abuse with much peril of life and limb, culture is good enough to point out to him that he need not have taken so much trouble: culture had seen the thing was falling; it would soon have fallen of its own accord; the crash has been unpleasant, and raised a good deal of disagreeable dust.

All this criticism of action is very valuable; but it is usually given in excess, just because, I think, culture is a little sore in conscience, is uncomfortably eager to excuse its own evident incapacity for action. Culture is always hinting at a convenient season, that rarely seems to arrive. It is always suggesting one decisive blow that is to be gracefully given; but it is so difficult to strike quite harmoniously, and without some derangement of attitude. Hence an instinctive, and, I think, irrational, discouragement of the action upon which less cultivated people are meanwhile spending themselves. For what does action, social action, really mean? It means losing oneself in a mass of disagreeable, hard, mechanical details, and trying to influence many dull or careless or bigoted people for the sake of ends that were at first of doubtful brilliancy, and are continually being dimmed and dwarfed by the clouds of conflict. Is this the kind of thing to which human nature is desperately prone, and into which it is continually rushing with perilous avidity? Mr. Arnold may say that he does not discourage action, but only asks for delay, in order that we may act with sufficient knowledge. This is the eternal excuse of indolence—insufficient knowledge: still, taken cautiously, the warning is valuable, and we may thank Mr. Arnold for it: we cannot be too much stimulated to study the laws of the social phenomena that we wish to modify, in order that "reason the card" may be as complete and accurate as possible. But we remember that we have heard all this before at much length from a very different sort of prophet. It has been preached to us by a school small, but energetic (energetic to a degree that causes Mr. Arnold to scream 'Jacobinism!'): and the preaching has been not in the name of culture, but in the name of religion and self-sacrifice.

I do not ask much sympathy for the people of action from the people of culture: I will show by an example how much. Paley somewhere, in one of his optimistic expositions of the comfortableness of things, remarks, that if he is ever inclined to grumble at his taxes, when he gets his newspaper he feels repaid; he feels that he could not lay out the money better than in purchasing the spectacle of all this varied life and bustle. There are more taxes now, but there are more and bigger newspapers: let us hope that Paley would still consider the account balanced. Now, might not Mr. Arnold imbibe a little of this pleasant spirit? As it is, no one who is doing anything can feel that Mr. Arnold hearing of it is the least bit more content to pay his taxes—that is, unless he is doing it in some supremely graceful and harmonious way.

One cannot think on this subject without recalling the great man who recommended to philosophy a position very similar to that now claimed for culture. I wish to give Mr. Arnold the full benefit of his resemblance to Plato. But when we look closer at the two positions, the dissimilarity comes out: they have a very different effect on our feelings and imagination; and I confess I feel more sympathy with the melancholy philosopher looking out with hopeless placidity "from beneath the shelter of some wall" on the storms and dust-clouds of blind and selfish conflict, than with a cheerful modern liberal, tempered by renouncement, shuddering aloof from the rank exhalations of vulgar enthusiasm, and holding up the pouncet-box of culture betwixt the wind and his nobility.

To prolong this fault-finding would be neither pleasant nor profitable. But perhaps many who love culture much —and respect the enthusiasm of those who love it more— may be sorry when it is brought into antagonism with things that are more dear to them even than culture. I think Mr. Arnold wishes for the reconciliation of antagonisms: I think that in many respects, with his subtle eloquence, his breadth of view, and above all his admirable temper, he is excellently fitted to reconcile antagonisms; and therefore I am vexed when I find him, in an access of dilettante humour, doing not a little to exasperate and exacerbate them, and dropping from the prophet of an ideal culture into a more or less prejudiced advocate of the actual.

III

THE POEMS AND PROSE REMAINS OF ARTHUR HUGH CLOUGH [1]

(*Westminster Review*, October 1869)

THESE two volumes contain all that will now be given to the world of a very rare and remarkable mind. The editor has, we think, exercised a wise confidence in transgressing what is usually a safe rule in posthumous publications, and including in the volume some prose that the author had probably not composed for permanence, and some verse that is either palpably unfinished, or at any rate not stamped with the author's final approval. Clough's productive impulse was not energetic, and only operated under favourable conditions, which the circumstances of his life but scantily afforded. Therefore the sum-total of his remains, when all is included, does not form an unwieldy book; and on the other hand his work is so sincere and independent that even when the result is least interesting it does not disappoint, while his production is always so rigidly in accordance with the inner laws of his nature, and expresses so faithfully the working of his mind, that nothing we have here could have been spared, without a loss of at least biographical completeness. There is much that will hardly be interesting, except to those who have been powerfully influenced by the individuality of the author. But the number of such persons (as every evidence shows), has not

---

[1] *The Poems and Prose Remains of Arthur Hugh Clough, with a Selection from his Letters, and a Memoir.* Edited by his WIFE. London: Macmillan and Co. 1869.

diminished, but largely increased during the ten years that have elapsed since his death: the circle of interest has gone on widening without becoming fainter, and now includes no small portion of a younger generation, to whom especially the publication of these volumes will afford timely and welcome gratification.

The tentative and gradual process by which Clough's remains have been published is evidence and natural result of the slow growth of his popularity. For this there seem to have been several reasons. It is partly due to the subject-matter of his writings. He was in a very literal sense before his age. His point of view and habit of mind are less singular in England in the year 1869 than they were in 1859, and much less than they were in 1849. We are growing year by year more introspective and self-conscious: the current philosophy leads us to a close, patient, and impartial observation and analysis of our mental processes: and the current philosophy is partly the effect and partly the cause of a more widespread tendency. We are growing at the same time more unreserved and unveiled in our expression: in conversations, in journals and books, we more and more say and write what we actually do think and feel, and not what we intend to think or should desire to feel. We are growing also more sceptical in the proper sense of the word: we suspend our judgment much more than our predecessors, and much more contentedly: we see that there are many sides to many questions: the opinions that we do hold we hold if not more loosely, at least more at arm's length: we can imagine how they appear to others, and can conceive ourselves not holding them. We are losing in faith and confidence: if we are not failing in hope, our hopes at least are becoming more indefinite; and we are gaining in impartiality and comprehensiveness of sympathy. In each of these respects, Clough, if he were still alive, would find himself gradually more and more at home in the changing world. In the second place his style, at least in his longer poems, is, though without any affectation, very peculiar: at the same time he has not sufficient loudness of utterance to compel public attention. Such a style is naturally slow in making way. Even a sympathising reader has to get accustomed to its oddities before he can properly feel its beauties. Afterwards, if it has real excellence, its peculiarity becomes an additional charm. Again, the chief excellence of Clough's style lies in a very delicate and precise adaptation of form to matter, attained with felicitous freshness and singular simplicity of manner; it has little superficial brilliancy wherewith to captivate a reader who through carelessness or want of sympathy fails to apprehend the *nuance* of feeling.

To this we may perhaps add, that the tone which many of Clough's personal friends have adopted in speaking of the author and his writings has, though partly the result, been also partly the cause of the slow growth of their popularity. It was, for example, certainly a misfortune that in issuing the first posthumous edition of these poems, Mrs. Clough prefaced them with a notice by Mr. Palgrave, a critic of much merit, but quite inappreciative of his friend's peculiar genius, and whose voluble dogmatism renders his well-meant patronage particularly depressing. There is a natural disposition among personal friends to dwell upon unrealised possibilities, and exalt what a man would, could, or should have done at the expense of what he actually did; and to this in Clough's case circumstances were very favourable. In the first place he produced very little, and the habit of demanding from candidates for literary fame a certain quantum of production seems inveterate, though past experience has shown the fallacy of the demand, and we may expect it to become still more patent in the future. Indeed, if we continue as we are now doing, to extend our own literary production and our sympathy and familiarity with past and alien literature *pari passu*, the reader of the future will have so much difficulty in distributing his time among the crowd of immortal works, that he certainly will contract a dislike to the more voluminous. And in the case of poems like these, that are attractive chiefly because they are characteristical and representative, because they express in an original and appropriate manner a side of human life, a department of thought and feeling, that waited for poetical expression, voluminous production seems not only unnecessary but even dangerous. On a subjective poet continence should especially be enjoined; if he writes much he is in danger of repeating words or tune; if he tries to write much he is in danger of mistaking his faculties and forcing his inspiration.

But besides this scantiness of production, there is much in the external aspect of Clough's career which justifies the disposition to regard his life as "wasted"—at best an interesting failure. We have before us a man always trying to solve insoluble problems, and reconcile secular antagonisms, pondering the "uralte ewige Räthsel" of existence, at once inert and restless, finding no fixed basis for life nor elevated sphere of action, tossed from one occupation to another, and exhausting his energies in work that brought little money and no fame; a man who cannot suit himself to the world nor the world to him, who will neither heartily accept mundane conditions and pursue the objects of ordinary mankind, nor effectively reject them as a devotee of something definite; a dreamer who will not even dream pleasant dreams, a man who "makes the worst of both worlds."

This is no doubt a natural complaint from a practical point of view, but it ignores the fact that the source of Clough's literary originality and importance lies precisely in what unfitted him for practical success. He was overweighted with certain impulses, felt certain feelings with a too absorbing and prolonged intensity; but the impulses were noble, at least an "infirmity of noble minds"; they are incident to most fine natures at a certain stage of their development, and generally are not repressed without a certain sense of loss and sacrifice. This phase of feeling is worthy of being worthily expressed, and it is natural that it should be so expressed by one who feels it more strongly than other men—too strongly for his own individual happiness.

It is the same with other phases of feeling. Out of many poets there are few Goethes; the most are sacrificed in some sort to their poetical function, and it is but a commonplace sympathy that loudly regrets it. Those at any rate who had no personal knowledge of Clough, may recognise that this life, apparently so inharmonious, was really in the truest harmony with the work that nature gave him to do. In one sense, no doubt, that work was incomplete and fragmentary; the effort of the man who ponders insoluble problems, and spends his passion on the vain endeavour to reconcile aspirations and actualities, must necessarily be so; the incompleteness is essential, not accidental. But his expression of what he had to express is scarcely incomplete, and though we have no doubt lost something by his premature death we can hardly think that we have lost the best he had to give. His poetical utterance was connected by an inner necessity with his personal experience, and he had already passed into a phase of thought and feeling which could hardly lead to artistic expression so penetrating and stirring as his earlier poems.

But we shall better discuss this question after a closer examination of his work, of what he had to express and how he expressed it.

In this examination we shall treat Clough as a poet. It is necessary to premise this, because he was a philosophic poet,—a being about whose nature and *raison d'être* the critical world is not thoroughly agreed. Philosophic poetry is often treated as if it was versified philosophy, as if its primary function was to 'convey ideas,' the only question being whether these should be conveyed with or without metre. Proceeding on this assumption, an influential sect maintains that there ought to be no philosophic poetry at all; that the 'ideas' it 'conveys' had much better seek the channel of prose. To us it seems that what poetry has to communicate is not ideas but moods and feelings; and that if a feeling reaches sufficient intensity, whatever be its specific quality, it is adapted for a poetical form, though highly intellectual moods are harder to mould to the conditions of metrical expression than others. The question is often raised, especially at the present day, when our leading poets are philosophic, whether such and such a poem—say Browning's *Christmas Eve*, or parts of *In Memoriam*—would not have been better in prose. And the question is often a fair one for discussion, but a wrong criterion is used for determining it. If such a poem is really unpoetical, it is not because it contains too much thought, but too little feeling to steep and penetrate the thought. Tried by this test, a good deal of Browning's thought-laden verse, and some of Tennyson's, will appear not truly poetical; the feeling is not adequate. Although Clough sometimes fails in this way, it may generally be said that with him the greater the contention of thought, the more intense is the feeling transfused through it. He becomes unpoetical chiefly when he becomes less eagerly intellectual, when he lapses for a moment into mild optimism, or any form of languid contentment; or when like Wordsworth he caresses a rather too trivial mood; very rarely when the depths of his mind are stirred. He is, then, pre-eminently a philosophic poet, communicator of moods that depend on profound and complex trains of reflection, abstract and highly refined speculations, subtle intellectual perceptions, and that cannot be felt unless these are properly apprehended. He is to a great extent a poet for thinkers; but he moves them not as a thinker, but as a poet.

We do not mean to say that Clough was not a thinker; but the term was somewhat indefinite, and in one sense he was not. His mind brooded over a few great questions, and was rather finely receptive than eagerly discursive; he did not enjoy the mere exercise of thought for its own sake. This is evidenced by the first of the volumes before us, especially the letters, which, except in the rare instances where he drops to his habitual depth of meditation, are perhaps somewhat disappointing. There is humour in them, but the vein is thin; and subtlety, perpetual subtlety, and from time to time a pleasant flow of characteristically whimsical fancy; there is also a permanent accuracy, propriety, *justesse* of observation, remarkable in compositions so carelessly thrown off; but fertility and rapid movement of ideas are wanting. They do not seem the work of a mind that ranges with pleasure and vigour over all subjects that come in its way. The critical essays, again, that have been republished, though exceedingly just, careful, and independent, and therefore always worth reading, are not very striking; with the exception of occasional passages where passionate utterance is given to some great general truth. But though he was too much of a poet to care greatly for the mere exercise of the cognitive faculties, though no one could less have adopted the "philosopher's paradox" of Lessing, we may still call him philosophic from his passionate devotion not to search after truth, but to truth itself—absolute, exact truth. He was philosophic in his horror of illusions and deceptions of all kinds; in his perpetual watchfulness against prejudices and prepossessions; against the Idols, as Bacon calls them, of the Cave and the Theatre, as well as of the Tribe and the Market-place. He was made for a free-thinker rather than a scientific inquirer. His skill lay in balancing assertions, comparing points of view, sifting gold from dross in the intellectual products presented to him, rejecting the rhetorical, defining the vague, paring away the exaggerative, reducing theory and argument to their simplest form, their "lowest terms." "Lumen siccum," as he calls it in one of his poems, is the object of his painful search, his eager hope, his anxious loyalty.

The intellectual function, then, which Clough naturally assumed was scepticism of the Socratic sort—scepticism occupied about problems on which grave practical issues depended. The fundamental assumptions involved in men's habitual lines of endeavour, which determined their ends and guided the formation of their rules, he was continually endeavouring to clear from error, and fix upon a sound basis. He would not accept either false solutions or no solutions, nor, unless very reluctantly, provisional solutions. At the same time, he saw just as clearly as other men that the continued contemplation of insoluble problems is not merely unpractical, but anti-practical; and that a healthy and natural instinct forces most men, after a few years of feverish youthful agitation, resolutely to turn away from it. But with this instinct Clough's fine passion for absolute truth conflicted; if he saw two sides of a question, he must keep seeking a point of view from which they might be harmonised. In one of the most impressive of the poems classed in this edition as *Songs in Absence*, he describes his disposition

> To finger idly some old Gordian knot,
> Unskilled to sunder, and too weak to cleave;

but the reluctance to cleave knots, in the speculative sphere, does not proceed from weakness.

It is this supreme loyalty to reason, combining and conflicting with the most comprehensive and profound sympathy with other elements of human nature, that constitutes the peculiar charm of Clough's scepticism, and its peculiar adaptation to poetical expression. Towards the beliefs to which other men were led by their desires, he was as strongly, or more strongly, impelled than others; the assertions in which they formulated their hopes he would gladly have made with the same cheerful dogmatism. His yearning for the ideal he never tried to quench or satisfy with aught but its proper satisfaction; but meanwhile the claims of the real, to be accepted as real, are paramount. He clings to the "beauty of his dreams;" but—two and two make four. It is the painfulness, and yet inevitableness of this conflict, the childlike simplicity and submissiveness with which he yields himself up to it; the patient tenacity with which he refuses to quit his hold of any of the conflicting elements; the consistency with which it is carried into every department of life; the strange mixture of sympathy and want of sympathy with his fellow-creatures that necessarily accompanies it—that makes the moods which he has expressed in verse so rare, complex, subtle, and intense.

We may classify these moods, according to a division suggested by this edition, into first, those of religious scepticism, where the philosophic impulse is in conflict with the mystical; secondly, those of ethical scepticism, where it contends with habitual active principles; thirdly, those where it is perplexed with the most clamorous and absorbing of human enthusiasms, the passion which forms the peculiar topic of poetry. It is this latter division that at once completes the consistency of Clough's scepticism, and forms its most novel, original, and least understood application. As he himself says, not only "saint and sage," but also "poet's dreams,"

> Divide the light in coloured streams;

the votary of truth must seek "lumen siccum."

The personal history of Clough's religious scepticism has rather to be guessed than known from the records of his life that lie before us. The memoir prefixed to the volume, written with great delicacy and dignity, but with an unreserve and anxious exactness in describing his phases of thought and feeling worthy of the subject and most grateful to the reader, can tell us little on this head. Nor do the letters that lead us up to the time when he must in effect have abandoned the beliefs of his childhood at all prepare us for so deep a change. At Rugby he seems to have yielded himself entirely to the influence of Arnold, and to have embraced with zealous docility the view of life which that remarkable man impressed so strongly, for good or for evil, on his more susceptible pupils. But though somewhat over-solemn and prematurely earnest, like many Rugby boys of the time, he was saved from priggishness by his perfect simplicity. At Balliol he shows nothing of the impulsiveness, vehemence, and restlessness, the spirit of dispute and revolt, which are supposed to precede and introduce deliberate infidelity. Thrown upon Oxford at the time when the "Newmanitish phantasm," as he calls it, was startling and exciting Young England, he writes of the movement to his friends with a mild and sober eclecticism—a tranquil *juste-milieu* temper which would become a dean. He is candidly observant, gives measured admiration for good points, notes extravagances, suggests the proper antidotes, seems disposed, on the whole, to keep out of the atmosphere of controversy and devote himself to his studies. Nothing could give smoother promise of untroubled orthodoxy. It is true that he speaks of being "exhausted by the vortex of philosophism"; and he must have been much more powerfully influenced by Newmanism than these letters indicate. He said afterwards, that for two years of this time he had been "like a straw drawn up the vortex of a chimney." His mind seems habitually to have been swayed by large, slow, deep-sea currents, the surface remaining placid, even tame; such a steady hidden movement it seems to have been that floated him away from his old moorings of belief. Gradually or suddenly the theologico-juridical, ecclesiastico-mystical dialectics that went on around him became shadowy and unreal: all his religious needs, hopes, aspirations remaining the same, a new view of the universe, with slowly accumulating force, impressed itself irresistibly on his mind, with which not only the intellectual beliefs entwined with these needs and aspirations seemed incompatible, but even these latter fundamentally incongruous. And thus began a conflict between old and new that was to last his life, the various moods of which the series of his religious poems, solemn, passionate, and ironical, accurately expresses.[1]

Perhaps the first characteristic that we notice in these is their rare reality and spontaneity. We feel that they are uttered, just as they appear, from an inner necessity; there was no choice to say them or not to say them. With

[1] A similar account is to be given of another event in his life, his abandonment of outward conformity to Anglicanism and its material appurtenances of an Oriel fellowship and tutorship. No reader of his life and writings can doubt that with him this step was necessarily involved in the change of opinions: yet many years elapsed between the two, and his biographer thinks that it was "some-half-accidental confirmation of his doubts as to the honesty and usefulness of his course" that finally led him to resignation. Such accident can surely have been but the immediate occasion, expressing the slow hidden growth of resolve. Lax subscription to articles was the way of Clough's world: and it belonged to his balanced temper to follow the way of his world for a time, not approving, but provisionally submitting and experimentalising. To do what others do till its unsatisfactoriness has been thoroughly proved, and then suddenly to refuse to do it any longer, is not exactly heroic, nor is it the way to make life pleasant; but as a *via media* between fanaticism and worldliness, it would naturally commend itself to a mind like Clough's.

some poets religious unbelief or doubt seems an abiding attitude of intellect, but only occasionally to engross the heart; their utterances have the gusty force of transitory passion, not the vitality of permanent feeling. But with Clough it is different: the whole man is in the poems—they spring from the very core of his being. The levity of some of them is as touching as the solemnity of others; it is a surface-mood, showing explored depths beneath it, in which an unrestful spirit finds momentary relief. Another characteristic is, that over the saddest cries of regret and struggles of checked aspiration is spread a certain tranquillity—not of hope, still less of despair, but a tranquillity that has something Aristotelian in it, the tranquillity of intellectual contemplation. It is curious, for example, to contrast the imperishable complaint of Alfred de Musset—

> Quand j'ai connu la vérité,
> J'ai cru que c'était une amie ;
> Quand je l'ai comprise et sentie,
> J'en étais déjà dégoûté ;

with Clough's

> It fortifies my soul to know
> That, though I perish, Truth is so.

The known order of the world, even without the certainty of a personal God, source or correlate of that order, afforded somewhat of philosophic satisfaction, however little it could content the yearnings of his soul. It was a sort of *terra firma*, on which he could set his feet, while his eyes gazed with patient scrutiny into the unanswering void. Further, we remark in these moods their balanced, complex character; there is either a solemn reconciliation of conflicting impulses, or a subtle and shifting suggestion of different points of view. Specimens of the former are two hymns (as we may call them), headed "*Qui laborat orat*," and ὕμνος ἄυμνος; they attempt to reconcile the intellectual resolve to retain clear vision with religious self-abandonment. The latter of these has a little too much intellectual subtlety and academic antithesis; but the former is one of Clough's most perfect productions; there is a deep pathos in the restrained passion of worship, and the clear-cut exactness of phrase, as it belongs to the very essence of the sentiment, enhances the dignity of the style. Somewhat similar in feeling, but more passionate and less harmonious, is the following fragment :—

> O let me love my love unto myself alone,
> And know my knowledge to the world unknown ;
> No witness to the vision call,
> Beholding, unbeheld of all ;
> And worship Thee, with Thee withdrawn apart,
> Whoe'er, whate'er Thou art,
> Within the closest veil of mine own inmost heart.
>
> .   .   .   .   .
>
> Better it were, thou sayest, to consent :
> Feast while we may, and live ere life be spent ;
> Close up clear eyes, and call the unstable sure,
> The unlovely lovely, and the filthy pure ;
> In self-belyings, self-deceivings roll,
> And lose in Action, Passion, Talk, the soul.
>
> Nay, better far to mark off so much air,
> And call it Heaven : place bliss and glory there ;
> Fix perfect homes in the unsubstantial sky,
> And say, what is not, will be by and by.

Sometimes the intellectual, or as we have called it, philosophical element, shows itself in a violence of sincerity that seems reckless, but is rather, to use a German word, *rücksichtslos*; it disregards other considerations, not from blind impulse but deep conviction. The tone of the poem is then that of one walking firmly over red-hot ploughshares, and attests at once the passion and the painfulness of looking facts in the face. In the fine poem called *Easter Day* (where a full sense of the fascination of the Christian story and the belief in immortality depending on it, and of the immensity of its loss to mankind, conflicts with scientific loyalty to the modern explanation of it), the intensity of the blended feeling fuses a prosaic material into poetry very remarkably.

>   What if the women, ere the dawn was grey,
>   Saw one or more great angels, as they say,
>   (Angels or Him himself)? Yet neither there, nor then,
>   Nor afterwards, nor elsewhere, nor at all,
>   Hath he appeared to Peter or the Ten ;
>   Nor, save in thunderous terror, to blind Saul ;
>   Save in an after Gospel and late Creed,
>   He is not risen, indeed,—
>   Christ is not risen.
>
>   .   .   .   .   .   .
>
>   As circulates in some great city crowd
>   A rumour changeful, vague, importunate, and loud,
>   From no determined centre, or of fact
>   Or authorship exact,
>   Which no man can deny
>   Nor verify ;
>   So spread the wondrous fame ;
>   He all the same
>   Lay senseless, mouldering, low :
>   He was not risen, no—
>   Christ was not risen !
>
>   Ashes to ashes, dust to dust ;
>   As of the unjust, also of the just—
>   Yea, of that Just one, too !
>   This is the one sad Gospel that is true,
>   Christ is not risen !

The complex and balanced state of Clough's moods shows itself in an irony unlike the irony of any other writer ; it is so subtle, frequently fading to a mere shade, and so all-pervading. In the midst of apparently most earnest expression of any view, it surprises us with a suggestion of the impossibility that that view should be adequate ; sometimes it shifts from one side of a question to the other, so that it is impossible to tell either from direct expression or ironical suggestion what the writer's decision on the whole is. In some of the later stanzas of the poem we have quoted the irony becomes very marked, as where the "Men of Galilee" are addressed—

>   Ye poor deluded youths, go home,
>   Mend the old nets ye left to roam,

> Tie the split oar, patch the torn sail :
> It was indeed an "idle tale,"
> He was not risen.

The truth is, that though Clough from time to time attempts to reconcile and settle, his deepest conviction is that all settlement is premature. We meet continually phrases like the

> Receive it not, yet leave it not,
> And wait it out, O man,

of one of his earlier poems. To use a favourite image of his, the universe, by our present arithmetic, comes to much less than we had fondly imagined. Our arithmetic is sound, and must be trusted; in fact, it is the only arithmetic we have got. Still the disappointing nature of the result (and let us never pretend to ourselves that it is not disappointing) may be taken as some evidence of its incompleteness.

This irony assumes a peculiar tone when it is directed to vulgar, shallow, unworthy states of mind. It is not that Clough passionately repudiates these, and takes up a censorial position outside and over against them; these, too, are facts, common and important facts of humanity; *humani nihil*—not even Philistinism—*a se alienum putat*. His contempt for them is deep, but not bitter; indeed, so far from bitter that a dull pious ear may misperceive in it an unpleasing levity. His mode of treating them is to present them in extreme and bald simplicity, so that the mind recoils from them. A penetrating observer describes something like this as a part of Clough's conversational manner. "He had a way," says Mr. Bagehot, "of presenting your own view to you, so that you saw what it came to, and that you did not like it." A good instance of this occurs in an unfinished poem, called *The Shadow* (published in this edition for the first time). We quote the greater part of it, as it also exemplifies Clough's powerful, though sparingly exercised, imagination; which here, from the combination of sublimity and quaintness, reminds one of Richter, only that we have antique severity instead of romantic profuseness :—

> I dreamed a dream : I dreamt that I espied,
> Upon a stone that was not rolled aside,
> A Shadow sit upon a grave—a Shade,
> As thin, as unsubstantial, as of old
> Came, the Greek poet told,
> To lick the life-blood in the trench Ulysses made—
> As pale, as thin, and said :
> "I am the Resurrection of the Dead.
> The night is past, the morning is at hand,
> And I must in my proper semblance stand,
> Appear brief space and vanish,—listen, this is true,
> I am that Jesus whom they slew."
>
> And shadows dim, I dreamed, the dead apostles came,
> And bent their heads for sorrow and for shame—
> Sorrow for their great loss, and shame
> For what they did in that vain name.
>
> And in long ranges far behind there seemed
> Pale vapoury angel forms ; or was it cloud ? that kept
> Strange watch; the women also stood beside and wept.
>   And Peter spoke the word :
> "O my own Lord,
> What is it we must do ?
> Is it then all untrue ?
> Did we not see, and hear, and handle Thee,
> Yea, for whole hours
> Upon the Mount in Galilee,
> On the lake shore, and here at Bethany,
> When Thou ascended to Thy God and ours ? "
>   And paler still became the distant cloud,
> And at the word the women wept aloud.
>
> And the Shade answered, "What ye say I know not ;
>   But it is true
>   I am that Jesus whom they slew,
> Whom ye have preached, but in what way I know not."
>
> *   *   *   *   *
>
> And the great World, it chanced, came by that way,
> And stopped, and looked, and spoke to the police,
> And said the thing, for order's sake and peace,
> Most certainly must be suppressed, the nuisance cease.

> His wife and daughter must have where to pray,
> And whom to pray to, at the least one day
> In seven, and something sensible to say.
>
> Whether the fact so many years ago
> Had, or not, happened, how was he to know ?
> Yet he had always heard that it was so.
> As for himself, perhaps it was all one ;
> And yet he found it not unpleasant, too,
> On Sunday morning in the roomy pew,
> To see the thing with such decorum done.
> As for himself, perhaps it was all one ;
> Yet on one's death-bed all men always said
> It was a comfortable thing to think upon
> The atonement and the resurrection of the dead
> So the great World as having said his say,
> Unto his country-house pursued his way.
> And on the grave the Shadow sat all day.

The effect of the latter part is like that of stripping an uncomely body, familiar to us as respectably draped and costumed, and showing it without disguise or ornament. That 'the world' has never seen himself in this nakedness we feel: but we also feel that here is the world which we know. The two lines before the three last show the felicitous audacity with which Clough sometimes manages metre: nothing could more sharply give the shallowness of the mood in contrast with the solemnity of the subject than the careless glibness of the lines,

> It was a comfortable thing to think upon
> The atonement and the resurrection of the dead.

The longest of the religious poems is an unfinished one called *The Mystery of the Fall*. The fundamental idea seems to be this. The legend of the Fall represents a permanent and universal element of human feeling, the religious conviction of sin, but only one element: the beliefs corresponding to it, even if intuitive consciousness is relied upon as their evidence, are not affirmed by the sum-total of valid consciousness — taking 'Sunday and work-days' together. Not only do our practical necessities and active impulses require and generate other conceptions of the universe which seem incompatible with the religious, but the latter is unsatisfying in itself: the notions of perfect creation, lapse, wrath, propitiation, though they correspond to a part of our religious experience, yet do not content our religious feeling as an adequate account of the relation of God to man. This Clough has tried to express, keeping the framework of the old legend, in dialogues between Adam, Eve, Cain, and Abel after expulsion from the garden. The transitions and blendings of the different moods are given with a close and subtle fidelity to psychological truth: and this putting of new wine into old bottles is perhaps justified by the prominence in human history of the Hebrew legend. There is no reason why Adam and his family should not be permanent machinery for serious fable, as Jove and his subordinates are for burlesque. Still the incongruity between the modern moods (and especially the perfect self-consciousness accompanying them) and the antique personages and incidents is here too whimsical: and, for poetry, the thought is too predominant, and the feeling not sufficiently intense; to some parts of the subject, as the murder of Abel, Clough's imagination is inadequate: and on the whole the result is interesting rather than successful, and we doubt whether the poem could ever have been completed so as to satisfy the author's severe self-criticism.

We take a very different view of the other unfinished long poem, *Dipsychus*. If it had received the author's final touches, a few trivialities and whimsicalities would no doubt have been pruned away: but we doubt whether the whole could have been much improved. It has certain grave defects which seem to us irremovable, and we should rank it as a work of art below either of his hexameter poems. There is not sufficient movement or evolution in it; the feeling is too purely egoistic to keep up our sympathies so long; and it is not sufficiently framed. The Venetian scenes in which the dialogue goes on, though appropriate to some of the moods, have no particular connection with the most important: whereas in *Amours de Voyage*, and still more in *The Bothie*, the harmonising of external and internal presentments is admirably managed. At the same time the composition is one of great interest. The stress of feeling is so sustained, the changes and fluctuations of mood are given with such perfect propriety, the thought and expression are so bold and novel yet free from paradox, so subtle without a particle of mere ingenuity. The blank verse too in parts, though only in parts, seems to have been carefully studied, and, though a little too suggestive of Elizabethan models, to attain a really high pitch of excellence. Perhaps no other poem of Clough's has so decidedly this one 'note' of genius, that its utterances are at once individual and universal, revealing the author to the reader, and at the same time the reader to himself.

The constructive idea of the poem, which is a dialogue between a man and an attendant spirit, is taken of course from *Faust*. But Goethe (as his half-apologetic prologue hints) sacrificed something in adapting his idea to the conditions of drama: and the issues in Clough's debate are so much finer, that we feel nothing imitative in his development of the conception. The suggestions of the spirit are never clearly fiendish in themselves; with much skill their fiendishness is made to lie in their relation to the man's thoughts. The spirit, in fact, is the "spirit of the world;" and the close of the debate is not between clear right and wrong (however plausible wrong), but between two sides of a really difficult question,—how far, in acting on society, rules and courses repugnant to the soul's ideal are to be adopted. True to himself, Clough does not decide the question; and though his sympathies are on the side of the ideal, we never know quite how far he would pronounce against the fiend.

The second part of the poem is almost too fragmentary to discuss. In it the man appears at the close of a successful career, having been attuned and attempered to the world by an immoral liaison. How far this means is justified by that end seems to us a disagreeable specialisation of the general problem of the first part, much more easy to decide. It is worked out, however, with much force. Several songs included in this poem were in the first edition published separately—by a great mistake, we cannot but think, as they have more force and beauty in their original setting; and it was a little unfair to Clough (though less than might be expected) to publish his fiend's utterances as his own.

We turn now to what we may call the amatory scepticism. This is a more proper subject of poetry, as thought here is in no danger of being too predominant over feeling; at the same time it is more novel and original, as on no subject do poets in general less allow thought to interfere with feeling. Poets, in fact, are the recognised preachers of the divinity, eternity, omnipotence of Love. It is true that with some of them fits of despair alternate with enthusiasm, and they proclaim that Love is an empty dream: but the notion of scrutinising the enthusiasm sympathetically, yet scientifically, and estimating the precise value of its claims and assertions, probably never entered into any poetic soul before Clough. Nor is it less alien to the habits of ordinary humanity. That the lover's state is a frenzy, innocuous indeed, delightful, perhaps even laudable as a part of nature's arrangements for carrying on the affairs of the world, but still a frenzy; that we all go into it and come out of it, take one view of things in general when in it and another when out of it—is what practical people accept with more or less playful or cynical acquiescence. Poets have a license to take an opposite view—in fact we should be disappointed if they did not; but we listen to them not for truth but for pleasant illusion. It will be seen how impossible it was for Clough's nature to acquiesce in this. Goethe sings of

> Den Drang nach Wahrheit und die Lust am Trug,

as part of the poet's endowment. It was Clough's peculiarity, perhaps his defect, as a poet, that he had not the "Lust am Trug." He feels the rapture that illusion gives, he quotes more than once with sympathy

Wen Gott betrügt ist wohl betrogen,

but such "wohl" he could not himself appropriate. Nor could he serenely separate idea from fact, as his friend Emerson does in the following passage :—

And the first condition [of painting Love] is, that we must leave a too close and lingering adherence to the actual, to facts. . . . Everything is beautiful seen from the point of the intellect. But all is sour, if seen as experience. Details are always melancholy: the plan is seemly and noble. It is strange how painful is the actual world,—the painful kingdom of time and place. There dwells care and canker and fear. With thought, with the ideal, is immortal hilarity, the rose of joy.

This well illustrates by contrast the fundamental mood of Clough. For his imagination at any time thus to abandon *terra firma* and console itself with cloudland would have been impossible. The fascination of the ideal was as strong for him as for other poets, but not stronger than the necessity of making it real. Hence in that period of youthful forecast and partial experience of passion, in which the finest love-fancies of most poets are woven, he perpetually feels the need of combining clear vision with exaltation. He keeps questioning Love as to what it really is, whence it comes, whither it goes: he demands a transcendent evaluation of it.

> Whence are ye, vague desires?
> Whence are ye?
>
> From seats of bliss above,
> Where angels sing of love;
> From subtle airs around,
> Or from the vulgar ground,
> Whence are ye, vague desires?
> Whence are ye?

'Is love spiritual or earthly?' is the passionate perplexity that tinges many of his songs. Or if this pearl of great price is to be found on earth, how shall we know it from its counterfeits, by what criterion discern the impulses that lead us to the true and the false? In one of the finer passages of the *Mari Magno* tales, this longing for direction is uttered.

> Beside the wishing gate which so they name,
> 'Mid northern hills to me this fancy came,
> A wish I formed, my wish I thus expressed:
> *Would I could wish my wishes all to rest,*
> *And know to wish the wish that were the best!*
> O for some winnowing wind, to the empty air
> This chaff of easy sympathies to bear
> Far off, and leave me of myself aware!
> While thus this over health deludes me still,
> So willing that I know not what I will;
> O for some friend, or more than friend, austere,
> To make me know myself and make me fear!
> O for some touch, too noble to be kind,
> To awake to life the mind within the mind!

But if love be after all only "a wondrous animal delight" in which nature's periodic blossoming culminates, the philosophic spirit, however deep its yearning, cannot submit to it, but has to contemplate it from the outside with tender and curious sympathy. This mood tinged with playfulness inspired the charming song in which he describes how he watched

> . . . in pleasant Kensington
> A 'prentice and a maid.
> That Sunday morning's April glow,
> How should it not impart
> A stir about the veins that flow
> To feed the youthful heart?

The rapture of this sympathetic contemplation is expressed in *Amours de Voyage*.

> And as I walk on my way, I behold them consorting and coupling;
> Faithful it seemeth and fond, very fond, very probably faithful,
> All as I go on my way, with a pleasure sincere and unmingled.
> Life is beautiful, Eustace . . . .
> . . . . and could we eliminate only
> This vile hungering impulse, this demon within us of craving,
> Life were beatitude, living a perfect divine satisfaction.

This leads us to the deepest issue of all—a thoroughly Platonic problem. Be this love as noble as it may, is its exaltation compatible with clear vision? Does not this individualised enthusiasm of necessity draw away from the centrality of view and feeling after which the philosophic spirit aspires? Is it not unworthy of us, for any pleasure's sake, to be tricked by its magic and take its coloured light for white?

But we are tired of reducing to prose the various phases of this subtle blending and conflict of enthusiasms. As expressed by Clough they have the perfect vitality and reality of all his moods. None of these perplexities is arbitrarily sought; the questions raised must each have been raised and decided by many human beings since self-consciousness began. If no poet has uttered them before, it is because in most men the state of mind in which they were felt is incompatible with the flow of feeling that poetry requires. Clough's nature was, perhaps, deficient in passion, but it had a superabundant tenderness and susceptibility to personal influence, which made him retain the full feeling of personal relations while giving free scope to his sceptical intellect.

In one of the two long hexameter poems published in his lifetime, *Amours de Voyage,* Clough has given a dramatic embodiment to the motives that we have been analysing. The poem is skilfully composed. Thoroughly apprehending the aversion which practical humanity feels for these perplexities, he somewhat exaggerates the egotism of the hero of the piece to whom he attributes them, handles him with much irony throughout, and inflicts a severe but appropriate Nemesis at the close. The caricature in 'Claude' is so marked that we are not surprised that Clough, the least egoistical of men, was indignant when a friend appeared to take the poem as an account of the author's own experiences. "I assure you," he writes, "that it is extremely not so." Still this attitude of the author could not reconcile the public to a hero who (as the motto has it) *doutait de tout, même de l'amour.* That the poem never attained the success of *The Bothie* we are not surprised. It has not the unique presentations of external nature which give such a charm to the earlier poem : it wants also the buoyant and vivacious humour which is so exuberant in *The Bothie*, and of which the fountain in Clough's later years seems almost to have dried up. But it shows greater skill in blending and harmonising different threads of a narrative, and a subtler management of the evolution of moods; it has a deeper psychological interest, and in its best passages a rarer, more original imagination. The 'amour' is very closely interwoven with the incidents of the French siege of Rome (of which, by the way, Clough's letters give us interesting details), so that the two series of events together elicit a complete and consistent self-revelation of the hero. The amative dubitations turn principally on two points—the immense issues that depend on amative selection compared with the arbitrary casual manner in which circumstances determine it, and the imperious claim of passion for a concentration of interest which to the innermost, most self-conscious, self is profoundly impossible. These play into one another in the following very characteristic passage :—

    Juxtaposition, in fine ; and what is juxtaposition ?
    Look you, we travel along in the railway carriage or steamer,
    And, *pour passer le temps*, till the tedious journey be ended,
    Lay aside paper or book, to talk with the girl that is next one ;
    And, *pour passer le temps*, with the terminus all but in prospect,
    Talk of eternal ties and marriages made in heaven.
    Ah, did we really accept with a perfect heart the illusion !
      Ah, did we really believe that the Present indeed is the Only !
    Or through all transmutation, all shock and convulsion of passion,
    Feel we could carry undimmed, unextinguished, the light of our
        knowledge !

      .   .   .   .

      But for the steady fore-sense of a freer and larger existence,
    Think you that man could consent to be circumscribed here into
        action ?
    But for assurance within of a limitless ocean divine, o'er
    Whose great tranquil depths unconscious the wind-tost surface
    Breaks into ripples of trouble that come and change and endure not,—
    But that in this, of a truth, we have our being, and know it,
    Think you we men could submit to live and move as we do here ?

Ah, but the women—God bless them! they don't think at all
about it.
Yet we must eat and drink as you say. And as limited beings
Scarcely can hope to attain upon earth to an Actual Abstract,
Leaving to God contemplation, to His hands knowledge confiding,
Sure that in us if it perish, in Him it abideth and dies not,
Let us in His sight accomplish our petty particular doings,—
Yes, and contented sit down to the victual that He has provided.

The three lines that we have italicised seem to us almost perfect specimens of the English hexameter, showing the extreme flexibility which the metre has in Clough's hands, and his only, and none of the over-accentuation which neither he nor any one else can generally avoid. Very opposite opinions have been delivered as to the merits of this hexameter. Some most appreciative readers of the poems declare that they read them continually under protest; that no interest in the subject and no habit can make the metre tolerable. Mr. Arnold, however, on this subject an especially Rhadamanthine critic, considers the success of Clough's experiment to be so decided as to form an important contribution to the question (which has occupied a most disproportionate amount of human intellect in our time), How Homer is to be translated? We do not take either view. We think Clough's metre, as he uses it, felicitous; but we do not think that this proves anything as to the appropriateness of the hexameter for translating Homer, or for any other application of 'the grand style.' Clough has not *naturalised* the metre. He has given it ease, but not simplicity; he has not tried to give it simplicity, and therefore he has succeeded with it. All English hexameters written quite *au sérieux* seem to us to fail; the line ought to be unconscious of being a hexameter, and yet never is. But Clough's line is, and is meant to be, conscious of being a hexameter: it is always suggestive of and allusive to the ancient serious hexameters, with a faint but a deliberate air of burlesque, a wink implying that the bard is singing academically to an academical audience, and catering for their artificial tastes in versification. This academic flavour suits each poem in a different way. It harmonises with the Oxonian studies of *The Bothie;* and here, indeed, the faint burlesque inseparable from the metre becomes from time to time mock-heroic. In *Amours de Voyage,* it suits the over-culture, artificial refinement of the hero's mind: he is, we may say, in his abnormal difficulties of action and emotion, a scholastic or academic personage. In short the metre seems to belong to a style full of characteristic self-conscious humour such as Clough has sustained through each of the poems; and we cannot analyse its effect separately. Clough we know thought differently; but we are forced to regard this as one instance out of many where a poet takes a wrong view of his own work. His experiment of translating Homer into similar hexameters is nearly as much a failure as Mr. Arnold's, or any other; and his still bolder experiment of writing hexameters by quantity and not accent results, in spite of the singular care and even power with which it is executed, in a mere monstrosity.

We consider then that it was a happy instinct that led him to the metre of *The Bothie.* In more ordinary metres he often shows a want of mastery over the technicalities of verse-writing. He has no fertility of rhymes, he is monotonous, he does not avoid sing-song, he wearies us with excessive, almost puerile, iterations and antitheses. It is very remarkable, therefore, how in this new metre, self-chosen, he rises to the occasion, how inventive he is of varied movements, felicitous phrases, and pleasant artifices of language, how emphatically yet easily the sound is adapted to the sense, in a way which no metre but blank verse in the hands of a master could rival. Another evidence of the peculiar fitness of this instrument for his thought is the amount that he can pack without effort into his lines; as *e. g.* in the following description of one of the members of the Oxford reading-party—

<blockquote>
Author forgotten and silent of currentest phrase and fancies,
Mute and exuberant by turns, a fountain at intervals playing,
Mute and abstracted, or strong and abundant as rain in the tropics;
Studious; careless of dress; inobservant; by smooth persuasions
Lately decoyed into kilt on example of Hope and the Piper;
Hope an Antinoüs mere, Hyperion of calves the Piper.
</blockquote>

It is hard to imagine so much said so shortly in any other style.

The flexibility of the metre aids in bringing out another great excellence of these poems; the ease and completeness with which character is exhibited. There is not one of the personages of *The Bothie*, or even of *Amours de Voyage*, where the sketching is much slighter, whose individuality is not as thoroughly impressed upon us as if they had been delineated in a three-volume novel by Mr. Trollope. We are made to understand by most happily selected touches, and delicately illustrative phrases, not only what they are in themselves, but precisely how they affect one another. It becomes as impossible for us to attribute a remembered remark to the wrong person as it would be in a play of Shakespeare. To say that Clough's dramatic faculty was strong might convey a wrong impression, as we imagine that he was quite devoid of the power of representing a scene of vivid action; but the power of forming distinct conceptions of character, and expressing them with the few touches that poetry allows, is one of the gifts for displaying which we may regret that he had not ampler scope.

The descriptions of natural scenery in *The Bothie* form probably the best-known and most popular part of Clough's poetry. In this, as in some of his most important poetical characteristics, he may be called, in spite of great differences, a true disciple of Wordsworth. His admiration for the latter appears to have been always strongly marked; and one of the more interesting of the prose remains now published is an essay on Wordsworth, perhaps somewhat meagre, but showing profound appreciation, together with the critical propriety and exactness of statement characteristic of Clough. His simplicity, sincerity, gravity, are all Wordsworthian; but especially his attitude towards nature. Through a manner of description quite different we trace the rapt receptive mood, the unaffected self-abandonment, the anxious fidelity of reproduction, which Wordsworth has taught to many disciples, but to no other poet so fully.

In the essay referred to we find a view of Wordsworth's

poetical merits, which to many persons will appear paradoxical, but which seems to us perfectly true, and applicable to some extent to Clough himself. He says that Wordsworth, the famous prefaces notwithstanding,—

"really derives from his style and his diction his chief and special charm"; . . . he bestowed "infinite toil and labour upon his poetic style"; "in the nice and exquisite felicities of poetic diction he specially surpassed his contemporaries"; and "his scrupulous and painstaking spirit, in this particular, constitutes one of his special virtues as a poet. . . . He has not . . . the vigour and heartiness of Scott, or the force and the sweep and the fervour of Byron. . . . But that permanent beauty of expression, that harmony between thought and word, which is the condition of '*immortal* verse,' they did not, I think—and Wordsworth did—take pains to attain. There is hardly anything in Byron and Scott which in another generation people will not think they can say over again quite as well, and more agreeably and familiarly for themselves; there is nothing which, it will be plain, has, in Scott or Byron's way of putting it, attained the one form which of all others truly belongs to it; which any new attempt will, at the very utmost, merely successfully repeat. For poetry, like science, has its final precision; and there are expressions of poetic knowledge which can no more be re-written than could the elements of geometry. There are pieces of poetic language which, try as men will, they will simply have to recur to, and confess that it has been done before them."

And he goes on to say that "people talk about style as if it were a mere accessory, the unneeded but pleasing ornament, the mere put-on dress of the substantial being, who without it is much the same as with it." Whereas really "some of the highest truths are only expressible to us by style, only appreciable as indicated by manner."

With all this we agree: but it seems to us that two conditions are necessary for the success in style spoken of, and that Clough has only given one. In order to attain it, a man must be conscious of very definite characteristic moods, and must have confidence in them, take an interest in and value their definite characteristics; then in expressing them he must work with a patient, single-minded effort to adapt the expression to the mood, caring always for the latter more than for the former. This was certainly the manner of Clough's composition, and hence many of his poetic utterances have, as he phrases it, "final precision." We do not mean to compare their effect to Wordsworth's. Clough has none of the prophetic dignity of his master, of the latter's organ-music he has not even an echo: and he far surpasses him in subtlety. There is a peculiar combination of simplicity and subtlety in his best things, the simplicity being as it were the final result and outcome of the subtlety, so that the presence of the latter is felt, and not distinctly recognised, which we find in no other poet except Goethe. It is this combination that fits him for his peculiar function of rendering conscious the feelings that pass half unconsciously through ordinary minds, without seriously modifying them. There is a pretty instance of this in an idyllic song which we will quote. Most of the song is rather commonplace; a peasant-girl driving she-goats homeward thinks alternately of the scene, and of her absent lover. Suddenly we are surprised with this very Cloughian sentiment.

> Or may it be that I shall find my mate,
> And he returning see himself too late?
> *For work we must, and what we see, we see,*
> *And God he knows, and what must be, must be,*
> When sweethearts wander far away from me.

The excellence of the lines that we have italicised we should describe paradoxically by saying that their naïveté is at once perfect, and as naïveté, impossible.

On the other hand, if Clough has many of Wordsworth's excellences, he certainly has his full share of the cognate defects. It is natural, perhaps, to the man who values the individuality of his thought and feeling so much as to spend great care on its expression, to want the power of discriminating between those parts of it that are, and those which are not worth expressing. Certainly Clough has not, any more than his master, the selective faculty that leads to the sustained elevation and distinction which we expect from a great poet, and which the adoption of a simple manner renders peculiarly indispensable. Commonplace thought and feeling in strikingly simple language does not make, perhaps, more really worthless poetry than commonplace thought and feeling in ornate language; but its worthlessness is more patent. There is this one advantage, that the critic is not forced to dwell upon it: no one's taste is perverted, except perhaps in the first charm of the poet's novelty. No one now pretends to admire the dulness and twaddle in Wordsworth; and in Clough even more than in Wordsworth the expression rises and falls with the matter: the dullest and most trivial things are the worst put. We will only say that the genius of twaddle, which often hovers near his muse, makes its presence especially felt in his last poems, the *Mari Magno* tales. These must, of course, be judged as unfinished productions; but no retouching could have enabled them to rank very high as poetry. They are easy, pleasant, even edifying reading, and they essentially want effectiveness. They are written in obvious emulation of Crabbe; and in a natural and faithful homeliness of style, which occasionally becomes a transparent medium for a most impressive tenderness, they certainly rival Crabbe; but their general level is much lower. The charm of Crabbe, when he is not tender, lies in the combination of unobtrusive dignity, and a certain rustic raciness and pregnancy, with a fair share of the artificial point and wit that properly belong to the Popian measure. Clough has nothing of this; and though in the best passages his characteristic fineness of apprehension makes amends, on the dead levels of narration the style is much inferior to Crabbe's: its blankness is glaring. In the first tale especially the genius of twaddle reigns supreme; it reminds us of—we will not say the worst, for it has no bad taste, but—the second-rate portions of Coventry Patmore.

The inferiority of these poems is due, as we before hinted, to a deeper cause than a temporary defect of vigour or a mistaken experiment of style. It is evident that we have here Clough without his peculiar inspiration—his talent, we may say, but not his genius. As an artist he is noteworthy—his production has many high qualities, viewed as technically as possible; it is not, however, as a mere artist, but as an utterer of peculiar yet representative moods, that he has the power to excite our deepest interest. But these moods are the moods, in the main, of youth; and when Clough, after a period of more than usually prolonged adolescence, finally adopted the adult attitude towards life, they ceased to dominate his habitual thought and feeling. Not that any abrupt change shows itself in him. There were two tempers singularly entwined in him throughout: his letters for the most part present a striking contrast to the contemporary poems. In the latter we find chiefly absorbing effort after an ideally clear vision, a perfect solution of problems: in the former mild practical wisdom, serene submission to the imperfections of life, cheerful acquiescence in "the best under the circumstances." And this quieter tone naturally grew upon him. Not that he could ever separate speculation from practice, or in either sphere settle down into smooth commonplace: but he grew tired of turning over the web of commonplace notions and rules, and showing their seamy side: he set himself rather to solve and settle instead of raising and exposing difficulties. At the same time the sincerity which had led him to emphasise his passionate perplexities, still kept him from exaggerating his triumph over them: he attains no fervour of confident hope, nor expansion of complacent optimism: he walks in the twilight, having adapted his eyes to it somewhat, but he does not mistake it for dawn. Whether in such twilight he would ever have seemed to see with sufficient clearness to impel him to utter his vision to the world, is doubtful: at any rate the utterance would, we imagine, have taken a prosaic and not a poetical form. He was looking at life steadily till he could see it whole: aspiring, as he says in an early poem, to

> . . . bring some worthy thing
> For waiting souls to see.

But the very loftiness of this aspiration, and the severity with which he would have judged his own claims to be a teacher, incline us to think that he would never have uttered the final outcome of his life's thought. What he wished to do for the world no one has yet done: we have scarcely reason to believe that he could have done it: and he would have been content to do nothing less. His provisional views, the temporary substitutes for "demonstrated faith" by which he was content to walk, he would hardly have cared to publish. That they would, however, have been interesting, we can see from the only fragment of them that the editor has been able to give us—a paper on *The Religious Tradition*. From this, as it illustrates a different side of Clough's mind to that on which we have been led chiefly to dwell, we will conclude by quoting some extracts :—

The more a man feels the value, the true import, of the moral and religious teaching which passes amongst us by the name of Christianity, the more will he hesitate to base it upon those foundations which, as a scholar, he feels to be unstable. Manuscripts are doubtful, records may be unauthentic, criticism is feeble, historical facts must be left uncertain. Even in like manner my own personal experience is most limited, perhaps even most delusive : what have I seen, what do I know? Nor is my personal judgment a thing which I feel any great satisfaction in trusting. My reasoning powers are weak ; my memory doubtful and confused; my conscience, it may be, callous or vitiated.

. . . I see not what other alternative any sane and humble-minded man can have but to throw himself upon the great religious tradition. But I see not either how any upright and strict dealer with himself—how any man not merely a slave to spiritual appetites, affections and wants—any man of intellectual as well as moral honesty—and without the former the latter is but a vain thing—I see not how anyone who will not tell lies to himself, can dare to affirm that the narrative of the four Gospels is an essential integral part of that tradition. I do not see that it is a great and noble thing . . . to go about proclaiming that Mark is inconsistent with Luke . . . it is no new gospel to tell us that the old one is of dubious authenticity. I do not see either . . . that it can be lawful for me, for the sake of the moral guidance and the spiritual comfort, to ignore all scientific or historic doubts, or if pressed with them to the utmost, to take refuge in Romish infallibility . . .

Where then, since neither in Rationalism nor in Rome is our refuge,—where then shall we seek for the Religious Tradition?

Everywhere; but above all in our own work: in life, in action, in submission, so far as action goes, in service, in experience, in patience, in confidence. I would scarcely have any man dare to say that he has found it, till that moment when death removes his power of telling it. Let no young man presume to talk to us vainly and confidently about it. Ignorant, as said Aristotle, of the real actions of life, and ready to follow all impressions and passions, he is hardly fitted as yet even to listen to practical directions couched in the language of religion. But this apart—everywhere . . . among all who have really tried to order their lives by the highest action of the reasonable and spiritual will.

[The following papers on Shakespeare's plays consist of parts of several lectures given at different times from 1889 to 1898 at Newnham College. As they did not form part of a course, but were delivered independently at considerable intervals of time, and to different audiences, it was almost inevitable that matters relating to Shakespeare's work generally should be treated of more than once in connexion with different plays, and these repetitions make it impossible to print all the lectures as they were given. Under the circumstances it seemed best to rearrange the lectures, with a few omissions and adjustments, adding only a very few words where required for connexion. —ED.]

IV

SHAKESPEARE'S METHODS, WITH SPECIAL REFERENCE TO *JULIUS CÆSAR* AND *CORIOLANUS*

JULIUS CÆSAR and *Coriolanus* are the first and last of the group of plays on which Shakespeare's unique position among modern poets mainly rests—the group or series of the seven great tragedies of his second and third periods—beginning with *Julius Cæsar* and *Hamlet*, and ending with *Antony and Cleopatra*, and *Coriolanus*, with *Othello, Lear*, and *Macbeth* intervening between the two. Before I say what I have to say about these plays, I should like to make clear what I shall try to do, and especially what I shall not try to do. I shall not try to give an abridged account of the story of the play, as told in successive scenes. I shall assume that we have probably all, at some time or other, read the play; and when I refer to points in the dramatic story, stages, or critical moments in its action, I shall do so chiefly with the aim of illustrating Shakespeare's method of work.

Still less shall I attempt to rival the admirable commentary of Mr. Aldis Wright, by dealing with any of the difficulties of interpretation which the play presents. But I should like to say a word as to the way in which commentaries of this kind should be used. Both the academic persons who manage examinations in English literature, and the commentators who assist in the preparation for them, are sometimes attacked as insidious foes of the culture that they profess to promote. It is said that under their influence the study of notes supplants and extinguishes the study of literature; and the story is told of a young lady who fastened up the text with an elastic band, that it might not distract her mind from the notes.

There is, perhaps, some justification for these sarcasms. The natural way of using a commentator is for occasional reference when we cannot understand the author; the systematic perusal of notes which an examination requires seems artificial and may be depressing. Still, I am persuaded, that with a view to reading Shakespeare with adequate intelligence, for literary enjoyment and culture, this close and thorough study of some one play is a valuable exercise. The most incurable defect in our ordinary reading of such an author lies in the misapprehensions of which we have no consciousness whatever;—the allusions that we merely miss, the subtle changes in the meaning of words and phrases that we simply ignore: but which, in the aggregate, interpose a thin impalpable mist between our mind and the author's, the source of which we cannot trace or remove. To correct this, it is very useful—whether with or without an examination in prospect—to take some one play and read it twice through carefully: the first time without a commentary, marking all the difficulties perceived: and the second time with a good commentary, marking all the meanings missed on the first reading as well as noting the solutions of the difficulties perceived. The immediate effect of the second process may be slightly depressing: but it will render all our subsequent reading of Shakespeare, for entertainment in hours of leisure, more intelligent than it would have been.

To-day, however, I am not concerned with the business of interpretation. My aim is chiefly to use these plays to illustrate Shakespeare's conception of dramatic work, and his method of working up his material, not forgetting the changes in his conception and method, and in the metrical instrument on which he plays such different tunes at different periods.

Let us begin by considering the date of the plays: for this is not a matter of merely biographical or bibliographical interest. The ardent and persistent scrutiny of Shakespeare and his times, during the present century, has produced no result of more value than the greater knowledge it has given us of the chronological order of the plays. For the chronological order is here markedly an order of development, and Shakespeare is a writer whose manner—both as regards style and versification, and as regards the deeper qualities of dramatic treatment—is in a continual process of change; and we cannot really attain to a full and delicate literary appreciation of his work if we read, say *Richard III.*, *Julius Cæsar*, and *Coriolanus*, as if they were the products of the same mind at the same time.

Fortunately, in the case of *Julius Cæsar* the date can be fixed, with a very high degree of probability, within very narrow limits. We can fix it at the commencement of the period in which Shakespeare's greatest work was done—in the latter part of 1600 or the beginning of 1601. It may be interesting to show how external and internal evidence combine to bring us to this result. We are very ignorant of Shakespeare's life: but there are a few points, a few milestones in his career, which we can recognise clearly; and these fortunately suffice to show us the general course of his work as a dramatist, and to mark its successive stages. We know that in 1585, at the age of twenty-one, he was married and father of three children baptized at Stratford-on-Avon. We know from a splenetic utterance in a pamphlet by Robert Greene, a leading dramatist of the time, written on his deathbed in 1592, that Shakespeare was then by profession a play-actor, who was at the same time rising into reputation as a playwright : he had risen enough to excite Greene's jealousy, but not enough to compel him to respectful treatment: he treats him as a conceited upstart Jack-of-all-trades, who absurdly supposes that he can write blank verse as well as the University men. Six years later, in 1598, his position is quite changed; for Francis Meres, M.A., in the *Wit's Treasury*, published that year, compares Shakespeare with Plautus and Seneca as a playwright for the stage, and calls him "among the English most excellent" both in comedy and tragedy. Meres mentions twelve plays, which include all the plays published in the first folio which we should on other grounds regard as Shakespeare's early work : he includes the obviously early comedies, *Love's Labour's Lost, Comedy of Errors, Two Gentlemen of Verona*, and the charming *Midsummer-Night's Dream ;* he includes also the crude exercise in bloody horrors called *Titus Andronicus*, and the fascinating but plainly youthful *Romeo and Juliet*. The other four plays that Meres classifies as tragedies belong to the group of English historical plays : *Julius Cæsar* is not among them. Shakespeare's serious work appears to have been concentrated at this time on the production of scenes from English chroniclers : he has not yet turned his attention to North's *Plutarch*.

Julius Cæsar, then, is not earlier than 1598 ; and as we have evidence that the second part of *Henry IV.* and *Henry V.* were written after Meres' book came out, but before the end of 1599, we may conceive Shakespeare as still occupied with English history to the end of the century. On the other hand, *Julius Cæsar* must have appeared before the end of 1601: because in Weever's *Mirror of Martyrs*, published that year, occur the lines—

> The many-headed multitude were drawne
> By Brutus' speech that Cæsar was ambitious.

This, as you know, is the simple and summary justification that Shakespeare's Brutus gives for his deed—

> As he was ambitious I slew him—

and the phrase is taken by Antony as the point which his
dexterous rhetoric has to repel, and is repeatedly quoted—

> But Brutus says he was ambitious, etc.

Now, though Plutarch indicates the lines of Antony's
funeral speech, which Shakespeare has followed, he says
nothing about this charge of ambition. This point is introduced by Shakespeare, and it is to Shakespeare's play that
Weever must refer. *Julius Cæsar*, then, is not later than
1601; and there are probable reasons for thinking it not
earlier than 1601.

And this date is confirmed by the internal evidence from
style and versification: which I shall presently illustrate.
Julius Cæsar, judged purely by its literary and metrical
quality, may be placed at the very point of transition from
Shakespeare's first to his second manner—so far as the
tragic style is concerned. It is, as I have said, the first of
the great series of plays of deep tragic interest—*i.e.* the
interest of sympathy with human beings of chequered but
not ignoble character, whose gloomy fate is partly woven
for themselves by the manifestation of their character under
pressure of their circumstances—in which Shakespeare's
unrivalled gifts of dramatic characterisation are exhibited
in full maturity.

In saying this, I do not, of course, mean to draw a broad
distinction between the first and second periods. Penetrating,
intense, versatile, imaginative sympathy with human nature
in all its varieties is a gift of Shakespeare's from the first;
and so far as comic characterisation goes, it is manifested
in one or two plays of the first period as fully as it ever is.
But in the more difficult characterisation of tragedy a somewhat longer interval of growth was required in which
Shakespeare's experience of life was widening and deepening,
and the mastery of his instrument becoming more complete.
It is not till we come to the second period—which we may
take to begin with *Julius Cæsar*, followed by *Hamlet*—that
Shakespeare's conception of character reaches its highest
point of subtlety, complexity, and coherence, and his pre-

sentation of character its highest point of vitality and impressiveness. Nor do I know any play earlier than *Julius Cæsar* in which is shown in an equally high degree the dramatist's art of combining incidents so as to exhibit the movement and working of character under stress of circumstances, and the art of framing situations and scenes so as to present effectively both the contrasts and the interaction of different characters in diverse moods.

And we may note a corresponding change in style and diction. In the plays of the first period the profusion and flow of poetic utterance does not always reveal an equal fulness of thought; there is sometimes, too, in the speeches too uniform a level of passion, a want of the gradual rise and fall of agitated emotion which is so striking a feature of Shakespeare's maturest work; there is a tendency to rhetorical amplification and rhetorical ingenuity—a liability to strain the natural imagery and inventiveness of passion into laboured conceits and extravagances.

Now, human improvement is usually gradual, and we cannot say that the style of *Julius Cæsar* is entirely free from these latter defects. For instance, at the crisis of the famous funeral oration of Antony, when he is showing the crowd the bloody garments of Cæsar, pierced by the assassins' swords—

> See what a rent the envious Casca made :
> Through this the well-beloved Brutus stabbed—

I am afraid that what follows is a conceit—

> And as he pluck'd his cursed steel away,
> Mark how the blood of Cæsar follow'd it,
> As rushing out of doors, to be resolved
> If Brutus so unkindly knock'd, or no.

Well, this image of the blood rushing out to see who is knocking is not the natural fantasy of passionate sorrow and indignation striving to communicate itself: it does not come from the heart, and we cannot conceive its finding its way to that organ. So before, when in Antony's pathetic outburst over the body of Cæsar, immediately after the murder, he cries—

> Here wast thou bay'd, brave hart;
> Here didst thou fall; and here thy hunters stand
> Sign'd in thy spoil and crimson'd in thy lethe—

the image is natural and moving: but when he goes on—

> O world, thou wast the forest to this *hart;*
> And this, indeed, O world, the *heart* of thee—

though the pun seems doubtless more grotesquely inappropriate to us than it would have seemed to an Elizabethan audience, it is difficult to believe that it can ever have seemed like the natural extravagance of emotion that finds ordinary expression feeble and inadequate. I do not think you will find such a pun at such a point of pathos in Shakespeare's later work.

These are spots in the sun. In the main the style of *Julius Cæsar* has freed itself from the immaturities of Shakespeare's earlier period. It is thoroughly dramatic: while there are many speeches in it which are eminently adapted for declamation—that is, for delivery apart from their dramatic context,—there is none that is in a bad sense declamatory: there is none that does not gain by its context, nor can be spared from it without some loss to the dramatic situation. It is interesting to compare the style of *Julius Cæsar* in this respect with that of *Coriolanus*, which exemplifies Shakespeare's third and latest manner. In this last stage the style suited to declamation has been altogether abandoned: the manner is purely dramatic. You can hardly find a single speech in *Coriolanus* calculated to give much pleasure, if severed from its context: though in their context the best speeches of *Coriolanus* have—with some loss of lucidity—a greater intensity of emphasis through greater concentration, and a more lifelike representation of the utterances of surging passion.

I will give here one illustration from *Julius Cæsar* of this double quality—declamatory and dramatic. On the eve of the Ides of March, when the last struggle in Brutus' mind is over, his servant tells him that Cassius and others have come with

> their hats plucked about their ears,
> And half their faces buried in their cloaks.

Brutus answers—
> Let 'em enter.
> They are the faction. O conspiracy,
> Shamest thou to show thy dangerous brow by night,
> When evils are most free ? O, then by day
> Where wilt thou find a cavern dark enough
> To mask thy monstrous visage ? Seek none, conspiracy ;
> Hide it in smiles, and affability :
> For if thou path, thy native semblance on,
> Not Erebus itself were dim enough
> To hide thee from prevention.[1]

This is a fine outburst, but it does not seem very appropriate to the actual moment when the conspirator's colleagues are being let in ; and at first one is disposed to think that Shakespeare in introducing it has aimed at theatrical effect rather than dramatic propriety. And perhaps Shakespeare would have felt this later on in his career. Still reflection will show that it has a deeper dramatic meaning. He has just shown us Brutus convincing himself, by a dry unemotional process of reasoning, that Cæsar must be killed ; he wants to shows us, that while stoically determined to act for the general good by the dry light of reason alone, Brutus is no cold passionless pedant : he feels intensely the moral repugnance that a fine nature must feel to the dreadful deed.

The passage recited may also serve to illustrate the change in versification which accompanies the change in style as we pass from the first to the second manner. The blank verse of the earliest period too much resembles rhymed verse in its structure : the lines usually end with a strong syllable and a stop, and are a little too regular for dramatic utterance. In the versification of *Julius Cæsar*,

[1] Act ii. Sc. i.

on the other hand, adequate variety and flexibility is introduced by varying the pauses, allowing the sense sometimes to run over from one line to another, and introducing extra syllables not only at the end of lines, but sometimes even in the middle.

> To hide thy monstrous visage. Seek none, conspiracy ;

—I do not think you will find a line like that in a play earlier than *Julius Cæsar*.

In the third manner the change is carried further in the same direction: the poet's aim often seems to be to conceal the metrical structure, preferring to have the breaks in the sense at the middle of the line rather than the end, and sometimes ending the line with a word on which the speaker cannot rest even for a moment. Take as an instance this speech of Coriolanus :—

> 'Shall'!
> O good but most unwise patricians ! why,
> You grave but reckless senators, have you thus
> Given Hydra here to choose an officer,
> That with this peremptory 'shall,' being but
> The horn and noise o' the monster's, wants not spirit
> To say he'll turn your current in a ditch,
> And make your channel his ? If he have power,
> Then vail your ignorance ; if none, awake
> Your dangerous lenity. If you are learn'd,
> Be not as common fools ; if you are not,
> Let them have cushions by you. You are plebeians,
> If they be senators : and they are no less,
> When, both your voices blended, the great'st taste
> Most palates theirs. They choose their magistrate,
> And such a one as he, who puts his 'shall,'
> His popular 'shall,' against a graver bench
> Than ever frown'd in Greece. By Jove himself !
> It makes the consuls base : and my soul aches
> To know, when two authorities are up,
> Neither supreme, how soon confusion
> May enter 'twixt the gap of both, and take
> The one by the other.[1]

I pass to examine Shakespeare's method of using his materials, in the composition of his plays and characterisa-

[1] Act iii. Sc. i.

tion of the personages. But here I must begin by saying that he has no uniform method: on the contrary, the striking characteristic of his method is that it varies so much with the nature of the materials.

I may quote a few sentences of Gervinus in which this is well put:—

"When he had an older drama before him, he discarded for the most part"—perhaps that is too strong—"the whole form, and retained only the story and the name. Was it a poor novel of Italian origin, he could seldom use the web of the action without first unweaving it, nor a character without creating it entirely afresh. We need only recollect the shallow narratives out of which he fashioned *All's Well that Ends Well*, *Measure for Measure*, *Cymbeline*, and the *Merchant of Venice*, to perceive with what a cold and regardless manner he treated the motives of the actions and the actions themselves. Even in the chronicles of his English histories, however conscientiously he observed the historical tradition, he was obliged, in order to put life into them, to lengthen them considerably and to introduce into them fictitious matter, and not unfrequently to invent the explanatory motives of the actions."

The case is startlingly different when we turn to the group of Roman plays, where the material is supplied by Plutarch —read in North's translation. In Plutarch's lives Shakespeare found history in the shape in which it suits the dramatist—he found it in the form of biography, written by one who had a genius for biography. Here there were historic plots ready made: characters fully drawn, with appropriate actions: striking situations, moving incidents, suggestions of effective dramatic scenes in abundance—and all belonging to the real world, not the world of fiction.

Under these circumstances the task of the dramatist did not call for creative originality in the largest sense: his business was mainly to select and combine the incidents of Plutarch's narrative, developing some aspects of the story and subordinating others, with a view to harmonious effect. And in expressing the character of his main personage— as in the case of Brutus, the *moral* hero of *Julius Cæsar*— what he has to do is, to a great extent, to work on the lines clearly drawn by Plutarch, and to reproduce and imitate the characteristic traits given in the incidents and utterances recorded by the biographer. This, at any rate, is what Shakespeare does. His least appreciative critics have rarely denied him creative and inventive powers of the first order: but to exercise these powers here would be inconsistent with the direct and simple manner in which he conceives the dramatist's task. What he has undertaken is to tell a true story by action, to bring on the stage a great historic event, which from its nature and the personages concerned is exceptionally adapted for dramatic treatment; and, as always when his undertaking is of this kind, he shows a reverent fidelity to the essential and vital facts of the history, though he allows himself some freedom in handling details. Even single expressions and phrases in which character is manifested, he is careful to note and use in composing his speeches.

I have said that the simple aim of Shakespeare is to tell a story dramatically. This is why so many of his plays resist the application of the traditional classification—handed down from the Greek stage—into comedies and tragedies. That is, they have usually either a preponderantly comic or preponderantly tragic quality; but very rarely is this quality maintained throughout: the interest of the comedy is deepened by the introduction of serious pathos, as in *Much Ado about Nothing*, and the tragic effects are relieved and heightened and rendered more lifelike by scenes and personages that are at least half comic, as the grave-diggers and the fop in *Hamlet*, the porter in *Macbeth*, the fool in *Lear*. Sometimes the comic and the serious interest is very evenly balanced, as in *Henry IV.*; sometimes the effect is not designed to be markedly either comic or tragic, but simply interesting, as in *Cymbeline* and the *Winter's Tale*. In *Julius Cæsar*, indeed, the comic element is very slight,—though I always think that the facetious citizen in the first scene rises above the rather low average standard of Shakespeare's verbal wit,—but I still feel that its plan of construction illustrates the conception of the drama on which I am now insisting. I think even the title shows this. Regarded as a tragedy, the hero is undoubtedly Brutus: it is in the interplay of his character and his circumstances that the deepest interest of the drama lies: but the central *event* is the death of Julius Cæsar, and it is the event that gives the title. The character of Cæsar is of quite subordinate interest; indeed, I think that Shakespeare deliberately presents it in the least attractive aspect which was compatible with fidelity to fact—emphasising his overweening and boastful consciousness of his exalted position—in order that the spectator's sympathies may not turn too decisively on Cæsar's side against Brutus. At the same time I do not doubt that Plutarch's life suggested to Shakespeare that arrogant egotism was an attribute of Cæsar. In another play Shakespeare speaks of Cæsar's famous letter—I once heard it described as Cæsar's famous telegram—" veni, vedi, vici " as a " thrasonical brag ";[1] and several other utterances of the great man would confirm this view—his divorcing his wife because Cæsar's wife must be above suspicion: his reassuring his boatman in a storm, " Thou hast Cæsar and his fortune with thee ": his lofty insolence to the tribune who resisted his spoliation of the public treasury, " Thou art mine, both thou and all them that have risen against me . . . it is harder for me to [threaten to kill] thee than to do it." All these would suggest a great man with an overblown and overweening consciousness of his greatness: a man who might be fitly made to exemplify—as Shakespeare makes him exemplify—the " pride that goeth before a fall," declaring himself unassailable and immutable just as the mine of conspiracy is exploding under his feet. The attractive qualities which Plutarch also shows us in Cæsar; his grace and *bonhommie*, his clemency and magnanimity, Shakespeare would doubtless have brought forward, if the plan of the drama had been different: he does not quite *conceal* these qualities, but he keeps them in the background, as I conceive, out of regard for the main dramatic effect at

[1] *As You Like it*, Act v. Sc. ii.

which he aims. He has to win a share of our sympathy for the noble aim that partly redeems the guilt of the assassins: he must not, therefore, dwell too much on the lovable qualities of the victim.

However this may be, Cæsar is not included among the characters of the play who have a leading interest for us as characters. These are Brutus, Cassius, and Antony; and it is instructive to note how far Plutarch has supplied matter for the striking contrast that Brutus presents alternately to either of the other two, and how Shakespeare has worked upon the material supplied. I will try to show this briefly in the case of Brutus and Cassius.

There is no doubt that Shakespeare's conception of the relation of Brutus to the conspiracy and to Cassius is simply Plutarch's. The lines with which Antony in the last scene pronounces Brutus' epitaph are simply Plutarch versified:—

> This was the noblest Roman of them all:
> All the conspirators save only he
> Did that they did in envy of great Cæsar;
> He only, in a general honest thought
> And common good to all, made one of them.[1]

It is from this moral elevation of Brutus, as Plutarch again tells us, that his moral support is thought indispensable by the conspirators. Cassius is the instigator of the conspiracy, and Plutarch makes clear that he would have practically guided it more wisely than Brutus, being "very skilful in wars," and better understanding the hard necessities of the cruel business he undertakes. He would not have saved Antony alive, and he would not have added the mistake of letting him make his funeral oration: Plutarch, like Shakespeare, expressly puts down these mistakes in the art of revolution to Brutus. But Cassius' *morale* is recognised as lower: "it is reported," says Plutarch, "that Brutus could evil away with the tyranny, and that Cassius hated the tyrant." Hence, when he begins to stir his friends against Cæsar, Plutarch tells us that they only

[1] Act v. Sc. v.

promised to take part with him, "so Brutus were the chief of their conspiracy . . . it stood them upon to have a man of such estimation as Brutus, to make every man boldly think, that by his only presence the fact were holy and just." This is the central point in Brutus' relation to the great event, as Shakespeare presents it.

Similarly all the main details of the event and its consequences: the appeal of Cassius to Brutus: the method of rousing him by anonymous letters adjuring him to wake from his lethargy: the relation of Portia to Brutus, her self-wounding to test her firmness, her appeal for her husband's confidence, her subsequent intense anxiety; later on, the death of Portia, the altercation between the two leaders in Brutus' tent, in which their moral difference is effectively brought out, their disagreement about the fatal battle, the apparition of the evil genius, the chief features of the battle itself, and of their double suicide,—all this is taken substantially from Plutarch, though some minor details are altered. Similarly the other features of Brutus' character, besides his moral elevation, are at least suggested in Plutarch. Plutarch's Brutus, like Shakespeare's, is a man who frames his manner of life by the study of philosophy; a bookish man, who falls to his book even on the day before a battle; and at the same time—what is not always the case with bookish philosophers—a man of cool self-restraint and rational firmness in trying crises of action, never carried away by passion or covetousness, never yielding to wrong or injustice. This outline Shakespeare has filled in with the figure of a thinker, studious of self-perfection, and self-revering; who guides his own actions, when most daring, by pure reason, and before he resolves to be an assassin, makes the premises and the steps of the formal process of reasoning that has led him to this conclusion almost pedantically precise. It is for the prevention of future mischief: Cæsar is not now a cruel tyrant, but experience shows that when he has attained the crown, the highest object of ambition, he is likely to become so:—

> Then, lest he may, prevent. And, since the quarrel
> Will bear no colour for the thing he is,
> Fashion it thus; that what he is, augmented,
> Would run to these and these extremities:
> And therefore think him as a serpent's egg,
> Which, hatch'd, would, as his kind, grow mischievous,
> And kill him in the shell.[1]

Contrast the manner in which Cassius has tried to sting him to resolve, by appealing to his personal sense of humiliation:—

> Why, man, he doth bestride the narrow world
> Like a Colossus, and we petty men
> Walk under his huge legs and peep about
> To find ourselves dishonourable graves.
> Men at some time are masters of their fates:
> The fault, dear Brutus, is not in our stars,
> But in ourselves, that we are underlings.
> Brutus and Cæsar: what should be in that "Cæsar"?
> Why should that name be sounded more than yours?
> Write them together, yours is as fair a name;
> Sound them, it doth become the mouth as well;
> Weigh them, it is as heavy; conjure with 'em,
> Brutus will start a spirit as soon as Cæsar.
> Now, in the names of all the gods at once,
> Upon what meat doth this our Cæsar feed,
> That he is grown so great? Age, thou art shamed!
> Rome, thou hast lost the breed of noble bloods!
> When went there by an age, since the great flood,
> But it was famed with more than with one man?
> When could they say till now, that talk'd of Rome,
> That her wide walls encompass'd but one man?
> Now is it Rome indeed and room enough,
> When there is in it but one only man.
> O, you and I have heard our fathers say,
> There was a Brutus once that would have brook'd
> The eternal devil to keep his state in Rome
> As easily as a king.[2]

This is the speech of a man who genuinely loves freedom, but in whom the love of freedom takes its lowest form of aversion to personal inferiority of position. There is force, however, in the concluding appeal to Brutus' ancestry: Brutus feels it, but is not to be moved to hasty

[1] Act ii. Sc. i. [2] Act. i. Sc. ii.

resolve: he replies with grave considerateness and defers decision. Rational himself, he expects rationality from others: he is even under the illusion that Antony will yield to the reasons which have led him to kill Cæsar: thus his address to the crowd before the funeral, though not without force, is jejune and academic.

At the same time, I think that Mr. Dowden in his interesting book on *Shakespeare's Mind and Art* has dwelt too exclusively on this side of Brutus' character. He is no mere Idealist, secluded in a world of abstractions: he has strong emotions and is in certain respects well fitted for action. This is Plutarch's conception of him, and it is clearly also Shakespeare's. Notice his cool self-command at the crisis just before the event, when the more passionate Cassius is giving way to premature despair, under the erroneous idea that Cæsar is being informed of the conspiracy. Observe with what firmness and calmness—though not altogether wisely—he directs the action of the conspirators immediately after the event. Observe the combination of feeling and self-mastery finely shown later on in his lament over the body of Cassius :—

> Friends, I owe more tears
> To this dead man, than you shall see me pay.
> I shall find time, Cassius, I shall find time.[1]

Nor is it mere *negative* self-mastery: he can not only restrain his mood but summon what mood the occasion demands. The change in Act ii. Scene i. from the mood of painful conflict and gloomy meditation to that of inspiriting resolve is very striking, and shows a man who, as far as *morale* is concerned, is eminently fit for action. Up to the moment when he gives his hand in final pledge he is almost like a brooding Hamlet :—

> Between the acting of a dreadful thing
> And the first motion, all the interim is
> Like a phantasma, or a hideous dream :
> The genius, and the mortal instruments,

---

[1] Act v. Sc. iii.

> Are then in council; and the state of man
> Like to a little kingdom, suffers then
> The nature of an insurrection.[1]

But then comes out another side of his nature: he springs to his right place as leader by virtue of moral superiority: and we feel that we have here the one man who can make conspiracy high-hearted, noble, magnanimous.

"Let us swear," says Cassius, " our resolution."

> *Brutus.* No, not an oath : if not the face of men,
> The sufferance of our souls, the time's abuse,—
> If these be motives weak, break off betimes,
> And every man hence to his idle bed ;
> So let high-sighted tyranny range on,
> Till each man drop by lottery. But if these,
> As I am sure they do, bear fire enough
> To kindle cowards and to steel with valour
> The melting spirits of women, then, countrymen,
> What need we any spur but our own cause
> To prick us to redress? what other bond
> Than secret Romans, that have spoke the word,
> And will not palter? and what other oath
> Than honesty to honesty engaged,
> That this shall be, or we will fall for it?
> Swear priests and cowards and men cautelous,
> Old feeble carrions and such suffering souls
> That welcome wrongs ; unto bad causes swear
> Such creatures as men doubt : but do not stain
> The even virtue of our enterprise,
> Nor the insuppressive mettle of our spirits,
> To think that or our cause or our performance
> Did need an oath ; when every drop of blood
> That every Roman bears, and nobly bears,
> Is guilty of a several bastardy,
> If he do break the smallest particle
> Of any promise that hath pass'd from him.[2]

Observe with what fidelity and inventiveness combined Shakespeare has used his materials. The moral superiority of Brutus, and the fact that the conspirators were not bound by oaths: these data he finds in Plutarch. But the combination of the two is all Shakespeare's: and it is impossible to imagine a more effective way of making his hero assume

---

[1] Act ii. Sc. i.   [2] Act ii. Sc. i.

the moral position that by right belongs to him. Observe, too, how well this speech is made to illustrate what Plutarch tells us of the style of Brutus' oratory. "When [his mind] was moved to follow any matter he used a kind of forcible and vehement persuasion that calmed not, till he had obtained his desire." Forcible and vehement persuasiveness is the exact description of the lines I have recited.

One word more before I leave Brutus and Cassius. There is a fine tragic effect in the way in which each friend misleads the other in turn: Brutus yielding to Cassius when he urges the need and the call of Rome; and Cassius allowing his superior practical insight to be overruled, in deference to his friend's moral superiority.

Perhaps of all the personages in the play, the character of Antony has the greatest dramatic capabilities: there is no room in this piece to develop them fully, but the presentation as far as it goes is excellent both in itself and in its contrast with Brutus. He is a man of genius without an ideal, with a rich nature capable of strong affections and loyal subordination: but intensely pleasure-loving and without *morale*: as Dowden well says, "looking on life as a game, in which he has a distinguished part to play, and playing that part with magnificent grace and skill," but with utter unscrupulousness. Shakespeare's unique power of presenting the elements of a mingled character—with good impulses but capable of the worst crimes—was never better shown. Antony is separated from Brutus by a moral gulf: the hideousness of the proscription by the Triumvirs, with their cold-blooded mutual sacrifice of friends and kinsmen to each other's vengeance, is used with fine tragic effect—we feel it an awful penalty for Brutus' noble crime, that the generosity and clemency of Cæsar has been exchanged for these bargaining butchers. Yet with all this, it is Antony not Brutus that has *le beau rôle* in the encounter over Cæsar's body, and at the funeral: because he shows not merely skilful management for his ends, but, genuinely and intensely, the human affection that Brutus has suppressed in himself. I know nothing subtler in Shakespeare than the way in which genuine feeling burns through the craftily planned speech with which he enters after the dreadful deed is done :—

> O mighty Cæsar ! Dost thou lie so low ?
> Are all thy conquests, glories, triumphs, spoils,
> Shrunk to this little measure ? Fare thee well.
> I know not, gentlemen, what you intend,
> Who else must be let blood, who else is rank :
> If I myself, there is no hour so fit
> As Cæsar's death's hour, nor no instrument
> Of half that worth as those your swords, made rich
> With the most noble blood of all this world.
> I do beseech ye, if ye bear me hard,
> Now, whilst your purpled hands do reek and smoke,
> Fulfil your pleasure. Live a thousand years,
> I shall not find myself so apt to die :
> No place will please me so, no mean of death,
> As here by Cæsar, and by you cut off,
> The choice and master spirits of this age.[1]

Turning to *Coriolanus,* also taken from North's *Plutarch,* we again find that Shakespeare's use of his materials throws light on the leading motives and aims that governed him in his choice and treatment of a subject. Professor Gervinus, a commentator from whom much may be learnt, begins his study of *Coriolanus* as follows :—

Fondness for the Roman State, whose mighty career Shakespeare contemplates in this play with the proud satisfaction of one belonging to it, seems to have induced the poet, after the completion of *Antony and Cleopatra,* to take up once more the better days of the first military greatness of this people and to treat a more noble subject out of its history. As in *Antony* he had represented the imperial time and its degeneracy, and in *Cæsar* the struggle of the republic with monarchy, in *Coriolanus* he brings before us the struggle between the aristocratic and democratic elements within the republic. The play is filled with the striving of the two powers, tribunes and consuls, plebeians and patricians, senate and people . . . The opposition between these two powers is everywhere exhibited as founded on their nature ; the implacable enmity between them is shown as a necessary result of the imprudence, unreasonableness, and harshness, of their contrast.

---

[1] Act iii. Sc. i.

Now, I do not say that there is nothing of all this in Shakespeare's mind, but I feel convinced that it occupied a much more subordinate place in his aims and motives than Professor Gervinus thinks. It is not fondness for the Roman State, but fondness for the Roman character, and a keen sense of its capabilities for dramatic representation that moved Shakespeare,—in my view. Plutarch, his source, is a biographer not a historian, and, as I have said, it is in the character of a biographer that he has so strong an attraction for our dramatist.

The fights of Romans and Volscians, the struggles of patricians and plebeians interest him mainly as constituting the element in which his hero first manifests his heroic qualities, and then weaves for himself his tragic destiny by his heroic excesses and errors of passion. I see no sign that he has more than the vaguest conception of Roman history as a whole: he makes Coriolanus say, when soliciting votes as a candidate, that "aged custom" will not permit him to be consul, except by the people's voices:[1] not being apparently aware that the whole affair happened—according to tradition—only twenty years after the expulsion of the kings from Rome.

It is not only that he has no general apprehension of the difference between the ancient and the modern world—he makes Coriolanus talk of "our divines" as persons with the functions of imparting virtues to the laity—and that he falls into the anachronisms of referring to Alexander, to Cato, even to Galen, as if they were characters familiarly known at the beginning of the 5th century B.C. This kind of thing we are accustomed to in Shakespeare. It is more striking to contrast the close and reverent fidelity with which he has studied and the skill with which he has used every scrap of information that Plutarch has given him about the characters and moods of his personages, with his carelessness and looseness in dealing with the purely political aspect of the story.

[1] Act ii. Sc. iii.

The central facts, from the political point of view, are the appointment of the tribunes and the bold proposal of Coriolanus to abolish the new-fangled plebeian magistracy. Now the *psychological* interest of these facts is most fully apprehended by Shakespeare: the self-assertive pride of office of these plebeian magistrates, contrasting with the arrogant consciousness of personal superiority shown by the patrician: their practised dexterity in managing the mob and working its feelings up to the point they desire, as contrasted with Coriolanus' reckless folly in provoking it by violent utterances of contempt: the collapse of the demagogues when the battle is transferred from the forum to the field:—all this is most vividly presented. But the political aspect of the matter has no similar interest for him, even on what seems to us its most dramatic side. Every schoolboy knows—I think this really is one of the things that every schoolboy does know—how the poorer plebeians were oppressed by the old harsh law of debt, reducing the defaulting debtor to practical slavery: how they were only induced to go out to fight an invading foe by the promise of relaxation of this harsh law: how the promise was not kept: how despairing of redress the plebeians marched away in orderly secession and encamped on the Holy Hill two miles off, threatening to leave Rome to the patricians and their 'clients. It is at this juncture that Menenius is sent to them, and persuades them to a compromise by the famous fable of the belly and its members, with which the play begins: and the chief point of this compromise is the appointment of tribunes. All this is clearly told by Plutarch—though not with perfect historical accuracy:—but all this does not interest Shakespeare. He mixes up this great historic secession of the plebs with a disturbance about the distribution of corn in time of dearth, which Plutarch describes at a later date: he makes Menenius tell his fable to a hungry company of mutinous citizens in a street: and he represents this eventful grant of the plebeian magistracy, the tribunate, as made to another similar crowd who

>   Said they were an-hungry ; sigh'd forth proverbs,
>   That hunger broke stone walls, that dogs must eat,
>   That meat was made for mouths, that the gods sent not
>   Corn for the rich men only.[1]

It is impossible to conceive that a dramatist moved—as Gervinus asserts—by "fondness for the Roman State" and desire to show what it was "in its better days," could have so degraded and vulgarised this most impressive incident in its history. Nor does he understand what the tribunes are appointed to do: he supposes that they are concerned in managing the election to the consulship and have to "endue" the candidate "with the people's voice": though I find no excuse for this blunder—as there is for other blunders—in North's *Plutarch*.

So again: he is in a muddle about Coriolanus' candidature for the consulship, which he describes after Plutarch: he thinks that it terminates in an election, and that Coriolanus actually *is* consul, by the people's voices: though as a subsequent confirmation is required, they have and use the power of revoking their votes. But this is a mere misunderstanding of Plutarch, who simply tells us that the people received the candidature of Coriolanus favourably, but changed their minds when it came to the election.

No, as I say, it is not the Roman State that interests Shakespeare but the Roman men and women of Plutarch, and their remarkable dramatic capabilities. The relation between patricians and plebeians had to be presented: but it was in order to bring out impressively the mingled qualities of Coriolanus. Hence it is rather irrelevant to inquire after Shakespeare's political sympathies: it is evident, indeed, that he is not a democrat, he does not think that one man is as good as another, or that *vox populi* is *vox Dei*, and there is no doubt an intention in this play to give an impression of the ignorance and short-sighted impulsiveness of the common people. But I conceive that this is done largely with the dramatic object of winning our sympathies for Coriolanus, whose contempt

[1] Act i. Sc. i.

for plebeians is thus partly justified. At the same time, he wishes no less to represent the people as impressible by valour, grateful for heroic services, easily led to follow and submit to a hero, if he will only keep his temper and use a little tact and discretion. It is the fatal defect of Coriolanus that he cannot condescend to exhibit these qualities.

As I have said, in combining the diverse qualities of Coriolanus—as well as in the other characters of the play— Shakespeare has followed and developed with the utmost care and fidelity the indications given by Plutarch. Pre-eminent alike in valour and physical strength, exercised in all kinds of activity, so that no competitor was ever a match for him, with "natural strength, and hardness of ward, that never yielded to any pain or toil he took upon him," he performs with a certain heroic inevitableness the great deeds of martial prowess that win him the surname of Coriolanus. Then when the victory is over, his magnanimity is no less marked: his refusal of the gifts that the consul presses on him, his determination to take simply his share with the rest of the soldiers, his single petition for the release of an old friend and host among the Volscian captives—these fine features of the hero's conduct are merely transferred from Plutarch's prose to the at once simple and dignified verse that Shakespeare has always at command for worthy occasions :—

> I thank you, general;
> But cannot make my heart consent to take
> A bribe to pay my sword : I do refuse it;
> And stand upon my common part with those
> That have beheld the doing.[1]

On the other hand, says his biographer, "he was so choleric and impatient, that he would yield to no living creature: churlish, . . . uncivil and altogether unfit for any man's conversation": so that while men marvelled "much at his constancy, that he was never overcome with pleasure, nor money," yet "for all that, they could not be acquainted

[1] Act ii. Sc. ix.

with him, as one citizen useth to be with another in the city. His behaviour was so unpleasant to them, by reason of a certain insolent and stern manner he had." Shakespeare admirably exemplifies this (in Act i. Sc. iv.) by the outburst of contemptuous fury at the cowardice of the common soldiers: on account of which, though his heroism excites admiration, he is always—so to say—on the verge of unpopularity. When he rushes gallantly into Corioli the soldiers' comment is

> *First Soldier.* See, they have shut him in.
> *All.* To the pot, I warrant him.

Hence, as Plutarch later on explains, he is altogether unapt for the political career to which his military services entitle him; being "a man too full of passion and choler, and too much given over to self-will and opinion," lacking "the gravity, and affability that is . . . to be looked for in a governor of State": and "thinking that to overcome always, and to have the upper hand in all matters, was a token of magnanimity." But having this imperious self-will, he lacks the highest kind of magnanimity—the greatness of soul that can forgive an injury: his rejection for the consulship fills him—Plutarch tells us—with "spite and malice," and his subsequent banishment produces a more profound and all-absorbing "vehemency of anger, and desire of revenge," that sweeps away all regard for friends and for country.

And here I would note a subtle trait skilfully introduced by Shakespeare into the earlier delineation of his hero. Knowing—as no reader of Plutarch could fail to know—how strong an element patriotism was in the character of a Roman of noble type, he thinks that, to explain the conduct of Coriolanus at this crisis, it should be hinted in the earlier part of the play that even in fighting his country's battles he is not in any high degree moved by patriotic ardour. As the first citizen says in the first scene, "What he hath done famously, though soft-conscienced men can be content to say it was for his country, he did it to please his mother, and to be partly proud." And his own casual phrase in the same scene, about his Volscian rival Tullus Aufidius, shows us delicately but sufficiently that it is chivalry and martial ardour rather than patriotic self-devotion that move him—

> Were half to half the world by the ears and he
> Upon my party, I'ld revolt, to make
> Only my wars with him.

Well, these traits make up an impressive and interesting moral figure, but not an attractive one: not a hero that can gain our sympathies—as Shakespeare always, I think, aims at gaining them, and always, I think, succeeds even when his choice of a character has imposed on him the greatest difficulties. Here, however, he has no difficulties to overcome: since a tender and amiable side to Coriolanus is given by the most interesting and ultimately important elements in his life, as told by Plutarch—his relation to his mother. "The only thing that made him to love honour," says the biographer, "was the joy he saw his mother did take of him. For he thought nothing made him so happy and honourable, as that his mother might hear everybody praise and commend him, and that she might always see him return with a crown upon his head." And it is not only love that he habitually pays her, but obedience in domestic life, for, "thinking all due to his mother, that had been also due to his father if he had lived," he took a wife at her desire, and "never left his mother's house therefore." It is this double habit of intense filial affection and submissive filial obedience that overcomes his passion of revenge at the crisis of his fate, when all other forces have given way before it, and saves him at the cost of life from the terrible crime of destroying his fatherland.

So far, then, as Shakespeare works out this relation between mother and son, conceiving them as similar in their characters—alike in haughty determination, and voluble vehemence and furious outbursts when their passion is roused—as well as bound by indissoluble ties of affection, he keeps still within the limits of the original Roman type as presented by Plutarch. At the same time, I always feel that in endeavouring to impress us with the charm of this side of Coriolanus' nature, he has mingled with the Roman original a good deal of the exuberant manliness, the eager chivalry, cordial friendship, enthusiastic courtesy, of the finest type of gentleman of the Elizabethan age. Plutarch tells us that Coriolanus was churlish, uncivil, and unfit for any man's conversation: but Shakespeare's Coriolanus only shows these qualities when moved by his exaggerated contempt and aversion for the weaker side of common human nature. He is not so to his intimates: the enthusiasm of old Menenius shows this—the relation between the older and the younger man is very natural and affecting. Again, his loyal and frank confidence in Aufidius—after they have sworn comradeship and even when the latter is plotting against him—is pathetically introduced at the crisis when he gives way to his mother's appeal:—

> Aufidius, though I cannot make true wars,
> I'll frame convenient peace. Now, good Aufidius,
> Were you in my stead, would you have heard
> A mother less? or granted less, Aufidius?
> . . . . .
> I'll not to Rome, I'll back with you; and pray you,
> Stand to me in this cause.[1]

Again, his tenderness to his wife is very beautifully though briefly presented: but for this, unlike what I have just noted, there is Plutarch's authority. Plutarch tells very well how, when the women come to him in his camp, affection overcomes his determination to be stern, "and nature so wrought with him, that . . . he could not keep himself from making much of them." The exquisite address on his return from Corioli is all of Shakespeare's invention; but it is quite in harmony with Plutarch. Nothing can be more simply effective than the contrast between the two women. Shakespeare has obviously asked himself what kind of daughter-in-law a woman like Volumnia would

[1] Act v. Sc. iii.

select to introduce into her household, and has decided that it would be a woman like Virgilia—and very unlike herself.

Round Coriolanus the other characters group themselves in effective contrast, and in relations that bring out his characteristics. First—Menenius, the genial popular nobleman, whose frankness the people like, though he tells them plain truths, and has no love for their leaders and tribunes, puts no restraint on his tongue. For an instance of Menenius' generally good-humoured roughness of speech, see his chaff of the leader of the mob in Act i. Scene i.—

> What do you think,
> You, the great toe of this assembly?
> *First Cit.* I, the great toe! why the great toe?
> *Men.* For that, being one o' the lowest, basest, poorest,
> Of this most wise rebellion, thou go'st foremost:
> etc.

This rough banter Shakespeare conceives as the right way to deal with the mob: it is effective at the time, and it leaves no sting behind, such as the insolence of Coriolanus leaves. There is not much of the Roman in Menenius: but it is a very vivid sketch of what an Elizabethan nobleman might be who could persuade a mob by a dexterously applied fable.

The character of Aufidius is more subtly mingled. His furious threats of unchivalrous assault in the last scene of Act i. contrast with Coriolanus' magnanimity—

> Nor sleep nor sanctuary,
> Being naked, sick, nor fane nor Capitol,
> The prayers of priests nor times of sacrifice,
> Embarquements all of fury, shall lift up
> Their rotten privilege and custom 'gainst
> My hate to Marcius.

Yet the very announcement of them, the very declaration that his "valour's poisoned," makes us feel that we are dealing with a mixed nature and not completely fallen; and prepares us for what follows when Coriolanus is banished: the first generosity, as appears in Act iv. Scene v. (the outburst of enthusiasm here is very Elizabethan—there is nothing more characteristic of the Elizabethan time than enthusiasm for human excellence), and then the clouds of jealousy settling down again, yet not without a certain sense of justice (see Act iv. Sc. vii.). So, again, the final treachery and penitence at the close is characteristic.

I have spoken of Shakespeare's fidelity to his original. This is shown in one way more strikingly here than in any other of the Roman plays, in the closeness with which he follows the speeches. He takes all the ideas and as many of the phrases as he can use, putting on emphasis and imagery when North's English prose does not seem to him sufficiently moving. There are three cases:—(1) The speech in the third Act, urging the abolition of the tribunate, already quoted from; (2) the address to Aufidius when he comes to him as a suppliant in Antium (Act iv. Sc. v.); (3) Volumnia's maternal appeal (Act v. Sc. iii.). A close comparison of these with North's original is very interesting and instructive : but this is the kind of comparison which, perhaps, a lecturer had better suggest than perform. I will only make a few remarks. In the first case —the speech about the tribunate—Shakespeare is not professedly giving the speech on the occasion on which the model in Plutarch is delivered, but a repetition on a different occasion : in the street, not in the senate : hence, perhaps, he has introduced more of his own matter. In the second case —the speech to Aufidius—he is very close to his original, only introducing a few images to make it more vivid. In the third case—Volumnia's appeal—he keeps very close to his original so far as it goes, only the appeal is skilfully divided, so as not to be too long, and the order slightly changed so as to lead to the climax; but I think it impresses him as not quite feminine enough in style, so he adds a more characteristically feminine though less classical passage at the end :—

> To his surname Coriolanus 'longs more pride
> Than pity to our prayers. Down : an end ;
> This is the last : so we will home to Rome,

And die among our neighbours. Nay, behold's :
This boy, that cannot tell what he would have,
But kneels and holds up hands for fellowship,
Does reason our petition with more strength
Than thou hast to deny 't. Come, let us go :
This fellow had a Volscian to his mother ;
His wife is in Corioli and his child
Like him by chance. Yet give us our dispatch :
I am hush'd until our city be afire,
And then I'll speak a little.

V

SHAKESPEARE AND THE ROMANTIC DRAMA, WITH SPECIAL REFERENCE TO *MACBETH*

.   .   .   .

THE easiest method of getting a precise notion of what is meant by the Romantic drama (of which the Shakespearian drama is the most splendid and impressive example) is to interpret it negatively. The Romantic drama is the type of drama that declines to be "cribbed, cabined, and confined" by the rules and restrictions which, under the influence of the scholars of the Rennaissance, came to be regarded as inviolable canons of classical art. In the Romantic drama no "unity" is considered indispensable for the general coherence of impression which dramatic like every other art requires, save and except the *unity of human interest* which a series of events acquires from the relations of all the events, in the way of cause and effect, to the life of a single human being, or closely connected group of human beings. If we may call this "unity of action," then the principle of the Romantic drama is that "unity of action" is the one unity needful; all other unities—unity of time, unity of place, unity of tone of sentiment, whether tragic or comic, unity of æsthetic level in the verbal instrument of expression, whether prose or verse—are all nonessential, and may be broken or kept according to convenience. These unities were maintained—not exactly and universally, but in the main—spontaneously and as a matter of course, by the great Greek tragedians: and they were imposed as rules resting on indubitable æsthetic principles on the so-called classical drama of France: but the Romantic drama holds it always lawful to violate them, though it may not always be expedient.

Unity of time and place are undoubtedly helpful in impressing the imagination of the audience with the inner unity of the action represented: but few critics would now maintain that they are indispensable for this purpose: and certainly in many cases their observance would render it impossible to bring directly before the spectators the most essential parts of the action—the most important consequences of the most important causes. Thus, *e.g.*, in witnessing the tragedy of *Othello*, the spectator must be dull whose imagination does not follow the wedded Othello and Desdemona from Venice to Cyprus, without the least sense of a break in the coherence of the action. So, again, if such an action as that of Macbeth is to be adequately represented —if the spectator is to see how " the assassination " cannot " trammel up the consequence," but " in these cases we still have judgment here,"—the time of the piece must be stretched to years. We must follow Macbeth from his appearance in the prime of manly vigour, fighting like " Bellona's bridegroom " against the enemies of his country, until after restless years of criminal rule, his

> way of life
> Is fall'n into the sear, the yellow leaf;
> And that which should accompany old age,
> As honour, love, obedience, troops of friends,
> I must not look to have ; but, in their stead,
> Curses, not loud but deep, mouth-honour, breath,
> Which the poor heart would fain deny, and dare not.[1]

The violation of unity in the tone of feeling stirred by the drama, the mingling of comic with tragic effects—this is at once a characteristic of deeper import, and more in need of defence. Even ardent admirers of Shakespeare have not always been able to approve the combinations of effects on which he ventures. Even Coleridge considered

Act v. Sc. iii.

that the "low soliloquy of the porter in *Macbeth* must have been written for the mob by some hand other than Shakespeare's"; and this view seems to have been accepted by Messrs. Clark and Wright. I see no reason for regarding this as less thoroughly Shakespearean than, *e.g.*, the utterances of the Fool in *King Lear*, at the crisis when the storm of the old man's passion is vying with the storm of the elements, which some readers have also found inharmonious with the pathetic situation in which they are introduced. Whether it is *right* æsthetically to appeal to our sense of the ridiculous at the very crisis of tragic interest, I do not venture dogmatically to decide. There seems to me both gain and loss in it. Undoubtedly the utterances (*e.g.*) of the porter in *Macbeth* break the harmony of the spectator's sentiment, and so far tend to diminish the intensity of the tragic impression. It may be replied that they relieve the strain on his feelings and so prevent him from being wearied: and I have no doubt that Shakespeare—writing for a mixed audience—had this effect in view. But this alone would not seem to me an adequate defence; an audience that required for mere relief such violent mixtures of tragic and comic as Shakespeare allows himself, would seem to me a vulgar audience: to cultivated spectators adequate relief might be given by more refined methods. For Shakespeare's mixtures, however, there is usually more to be said. Firstly, since in actual life the trivial and ridiculous does thus mingle itself with the gravest events, its introduction often increases in a startling way the life-likeness of the whole; the combination of the two elements enables the poet to bring before us the whole scene, the whole story, in its fulness. Sometimes it does even more than this: the ludicrous element, even while it amuses, heightens the pathos, intensifies the tragedy of the situation. This, I think, is the case in the scene in *Lear* to which I referred; the grotesque accompaniment of the faithful fool renders the outpourings of the desolate king's wounded heart more and not less pathetic. I do not say that the additional vividness and intensity thus gained always makes up for the loss through discordance of effects: but at any rate it is characteristic of the Romantic drama that it prefers to seize this kind of gain at the risk of this kind of loss.

The same general preference is shown in other ways than in the mingling of tragedy and comedy; the Romantic —and especially the Shakespearean—drama will aim at *naturalness* at the risk of offending our sense of taste and decorum: it will aim at emphasis and force in the expression of feeling at the risk of repelling us by violence and uncouthness: it will aim at volume and richness of effect at the risk of wearying by profusion or bewildering by variety. It has the defects of its qualities; what can be fairly claimed for it is, that for its central object of presenting impressively the complex content of a human story, its method, in a master's hand, is surpassingly effective.

This disregard of unity or homogeneity in tone of sentiment is naturally accompanied by the license of variation in the method of verbal expression which characterises this type. The Shakespearean drama descends to prose, rises to blank verse, and occasionally dances into rhyme at its own sweet will, according as it finds one or other of these modes of expression more appropriate. In Shakespeare's use of these different verbal instruments important changes occur as his art develops; thus, except in two or three of the earliest comedies, rhyme occupies a quite subordinate place, and towards the close of his period of production he seems to be abandoning it: still it is used, though sparingly, for definite effects even in his best tragedies. To speak frankly, I cannot always explain why it is used, nor can I always explain the subtle instinct by which Shakespeare divides the less impressive part of the dialogue between blank verse and prose; but one may say broadly, that in Shakespeare's mature work blank verse is used ordinarily for passionate, earnest, and dignified utterance, prose ordinarily for what is either comic, trivial, or markedly unemotional, while rhymed verse may come in where deliberate sententiousness seems to be in place, as at the conclusion of a scene, or where a combat of polite wits is designed, the entertainment of which is not impaired by a touch of artificiality.[1]

It follows from what has been said, that it is not always possible to classify the products of the Romantic dramatist as definitely tragedies or comedies. To apply such a classification rightly would be to miss the essential features of the type. They may be either or both in varying degrees: mainly tragic with comic elements, or mainly comic with pathetic effects produced by an introduction of the style of tragedy. Thus, in *Much Ado about Nothing*, the effect is preponderantly comic and most of the dialogue is in prose; but when, in the fourth act, the wedding is broken off by a vile conspiracy of calumny against the bride, it rises into blank verse; and the passionate outbreak of the father, under the shock of his daughter's dishonour, is in the finest tragic manner of Shakespeare's middle period.

> Do not live, Hero; do not ope thine eyes:
> For, did I think thou wouldst not quickly die,
> Thought I thy spirits were stronger than thy shames,
> Myself would, on the rearward of reproaches,
> Strike at thy life. Grieved I, I had but one?
> Chid I for that at frugal nature's frame?
> O, one too much by thee! Why had I one?
> Why ever wast thou lovely in my eyes?
> Why had I not with charitable hand
> Took up a beggar's issue at my gates,
> Who smirched thus and mired with infamy,
> I might have said " *No part of it is mine,*
> *This shame derives itself from unknown loins* " ?
> But mine and mine I loved and mine I praised
> And mine that I was proud on, mine so much
> That I myself was to myself not mine,
> Valuing of her—why she, O, she is fallen
> Into a pit of ink.[2]

The conspiracy is, as you know, unmasked, and the calumny refuted, and all ends happily: so we have no scruple in classifying the play as a comedy; but when from the lively

---

[1] When I say that blank verse is used for dignified utterance, it is to be noted that it is sometimes the dignity of the person, rather than of the matter spoken, that determines the choice of this form.

[2] Act iv. Sc. i.

repartees of Beatrice and Benedict, and the merry jest of making each believe that the other is pining for love of him or her, we are suddenly swept into this passage of elevated pathos, we feel to the full the mingled quality of the Romantic drama.

Still, such plays as this we can classify by their predominant quality; but there are others in which we find no such definite predominance of quality at all; and in some of these latter the aim of presenting an interesting story is more prominent than any design of being either tragic or comic. Thus, in *Cymbeline, The Winter's Tale*, and *The Tempest*, the dramatist does not aim specially at moving us to pity and terror, or amusing us with droll situations and witty sayings—any more than a modern novelist does, —but at exciting our sympathy with the joys and sorrows, hopes and fears, of interesting persons to whom interesting events happen.

I have mentioned three plays that belong to Shakespeare's latest work, because it is important to note that this mixed and variegated quality of the effects aimed at by the Romantic drama is not a characteristic that Shakespeare's art has any tendency to outgrow,—as he seems to have a tendency to outgrow the use of rhyme. Quite the contrary; it is in his earliest work that we have comedy without any pathetic or dignified scenes, and tragedy without any touch of the humorous. *Love's Labour's Lost* and the *Comedy of Errors* are both the purest comedies though of very different kinds; and *Titus Andronicus*—which, I am sorry to say, I can find no adequate reason for *not* regarding as an early production of Shakespeare's—is the most perfectly unrelieved tragedy, and blank verse—often very blank—from beginning to end. Whereas of the later tragedies there is not one of which the predominant tone is not relieved or varied—it may be heightened—by some other element than the serious tragic style.

Partly, this may be referred to the tendency of development of Shakespeare's own genius; we seem to find in him a growing determination to combine fulness and pregnancy with impressiveness—at some sacrifice of harmoniousness—in all his representation and expression of human life. But it is partly to be regarded in a less personal way, as exhibiting the final and complete triumph of the popular conception of the drama over the scholarly conception, between which, for some time before Shakespeare, there has been a conflict going on.

. . . . .

In the present lecture it is my object to characterise and illustrate some of the special features of Shakespeare's own work; and I have thought it best to take as a kind of centre the play of *Macbeth,* and dwell most on those aspects of Shakespeare's work which *Macbeth* exemplifies. That is, I shall have in view mainly the plays classified as Tragedies or Histories—not Comedies; I say Tragedies *or* Histories, because *Macbeth* is to be regarded as partaking of both characters. I see no reason for thinking that Shakespeare regarded Holinshed's *Chronicle*—from which he took the story of the play—as materially less historical and trustworthy in its account of Duncan's murder and Macbeth's reign, than in the later events of English history in which he similarly followed its guidance.

And when I distinguish these from Comedies I wish you to bear in mind that, as I have said, the separation between the two is only partial, since it is a fundamental characteristic of the Romantic drama that the dramatist can mingle the two elements in any proportion he likes. Still, allowing for this mingled quality of the Romantic drama, there are still many plays which we can fairly classify as Tragedies or Comedies. And when we compare the two sets, I think it ought to be admitted—notwithstanding the delight that so many of his comic personages have given us—that Shakespeare's fame as the greatest of modern dramatists rests more indubitably on his tragedies. For, first, Shakespearean tragedy impresses me as a higher type of drama than Shakespearean comedy, because of its greater unity of interest. In the great tragedies—in *Hamlet, Macbeth, Lear, Othello*—the fate of the central personage, or closely united pair of personages, as woven by the interaction of character and circumstances, supplies a dominant central thread of interest round which the interests of all other events and personages are hung, and from their relation to which these minor interests derive most of their vitality. Now in the best Shakespearean comedy this unity of central interest is wanting, and therefore there is less coherence in total effect. Thus, though I individually enjoy Shakespeare's comedies more than Molière's, I cannot deny that Molière's type has the decided advantage in cohesion and unity of interest. Something similar may be said of Ben Jonson. When I pass from the Shakespearean comedy to the Jonsonian, I have to admit, along with a great loss of charm, a certain progress in type, an increase in coherent interest; but in tragedy after Shakespeare there is no similar advance. Secondly, in one important element of a comedian's stock-in-trade, Shakespeare's stock-in-trade seems to me inferior in quality: I mean *wit*. He has plenty of it; he delights in quips and quirks and happy hits, neat turns of phrase and smart repartees; and—in the earlier part of his career at least— is inventive and profuse in his efforts to produce them. But the results are disappointing; his sallies and retorts are ingenious but not felicitous; his word-plays rarely make us laugh, and often make us blush to contemplate our greatest comic poet lingering so complacently over puns so poor. And we feel this all the more, as the pleasure we get from his humour—from laughter-provoking incongruities between what men are and what they think themselves to be or what their situation calls on them to be—is so varied and inexhaustible, whether we simply laugh at the humorous personage, as at Bottom and Dogberry and Malvolio; or, better still, partly at and partly with them, as with Falstaff and Touchstone. This humour is only one aspect of Shakespeare's subtle and comprehensive grasp of human life in its strangely varied divergences from the human ideal: but his combats of wit and ingenuities of vivacious dialogue—I humbly think that they were for an age, and not for all time.

And it ought to be said that as Shakespeare's art develops, this element is valued less and less for its own sake, and more and more as a means of exhibiting character. Of comedy then I shall say no more in detail, but only refer to it generally, so far as may be necessary in speaking of Shakespeare's work as a whole.

. . . . . .

It is clear that—at least during a great part of Shakespeare's career — his literary reputation, which was considerable, was not based mainly on his plays, but on his poems, *Venus and Adonis*, and *Lucrece*, and on the sonnets handed round among his friends, and not published till 1609. This is shown by his being mentioned with praise as a poet by writers who do not even allude to his plays.

I conceive, then, that Shakespeare, who seems to have been quite devoid of the self-assertive egotism that characterised his rival Ben Jonson, regarded his plays much as the public regarded them: he constructed them for the stage, and so long as they retained their popularity on the boards it was not in the way of business to collect them in a book. There is no reason to suppose him indifferent to their ultimate fate; he died prematurely at fifty-two, and may easily have designed for his old age the task of presenting his work in final literary form: which, as it was, had to be undertaken seven years after his death by surviving members of his company. But, primarily, he wrote with an eye to his business, as playwright, play-actor, and shareholder in the Globe Theatre,—a business which he pursued with steady resolution, but always looking forward to leaving it and living like a gentleman at Stratford, when he had restored the decayed fortunes of his family.

I dwell on this business aspect of Shakespeare's work, because I think that not only the difficulty of making out exactly where his work begins and ends, but also the characteristic qualities of what is undoubtedly his—both good and bad qualities—are largely due to this cause, that what he had to write was first and foremost an acting play, made to tell on a certain given audience, whose capacities and susceptibilities he had, as actor as well as playwright, learned to know thoroughly. We must conceive it as an audience of a very mixed character: containing doubtless a refined and cultivated element, who could appreciate his deeper reflection, his subtleties and ingenuities, and catch the meaning of the compact allusive phrases with which his later style is rife: but containing also a vulgarer element that had to be amused by broad drollery, entertained by varied scenes and startling transitions, impressed with contrasts of character and changes of moods by violent and profuse manifestations. I think that, in the eager sustained effort to satisfy these diverse needs the genius of Shakespeare was drawn out, but was also here and there made to stoop to work quite below the level of his own taste. And as the demand for new plays was surprisingly incessant,—in one part of his career at least it would seem that a new play was wanted about every seventeen days,—it is not strange that even Shakespeare's facile pen and unflagging industry could not unassisted meet the demand, so that he was led to collaborate with others, and take old plays and work them up into a more effective form. I cannot doubt that in most, if not all, of the plays regarded by at least some important critics as doubtful,[1] a mingling of Shakespearean and non-Shakespearean elements has been caused in one or other of these two ways.

But if this alien element be admitted in so many of the plays published as Shakespeare's by his fellow-actors, how can we define its limits? Well, I think the decision is difficult, and that we must candidly admit that the work of other hands may possibly lurk unrecognised in plays that have hitherto been unquestioningly received. For example, I agree with the Cambridge editors[2] in tracing such an element in *Macbeth* from the combined effect of internal and external evidence; but I do not think that a sober-

[1] *Titus Andronicus*, the three parts of *Henry VI.*, *The Taming of the Shrew*, *Timon of Athens*, *Pericles*, *Henry VIII*.
[2] Messrs. Clark and Wright.

minded critic will extend the alien element far, in the plays on which the world sets a real value. And I would add that I do not think the general possibility of this foreign admixture ought to be used as a means of relieving Shakespeare of the responsibility of bad writing; indeed, however strong my impression might be that the style of a passage was un-Shakespearean, I should never rely on the evidence of style alone unsupported by other tests. Experiences of my own many years ago, when I knew more about the authorship of anonymous reviews than I do now, convinced me that cultivated persons generally overrate their power of knowing an author by his style. I think, therefore, that when Messrs. Clark and Wright say that "Shakespeare has always a manner which cannot well be mistaken," they are not allowing enough for the general feebleness of human discernment of literary qualities. In the particular case of *Macbeth*, however, I agree with the Cambridge editors in thinking the second scene of Act i., in which the sergeant reports the martial deeds of Macbeth and Banquo, is un-Shakespearean in its laboured and level bombast unsuited to the personage, and that most of the utterances of Hecate and some of those of the witches, are un-Shakespearean in their flat and fluent triviality.

Let me explain. I do not think that Shakespeare in his maturity writes exactly *bombast*, as I should use the word. I admit that his expressions are what might loosely be called "bombastic"; *i.e.* I admit that they are sometimes violent, exaggerated, extravagant,—if you like, unnatural. Excessive emphasis is a sin of the Elizabethan drama generally, and Shakespeare is undoubtedly among the sinners. But his violent and extravagant phrases are at any rate carefully prepared and worked up to: they belong to the character, the situation, and correspond to some adequate cause of strong emotion: they do not produce on us the effect of mere rhetorical effort gone wrong: of a man swelling out his phrases and talking big in order to impress us, and not impressing us after all. And I think that there is no play of Shakespeare's better adapted to illustrate this difference than *Macbeth* : none in which the violent utterances are more carefully prepared and worked up to. Take, *e.g.*, the meditation of Macbeth just before the murder of Banquo :—

> To be thus is nothing ;
> But to be safely thus.—Our fears in Banquo
> Stick deep ; and in his royalty of nature
> Reigns that which would be fear'd : 'tis much he dares ;
> And, to that dauntless temper of his mind,
> He hath a wisdom that doth guide his valour
> To act in safety. There is none but he
> Whose being I do fear : and, under him,
> My Genius is rebuked ; as, it is said,
> Mark Antony's was by Cæsar. He chid the sisters
> When first they put the name of king upon me,
> And bade them speak to him : then prophet-like
> They hailed him father to a line of kings :
> Upon my head they placed a fruitless crown,
> And put a barren sceptre in my gripe,
> Thence to be wrench'd with an unlineal hand,
> No son of mine succeeding. If 't be so,
> For Banquo's issue have I filed my mind ;
> For them the gracious Duncan have I murder'd ;
> Put rancours in the vessel of my peace
> Only for them ; and mine eternal jewel
> Given to the common enemy of man,
> To make them kings, the seed of Banquo kings !
> Rather than so, come fate into the list,
> And champion me to the utterance ! [1]

Observe how out from the meditative calmness of the intellectual state of analysis of his rival's character, the passion of jealousy—naturally imperious in a powerful mind that has given itself to criminal ambition—is gradually worked up to increasing violence of expression. The last phrase is just what might have been bombastic if it had not been thus prepared ; but as it comes in it seems to me right.

I will take another instance where there is an extravagance of image which I cannot quite defend, but which yet is not bombast :—

[1] Act iii. Sc. i.

> If it were done when 'tis done, then 'twere well
> It were done quickly : if the assassination
> Could trammel up the consequence, and catch
> With his surcease success ; that but this blow
> Might be the be-all and the end-all here,
> But here, upon this bank and shoal of time,
> We'd jump the life to come.   But in these cases
> We still have judgment here ; that we but teach
> Bloody instructions, which, being taught, return
> To plague the inventor : This even-handed justice
> Commends the ingredients of our poison'd chalice
> To our own lips.   He's here in double trust ;
> First, as I am his kinsman and his subject,
> Strong both against the deed ; then, as his host,
> Who should against his murderer shut the door,
> Not bear the knife myself.   Besides, this Duncan
> Hath borne his faculties so meek, hath been
> So clear in his great office, that his virtues
> Will plead like angels, trumpet-tongued, against
> The deep damnation of his taking-off :
> And pity, like a naked new-born babe,
> Striding the blast, or heaven's cherubim, horsed
> Upon the sightless couriers of the air,
> Shall blow the horrid deed in every eye,
> That tears shall drown the wind.   I have no spur
> To prick the sides of my intent, but only
> Vaulting ambition, which o'er-leaps itself,
> And falls on the other.[1]

I confess that the idea of " tears drowning the wind " seems to me too extravagant to be approved anywhere : but if anywhere we can tolerate it here, where it comes as the one burst of violent emotion in a speech of which the general language expresses admirably the tranquil tension of anxious meditation at a tremendous crisis of life.

Observe, again, how subtly these speeches—and other speeches of Macbeth—are suited to the character that Shakespeare requires for the effectiveness of the drama. *Macbeth* is the only one of the great group of tragedies that belongs to Shakespeare's middle period, in which the leading villain of the piece is at the same time the hero, on whose career (along with his wife's) the spectators have to

[1] Act i. Sc. vii.

concentrate their main interest: the dramatist has therefore the difficult problem of exciting our sympathies for a man whom he has to show descending through a series of hideous crimes to a depth of utter wickedness. And the difficulty is doubled because the story he has to tell precludes him from attributing to Macbeth, at the great crisis of the action, the only moral excellences appropriate to a thorough-going criminal—high-hearted courage and manly resolution. It is the wife who has to exhibit these qualities: and if it is awkward for a hero to be a villain, it is even more awkward for him to play second fiddle to a woman.

But it is in triumphing over difficulties of this kind that Shakespeare's dramatic genius is most strikingly shown: for if there is anything in which Shakespeare's genius is incontestable it is in his power of winning for his personages —under the most unfavourable circumstances—at least the *quantum* of human sympathy required for dramatic interest. He achieves this in the case of Macbeth by giving him an intellectual comprehensiveness and penetration, and at the same time an emotional susceptibility remarkably deep and delicate. Thus his vacillation at the crisis, before the crime, and the terrifying collapse and overthrow of his rational self-control immediately after it, are felt by the spectator to be due not to the feebleness of his nature but to its intellectual range and emotional fineness. It is because he can see clearly the consequences of his crime, and even feel with sympathetic intensity the pity and horror it will excite in others—though this gift of sympathy is perfectly dominated by selfish ambition—that he hesitates at the crisis; it is through the same fineness of nature that he feels so intensely afterwards how the springs of true human life are for him so irrevocably poisoned.

The same characteristics give a singular charm to his meditative utterances even at the later period of his career, when not only morality but natural affection has been eaten out of him by his course of relentless crime. Thus in his speech, on hearing of his wife's death—

> She should have died hereafter ;
> There would have been a time for such a word.
> To-morrow, and to-morrow, and to-morrow,
> Creeps in this petty pace from day to day
> To the last syllable of recorded time,
> And all our yesterdays have lighted fools
> The way to dusty death. Out, out, brief candle !
> Life's but a walking shadow, a poor player
> That struts and frets his hour upon the stage
> And then is heard no more : it is a tale
> Told by an idiot, full of sound and fury,
> Signifying nothing.[1]

In this speech he shows that conjugal love—so strong in the crisis before the murder, so powerful in deciding him to action—has withered away : the relic of it is only able to stir in him a vague sense of the hollowness of life : but his expression of this feeling irresistibly wins for him the interest attaching to a fine nature in moral ruin.

[1] Act. v. Sc. v.

VI

BENTHAM AND BENTHAMISM IN POLITICS AND ETHICS

(*Fortnightly Review*, May 1877)

In the critical narrative, equally brilliant and erudite, which Mr. Leslie Stephen has given us of the course of English thought in the eighteenth century, there is one gap which I cannot but regret, in spite of what Mr. Stephen has said in explanation of it. The work of Bentham is treated with somewhat contemptuous brevity in the chapter on Moral Philosophy; while in the following chapter on Political Theories his name is barely mentioned. The present paper is an attempt in some measure to supply this deficiency. I should not have ventured on it if Bentham's teaching had become to us a matter of merely historical interest; as I cannot flatter myself that I possess Mr. Stephen's rare gift of imparting a sparkle to the dust-heaps of extinct controversy. But no such extinction has yet overtaken Bentham: his system is even an important element of our current political thought; hardly a decade —though an eventful one—has elapsed since it might almost have been called a predominant element. Among the other writers to whom Mr. Stephen has devoted many entertaining pages in his tenth chapter, there is not one of whom this can be said. It would be almost ostentation, in polite society at the present day, to claim familiarity with Bolingbroke; it would be even pedantry to draw attention to Hoadly. The literary sources of the French Revolution are studied with eager and ever-increasing interest; but they are studied, even by Englishmen, almost entirely in the writings of France: the most ardent reader of revolutionary literature is reluctant to decline from Rousseau to Tom Paine. Mr. Kegan Paul's entertaining biography has temporarily revived our interest in Godwin, otherwise *Political Justice* would be chiefly known to this generation through the refutation of Malthus; and Malthus's own work is now but seldom taken from the shelf. There are probably many schoolboys feeding a nascent taste for rhetoric on the letters of Junius; but Mr. Stephen has felt that the inclusion of these in an account of Political Theories requires something like an apology. Burke lives, no doubt, not merely through the eloquence which immortalises even the details of party conflicts, but through a kind of wisdom, fused of intellect and emotion, which is as essentially independent of the theorising in which it is embedded as metal is of its mine. But though Burke lives, we meet with no Burkites. The star of Hume's metaphysical fame has risen steadily for a century; but his warmest admirers are rather irritated by his predominant desire for literary popularity, and are perhaps too much inclined to turn aside from the philosophic material that was wasted in furnishing elegant essays on National Character and The Idea of a Perfect Commonwealth. In short, of all the writers I have mentioned, regarded as political theorists, it is only the eccentric hermit of Queen's Square Place whose name still carries with it an audible demand that we should reckon with his system, and explain to ourselves why and how far we agree or disagree with his opinions.

Mr. Stephen, it should be said, is so far from denying this exceptional vitality of Benthamism, that he even puts it forward as an explanation of his cursory treatment of this system. "The history of utilitarianism as an active force belongs," he tells us, to the new post-revolutionary era, on the threshold of which his plan compels him to stop. This argument would have been sound if Bentham had really been a man of the nineteenth century, born before his time in the eighteenth, and thus naturally not appreciated till later, when the stream of current thought had at length caught him up. Such freaks of nature do sometimes occur, to the very considerable perplexity of the philosophical historian, in his efforts to exhibit a precise and regular development of opinion. But this is so far from being the case with Bentham, that when J. S. Mill, in his most eclectic phase, undertook to balance his claims as a thinker against those of Coleridge, he described the conflict between these two modes of thought as the "revolt of the nineteenth century against the eighteenth." The appropriateness of the phrase is surely undeniable. No doubt it is also true, as Mr. Stephen says, that Benthamism as an active force—and Benthamism is nothing if it is *not* an active force—belongs rather to the nineteenth century. It is just because both these views are equally true that Bentham deserves the special attention of the historian of opinion. In England, at least in the department of ethics and politics, Benthamism is the one outcome of the Seculum Rationalisticum against which the philosophy of Restoration and Reaction has had to struggle continually with varying success. It is, we may say, the legacy left to the nineteenth century by the eighteenth; or rather, perhaps, by that innovating and reforming period of the eighteenth century in which Enlightenment became ardent, and strove to consume and re-create. In his most characteristic merits, as well as his most salient defects, Bentham is eminently a representative of this stirring and vehement age : in his unreserved devotion to the grandest and most comprehensive aims, his high and sustained confidence in their attainability, and the buoyant, indefatigable industry with which he sought the means for their attainment—no less than in his exaggerated reliance on his own method, his ignorant contempt for the past, and his intolerant misinterpretation of all that opposed him in the present.

It must be admitted that, though distinctly a child of its age, Benthamism was not exactly a favourite child. The

Fragment on Government (1776), and the *Principles of Morals and Legislation* (published 1789), had found comparatively few sympathising readers at the time when *Political Justice* and *The Rights of Man* were being greedily bought. At the age of forty-two (1790) Bentham speaks, in a letter to his brother, of "the slow increase of my school." Yet we observe very clearly that from the first Bentham appears as a teacher and master of political science—one who has, or ought to have, a "school"—and is accepted as such by competent judges. In 1778, only two years after the publication of the *Fragment*, D'Alembert writes to him, in the style of the time, as a philosopher and professional benefactor of the human race. Two years later he was taken up by Lord Lansdowne, who seems to have had the eager receptivity for abstract theory which is often found in powerful but imperfectly trained intellects, even after the fullest acquisition of all that experience can teach. The retired statesman bore with really admirable patience the humours of the sensitive and self-conscious philosopher: and in the circle at Bowood Bentham found —besides the one romance of his life—invaluable opportunities for extending his influence as a thinker. It was there that he first met Romilly, the earliest of the band of reformers who, in the next century, attempted the practical realisation of his principles; and there, too, he laid the foundation of his remarkable ascendency over Dumont. The self-devotion with which a man of Dumont's talents and independence of thought allowed himself to be absorbed in the humble function of translating and popularising Bentham was a testimony of admiration outweighing a bushel of complimentary phrases : of which, however, Bentham had no lack, though they came from a somewhat narrow circle. "The suffrages of the few," writes Dumont in one of his earlier letters, "will repay you for the indifference of the many . . . Write and bridle my wandering opinions." Through Dumont he became known to Mirabeau: and a good deal of Benthamite doctrine found its way into that hero's addresses to his constituents, which Dumont assisted in composing. Brissot again, who saw a good deal of Bentham in London, some years before 1789, always spoke and wrote of him with the utmost enthusiasm : to which it may be partly attributed that, in August 1792, a special law of the National Assembly made him (as he tells Wilberforce afterwards) "an adopted French citizen, third man in the universe after a natural one"; Priestley and Paine being the first two. As soon as Dumont published the *Principes de la Code Civile et Pénale* (1802), expressions of even hyperbolical admiration were sent to the philosopher from different parts of Europe. A Swiss pastor subscribes himself, rather to Bentham's amusement, "un homme heureux, regénéré par la lecture de vos ouvrages." A Russian general writes that his book "fills the soul with peace, the heart with virtue, and dissipates the mists of the mind"; and conjures him to dictate a code to Russia. Another Russian admirer ranks him with Bacon and Newton as the "creator of a new science," and writes that he is "laying up a sum for the purpose of spreading the light which emanates" from his writings. Nor is he without similar honour even in his own country. Lord Lansdowne, answering good-humouredly a reproachful epistle of sixty pages, says that it is a letter which "Bacon might have sent to Buckingham." In 1793 a gentleman whom he has asked to dinner writes expressing "a woman's eagerness to meet a gentleman of so enlightened a mind." A few years later we find that the great Dr. Parr is never tired of praising his "mighty talents, profound researches, important discoveries, and irresistible arguments." On the whole we may say that as even in his revered old age he never attained the kind of popularity that adapts a man's name for utterance on platforms : so even in the earlier part of his career he often met with respect that almost amounted to homage from men more or less influential and representative.

The degree and kind of influence which Bentham exercised in the revolutionary period corresponds tolerably well to the degree of affinity between his teaching and the principles on which the revolutionary movement proceeded. In the combat against prejudices and privileges any ally was welcome; and Bentham was as anxious as any revolutionist to break with the past, and reform all the institutions of society in accordance with pure reason. It is true that, from our point of view, the reason of Bentham appears the perfect antithesis of the reason of Rousseau; but it is very doubtful whether this would have been evident to Rousseau himself. The mainspring of Bentham's life and work, as his French friends saw, was an equal regard for all mankind: whether the precise objects of this regard were conceived as men's "rights" or their "interests," was a question which they would not feel to be of primary concern. He himself, indeed, was always conscious of the gulf that separated him from his fellow-citizens by adoption. "Were they," he writes in 1796, "to see an analysis I have by me of their favourite Declaration of Rights, there is not perhaps a being upon earth that would be less welcome to them than I could ever hope to be." But the *Anarchical Fallacies*, like some other fruits of Bentham's labours, remained on the philosopher's shelves till the end of his life; only a meagre fragment of them found its way into Dumont's *Principes*; and by the time that this came out, anarchical theories were somewhat obscured behind military facts. And unless the "principle of utility" explicitly announced itself as hostile to the fundamental principles of the common revolutionary creed, it certainly would not be generally perceived to be so. I should almost conjecture from what Mr. Stephen says of Bentham, compared with the references to utilitarianism in his discussion of earlier writers, that he has hardly enough recognised that Bentham's originality and importance lay not in his verbal adoption of utility as an end and standard of right political action, but in his real exclusion of any other standard; in the definiteness with which he conceived the "general good"; the clearness and precision with which he analysed it into its empirically ascertainable constituents; the exhaustive and methodical consistency with which he applied this one standard to all departments of practice; and the rigour with which he kept its application free from all alien elements. Merely to state "utility" as an ultimate end was nothing; no one would have distinguished this from the "public good" at which all politicians had always professed to aim, and all revolutionary politicians with special amplitude of phrase. The very Declaration of the National Assembly, that solemnly set forth the maintenance of the "natural, imprescriptible, and inalienable" rights of man, as the sole end of government, announced in its very first clause, that "civil distinctions, *therefore*, can be founded only on public utility." It was not then surprising that Morellet, Brissot, and others, recognising the comprehensiveness of view and clearness of grasp that were so remarkably combined in Bentham's intellect, the equal distribution of his sympathies, and the elevated ardour of his philanthropy, should have hailed him as worthy to "serve in the cause of liberty."

And yet the almost comical contrast that we find between Bentham's temper and method in treating political questions, and the habitual sentiments and ideas of his revolutionary friends, could hardly fail to make itself felt by the latter. Let us take, for example, the *Essay on Parliamentary Tactics* which he offered for the guidance of the new Assembly in 1789; and let us imagine a French deputy—a member of the "Tiers" that has so recently been "Rien" and is now conscious of itself as "Tout"—attempting its perusal. He finds in it no word of response to the sentiments that are filling his breast; nothing said of privileged classes whose machinations have to be defeated, in order that the people may realise its will; instead of this, he is met at the outset with an exhaustive statement of the various ways in which he and other servants of the people are liable to shirk or scamp their work, or otherwise to miss attainment of the general good. The object of the treatise, as the author explains, is—

To obviate the inconveniences to which a political assembly is exposed in the exercise of its functions. Each rule of this tactics can therefore have no justifying reason, except in the *prevention of an evil.* It is therefore with a distinct knowledge of these evils that we should proceed in search of remedies. These inconveniences may be arranged under the ten following heads :—

    1. Inaction.
    2. Useless decision.
    3. Indecision.
    4. Delays.
    5. Surprise or precipitation.
    6. Fluctuations in measures.
    7. Quarrels.
    8. Falsehoods.
    9. Decisions, vicious on account of form.
    10. Decisions, vicious in respect of their foundation.

We shall develop these different heads in a few words.

Under the head of delays, we find—

may be ranked all vague and useless procedures—preliminaries which do not tend to a decision—questions badly propounded, or presented in a bad order—personal quarrels—witty speeches, and amusements suited to the amphitheatre or the playhouse.

The last and most important head is thus further analysed :

When an assembly form an improper or hurtful decision, it may be supposed that this decision incorrectly represents its wishes. If the assembly be composed as it ought to be, its wish will be conformed to the decision of public utility; and when it wanders from this it will be from one or other of the following causes :—

1. *Absence.*—The general wish of the assembly is the wish of the majority of the total number of its members. But the greater the number of the members who have not been present at its formation, the more doubtful is it whether the wish which is announced as general be really so.

2. *Want of Freedom.*—If any restraint have been exercised over the votes, they may not be conformable to the internal wishes of those who have given them.

3. *Seduction.*—If attractive means have been employed to act upon the wills of the members, it may be that the wish announced may not be conformable to their conscientious wish.

4. *Error.*—If they have not possessed the means of informing themselves—if false statements have been presented to them—their understandings may be deceived, and the wish which has been expressed may not be that which they would have formed had they been better informed.

And so on for page after page of dull and beggarly elements, methodised no doubt in a masterly manner, and calculated to have a highly salutary and sobering effect on the mind of any legislator who can be persuaded to read them. One defect which Bentham is most seriously concerned to cure is the imperfect acquaintance that legislators are liable to have with the motions on which they vote.

"Nothing is more common," he says, "than to see orators, and even practised orators, falling into involuntary errors with respect to the precise terms of a motion." This evil, he thinks, may be obviated by "a very simple mechanical apparatus for exhibiting to the eyes of the assembly the motion on which they are deliberating."

"We may suppose a gallery above the president's chair, which presents a front consisting of two frames, nine feet high by six feet wide, filled with black canvas, made to open like folding doors;—that this canvas is regularly pierced for the reception of letters of so large a size as to be legible in every part of the place of meeting. These letters might be attached by an iron hook, in such manner that they could not be deranged. When a motion is about to become the object of debate, it would be given to the compositors, who would transcribe it upon the table, and by closing the gallery, exhibit it like a placard to the eyes of the whole assembly."

One would think that these suggestions were sufficiently particular; but Bentham feels it needful to give a page more of minute directions as to size of letters, method of fixing them, composition of the table, etc.

The salutary working of this machinery is obvious:—

When the orator forgets his subject, and begins to wander, a table of motions offers the readiest means for recalling him. Under the present régime, how is this evil remedied? It is necessary for a member to rise, to interrupt the speaker, and call him to order. This is a provocation—it is a reproach—it wounds his self-love. The orator attacked, defends himself; there is no longer a debate upon the motion, but a discussion respecting the application of his arguments. . . . But if we suppose the table of motions placed above [the president], the case would be very different. He might, without interrupting the speaker, warn him by a simple gesture; and this quiet sign would not be accompanied by the danger of a personal appeal.

The faithful Dumont is unbounded in his eulogy of this "absolutely new and original" work, which "fills up one of the blanks of political literature," and reports that Mirabeau and the Duc de la Rochefoucauld admired this "truly philosophical conception." Still the reader will hardly be surprised to learn that Morellet thinks it not likely to be appreciated by "light-minded and unreflecting persons" in the crisis of 1789. Bentham, we feel, must often have appeared to his French friends as a perfect specimen of the cold unsentimental type of Englishman; though with an epistolary prolixity which Sir Charles Grandison could hardly surpass. On one occasion the admiring Brissot cannot repress a murmur at the "dryness and drollery" with which he responds to sentiment. "You have then never loved me!" he exclaims,—"me whose sensibilities mingle with legislation itself!" And in truth, though Bentham had plenty of sensibilities beneath his eccentric exterior, he was not in the habit of letting them mingle with legislation.

The above extracts have sufficiently illustrated another marked characteristic of Bentham's work in politics, besides his severe exclusion of fine sentiments: his habit, namely, of working out his suggestions into the minutest details. This tendency he often exhibits in an exaggerated form, so that it becomes repellent or even ridiculous; especially as Bentham, with all his desire to be practical, is totally devoid of the instinctive self-adaptation which most men learn from converse with the world. Still the habit itself is an essential element of the force and originality of his intellectual attitude. "A man's mind," says the representative scientific man in *Middlemarch*, " must be continually expanding and shrinking between the whole human horizon and the horizon of an object-glass." Bentham's mind was continually performing a similar " systole and diastole " ; and thus, in spite of the unduly deductive method that he generally employs, he really resembles the modern man of science in the point in which the latter differs most strikingly from the ancient notion of a philosopher. His apprehension, whether of abstract theory or of concrete fact, has marked limitations ; but as regards the portion of human life over which his intellectual vision ranges, he has eyes which can see with equal clearness in the most abstract and the most concrete region ; and he as naturally seeks completeness in working out the details of a practical scheme as in defining the most general notions of theoretical jurisprudence. He aims at a perfectly reasoned adaptation of means to ends in constructing a " frame of motions," no less than in constructing a code of laws ; and he passes from the latter to the former without any abatement of interest or any sense of incongruity. Thus, for twenty years (from 1791 to 1811), while his fame as a philosophical jurist was extending through the civilised world, he was probably better known to the Government at home as belonging to the rather despised class of beings who were then called " projectors," from his favourite plan of a " Panopticon " Penitentiary, which was continually urged on their notice by himself and his friends.

Panopticon or Inspection House was a circular building, in which prisoners' cells were to occupy the circumference and keepers the centre, with an intermediate annular wall all the way up, to which the cells were to be laid open by an iron grating. This construction (which with proper modifications could be adapted to a workhouse) fills a much larger space in Bentham's correspondence than all his codes put together. Indeed, among the numerous wrongs, great and small, on which the philosopher in his old age used to dilate with a kind of cheerful acrimony peculiar to himself, there was none which roused so much resentment as the

L

suppression of Panopticon, which he always attributed to a personal grudge on the King's part. He composed a whole volume on "the war between Jeremy Bentham and George III., by one of the belligerents." "But for George III." the narrative begins, "all the prisons and all the paupers in England would long ago have been under my management." For the administration of his prisons he had devised a complete scheme, to the realisation of which he was prepared to devote himself. The expense of prisoners was to have been reduced ultimately to zero by a rigid economy, which yet, when mitigated by the indulgences that were to be earned by extra labour, would only produce about sufficient discomfort to make the punishment deterrent. Idle prisoners were to be fed on potatoes and water *ad lib.*, clothed in coats without shirts, and wooden shoes without stockings, and made to sleep in sacks in order to save the superfluous expense of sheets. Existence being thus reduced to its lowest terms, a means of ameliorating it was provided in a certain share of the profits of industry; and Bentham was sanguine enough to suppose that fifteen hours a day of sedentary labour and muscular exercise combined, could be got out of each prisoner by this stimulus. Contract-management was an essential feature of the scheme; it must be made the manager's interest to extract from his prisoners as much work as he could without injuring them; while the prisoners would be sufficiently protected against the manager's selfishness by the terms of his contract, by the free admission of the public to inspect the prison, and by a fine to be paid for every prisoner's death above a certain average.

The amount of labour that Bentham spent in elaborating the details of this scheme, defending it against all criticisms, urging it on ministers and parliamentary friends, and vituperating all whom he believed to have conspired to prevent its execution, would have alone sufficed to fill the life of a man of more than average energy; while the total disappointment of the hopes of twenty years, after coming within sight of success—for in 1794 Parliament had authorised such a contract as Bentham proposed—would have damped any ordinary philanthropic zeal. But Panopticon and all that belongs to it, including all that he wrote on the Poor Law and Pauper Management, might be subtracted from Bentham's intellectual labours, without materially diminishing the impression produced on the mind by their amount and variety. Nay, even if the whole of his vast work on Law and its administration, including innumerable pamphlets on special points and cases, were left out of sight,—if we knew nothing of Bentham the codifier, or Bentham the radical reformer,—his life would still seem fuller of interests and activities than most men's. Besides his well-known pamphlet in defence of usury, he composed a *Manual of Political Economy*, in which the principles of *laisser-faire* are independently expounded and applied. The Bell and Lancaster method of instruction inspired him to enthusiastic emulation : he immediately planned an unsectarian Chrestomathic day-school to be built in his own garden in Queen's Square Place. The school itself never came into existence; for this, like some other educational schemes, was wrecked on the rock of theology. But Bentham fulfilled his part in composing a *Chrestomathia*, which contained, besides a full and original exposition of pedagogic principles, a sort of manual of geometry, algebra, and physics, and an encyclopædic discussion of scientific nomenclature and classification. And this is only one striking specimen of his habitual practice. *Quicquid agunt homines*—whatever men do for men's happiness—is certainly the farrago of his inexhaustible MSS. Whatever business suggests to him an idea of amelioration he immediately studies with minute and intense interest, until he believes himself to have perfectly penetrated it by his exhaustive method, and is ready with a completely reasoned scheme of improvement. Currency projects, banking regulations, proposals for an "unburthensome increase of the revenue," reform of the Thames police, a new mode of taking the census, a device for preventing forgery, a prospect of abolishing the slave-trade, a plan for morally improving Irish labourers in New York—each subject in its turn is discussed with a fresh eagerness and an amplitude of explanation that seem to belong to the leisured amateur of social science. Nor is his attention confined to matters strictly social or political. He is not too much engaged in applying his method of study to expound it in an *Essay on Logic,* supplemented by a characteristic dissertation on Language and Universal Grammar. Chemistry and botany, from their rich promise of utility, are continually attractive to him. He is never too busy to help in experiments which may enrich mankind with a new grass or a new fruit. At one time he is anxious to learn all about laughing gas; at another he corresponds at length about a Frigidarium, in which fermentable substances may be preserved from pernicious fermentation while remaining unfrozen. Nothing seems to him too trivial an object for his restless impulse of amelioration; and he cannot understand why it should seem so to any one else. There is an amusing instance of this in one of his letters to Dumont at the crisis of a negotiation in which the latter, having won Talleyrand's patronage for the *Civil and Penal Codes,* is delicately endeavouring to secure a favourable notice for Panopticon. Dumont has asked his master to send Talleyrand a set of economical and political works. It occurs to Bentham that it will be a stroke of diplomacy to forward along with the books " a set or two sets of my brother's patent but never-sold fire-irons of which the special and characteristic property is levity." They would serve, he thinks, " as a specimen of the Panopticon system. One might be kept by T. (Talleyrand), the other, if he thought fit, passed on to B. (Bonaparte)." Even the sympathetic Dumont declines to extend his interest to patent fire-irons, and coldly intimates that he is " not familiar with such instruments." The humblest games, we find, are not unworthy of utilitarian consideration, and may be treated in the same confident deductive fashion as governments. At Ford Abbey—where Bentham lived from 1814 to 1817, and where the youthful J. S. Mill found the " sentiment of a larger and freer existence " in the " middle-age architecture, baronial hall, and spacious and lofty rooms "—battledores and shuttlecocks were kept in frequent exercise; and any tendency in manufacturers to deviate from the true type of shuttlecock was severely repressed. " Pointed epigrams, yes," writes the philosopher; " but pointed shuttlecocks never were, nor ever will be, good for anything. These, it is true, have not been tried; but trial is not necessary to the condemnation of such shuttlecocks as these." Bentham was strictly temperate in his diet: he ate meat but once a day, and then very moderately, and was almost a teetotaler. But the pleasures of the table were too important to be diminished by a stupid adherence to custom; and being particularly fond of fruit, he used often to maximise his prandial happiness by commencing with the dessert, before the sensibility of his palate had been impaired by coarser viands.

I have dwelt at some length on this side of Bentham's character, because it seems to me that we get the right point of view for understanding his work in politics and ethics, if we conceive it as the central and most important realisation of a dominant and all-comprehensive desire for the amelioration of human life, or rather of sentient existence generally. A treatise on deontology, a code, an inspection-house, a set of fire-irons, may all be regarded as instruments more or less rationally contrived for the promotion of happiness; and it is exclusively in this light that Bentham regards them. Thus, perhaps, we may partly account for the extreme unreadableness of his later writings, which are certainly " biblia abiblia." The best defence for them is that they are hardly meant to be criticised as books; they were written not so much to be read as to be used. Hence if, after they were written, he saw no prospect of their producing a practical effect, he kept them contentedly on his shelves for a more seasonable opportunity. In his earlier compositions he shows considerable literary faculty: his argument is keen and lucid, and his satirical humour often excellent, though liable to be too prolix. But the fashion in which he really liked to express his thoughts was the proper style of legal documents—a style, that is in which there are no logically superfluous words, but in which everything that is intended is fully expressed, and the most tedious iteration is not shunned if it is logically needed for completeness and precision. And as years went on, and Dumont saved him the necessity of making himself popular, he gave full scope to his peculiar taste. Such a manner of expression has indeed a natural affinity to the fulness of detail with which his subjects are treated. But the tedium caused by the latter is necessarily aggravated by the former; and therefore the "general reader" has to be warned off from most of Bentham's volumes; or perhaps such warning is hardly needed. Those, however, who study him as he would have wished to be studied, not for literary gratification, but for practical guidance, will feel that his fatiguing exhaustiveness of style and treatment has great advantages. It to some extent supplies the place of empirical tests to his system; at least, whatever dangers lurk in his abstract deductive method of dealing with human beings, we certainly cannot include among them the "dolus" which "latet in generalibus." If in establishing his practical principles he has neglected any important element of human nature, we are almost certain to feel the deficiency in the concrete result which his indefatigable imagination works out for us. Often, indeed, the danger rather is that we shall be unduly repelled by the mere strangeness of the habits and customs of the new social organisation into which he transports us.

Thus from different points of view one might truly describe Bentham as one of the *most* or the *least* idealistic of practical philosophers. What is, immediately suggests to him what ought to be; his interest in the former is never that of pure curiosity, but always subordinated to his purpose of producing the latter; there is no department of the actual that he is not anxious to reconstruct systematically on rational principles, and so in a certain sense to inform and penetrate with ideas. While again his ideal is, to borrow a phrase of John Grote's, as much as possible *de-idealised*, positivised, some might say philistinised, his good is purged of all mystical elements, and reduced to the positive, palpable, empirical, definitely quantitative notion of "maximum balance of pleasure over pain"; and his conception of human nature and its motives—the material which he has to adapt to the attainment of this good—is not only un-ideal, but even anti-ideal, or idealised in the wrong direction. While he is as confident in his power of constructing a happy society as the most ardent believer in the moral perfectibility of mankind, he is as convinced of the unqualified selfishness of the vast majority of human beings as the bitterest cynic. Hence the double aspect of his utilitarianism, which has caused so much perplexity both to disciples and to opponents. It is as if Hobbes or Mandeville were suddenly inspired with the social enthusiasm of Godwin. Something of the same blending of contraries is found in Helvetius; and he, perhaps, rather than Hume, should be taken as the intellectual progenitor of Bentham. In Helvetius, however, though utilitarianism is passing out of the critical and explanatory phase in which we find it in Hume, into the practical and reforming phase, the transition is not yet complete. Still the premises of Bentham are all clearly given by Helvetius; and the task which the former took up is that which the latter clearly marks out for the moralist. Indeed, if we imagine the effect of *L'Esprit* on the mind of an eager young law-student, we seem to have the whole intellectual career of Bentham implicitly contained in a " pensée de jeunesse."

Helvetius puts with a highly effective simplicity, from which Hume was precluded by his more subtle and complex psychological analysis, these two doctrines : first, that every human being " en tout temps, en tout lieu " seeks his own interest, and judges of things and persons according as they promote it : and secondly, that, as the public is made up of individuals, the qualities that naturally and normally gain public esteem and are called virtues are those useful to the public. Observation, he says, shows us that there are a few men who are inspired by " un heureux naturel, un désir vif de la gloire et de l'estime," with the same passion for justice and virtue which men generally feel for wealth and greatness. The actions which promote the private interest of these virtuous men are actions that are just, and conducive, or not contrary, to the general interest. But these men are so few that Helvetius only mentions them " pour l'honneur de l'humanité." The human race is almost entirely composed of men whose care is concentrated on their private interests. How, under these circumstances, are we to promote virtue? for which Helvetius really seems to be genuinely concerned, though he is too well bred to claim for himself expressly so exceptional a distinction. It is clear, he thinks, that the work will not be done by moralists, unless they completely change their methods. " Qu'ont produit jusqu'aujourd'hui les plus belles maximes de la morale?" Our moralists do not perceive that it is a futile endeavour, and would be dangerous if it were not futile, to try to alter the tendency of men to seek their private happiness. They might perhaps gain some influence if they would substitute the " langage d'intérêt" for the " ton d'injure " in which they now utter their maxims; for a man might then be led to abstain at least from such vices as are prejudicial to himself. But for the achievement of really important results the moralist must have recourse to legislation. This is a conclusion which Helvetius is never tired of enforcing. " One ought not to complain of the wickedness of man, but of the ignorance of legislators who have always set private interest in opposition to public." " The hidden source of a people's vices is always in its legislation; it is there that we must search if we would discover and extirpate their roots." " Moralists ought to know that as the sculptor fashions the trunk of a tree into a god or a stool, so the legislator makes heroes, geniuses, virtuous men, as he wills: . . . reward, punishment, fame, disgrace, are four kinds of divinities with which he can always effect the public good." In short, Helvetius conceives that universal self-preference might by legislative machinery be so perfectly harmonised with public utility that " none but madmen would be vicious": it only wants a man of insight and courage, " échauffé de la passion du bien général," to effect this happy consummation.

Such, then, was the task that Bentham, at the age of twenty-five, undertook; and perhaps his bitterest opponent, surveying his sixty years of strenuous performance, will hardly blame him severely for presumption in deeming himself to possess the requisite qualifications. The young Englishman, indeed, with his faith in our " matchless constitution " as yet unshaken, conceives himself to be in an exceptionally favourable position for realising this union of morals and legislation. " France," he writes in his commonplace-book for 1774-75, " may have philosophers. The world is witness if she have not philosophers. But it is England only that can have patriots, for a patriot is a philosopher in action." Such a " philosopher in action " might hope not merely to delineate, but actually to set on foot that reformation in the moral world which could only come from improvement in the machine of law. But in the moral no less than in the physical world one cannot improve a machine without understanding it; the study of it as it exists must be separated from the investigation of what it ought to be, and the former must be thoroughly performed before the latter can be successfully attempted. This is to us so obvious a truism that it seems pedantic to state it expressly; but it is a truism which Bentham found as much as possible obscured in Blackstone's famous *Commentaries*. The first thing then which he had to do was to dispel that confusion between the expository and the censorial functions of the jurist, which seemed to be inherent in the official account of the laws and constitution of England. The clearness and completeness with which this is done are the chief merits of the *Fragment on Government*. In this elaborate attack on Blackstone's view of municipal law Bentham does not as yet criticise the particulars either of the British constitution or of British administration of justice: his object is merely to supply the right set of notions for apprehending what either actually is, together with the right general principles for judging of its goodness or badness. His fundamental idea is taken, as he says, from Hume; but the methodical precision with which it is worked out is admirable; in fact, the *Fragment* contains the whole outline of that system of formal constitutional jurisprudence which the present generation has mostly learnt from his disciple John Austin. Among other things we may notice as characteristic the manner in which he throws aside the official nonsense about the "democratic element" in the unreformed British Parliament, which half imposed even on the clear intellect of Paley. "A duke's son," he says, "gets a seat in the House of Commons; it needs no more to make him the very model of an Athenian cobbler." In a similar spirit he banters Blackstone's account of the "wisdom and valour" for which our lords temporal are selected. He remarks that in Queen Anne's reign, in the year 1711, "not long after the time of the hard frost," there seems to have been such an exuberance of these virtues as to "furnish merit enough to stock no fewer than a dozen respectable persons, who upon the strength of it were all made barons in a day"; a phenomenon, he adds, which a contemporary historian has strangely attributed to the necessity of making a majority. It is evident that whatever constitution Bentham may prefer, he will not be put off by any conventional fictions as to the relations of its parts; his preference will depend entirely on what he believes to be their actual working.

More than thirty years, however, were to elapse before Bentham seriously turned his attention to constitutional construction. Indeed nothing is more characteristic of the Benthamite manner of thought, in its application to politics, than the secondary and subordinate position to which it relegates the constitutional questions that absorbed the entire attention of most English politicians of the eighteenth century. Such politicians, even when most theoretical, seem to have had no notion that the political art properly includes a systematic survey of the whole operation of government, and a thorough grasp of the principles by which that operation should be judged and rectified. Their philosophy was made up of metaphysico-jural dissertations on the grounds and limits of civil obedience, and loose historical generalisations as to the effects of the "three simple forms" of government, conceived as chemical elements out of which the British constitution was compounded. What they habitually discussed was not how laws should be made or executed, but what the terms of the social compact were, and whether the balance between Crown and Commons could be maintained without corruption. It is perhaps some survival in Mr. Stephen's mind of this now antiquated way of viewing politics which has led him, while speaking respectfully of Bentham's labours in the sphere of jurisprudence, to refer so slightly to him in describing the course of political thought. And no doubt Bentham's determination to maintain a purely and exhaustively practical treatment in all his writings on law and its administration, render it almost necessary to leave the greater part of his work to the criticism of professional experts. But the general principles by which the whole course of his industry was guided; that government is merely an organisation for accomplishing a very complicated and delicate work, of which the chief part consists in preventing, by the threatened infliction of pain or damage for certain kinds of conduct, some more than equivalent pain or loss of happiness resulting from that conduct to some of the governed; that the primary end of the political art is to secure that this work shall be done in the best possible way with the utmost possible precision and the least possible waste of means; and that the rules controlling the appointment and mutual relations of different members of the government should be considered and determined solely with a view to this end,— these were surely worth mentioning among political theories. For it is this fundamental creed that has given Benthamism its vitality; when once these principles were clearly and firmly apprehended by a man with the "infinite capacity for taking trouble" which has been said to constitute genius, though the eighteenth century, ideally speaking, was not yet over, the nineteenth had certainly begun. A theory that is exclusively positive and unmetaphysical, at the same time that it is still confidently deductive and unhistorical, forms the natural transition from the "Age of Reason" to the period of political thought in which we are now living.

When we consider that Bentham's early manhood coincided with the intensest period of revolutionary fervour, and that he was in close personal relations with some influential Frenchmen of this age, it seems a remarkable evidence of his intellectual independence that he should have so long kept his attention turned away from constitutional reform. Probably the aversion he felt for the metaphysics in which the conception of rational and beneficent government seemed to be commonly entangled, co-operated to concentrate his attention on that department of reform in which alone he felt himself in full sympathy with the party of movement. At the outset of the American war he was altogether hostile to the colonists, owing to the "hodgepodge of confusion and absurdity" which he found in their Declaration of Rights. Six years later he was content to regard the English constitution as "resting at no very great distance, perhaps, from the summit of perfection." In 1789 he went so far with his French friends as to offer the cause of liberty his treatise on Parliamentary Tactics. Still, as we have seen, the dry practicality of this dissertation could hardly be surpassed; it does not touch on a single "burning question" except Division of Chambers, which it treats very abstractly and neutrally. In 1793 whatever sympathy he may have felt for the revolutionists had quite vanished. "Could the extermination of Jacobinism be effected," he writes to his cousin Metcalf, "I should think no price that we could pay for such a security too dear"; and about the same time he tells Dundas that though some of the MSS. he sends him might "lead to his being taken for a republican," he is "now writing against even Parliamentary Reform, and that without any change of sentiment." It is evident that he is thoroughly absorbed in schemes of legislative and administrative improvement: his interest in the French Revolution was due to the unexampled opportunity it seemed to offer for new codes, new judicial establishments, Panopticons, etc.; he has no desire to quarrel with the English Tory Government if it will find employment for his inventions in this line. Until 1791 he seems to have hoped that Lord Lansdowne would place him in Parliament; he even obtained a vague promise to that effect, though for some reason or other the idea was afterwards dropped. Then during the twenty years (from 1791 to 1811) in which Panopticon was in suspense, he would naturally shrink from risking its prospects by any open breach with the Government. Still it is pretty clear that his opinion of the practical efficiency of the Matchless Constitution was growing rapidly worse during the latter part of this period, until in 1809 he wrote his first plan of Parliamentary Reform. This, however, remained unpublished till 1817; and in a letter to President Madison in 1811, in which he proposes to codify for the United States, he takes care to say that " his attention has not turned and is not disposed to turn itself" to changes in the form of their government. Indeed, since the enthusiastic reception which his Civil and Penal Codes, in Dumont's rendering, had met with throughout Europe, his hopes of benefiting the human race by codification had taken so wide a range as almost necessarily to keep him neutral even towards the most despotic kind of rule. In no country was this reception more enthusiastic than in Russia. Accordingly in 1814, Panopticon being finally suppressed, and code-making being in hand in Russia, Bentham considers that the time has come to offer his services for this purpose. The Emperor, with every expression of courtesy and respect, requests him to communicate with the Commission that is sitting on legislation. But this seems to him useless. Alone he must do it; and he somewhat sourly rejects all compliments not accompanied with legislative *carte blanche*. When he is convinced that he cannot be employed on these conditions, his last reason for keeping terms with the traditional forms of government would seem to have vanished; and he prepares, when already verging on threescore and ten, to crown the edifice of his jurisprudence with a Constitutional Code.

It is not often that an energetic practical philanthropist throws himself into constitutional reform at the age of sixty-eight. When he does so, it is likely to be with the accumulated bitterness resulting from a lifetime of baffled attempts to benefit his fellow-men under their existing constitution. And all that Bentham writes after 1817 is full of the heated and violent democratic fanaticism which is incident to the youth of many Liberals who in later years become "tempered by renouncement," but which, as we have seen, was conspicuously absent from the earlier stages of Bentham's political activity. No doubt this may be partly attributed to the spirit of the time. From 1817 to 1830 the tide of Liberalism was rapidly rising, and the flavour of the rising Liberalism was peculiarly bitter. Still a man of sixty-eight is not usually carried away by an upsurging wave of opinion; and we can hardly explain Bentham's mood without taking into account the acrimony of the disappointed projector. It is the persistent rejection of Panopticon and many other fair schemes which has inspired him with so intense a conviction that governments of One or Few invariably aim at the depredation and oppression of the Many. He tells us himself, in the "historical preface" (published 1828) intended for the second edition of the *Fragment on Government*, that it is only after the experience and observation of fifty years that he has learnt to see in the imperfections of the British constitution "the elaborately organised and anxiously cherished and guarded products of sinister interest and artifice." Had George III., any time between 1793 and 1811, made peace with Panopticon, had Alexander in 1814 allowed free play to the great codifier's energies, the Constitutional Code, we may well believe, would have remained unwritten, and the philosophy of modern English Radicalism would have acknowledged a different founder.

And yet, when we examine the rational basis of his constitutional construction, whether as given in the introduction to his *Plan of Parliamentary Reform* (1817), or more fully and characteristically developed in the elaborate work just mentioned, we find that it consists in a few very natural inferences from the ethical and psychological premises on which his whole social activity proceeded; inferences, indeed, so simple and obvious, that we can hardly suppose him not to have tacitly drawn them, even in the earliest stage of his career. If once we regard the administration of law as a machinery indispensable for identifying the interest of individuals with the conduct by which they will most promote the general happiness, so that through a skilful adjustment of rewards and punishments the universally active force of self-preference is made to produce the results at which universal benevolence would aim, it is plain that our arrangements are incomplete unless they include means for similarly regulating the self-preferences of those who are to work and repair the machine. And this, of course, must be done by a combination of rewards and punishments; the problem is, how to apply these so as to produce an adequate effect. It is obviously a far more difficult problem than that with which Bentham had to deal in regulating private relations. For what the private man, in his view, has for the most part to *do*, in order to promote the general happiness, is to consult the interests of himself and his family; whatever private services it is desirable he should render to others should rarely be made legally obligatory, except when he has freely bound himself by special and definite contracts. But from governors, if government is to be well performed, we require the energetic and sustained exercise of all their faculties in the service of their fellow-citizens generally—even more sustained energy than most men spend on their own affairs, in proportion as government is a more difficult business; while at the same time this business is of such a nature that it is necessary to give the managers of it an indefinite power of interfering with the liberty, property, and even life of their fellow-citizens generally. For to set definite limits to this power in the prescriptions of a constitutional code is, from a utilitarian point of view, manifestly irrational. The only rational limits—those which utility would prescribe in any case—cannot be foreseen and fixed once for all; hence any such constitutional restrictions, if observed, are likely to prevent salutary laws and ordinances as well as mischievous ones; while, if they are to be overruled by the "salus populi," their announcement was worse than useless—it was an express incitement to groundless rebellion. The only plan that remains, and the only one that can possibly secure the requisite junction of interests, is to provide that government, while supreme over individuals, shall be under the continual vigilant control of the citizens acting collectively. Every citizen who is not childish, insane, etc., should *primâ facie* have a share in this control, otherwise his interests will presumably be neglected; and every one an equal share, in so far as we have no ground for considering one man's happiness of more importance than any other man's.

We are thus led to the familiar system of Representative Democracy, with universality and equality of suffrage; but, be it observed, without any of the metaphysical fictions which had commonly been involved in the construction of this system. Bentham's system is not a contrivance for enabling every one to "obey himself alone": such an end would have seemed to him chimerical and absurd: it is merely an arrangement for securing that every one's interests shall be as well as possible looked after. To this difference of *rationale* corresponds naturally a difference of constitutional sentiment. Bentham's supreme legislative assembly is not a majestic incarnation of the sovereignty of the people; it is merely a collection of agents, appointed by the people to manage a certain part of their concerns, liable, like other agents, to legal punishment if they can be proved to have violated their trust, and to instant dismissal if it seem probable that they have done so.

Another important difference appears at once in comparing the *rationale* of utilitarian democracy with that based on natural rights. The former, however dogmatically it may be announced, depends necessarily upon certain psychological generalisations, the truth of which may be continually brought to the test of experience. Between traditional legitimacy and natural freedom there was no common ground, and therefore really no argument possible. If I maintain that I and my fellow-citizens have an imprescriptible right to be governed only by laws to which we have consented, I can find no relevancy in the answer that certain persons have inherited a prescriptive right to govern me. But if I maintain that our common interests are most likely to be well looked after by managers whom we can dismiss, however confident I may be in my deduction of this probability from the " universality of self-preference," I must admit arguments from experience tending to prove the opposite. And when these are once admitted, the descent from the position of Bentham and James Mill, that democracy is absolutely desirable, to John Stuart Mill's relative and qualified assertion of its desirability, is logically inevitable; though, like many other logically inevitable steps, it took a generation to make it.

The chief peculiarities, however, in the main outline of Bentham's constitution are due not to his conception of the political end, but to his intense sense of the need of guarding his government against the danger of perversion: a danger which democrats of the older type, from their confidence in ordinary human nature, had commonly overlooked. If the oppressions of kings and aristocrats are connected with the prevalence of prejudice and superstition, it is natural to suppose that when these are removed the business of government is as likely to go on well as any other business. But in Bentham's view governors, under however enlightened a constitution, will be ordinary human beings exposed to extraordinary temptations, to which, therefore, we must presume that they will certainly yield unless very exceptional securities are provided. All the members of government will have natural appetites for power, wealth, dignity, ease at the expense of duty, vengeance at the expense of justice, which are obviously all forces acting in the direction opposed to the general happiness. And since for the exercise of their normal functions governors, or at least the chief among them, must have power not definitely limited, and must have at their disposal a similarly indefinite amount of wealth, it cannot but be profoundly difficult to prevent them from satiating—if it be possible to satiate—all their mischievous appetites. To set one part of government to watch another will avail little: corrupt mutual connivance is too obviously their common interest. The utmost frequency in the elections of the members of the legislative assembly is a desirable, but not an adequate security: it will be the interest of each legislator to corrupt his leading constituents by patronage, and it will be their interest to be corrupted; and the claim of experience which the sitting member can put forward will be so plausible that it will be easy for the leading constituents to hoodwink the rest. How then shall we prevent legislators, administrators, and leading constituents from being thus driven by the combined force of their self-preferences into a conspiracy against the general happiness? We must do what we can by "minimising confidence and maximising control," through the concentration of responsibility, together with arrangements for securing to the public easy and complete cognisance of all official acts. We must "minimise the matter of corruption" by continually keeping down the amount of wealth and power disposable by each official: in order to reduce salaries, Bentham proposes to institute a pecuniary competition among the properly qualified candidates for any office, on the principle of choosing the man who will take least, or perhaps will even pay, to perform its functions. We must render bargains with electors difficult by secret voting. But, above all, we must be in a position to stamp out the virus of corruption as soon as it appears by immediately dismissing—or, as he prefers to say, "dislocating"—the peccant official. He considers that direct "location" by the people is incompatible with good government, except in the case of members of the legislature; even the appointment of the head of the executive, who has to make or sanction other administrative appointments, he would give to the supreme assembly; but "universal dislocability" by a vote of the majority of citizens seems to him absolutely indispensable: all other securities will be inadequate without this.

After all is done, the readers of the *Constitutional Code* will probably feel that, when Helvetius proposed to ardent philanthropy the noble task of moralising selfish humanity by legislation, he had not sufficiently considered the difficulty of moralising the moralisers, and that even the indefatigable patience and inexhaustible ingenuity of Bentham will hardly succeed in defeating the sinister conspiracy of self-preferences. In fact, unless a little more sociality is allowed to an average human being, the problem of combining these egoists into an organisation for promoting their common happiness is like the old task of making ropes of sand. The difficulty that Hobbes vainly tried to settle summarily by absolute despotism is hardly to be overcome by the democratic artifices of his more inventive successor.

Bentham's final treatise on politics was never absolutely completed. Only about one half had been printed or revised for the press when his long career of intellectual toil was terminated. On the 6th of June 1832, there remained for the indefatigable old man but one last contribution to the balance of human happiness, which was faithfully rendered: to "minimise the pain" of the watchers round his dying bed. His treatise on private ethics, or, as he calls it, *Deontology* (the place of which in his system had been indicated fifty years before in his *Treatise on Morals and Legislation*), was left a mere mass of undigested fragments. The task of preparing it for publication was, however, at once undertaken by Bowring, the favourite disciple of the master's later years; and so much of Bentham's work had been given to the world through the medium of a disciple, that there seemed no reason why the *Deontology* should not take rank with *The Civil and Penal Codes* as a generally trustworthy exposition of Benthamite doctrine.

But the book had no sooner appeared than it was formally repudiated by that section of the school whose opinions were likely to have most weight with the public. J. S. Mill, writing August 1838, in the *London and Westminster Review*, urged that, considering its dubious origin and intrinsic demerits together, it should be omitted from any collected edition of Bentham's works; its demerits being that instead of "plunging boldly into the greater moral questions," it treated almost solely of "the *petite morale*, and that with pedantic minuteness, and on the *quid pro quo* principles which regulate trade." That the *Deontology* corresponds to this description is undeniable; the only question is whether a disciple of Bentham's ought to have been surprised at it. The surprise, at any rate, is a phenomenon demanding explanation; for Bentham is not a Hegel, to be understood by one disciple only, and misunderstood by him; he is commonly liable to be wearisome from obtrusive consistency, and unreadable from an excessive desire to be unmistakable.

The truth is that an ethical system constructed on Bentham's principles is an instrument that may be put to several different uses; so that it is not unnatural that his disciples, employing and developing it each in his own way, should insensibly be led to widely divergent views as to the really essential characteristics of the master's doctrine. The theory of virtue which he received from Helvetius has two aspects, psychological and ethical. Psychologically analysed, common morality appears as a simple result of common selfishness. "Each man likes and approves what he thinks useful to him; the public (which is merely an aggregate of individuals) likes and praises what it thinks useful to the public; that is the whole account of virtue." How, on this theory, men's moral judgments come to agree as much as they actually do is not sufficiently explained; and in any case there is no rational transition possible from this psychological theory to the ethical principle that "the standard of rectitude for all actions" is "public utility." Nor does Bentham really maintain that there is: when he is pressed, he explains frankly that his first principle is really his individual sentiment; that, in fact, he aims at the general happiness because he happens to prefer it. Still, for all practical purposes, he does accept "greatest happiness"[1] as (to use his own words) "a plain as well as true standard for whatever is right or wrong, useful, useless, or mischievous in human conduct, whether in the field of morals or of politics." The primary function, then, of the utilitarian[2] moralist is to apply this standard to the particulars of human life, so as to determine by it the different special virtues or rules of duty, so far as such determination is possible in general terms; and, in fact, several of the fragments put together in the *Deontology* were written with this aim. But suppose this has been accomplished, and the code of duty clearly made out: we have still to ask what the exact use of it will be. It will, of course, give a complete practical guidance to persons whose ruling passion is a desire to promote universal happiness; but Bentham, no less than Helvetius, regards such persons as so exceptional that it would be hardly worth while to print a book for them. What, then, is the relation of the utilitarian moralist to the great mass of mankind, in whose breasts universal benevolence holds no such irresistible sway? This is the practically important question. One answer to it is that given by Paley (and afterwards by John Austin), which treats the rules of utilitarian duty as a code of Divine Law, adequately supported by religious sanctions. Such an answer avoids some of the objections to utilitarianism, at the cost, perhaps, of introducing greater ones; but in any case it is not Bentham's, though it is not expressly excluded by him. If we put this aside, there remain two entirely different ways of dealing with the question, each of which,

---

[1] The phrase which he used during the greater part of his life, and which has become current—"The greatest happiness of the greatest number"—he found, at the age of twenty-two, in an early pamphlet of Priestley's. In the *Deontology*, however, he proposes to drop the latter half of the phrase, as superfluous and liable to misinterpretation.

[2] J. S. Mill tells us in his *Autobiography* that he introduced this term into currency from one of Galt's novels. It was, however, suggested by Bentham, in a letter to Dumont in June 1802, as preferable to "Benthamite."

from a utilitarian point of view, is perfectly appropriate. In the first place, the code as above deduced may be offered to mankind as a standard for rectifying their ordinary judgments of approbation and disapprobation, clearing them from a certain amount of confusion and conflict which now perplexes them, and so increasing their beneficent effect. Even if few persons are sufficiently benevolent to take the general happiness as the one ultimate end of their own conduct, it may still be generally accepted as a standard for apportioning praise and blame to others; and much would be gained for the general happiness if the whole force of these powerful motives could be turned in the direction of promoting it. In all Bentham says of the "moral sanction" in his *Morals and Legislation*, this conception of morality as a system of distributing praise and blame is implied; and such, I gather, was the view taken by James Mill of the practical function of the utilitarian moralist (except in so far as his associational psychology led him to recognise the love of virtue as a distinct though derivative impulse). But this view, though not absent from the *Deontology*, is certainly not prominent there; and it is plain from Bentham's earlier treatise [1] that he conceived "private ethics" not merely as an art of praising and blaming, but rather as an art of conduct generally, from the individual's point of view—"art of self-government" he calls it. But in counselling individuals Bentham thought, like Helvetius, that it was useless to "clamour about duty"; the only effective way of persuading a man to its performance was to show him its coincidence with interest. In such a demonstration the pleasures of pure benevolence are, of course, not neglected: but he obviously cannot lay much stress on them. Hence the necessity for the "*quid pro quo*" treatment of which Mill complains. The erroneousness of the estimate which the vicious man makes of pains and pleasures has to be shown in every possible way; honesty has to be exhibited as the best policy, extra-regarding beneficence as an investment in a sort of bank of general

[1] Cf. esp. c. xix. of the *Principles of Morals and Legislation*, §§ 2, 3, 6, 7.

good-will, etc. We can see at the same time why, from this point of view, the *petite morale* is so prominent. For the more important part of the coincidence between interest and duty it belongs to the legislator to effect and enforce; and his share of the code ought to be written, to use a Platonic image, in large print, needing no comment; the moralist's task is to decipher and exhibit the minor supplementary prescriptions of duty. And that Bentham, when he had once undertaken this task, should have performed it with a "minuteness" which a hostile critic might call "pedantic," can hardly have surprised any one so familiar with his works as Mill was.

So far, I think, there can be no doubt that Bowring has given us the genuine Bentham, and that the faithful historian must refuse to follow Mill in rejecting the *Deontology*. But it is one thing to hold that the moralist ought chiefly to occupy himself in showing men how much of their happiness is bound up with their duty: it is quite another thing to maintain that the two notions are universally coincident in experience, and that (from a purely mundane point of view) "vice may be defined to be a miscalculation of chances." This latter is the ground implicitly taken throughout the greater part of the *Deontology*, and expressly in one or two passages. No doubt the step to this from the former position is a very natural one for an enthusiastic and not very clear-headed disciple; for if it is tenable, the moralist's task can be much more triumphantly achieved. But that Bentham himself would ever have deliberately maintained this position is very difficult to believe. Certainly in the passage of his earlier treatise above referred to, where he defines the relation of "private ethics" to legislation, he distinctly avoids taking it. "It cannot but be admitted," he says, "that the only interests which a man at all times and on all occasions is sure to find adequate motives for consulting are his own." All he can maintain is that "there are no occasions on which he has not *some* motives for consulting the happiness of other men." And with his purely practical view of the moralist's function, he would naturally, in writing his notes for the *Deontology*, exhibit these motives without dwelling on their occasional inadequacy, and would thus encourage his editor to take the critical step from the actual to the ideal, and assert that they are always adequate. But if, as we have seen, the author of the *Principles of Morals and Legislation* shrank from asserting this, we can hardly suppose that the author of the *Constitutional Code* had seen reason to change his mind. For if it is always every man's interest, on a rational computation of chances, to promote the general happiness, what becomes of his anti-monarchical and anti-oligarchical deductions from the principle of self-preference? It may of course be said that monarchs and oligarchs may and do mistake their true interests. But Bentham's argument goes far beyond this. He repeatedly states it as certain and inevitable that, without such artificial junction of interests as is provided by the *Constitutional Code*, governors will sacrifice the happiness of the governed to their own appetites for power, wealth, ease, and revenge. There are some inconsistencies so flagrant that even a philosopher should be held innocent of them till he is proved guilty; and to hold the serene optimism of the *Deontology* as to human relations generally, together with the bitter pessimism of the *Constitutional Code* as to the relation of rulers and subjects, would surely be an inconsistency of this class.

At the same time I must admit that there were other utilitarians besides Bowring who did not perceive the incongruity, and that even after it had been explained to them by a writer who generally succeeded in making his explanations pretty clear. In the famous passage of arms between the *Edinburgh* and the *Westminster* in 1829-30, Macaulay no doubt ventured into a region where he was not altogether at home; still his clear common sense, wide knowledge of historical facts, and a dialectical vigour and readiness which few philosophers could afford to despise, rendered him by no means ill matched even against James Mill; in fact, both combatants, on the ground on which they met, were better equipped for offensive than for defensive warfare; and if the author of the *Essay on Government* had himself replied to his assailant, the conflict would probably have been bloody, but indecisive. But when Macaulay's article came out, the split between Bowring and the Mills had taken place, and the management of the *Westminster* had passed into the hands of Colonel Perronet Thompson, who accepted to the full Bowring's view of utilitarian ethics, and in fact regarded the coincidence of utilitarian duty with self-interest properly understood as Bentham's cardinal doctrine. Colonel Thompson was a writer of no mean talents, and if he had only had to defend his own view of the "greatest happiness principle" he might have come off with tolerable success. Unfortunately the conditions of the controversy rendered it incumbent on him to defend James Mill's at the same time; and against the compound doctrine that it is demonstrably the interest of kings and aristocracies to govern well, and yet demonstrably certain that they will never think so, Macaulay's rejoinder was delivered with irresistible force.

Macaulay's articles had other consequences, more important than that of exhibiting the ambiguities of the greatest happiness principle. His spirited criticism of the deductive politics of James Mill, though it was treated with contempt by its object, had a powerful effect on the more impartial and impressible mind of the younger Mill; and the new views of utilitarian method which were afterwards propounded in the latter's *Logic of the Moral Sciences*[1] owe their origin in some measure to the diatribes of the *Edinburgh*. If space allowed, it would be interesting to trace the changes that Bentham's system underwent in the teaching of his most distinguished successor, under the combined influences of Comtian sociology, Associational psychology, and Neo-Baconian logic. But such an undertaking would carry us far beyond the limits of the present historical sketch, and right into the midmost heats of contemporary controversy.

[1] Cf. J. S. Mill's *Logic*, B. vi. ch. vii. viii.; and his *Autobiography*, p. 158.

VII

THE SCOPE AND METHOD OF ECONOMIC SCIENCE

AN ADDRESS DELIVERED TO THE ECONOMIC SCIENCE AND STATISTICS SECTION OF THE BRITISH ASSOCIATION AS PRESIDENT OF THE SECTION IN 1885.

I HAVE chosen for the subject of the discourse, which by custom has to be delivered from the chair that I am called upon to occupy, the scope and method of economic science, and its relation to other departments of what is vaguely called 'social science.' If the abstract and academic nature of the subject, together with my own deficiencies as an expositor, should render my remarks less interesting to the audience than they have a right to expect, I trust that they will give me what indulgence they can; but, above all, that they will not anticipate a corresponding remoteness from concrete fact in the discussions that are to follow. I see from the records of the Association that it has been the custom in this department—and it seems to me a good custom—to give to the annual addresses of the presidents the variety that naturally results when each speaker in turn applies himself unreservedly to that aspect of our complex and many-sided inquiry which his special studies and opportunities have best qualified him to treat; and as my own connection with economic science has been in the way of studying, criticising, and developing theories, rather than collecting and systematising facts, I have thought that I should at any rate have a greater chance of making a useful contribution to our discussions if I allowed myself to deal with the subject from the point of view that is most familiar to me.

I have the less scruple in adopting this course because I do not think that any who may listen to my remarks are likely to charge me with overrating the value of abstract reasoning on economic subjects, or regarding it as a substitute for an accurate and thorough investigation of facts instead of an indispensable instrument of such investigation. There is indeed a kind of political economy which flourishes in proud independence of facts; and undertakes to settle all practical problems of Governmental interference or private philanthropy by simple deduction from one or two general assumptions—of which the chief is the assumption of the universally beneficent and harmonious operation of self-interest well let alone. This kind of political economy is sometimes called 'orthodox,' though it has the characteristic unusual in orthodox doctrines of being repudiated by the majority of accredited teachers of the subject. But whether orthodox or not, I must be allowed to disclaim all connection with it; the more completely this survival of the *à priori* politics of the eighteenth century can be banished to the remotest available planet, the better it will be, in my opinion, for the progress of economic science. Since, however, this kind of political economy is still somewhat current in the market-place,—since the language of newspapers and public speakers still keeps up the impression that the professor of political economy is continually laying down laws which practical people are continually violating, —it seems worth while to try to make clear the relation between the economic science which we are concerned to study and the principles of Governmental interference—or rather non-interference—which are thought to have been of late so persistently and in some cases so successfully outraged.

It must be admitted at once that there is considerable excuse for the popular misapprehension just mentioned; since for more than a century the general interest taken in the analysis of the phenomena of industry has been mainly due to the connection of this analysis with a political movement towards greater industrial freedom. No researches into the historical development of economic studies before Adam Smith can displace the great Scotchman from his position as the founder of modern political economy considered as an independent science, with a well-marked field of investigation and a definite and characteristic method of reasoning. And no doubt the element of Adam Smith's treatise which makes the most impression on the ordinary reader is his forcible advocacy of the "system of natural liberty"; his exposition of the natural "division of labour" —tending, if left alone, to become an international division of employments—as the main cause of the "universal opulence" of "well-governed" societies; and of the manner in which, in this distribution of employments, individual capitalists seeking their own advantage are led "by an invisible hand" to "prefer that employment of their capital which is most advantageous to society."

At the same time Adam Smith was too cool and too shrewd an observer of facts to be carried, even by the force and persuasiveness of his own arguments, into a sweeping and unqualified assertion of the universality of the tendency that he describes. His advocacy of natural liberty in no way blinds him to the perpetual and complex opposition and conflict of economic interests involved in the unfettered efforts of individuals to get rich. He even goes the length of saying that "the interest of the dealers in any particular branch of trade or manufacture is always in some respects different from, and even opposite to, that of the public." To take a particular case, he is decidedly of opinion that the natural liberty of bankers to issue notes may reasonably be restrained by the laws of the freest Governments. He is quite aware, again, that the absence of Governmental interference does not necessarily imply a state of free competition, since the self-interest of individuals may lead them, on the contrary, to restrict competition by "voluntary associations and agreements." He does not doubt that Governments, central or local, may find various ways of employing wealth

—of which elementary education is one of the most important—which will be even economically advantageous to society, though they could not be remuneratively undertaken by individual capitalists. In short, however fascinating the picture that Adam Smith presents to us of the continual and complex play of individual interests constituting and regulating the vast fabric of social industry, the summary conclusion drawn by some of his disciples that the social production of wealth will always be best promoted by leaving it altogether alone, that the only petition which industry should make to Government is the petition of Diogenes to Alexander that he would cease to stand between him and the sunshine, and that statesmen are therefore relieved from the necessity of examining carefully the grounds for industrial intervention in any particular case—this comfortable and labour-saving conclusion finds no support in a fair survey of Adam Smith's reasonings, though it has been no doubt encouraged by some of his phrases. To attribute to him a dogmatic theory of the natural right of the individual to absolute industrial independence—as some recent German writers are disposed to do [1]—is to construct the history of economic doctrines from one's inner consciousness.

It is true, as I have said, that among Adam Smith's disciples there were not a few who rushed to the sweeping generalisations that the master had avoided. In England, in particular, the influence of the more abstract and purely deductive method of Ricardo tended in this direction. It was natural, again, that in the heat of a political movement absolute and unqualified statements of principle should come into vogue, since the ease and simplicity with which they can be enunciated and apprehended makes them more effective instruments of popular agitation: hence it is not surprising to find the anti-corn-law petitions declaring the " inalienable right of every man freely to exchange the result of his labour for the productions of other people," to

[1] *E.g.* v. Scheel, in Schönberg's *Handbuch der politischen Oekonomie*, p. 89, speaks of "Die naturrechtliche Wirthschaftstheorie oder der Smithianismus."

be "one of the principles of eternal justice." But under the more philosophic guidance of J. S. Mill, English political economy shook off all connection with these antiquated metaphysics, and during the last generation has been generally united with a view of political principles more balanced, qualified, and empirical, and therefore more in harmony with the general tendencies of modern scientific thought.

If, indeed, *laisser-faire* were—as many suppose—the one main doctrine of modern political economy, there can be no doubt that the decisive step forward that founded the science ought to be attributed not to Adam Smith, but to his French predecessors the 'Physiocrats.' It is to them— to Quesnay, De Gournay, De la Rivière, Turgot—that the credit, whatever it may be, is due of having first proclaimed to the world with the utmost generality and without qualification that what a statesman had to do was not to make laws for industry, but merely to ascertain and protect from encroachment the simple, eternal, and immutable laws of nature, under which the production of wealth would regulate itself in the best possible way if men would abstain from meddling.

This doctrine formed one part of the impetuous movement of thought against the existing political order which characterised French speculation during the forty years that preceded the great Revolution. It was, we may say, the counterpart and complement of the doctrine of which Rousseau was the chief prophet. The sect of the Économistes and the disciples of Rousseau were agreed that the existing political system needed radical change; and in both there was a tendency to believe that an ideal political order could at once be constituted. At this point, however, their courses diverged: the school of Rousseau held that the essential thing was to alter the *structure* of government, and to keep legislation effectually in the hands of the sovereign people; the Économistes thought that the all-important point was to limit the *functions* of government, holding that the simple duty of maintaining the natural rights of the individual to liberty and property could be best performed by an absolute monarch. Both movements had much justification; both have had effects on the political and social life of Europe of which it is difficult to measure the extent; but both doctrines—attained, as they were, by a fallacious method—involved a large element of exaggeration, suitable to the ardent and sanguine period that brought them forth, but which gives them a curious air of absurdity when they are resuscitated and offered for the acceptance of our more sober, circumspect, and empirically-minded age. In the most civilised countries of Europe it is now a recognised and established safeguard against oppressive laws that an effective control over legislation is vested in the people at large; but no serious thinker would now maintain with Rousseau that the predominance of the will of the sovereign people has a necessary tendency to produce just legislation. Similarly, the doctrine of the Physiocrats has prevailed, in the main, as regards the internal conditions of national industry in modern civilised societies. The old hampering privileges, restraints, and prohibitions have been almost entirely swept away, to the great advantage of the community; but the absolute right of the individual to unlimited industrial freedom is now only maintained by a scanty and dwindling handful of doctrinaires, whom the progress of economic science has left stranded on the crude generalisations of an earlier period.

There will probably always be considerable disagreement in details among competent persons as to the propriety of Governmental interference in particular cases; but, apart from questions on which economic considerations must yield to political, moral, or social reasons of greater importance, it is an anachronism not to recognise fully and frankly the existence of cases in which the industrial intervention of Government is desirable, even with a view to the most economical production of wealth. Hence, I conceive, the present business of economic theory in this department is to give a systematic and carefully-reasoned exposition of these cases, which, until the constitution of human nature and society are fundamentally altered, must always be regarded as exceptions to a general rule of non-interference. The statesman's decision on any particular case it does not belong to abstract theory to give; this can only be rationally arrived at after a careful examination of the special conditions of each practical problem at the particular time and place at which it presents itself. But abstract reasoning may supply a systematic view of the general occasions for Governmental interference, the different possible modes of such interference, and the general reasons for and against each of them, which may aid practical men both in finding and in estimating the decisive considerations in particular cases. Thus it may show, on the one hand, under what circumstances the inevitable drawbacks of Governmental management are likely to be least, and by what methods they may be minimised; and where, on the other hand, private enterprise is likely to fail in supplying a social need —as where an undertaking socially useful is likely for various reasons to be unremunerative to the undertakers— or where private interests are liable to be markedly opposed to those of the public, as is generally the case with businesses that tend to become monopolies.

It would be tedious now to dwell at more length on these generalities; but there is one special exception to the triumph of the system of natural liberty in the civilised countries of Europe which has too much historical importance to be passed over without a word in this connection. As we are all aware, this triumph has only been decided as regards the *internal* conditions of industry and trade; the practice of imposing barriers on *international* exchange, with a view to the protection of native industry, still flourishes in the most advanced communities, and shows no immediate tendency to come to an end. It is not, I conceive, reasonable to attribute this result entirely, as some Free-traders are disposed to do, to the incapacity of mankind to understand elementary economic truths, and the interested efforts of a combination of producers to prey in a comfortable and legal way on the resources of the confiding consumers. I do not deny that both these causes have operated; but, in view of the evident ability and disinterestedness of many of the writers and statesmen who have supported the cause of Protection on the Continent or in the United States, I cannot find in them an adequate explanation of the phenomenon.

A part of the required explanation is, I think, suggested when we examine the arguments by which Free Trade was actually recommended to intelligent Englishmen at the time when England's policy was taking the decisive turn in this direction, and imagine their effect on the mind of an intelligent foreigner. Suppose, for instance, that the intelligent foreigner is studying the *Edinburgh Review* in 1841, when it came forward as a vigorous and decided advocate of Free Trade. In the January number he would find the cosmopolitan and abstract argument with which we are so familiar; he would learn how, under Free Trade, "every country will exert itself in the way that is most beneficial in the production of wealth"; how labour and capital will be employed in each country to produce those things which the varieties of climate, situation, and soil enable it to produce with greater advantage than other countries, so that "the greatest possible amount of industry will be kept constantly in action, and all commodities will exist in the greatest abundance." But in the July number of the same organ he would find a recommendation of Free Trade from a national point of view, which, though more restricted in its scope, would appear to contain matter no less important for practical consideration. He would find that the immediate introduction of Free Trade was held to be essential in order to keep what remained of the manufacturing and commercial supremacy of England. He would learn that "the early progress of any nation that attempts to rival us in manufactures must be slow"; for "it has to contend with our great capital, our traditionary skill, our almost infinite division of labour, our long-established perseverance, energy, and enterprise, our knowledge of markets, and with the habits of those who have been bred up to be our customers." He would learn that there was "no reason to to believe that," in the "absence of disturbing causes," we should ever lose our present command of the world's market; that we might have preserved our superiority for centuries; but that "if these difficulties were once surmounted, this superiority—so far at least as respects the commodity in which we find ourselves undersold—would be gone for ever," in consequence of "the well-known law of manufacturing industry that, *ceteris paribus*, with every increase of the quantity produced, the relative cost of production is diminished." It cannot be denied that a consideration of this law, and of the *vis inertiæ* here attributed to an established superiority in manufactures and commerce, supplies an important qualification of the general argument for Free Trade. For, along with the tendency of industry to go where it can be most economically carried on, we have also to recognise a tendency for it to stay and develop where it has been once planted; and the advantage of leaving this latter tendency undisturbed would naturally be less clear to the patriotic foreigner than to the patriotic Englishman. The proclamation of a free race for all, just when England had a start which she might probably keep "for centuries," would not seem to him a manifest realisation of eternal justice; to delay the race for a generation or two, and meanwhile to apply judiciously "disturbing causes" in the form of protective duties, would seem likely to secure a fairer start for other nations, and ultimately, therefore, a better organisation of the world's industry even from a cosmopolitan point of view.

Nor would it seem to him a conclusive argument against this course that protective duties impose great present pecuniary sacrifices on the protecting nation; especially when he learnt, from an impartial English source, of the great sacrifices which private capitalists in England were in the habit of making to assist the tendency of free competition in their favour. He would find, for instance, in the Report of a Commission published in 1854,[1] an appeal to

[1] See p. 20 of Report by Mr. H. S. Tremenheere, Commissioner appointed to inquire into the operation of Act 5 & 6 Vict. c. 99, and into the state of the population in the mining districts (Vol. XIX. of Parl. Papers for 1854).

the working-classes to consider " the immense losses which their employers voluntarily incur in bad times, in order to destroy foreign competition, and to gain and keep possession of foreign markets." Should the efforts of Trade Unionists, urges the writer, be successful for any length of time, they would interfere with the " great accumulations of capital which enable a few of the most wealthy capitalists to overwhelm all foreign competition in times of great depression," and which thus constitute " the great instruments of warfare against the competing capital of foreign countries." If it was the view of shrewd English men of business that these great sacrifices of private wealth were needed and were worth making, to maintain the industrial start once gained, the intelligent foreigner would naturally conclude that the other combatants in the industrial battle must be prepared to make corresponding sacrifices; that each nation must fight with its own weapons; and that where there were no great accumulations of capital in private hands, the instruments of warfare must be obtained by a general contribution.

I have given these considerations, not because I agree with the practical conclusion which they tend to support, but because I think that they require to be met by a line of argument different from that which English economists have usually adopted. I think it erroneous to maintain, on the ordinary economic grounds, that temporary Protection must always be detrimental to the protecting country, even if it were carried out by a perfectly wise and strong Government, able to resist all influences of sinister and sectarian interests, and to act solely for the good of the nation. The decisive argument against it is rather the political consideration that no actual Government is competent for this difficult and delicate task; that Protection, as actually applied under the play of political forces, is sure to foster many weak industries that have no chance of living without artificial support, and to hamper industries that might thrive independently, by the artificial dearness of some of their materials and instruments; so that it turns out a dangerous and clumsy, as well as a costly, instrument of industrial competition, and is not likely on the whole to bring the desired victory, though it may give a partial success here and there. And some such conclusion as this is, I think, now prevalent even among those German economists who are most decided in their rejection of the claims of *laisser-faire* to absolute and unqualified validity.

So far I have been speaking of the function of economic science in determining principles of Governmental intervention in matters of industry, because this is the function prominent in the popular view of political economy. But I need hardly say to the present audience that this is not the view that English economists generally have taken as to their primary business. Indeed, during the last generation our leading economists—even those who come nearest to the so-called 'orthodox' type — have gone even further than I should myself go in declaring that economic science had nothing to do with the doctrine of *laisser-faire*. No one (*e.g.*) has stated this more strongly than Cairnes, whom I select as a conspicuous and effective advocate of Free Trade. "The maxim of *laissez-faire*," he says, " has no scientific basis whatever"; it is a "mere handy rule of practice," though " a rule in the main sound." According to this view, the 'laws' with which economic science is primarily concerned are the laws that determine economic quantities—the amount of the aggregate of wealth, its annual increase, the relative values of its different elements, and the shares of the economic classes that have combined to produce it—as they would be apart from special Governmental interference; and not the rules for deciding when and how far such interference is justifiable.

And it is the additional light that Adam Smith threw on the general determination of such economic quantities—and not his advocacy of natural liberty—which in the view of economists constitutes his chief claim to his place in the historical development of economic science. And I may observe that, from this point of view, the important predecessors of Adam Smith are not the Physiocrats only, but even more Cantillon, who wrote a generation before, to whom Jevons drew attention some years ago in a remarkable essay; nor should we overlook his English predecessors of a still earlier age such as Petty and Locke—the former of whom has a special interest for us as a pioneer in each of the two lines of investigation of which we here maintain the union, since he was the first in England to combine a serious effort to establish the general relations of economic quantities by abstract reasoning and analysis with patient endeavours to ascertain particular economic facts by statistical inquiries. When we trace the gradual evolution of the modern economic view as to the manner in which the play of individual self-interests tends to determine prices and shares—from the rude beginnings of Petty and Locke, through the more systematic and penetrating theory of Cantillon, the fuller analysis and exposition of Adam Smith, and the closer reasoning of Ricardo, down to the important rectifications and additions of Jevons—we see clearly that the progress of the theory has no necessary connection with any doctrine as to the limits of the industrial intervention of Government.

And it is to be observed that neither Adam Smith nor the predecessors to whom I have referred had any design of maintaining that the distribution which they were endeavouring to analyse satisfied either the claims of ideal equity by giving each individual his deserts, or the claims of expediency by giving him what was most conducive to general happiness. Nor, since Adam Smith, has any leading English economist maintained the former of these propositions; and so far as the school of Ricardo may have seemed to maintain the latter—so far as they certainly have taught that direct Governmental interference with distribution was undesirable—it has not been from any prevalence among them of the shallow optimism of Bastiat and his followers. It is pessimism rather than optimism which is to be laid to their charge; not a disposition to underrate or ignore the hardships that the "natural" rate of wages might entail; but a conviction that, however bad things might be naturally, the direct interference of Government could only make them worse. I am not arguing that they did not go too far in this view; I am now chiefly desirous to remove a profound and widespread misunderstanding as to the general aim and drift of their investigations, which I find in certain German and other Continental critics of English political economy,—and, I may add, in certain English critics who repeat the foreign objections. Such critics either fail to see, or continually forget, that the English economist, in giving an explanation of the manner in which prices, wages, profits, etc., are determined, is not attempting to justify the result; he is not trying to show that in getting the market price of his services the labourer, capitalist, or landlord gets what he deserves. Thus when Senior called interest the " reward of abstinence," he did not mean to imply that it was normally proportioned to the capitalist's merit in abstaining, but merely that capital is increased by individuals saving instead of spending, and that they require the inducement given by the actual rate of interest to save to the extent to which they actually are saving. Whether any other rate of interest would be *juster* is a question of ideal politics to which the English economist has usually nothing to say so long as it is stated in this abstract form; it is only when the political idealist descends to practice, and proposes a scheme for realising his conception of justice, that it comes within the province of economic science to discuss the probable effects of this scheme on production and distribution. But it is not with such far-reaching proposals of change that the English economist is mainly concerned; his primary business is to ascertain the causes which determine actual prices of products and services.

Hence, when the most recent German school of economists — variously known as the 'historical,' 'ethical,' or 'social' school—claims to have moralised political economy by throwing over the assumption of egoism, which they regard as characteristic of 'Smithianismus,' they usually appear to the English economist to confound what is with what ought to be. The assumption that egoism ought to be universal—that the universal prevalence of self-interest leads necessarily to the best possible economic order—has never been made by leading English writers; and it is an assumption with which they generally conceive themselves in no way concerned—in that part, at least, of the science which deals with distribution. It is the actual prevalence of self-interest in ordinary exchanges of products and services which constitutes their fundamental assumption.

But I admit that this reply does not end the controversy. The critic may rejoin that, if egoism is not what ought to be, the tranquil way in which the economist treats it as universally predominant is objectionable, as tending to give dangerous encouragement to the baser side of human nature. And, secondly, he may deny that self-interest actually has any such predominance as English economists assume; hence, he may argue, their fundamental assumption must lead to serious errors in the analysis and forecast of actual facts.

The first of these points I should concede to some extent. If we regarded it as blameworthy that a man should, under ordinary circumstances, try to get the highest price for any commodity he sells, and give the lowest for what he buys, then, though the analysis of economic facts, as they exist in the present selfish and wicked world, might still be conducted on the present method, I certainly think its results ought to be—and would be—expounded in a different tone. I should say, therefore, that our economists generally do not hold to be censurable, in a broad and general way, the self-regard which they assume as normal. I conceive, however, that this view is commonly held with the following important qualifications.

Firstly, it is not implied that the right of free exchange ought not to be legally limited in respect of certain special commodities. Thus, when it is urged by statesmen or philanthropists that the sale of opium, or brandy, or lottery-tickets, or children's labour, ought to be prohibited or placed under certain restrictions, the political economist, as such, is not to be regarded as holding a brief on the other side—at most he only throws the *onus probandi* on those who advocate interference, adding perhaps a warning that the consequences of their measure may possibly be different from what they anticipate, owing to the play of ordinary self-regard working under the new conditions that they aim at imposing.

Secondly, it is not implied that similar limitations may not be effectively imposed by the force of moral opinion. It has, indeed, to be pointed out that morality, like law, may produce effects other than what are designed—*e.g.* that the discredit attaching to usury may cause the unhappy debtor to pay more instead of less for his inevitable loan, since the usurer has to be compensated for the social drawbacks of his despised employment. But it does not follow that there are no cases in which this disadvantage has to be faced as the least of two evils.

Thirdly, the economist does not assume that his economic man is *always* buying in the cheapest and selling in the dearest market, and never rendering services to his fellow-creatures on any other terms. He does not lay down that the economic distribution which it is his business to analyse will not be supplemented to an indefinite extent by a distribution prompted by other motives:—indeed, it should be noted that the ordinary economic man is always understood to be busily providing for a wife and children; so that his dominant motive to industry is rather domestic interest than self-interest, strictly so-called. And it has never been supposed that outside his private business—or even in connection with it if occasion arises—a man will not spend labour and money for public objects, and give freely gratuitous services to friends, benefactors, and persons in special need or distress.

The political economists, it is true, have often felt called upon to criticise the proceedings of philanthropists; but those who have assumed in enunciating these criticisms a grave air of giving the results of abstruse scientific reasoning are partly to blame, I think, for having drawn on political economy a kind of odium which ought to have been thrown on the broader back of plain common sense. We may say, indeed, with special force of a great part of economic science what Huxley has said of science generally—that it is only "organised common-sense." But it needs little organisation to show that the motives to industry and thrift are impaired by the indiscriminate relief of the idle and improvident; that you help men best by encouraging them to help themselves, by widening the opportunities for the display of energetic activity and enterprise, and diffusing the knowledge that will save it from being wasted, rather than by diminishing the inducements that stimulate it. To apprehend the truth of propositions like these, a man need not even have read a shilling handbook; and yet these commonplaces constitute the greater part of the "hard-hearted economist's" criticism of sentimental philanthropy. If, indeed, the economist has gone on to say that therefore no efforts ought to be made to relieve distress, and raise those who have temporarily stumbled in the struggle for existence, or if he has prophesied failure to all larger attempts on the part of philanthropists, to improve the condition of the classes at the base of the industrial pyramid—if, I say, an individual economist has here and there been found lecturing and prognosticating in this sweeping manner, he has only exemplified the common human tendency to dogmatise beyond the limits of his knowledge; and I trust the blame will not be laid on the science whose exacter methods he has deserted or misapplied.

The important question of method, then, at issue between the English economists and their German critics is not whether the play of the ordinary motives of self-interest ought to be limited and supplemented by the operation of other motives; but whether these other motives actually do, or can reasonably be expected to, operate in such a way as to destroy the general applicability of the method of economic analysis which assumes that each party to any free exchange will prefer his own interest to that of the other party. And in speaking of the German historical school as antagonists on this question, I ought to say that I refer only to what I may call their more aggressive left wing. With the more moderate claims of the historical method as set forth by the distinguished leader of the school, William Roscher, the English economists who maintain the tradition of Adam Smith and Ricardo have no sort of quarrel; and Roscher expressly disclaims any quarrel with them. He has sought, as he says, "gratefully to avail himself" of the results of Ricardian analysis, and we can no less gratefully profit by the abundant historical researches that he has led and stimulated. It is no doubt true that our older economists often had an insufficient appreciation of the historical variations in economic conditions; and, in particular, did not adequately recognise the greater extent to which competition was limited or repressed by law or custom in states of society economically less advanced than our own. But for a generation there has been no serious dispute about this; nor has there ever been any fundamental disagreement between Ricardians and Roscherians as to the right method of studying the history of economic facts. The most deductive English economist has never gone so far as to maintain that this can be constructed *à priori*, any more than any other history; and if a generation ago he was sometimes wont to dogmatise with insufficient information as to the causes of industrial changes and the economic effects of political measures in other ages and countries, he has grown wiser, like other persons, through the great development of historical study—and of what I may call the common historic sense of educated persons—which has taken place in the interval. Indeed, I think the danger now is rather that we should go into the opposite extreme, and not give sufficient attention to the more latent and complicated but very effective manner in which competition is found operating even in states of society where the barriers of custom are strongest.

But further, even as regards the present condition of industry in the more advanced countries, to which the theory of modern economic science primarily relates, there is, I conceive, no dispute as to the need of what is called a "realistic" or "inductive" method—*i.e.* as to the need of accurately ascertaining particular facts when we are inquiring into the particular causes of particular values, or of the shares of particular economic classes at any given place and time. All that the deductive reasonings of English economists supply is a method of analysing the phenomena and a statement of the general causes that govern them, and of the manner of their operation. In this analysis, no doubt, the assumption is fundamental that the individuals concerned in the actual determination of the economic quantities resulting from free exchange will aim, *ceteris paribus*, at getting the most they can for what they sell and giving the least they can for what they buy. And when we find the legitimacy of this assumption, and the scientific value of the analysis based upon it, broadly assailed by Hildebrand,[1] Knies,[2] and others, we are no doubt seriously concerned to meet their criticism.

For my own part, I can only say that, having searched their works with the interest and respect which are due to the indefatigable research and the scientific fertility of the German intellect, I am quite unable to discover what other scientific treatment of the general theory of distribution and exchange they propose to substitute for the treatment which they sweepingly criticise. I cannot perceive that their higher view of man as a moral, sympathetic, public-spirited being, habitually rising above the sordid huckstering considerations by which English economists assume him to be governed, has any material effect on their theory of the determination of economic quantities when it comes to be actually worked out. When Knies,[3] for instance, is discussing the nature and functions of capital, money and credit, or when he is arguing with more subtlety than success against

---

[1] See two papers on "Die gegenwärtige Aufgabe der Wissenschaft der politischen Oekonomie," in the first volume (1863) of Hildebrand's *Jahrbuch für National-Oekonomie u. Statistik*, p. 5 ff. and p. 137 ff.: especially his criticism of J. S. Mill (p. 23), quoted with approval by Schönberg in the introduction to his *Handbuch*.
[2] See his *Politische Oekonomie vom geschichtlichen Standpunkte*, iii. § 3.
[3] See his *Geld und Credit*—in particular, *Credit*, pt. ii. ch. xii. § 2.

the Ricardian doctrine of rent, we find that the capitalists and landlords, the lenders and borrowers, whose operations are contemplated, exhibit throughout the familiar features of the old economic man. So, again, when, in the *Encyclopædia of Political Economy*[1] recently published by this school, we examine the definitions of fundamental notions, or the explanation of prices, or the theory of distribution, we meet, indeed, with some interesting variations on the old doctrines, but we find everywhere the old economic motives assumed and the old method unhesitatingly applied. The proof of the pudding, as the proverb says, is in the eating; but our historical friends make no attempt to set before us the new economic pudding which their large phrases seemed to promise. It is only the old pudding with a little more ethical sauce and a little more garnish of historical illustrations.

In saying this I should be sorry to seem to underrate the debt that economic science owes to the labours of the school now dominant in Germany. Much of the positive work that they have produced is in its way excellent; even their criticism of the older method has been, in my opinion, most useful; and if I complain that they have by no means done what they announced, with some flourish of trumpets, that they were going to do, it is chiefly because their exaggerated phrases have led critics of a looser sort to misunderstand and misrepresent the recent progress and actual condition of economic thought. I fully recognise that the elaborate and careful study of economic facts in all departments, which the historical school has encouraged and carried out, is an indispensable aid to the due development of general economic theory. In all abstract economic reasoning which aims at quantitative precision, there is necessarily a hypothetical element; the facts to which the reasonings relate are not contemplated in their actual complexity, but in an artificially simplified form; if, therefore, the reasoning is not accompanied and checked by a careful study of facts, the required simplification may easily go too far or be

[1] See Schönberg's *Handbuch*, iv. v. and xi.

inappropriate in kind, so that the hypothetical element of the reasoning is increased to an extent which prevents the result from having any practical value. And this danger is enhanced by the great, though generally gradual, changes in economic facts which accompany or constitute industrial development. Thus, for instance, a theoretical investigation of the purchasing power of money, which assumes for simplicity that coin and bank notes form the sole medium of exchange, might easily lead to serious practical errors in the existing condition of industry; and a theory of capital which ignores the great and growing preponderance of auxiliary over remuneratory capital is liable to be similarly delusive. The general study of economic history is important as calling attention to this source of error; but for effective protection against it we must look to that patient and systematic development of statistical inquiry which it is one of our main functions here to watch and to foster.

I must observe, however, that the historical economists are apt to insist too one-sidedly on the progress in economic theory attained by studying the industrial organisation of society in different stages of its development; they do not sufficiently recognise that other kind of progress which consists in conceiving more clearly, accurately, and consistently, the fundamental facts that remain without material change. But this latter kind of progress is very palpable to one who traces back the history of economic doctrines. Indeed, if our active controversy on principles and method has led anyone to think that political economists are always wrangling, and never establishing anything, he may easily correct this impression by turning to the older writers, and noting the confusions they make on points that are now clear to all instructed persons, and the inferences they unhesitatingly draw, which all would now admit to be in whole or in part erroneous. And by the "older writers" I do not mean merely those who lived before Adam Smith: what I have just said is no less true of the *Wealth of Nations* and its most distinguished successors. A tiro can now see the fallacy of Adam Smith's statement, that "labour never varying in its own value" is a "universal" and "accurate standard of the exchangeable value of all commodities at all times and places"; the staunchest Ricardian would refuse to follow his master in maintaining that a tax on corn would cause labourers "no other inconvenience than that which they would suffer from any other mode of taxation"; the most faithful disciple of J. S. Mill would not fall into the confusion between "interest" and "profit" which seriously impairs the value of important parts of his discussions. Much progress, I doubt not, still remains to be made, by steadily continuing that labour of reflective analysis through which our conception of fundamental economic facts has grown continually fuller and more exact; but no one who examines impartially the writings of our most eminent predecessors can ignore the progress that has already been made.

I now pass to consider another old charge against political economists, which has been recently revived: the charge of confining their attention too much to the special group of phenomena with which they are primarily concerned, and neglecting the relations of these to other social facts. There have, no doubt, been writers—Senior is, perhaps, the most important—in whom such neglect was deliberate and systematic; but their peculiar view of economic method has long ceased to have much influence on current thought; and I hardly think that political economists are now more open to the charge of systematic narrowness than any other set of students who do not "take all knowledge for their province," but accept the limitations which the present state of research imposes as the inevitable condition of thorough work in any department. And so far as the charge hits a real defect, I doubt whether vague generalities about the "consensus of the different functions of the social organism," and the impossibility of "isolating the study of one organ from that of the rest," will be found of much practical use in correcting the defect; since the relations of other social phenomena to those which primarily concern the economist vary indefinitely in closeness and importance; so that the question how far it is needful to investigate them is one which has to be answered very differently in relation to different economic inquiries. Thus, in considering generally the first subject of Adam Smith's investigation—" the causes of the improvement in the productive powers of labour"—the importance of a healthy condition of social morality must not be overlooked; but it is not therefore the economist's duty to study in detail the doctrine or discipline of the different Christian churches: while any reference he may make to the history of the Fine Arts will obviously be still more remote and brief. If, however, we are considering historically the causes that have affected the interest of capital, the views of Christian theologians with regard to usury will require careful attention; if, again, we are investigating the share taken by a particular community in the international organisation of industry, the higher average of artistic sensibility among its members may be a consideration deserving of notice—as in the case of France.

Or again, we may illustrate the different degrees in which economic science is connected with different departments of social fact by comparing the chief classes of statistics with which it has been our custom here to deal. Some of the most important of these—such as the statistics of taxation, trade, railways, land-tenure and the like, and a great part of the statistics of population—supply the indispensable premisses of much of the economist's reasoning, so far as it aims at being precise and particular, and the indispensable verification of many of his conclusions. In other cases again,—as, for instance, the great departments of sanitary and educational statistics,—the interest of the economist is more general and limited: for though both sanitation and education have important bearings on the productiveness of national labour, the details of the organisation for promoting either end lie in the main beyond the scope of his investigation; while he has manifestly still less to do with criminal statistics, military and naval statistics, and several other species of social facts which governmental or private agencies now enable us to ascertain with approximate quantitative exactness.

At this point, however, our critics will probably say that it is not so much a knowledge of the separate relations of different groups of social phenomena that the political economist lacks, but rather a true conception of the social organism as a whole, and of the fundamental laws of its development; he does not recognise that his study can only be legitimately or profitably pursued as a duly subordinated branch of the general science of sociology. This view was strongly urged by Mr. Ingram in his presidential address to this Section seven years ago in Dublin[1]; and it was enforced by pointing contemptuously to the limited function which well-instructed economists at the present day are careful to allot to their science in the settlement of practical questions. When we explain, with Cairnes, that political economy furnishes certain data that go towards the formation of a sound opinion on such questions, but does not undertake to pronounce a final judgment on them, we are told that this "systematic indifferentism amounts to an entire paralysis of political economy as a social power"; and that the time has come for it to make way for, or be absorbed into, the "scientific sociology" which is now in the field, and which certainly seems ready to offer statesmen the dogmatic, comprehensive, and complete practical guidance that mere economic science confesses itself inadequate to supply.

It appears to me that Mr. Ingram and his friends somewhat mistake the point that they have to prove. It is not necessary to show that if we could ascertain from the past history of human society the fundamental laws of social evolution as a whole, so that we could accurately forecast the main features of the future state with which our present social world is pregnant,—it is not needful, I say, to show that the science which gave this foresight would be of the

---

[1] It has been recently expressed again, with no less emphasis, in Mr. Ingram's article on "Political Economy," in the nineteenth volume of the *Encyclopædia Britannica*.

highest value to a statesman, and would absorb or dominate our present political economy. What has to be proved is that this supremely important knowledge is within our grasp; that the sociology which professes this prevision is really an established science. To deny this may perhaps seem presumptuous, in view of the voluminous works that we possess on the subject, which it would be quite out of place for me to attempt to criticise methodically on the present occasion. Fortunately, however, such methodical criticism is not required to justify my negative conclusion: since there are two simple tests of the real establishment of a science—emphatically recognised by Comte in his discussion of this very subject—which can be quickly and decisively applied to the claims of existing sociology. These tests may be characterised as (1) Consensus or Continuity, and (2) Prevision. The former I will explain in Comte's own words:—" When we find that recent works, instead of being the result and development of what has gone before, have a character as personal as that of their authors, and bring the most fundamental ideas into question "—then, says Comte, we may be sure we are not dealing with any doctrine deserving the name of positive science. Now, if we compare the most elaborate and ambitious treatises on sociology, of which there happens to be one in each of the three leading scientific languages,—Comte's *Politique Positive*, Spencer's *Sociology*, and Schäffle's *Bau und Leben des socialen Körpers*,—we see at once that they exhibit the most complete and conspicuous absence of agreement or continuity in their treatment of the fundamental questions of social evolution.

Take, for example, the question of the future of religion. No thoughtful person can overlook the importance of religion as an element of man's social existence; nor do the sociologists to whom I have referred fail to recognise it. But if we inquire after the characteristics of the religion of which their science leads them to foresee the coming prevalence, they give with nearly equal confidence answers as divergent as can be conceived. Schäffle cannot comprehend that the place of the great Christian Churches can be taken by anything but a purified form of Christianity; Spencer contemplates complacently the reduction of religious thought and sentiment to a perfectly indefinite consciousness of an Unknowable and the emotion that accompanies this peculiar intellectual exercise; while Comte has no doubt that the whole history of religion—which, as he says, " should resume the entire history of human development "—has been leading up to the worship of the Great Being, Humanity, personified domestically for each normal male individual by his nearest female relatives. It would certainly seem that the science which allows these discrepancies in its chief expositors must be still in its infancy. And when we go on to ask how these divergent forecasts of the future are scientifically deduced from the study of the past evolution of mankind, we are irresistibly reminded of the old epigram as to the relation of certain theological controversialists to the Bible :

> Hic liber est in quo quærit sua dogmata quisque,
> Invenit et pariter dogmata quisque sua.

I do not doubt that our sociologists are sincere in setting before us their conception of the coming social state as the last term of a series of which the law has been discovered by patient historical study; but when we look closely into their work it becomes only too evident that each philosopher has constructed on the basis of personal feeling and experience his ideal future in which our present social deficiencies are to be remedied ; and that the process by which history is arranged in steps pointing towards his Utopia bears not the faintest resemblance to a scientific demonstration.

This is equally evident when we turn from religion to industry, and examine the forecasts of industrial development offered to the statesman in the name of scientific sociology as a substitute for the discarded calculations of the mere economist. With equal confidence, history is represented as leading up, now to the naïve and unqualified individualism of Spencer, now to the carefully guarded and elaborated socialism of Schäffle, now to Comte's dream of securing seven-roomed houses for all working-men—with other comforts to correspond—solely by the impressive moral precepts of his philosophic priests. Guidance, truly, is here enough and to spare: but how is the bewildered statesman to select his guidance when his sociological doctors exhibit this portentous disagreement?

Nor is it only that they adopt diametrically opposite conclusions: we find that each adopts his conclusion with the most serene and complete indifference to the line of historical reasoning on which his brother sociologist relies. Schäffle, *e.g.*, appears not to have the least inkling of the array of facts which have convinced Spencer that the recent movement towards increased industrial intervention of government in Germany and England is causally connected with the contemporaneous recrudescence of "militancy" in the two countries. And similarly, when Spencer explains how, under a régime of private property and free contract, there is necessarily a "correct apportioning of reward to merit," so that each worker "obtains as much benefit as his efforts are equivalent to—no more and no less," he exhibits a total ignorance of the crushing refutation which, according to Schäffle, this individualistic fallacy has received at the hands of socialism. The tendency of free competition to annihilate itself, and give birth to monopolies exercised against the common interest for the private advantage of the monopolists; the crushing inequality of industrial opportunities, which the legal equality and freedom of modern society have no apparent tendency to correct; the impossibility of remunerating by private sale of commodities some most important services to the community; the unforeseen fluctuations of supply and demand which a world-wide organisation of industry brings with it, liable to inflict, to an increasing extent, undeserved economic ruin upon large groups of industrious workers; the waste incident to the competitive system, through profuse and ostentatious advertisements, needless multiplication of middlemen, inevitable non-employment, or half-employment, of many competitors; the demoralisation, worse than waste, due to the reckless or fraudulent promotion of joint-stock companies, and to the gambling rife in the great markets, and tending more and more to spread over the whole area of production,—such points as these are unnoticed in the broad view which our English sociologist takes of the modern industrial society gradually emancipating itself from militancy : it never enters his head that they can have anything to do with causing the movement towards socialism to which his German *confrère* has yielded.[1]

However, whether Spencer or Schäffle is a true prophet —whether the decay of war will bring us to a more complete individualism, or whether the increasing scale of the organisation of industry and its increasingly marked deficiencies are preparing the way for socialism—cannot certainly be known before a date more or less distant. But as Comte's sociological treatise was written a generation ago, we are fortunately able to bring his very definite predictions and counsels to the test of accomplished facts. In 1854 he announced that the transition which was to terminate the Western Revolution, would be organised from Paris, the "religious metropolis of regenerate humanity," where an "irreversible dictatorship" had just been established, within the space of a generation. In the initial phase of the transition, which ought to last about seven years, perfect freedom of the press would "rapidly extinguish journalism," owing to the "inability of the journal to compete with the placard." By a "judicious use of placards, with a few occasional pamphlets," Positivism would regenerate public opinion. The budget of the clergy, the University of France, the Academy of Sciences, must be suppressed, and the proximate abolition of copyright announced. By these moderate measures Louis Napoleon's irreversible dictatorship might be "perfected and consolidated," so that the dictator

---

[1] See Schäffle's "Kritik der kapitalistischen Epoche," in *Bau und Leben des socialen Körpers*, vol. iii. pp. 419-457.

might assume complete legislative power, reducing the Representative Assembly—which would sit once in three years—to the purely financial function of voting the Budget. In the second phase of the transition, which should last about five years, the "dictatorial government, now unquestionably progressive," would suppress the French army, substituting a constabulary of 80,000 gendarmes. This would suffice to maintain order, internal and external, as the oppressive military establishments of neighbouring states would everywhere fall as soon as France had put down her army. The dictator would then break up France into seventeen separate intendancies, as a step towards the ultimate Positive régime, under which the peoples of Western Europe are to be distributed into seventy republics, comprising about 300,000 families each. The third and last phase of the transition, which should occupy about twenty-one years, might be expected to be opened by the voluntary abdication of the dictator in favour of a triumvirate, consisting probably of a banker to manage foreign affairs, an "agricultural patrician" as minister of the interior, and a working-man to take charge of the finances. Their names would be suggested by the High Priest of Humanity—indeed, Comte tells us that he had been "working for several years at the choice of persons," in order to be ready for this momentous nomination: for the immense influence which Positivist doctrine ought to have gained by this time would enable the political direction of France to be placed completely in the hands of Positivists. This triumvirate would transform the seventeen intendances into separate republics: the *bourgeoisie* would then be gradually "eliminated" by the extinction of *littérateurs*, lawyers, and small capitalists, so that society would pass easily into the final régime.[1]

I need not go on to this final régime: I have already given you more than enough of these extravagances; but it seemed important to show how completely the delusive

---

[1] These details are taken from Comte's *Système de Politique Positive*, vol. iv. chap. v.

belief that he had constructed the science of sociology could transform a philosopher of remarkable power and insight into the likeness of a crazy charlatan. I trust that our Association will take no step calculated to foster delusions of this kind. There is no reason to despair of the progress of general sociology; but I do not think that its development can be really promoted by shutting our eyes to its present very rudimentary condition. When the general science of society has solved the problems which it has as yet only managed to define more or less clearly—when for positive knowledge it can offer us something better than a mixture of vague and variously applied physiological analogies, imperfectly verified historical generalisations, and unwarranted political predictions—when it has succeeded in establishing on the basis of a really scientific induction its forecasts of social evolution—it will not require any formal admission to the discussions of this Section; its existence will be irresistibly felt throughout the range of the more special inquiries into different departments of social fact to which we have hitherto restricted ourselves. It is our business in the meantime to carry on our more limited and empirical studies of society in as scientific a manner as possible. Of the method of statistical investigation I have not presumed to speak, as I have not myself done any work of this kind, but have merely availed myself gratefully of the labours of others. But, even so, it has been impossible for me not to learn that to do this work in its entirety, as it ought to be done, repuires scientific faculties of a high order. For duly discerning the various sources of error that impede the quantitative ascertainment of social facts, eliminating such error as far as possible, and allowing for it where it cannot be eliminated—still more for duly analysing differences and fluctuations in the social quantities ascertained, and distinguishing causal from accidental variations and correspondences—there is needed not only industry, patience, accuracy, but a perpetually alert and circumspect activity of the reasoning powers; nor is the statistician completely equipped for his task of discovering empirical laws unless he can effectively use the assistance of an abstract and difficult calculus of probabilities. It is satisfactory to think that there is every prospect of statistical investigations being carried on, in an increasingly comprehensive and systematic manner, throughout an ever widening range of civilised countries. The results of this development cannot fail to be important from the statesman's no less than the theorist's point of view: for though the statistician, as such, does not profess to guide public opinion on political questions, there can be no doubt—as Mr. Giffen has recently pointed out—that the knowledge attained by him tends to exercise on the general discussion of such questions an influence, on the whole, no less salutary than profound.

VIII

ECONOMIC SOCIALISM

(*Contemporary Review*, November 1886)

OBSERVERS of the current drift of political thought and practice, however widely they may diverge in their judgments of its tendencies, appear to be generally agreed upon one point—viz. that Socialism is flowing in upon us with a full tide. Whether, like M. de Laveleye, they regard this phenomenon complacently as a "good time coming," or whether, with Mr. Spencer, they hold that what is coming is "slavery," they seem to have no doubt that the political signs are pointing to a great extension of governmental interference in the affairs of private members of the community. And a second point on which they appear to agree is that this socialistic movement—as it is often called—is altogether opposed to 'orthodox political economy'; that the orthodox political economist teaches us to restrict the intervention of Government on all the lines on which the socialistic movement aims at extending it. The object of the present paper is not to argue directly for or against any proposed governmental interference, but to reduce to its proper limits the supposed opposition between orthodox political economy and what is vaguely called socialistic, or semi-socialistic, legislation. I admit that the opposition really exists to some extent; and, so far as it exists, I am —for the most part—on the side of orthodox political economy; but I think that the opposition has been dangerously and misleadingly exaggerated for want of a proper distinction of the different grounds on which different kinds of governmental interference are reasonably based.

I will begin by stating briefly the general argument by which orthodox political economy seeks to show that wealth tends to be produced most amply and economically in a society where Government leaves industry alone;—that is, where Government confines itself to the protection of person, property, and reputation, and the enforcement of contracts not obtained by force or fraud, leaving individuals free to produce and transfer to others whatever utilities they may choose, on any terms that may be freely arranged. The argument is briefly that—assuming that the conduct of individuals is generally characterised by a fairly intelligent and alert pursuit of their private interests—regard for self-interest on the part of consumers will lead to the effectual demand for the commodities that are most useful to society, and regard for self-interest on the part of producers will lead to the production of such commodities at the least cost. If any material part of the ordinary supply of any commodity A were generally estimated as less adapted for the satisfaction of social needs than the quantity of another commodity B that could be produced at the same cost, the demand of consumers would be diverted from A to B, so that A would fall in market value and B rise; and this change in values would cause a diversion of the efforts of producers from A to B to the extent required. On the other hand, the self-interest of producers will tend to the production of everything at the least possible cost; because the self-interest of employers will lead them to purchase services most cheaply, taking account of quality, and the self-interest of labourers will make them endeavour to supply the best paid—and therefore most useful—services for which they are adapted. Thus the only thing required of Government is to secure that every one shall be really free to buy the utility he most wants, and to sell what he can best furnish.

If the actual results of the mainly spontaneous organisation by which the vast fabric of modern industry has been constructed do not altogether realise the economic ideal above delineated, they at any rate exhibit, on the whole, a very impressive approximation to it. The motive of self-interest does, I hold, work powerfully and continually in the complex manner above described; and I am convinced that no adequate substitute for it, either as an impulsive or as a regulating force, has as yet been found by any socialistic reformer. Still, the universal practice of modern civilised societies has admitted numerous exceptions to the broad rule of *laisser-faire* with which the argument above given concludes; and it seems worth while to classify these exceptions, distinguishing as clearly as possible the principles on which they are based, in order that, in any novel or doubtful case, we may at least apply the appropriate general considerations for determining the legitimacy of the exception, and not be misled by false analogies.

Let us begin by marking off a class of exceptions with which political economy, as I conceive it, is only indirectly or partially concerned;—exceptions which are due to the manifest limitations under which abstract economic theory is necessarily applied in the art of government. Thus, in the first place, the human beings with whom economic science is primarily concerned—who, in the general argument for *laisser-faire*, are assumed to be capable of a sufficiently alert and careful regard for their private interests— are independent adults. The extremest advocate of *laisser-faire* does not extend this assumption to children; hence the need of governmental interference to regulate the education and employment of children has to be discussed on principles essentially different from those on which we determine the propriety of interfering with the industry of adults. It is, no doubt, a very tenable proposition that parents are the best guardians of their children's interests, but it is quite a different proposition from that on which the general economic argument for industrial non-interference is based—viz., that every one is the best guardian of his own interests; and the limitations within which experience leads us to restrict the practical application of the two principles respectively differ to an important extent.

But, secondly, what the political economist is primarily concerned with is the effect on the *wealth*[1] of the community caused by interference or non-interference; but we all agree that from the statesman's point of view considerations of wealth are not decisive; they are to be subordinated to conditions of physical or moral well-being. If we regard a man merely as a means of producing wealth, it might pay to allow a needle-grinder to work himself to death in a dozen years, as it was said to pay some American sugar-planters to work their slaves to death in six or eight; but a civilised community cannot take this view of its members; and the fact that a man will deliberately choose to work himself to death in a dozen years for an extra dozen shillings a week is not a decisive reason for allowing him to make the sacrifice unchecked. In this and similar cases we interfere on other than economic grounds: and it is by such extra-economic considerations that we justify the whole mass of sanitary regulations; restrictions on the sale of opium, brandy, and other intoxicants; prohibitions of lotteries, regulation of places of amusement; and similar measures. It is, no doubt, the business of the political economist to investigate the effects of such interference; and, if he finds it in any case excessively costly, or likely to be frustrated by a tenacious and evasive pursuit of private interest on the part of persons whose industry or trade is interfered with, he must direct attention to these drawbacks; but the principles on which the interference is based carry him beyond the scope of his special method of reasoning, which is concerned primarily with effects on wealth.

This last phrase, however, suggests another fundamental distinction to which attention must be drawn. We have to distinguish effects in the *production* of wealth from effects on its *distribution*. The argument for *laisser-faire*, as given

---

[1] I use the term wealth for brevity; but I should include along with wealth all purchased utilities—whether "embodied in matter" or not—so far as they are estimated merely at their value in the market.

above, dealt solely with its tendency to promote the most economical and effective production of wealth: it did not aim at showing that the wealth so produced tends to be distributed among the different classes that have co-operated in producing it in strict accordance with their respective deserts. On this latter point there has, I think, always been a marked difference between the general tone of English political economists and the general tone of leading continental advocates of *laisser-faire*, of whom Bastiat may be taken as a type. Bastiat and his school do boldly attempt to show that the existing distribution of wealth—or rather that which would exist if Government would only keep its hands off—is "conformable to that which ought to be"; and that every worker tends to get what he deserves under the economic order of unmodified competition. But the English disciples of Adam Smith have rarely ventured on these daring flights of optimistic demonstration: when, *e.g.*, Ricardo talked of "natural wages," he had no intention of stamping the share of produce so designated as divinely ordered and therefore just; on the contrary, a market-price of labour above the natural price is characteristic, in Ricardo's view, of an "improving society." And, generally speaking, English political economists, however 'orthodox,' have never thought of denying that the remuneration of workers tends to be very largely determined by causes independent of their deserts—*e.g.* by fluctuations in supply and demand, from the effects of which they are quite unable to protect themselves. If our economists have opposed—as they doubtless have always opposed—any suggestion that Government should interfere directly to redress such inequalities in distribution, their argument has not been that the inequalities were merited; they have rather urged that any good such interference might do in the way of more equitable distribution would be more than outweighed by the harm it would do to production, through impairing the motives to energetic self-help; since no Government could discriminate adequately between losses altogether inevitable and losses that might be at least largely reduced either by foresight or by promptitude and energy in meeting unforeseen changes. If, however, we can find a mode of intervention which will reduce inequalities of distribution without materially diminishing motives to self-help, this kind of intervention is not, I conceive, essentially opposed to the teaching even of orthodox political economy —according to the English standard of orthodoxy; for orthodox economy is quite ready to admit that the poverty and depression of any industrial class is liable to render its members less productive from want of physical vigour and restricted industrial opportunities. Now, an important part of the recent, and the proposed, enlargement of governmental functions, which is vaguely attacked as socialistic, certainly aims at benefiting the poor in such a way as to make them more self-helpful instead of less so, and thus seeks to mitigate inequalities in distribution without giving offence to the orthodox economist. This is the case, *e.g.*, with the main part of governmental provision for education, and the provision of instruments of knowledge by libraries etc. for adults. I do not say that all the money spent in this way is well spent; but merely that the principle on which a great part of it is spent is one defensible even in the court of old-fashioned political economy; so far as it aims at equalising, not the advantages that should be earned by labour, but the opportunities of earning them.

At this point it will probably be objected that the means of equalising opportunities in the way proposed can only be raised by taxation, and that it cannot be economically sound to tax one class for the benefit of another. If, however, the result sought is really beneficial to the production of the community as a whole, it may, I conceive, be argued—on the premises of the most orthodox political economy—that the expense of it may be legitimately thrown on the community as a whole—*i.e.* may be raised by taxation equitably distributed. In order to make this plain, it will be convenient to pass to the general consideration of a kind of exceptions to *laisser-faire* differing fundamentally in principle from those which we have so far considered; cases in which it may be shown *à priori* that *laisser-faire* would not tend to the most economic production of wealth or other utilities, even in a community whose members were as intelligent and alert in seeking and guarding their private interests as any human beings can reasonably be expected to be. I do not argue that in all such cases Government ought to interfere: in human affairs we have often only a choice of evils, and even where private industry fails to bring about a satisfactory result, it is possible that governmental interference might on the whole make matters worse. All I here maintain is, that in such cases the general economic presumption in favour of leaving social needs to be supplied by private enterprise is absent, or is balanced by strictly economic considerations on the opposite side.

To give a complete systematic account of these exceptional cases would carry me beyond the limits of an article: my present object is merely to illustrate the general conception of them by a few leading examples, in choosing which I shall try as far as possible to avoid matters of practical controversy.

We may begin by noticing that there are certain kinds of utility—which are, or may be, economically very important to individuals—which Government, in a well-organised modern community, is peculiarly adapted to provide. Complete security for savings is one of these. I do not of course claim that it is an attribute of Governments, always and everywhere, that they are less likely to go bankrupt, or defraud their creditors, than private individuals or companies. History would at once refute the daring pretension. I merely mean that this is likely to be an attribute of governments in the ideal society that orthodox political economy contemplates. Of this we may find evidence in the fact that even now, though loaded with war debts and in danger of increasing the load, the English Government can borrow more cheaply than the most prosperous private company. We may say, therefore, that Government is theoretically fit to be the keeper of savings for which special security is required. So again—without entering dangerously into the burning question of currency—we may at least say that if *stability* in the value of the medium of exchange can be attained at all, without sacrifices and risks outweighing its advantages, it must be by the intervention of Government: a voluntary combination powerful enough to produce the result is practically out of the question.

In other cases, again, where *uniformity* of action or abstinence on the part of a whole class of producers is required for the most economical production of a certain utility, the intervention of Government is likely to be the most effective way of attaining the result. It should be observed that it is not the mere need of an extensive combination of producers which establishes an exception to the rule of *laisser-faire*, for such need can often be adequately met by voluntary association: the case for governmental interference arises when the utility at which the combination aims will be lost or seriously impaired if even one or two of the persons concerned stand aloof from the combination. Certain cases of protection of land below the sea-level against floods, and the protection of useful animals and plants against infectious diseases, exemplify this condition. In a perfectly ideal community, indeed, we might perhaps assume that all the persons concerned would take the requisite precautions; but in any community of human beings that we can expect to see, the most that we can hope is that the great majority of any industrial class will be adequately enlightened, vigilant, and careful in protecting their own interest; and in the cases just mentioned, the efforts and sacrifices of a great majority might easily be rendered almost useless by the neglect of one or two individuals.

But the case for governmental interference is still stronger where the very fact of a combination among the great majority of a certain industrial class to attain a certain result materially increases the inducement for individuals to stand aloof from the combination. Take, for instance, the case of certain fisheries, where it is clearly for the general interest that the fish should not be caught at certain times, or in certain places, or with certain instruments; because the increase of actual supply obtained by such captures is much overbalanced by the detriment it causes to prospective supply. We may fairly assume that the great majority of possible fishermen would enter into a voluntary agreement to observe the required rules of abstinence; but it is obvious that the larger the number that thus voluntarily abstain, the stronger inducement is offered to the remaining few to pursue their fishing in the objectionable times, places, and ways, so long as they are under no legal coercion to abstain.

So far I have spoken of cases where it is difficult to render a voluntary association as complete as the common interest requires. But we have also to consider cases where such a combination may be too complete for the public interest, since it may give the combiners a monopoly of the article in which they deal. This is, perhaps, the most important of all the theoretical exceptions to the general rule of *laisser-faire*. It is sometimes overlooked in the general argument for leaving private enterprise unfettered, through a tacit assumption that enlightened self-interest will lead to open competition; but abstract reasoning and experience equally show that under certain circumstances enlightened self-interest may prompt to a close combination of the dealers in any commodity: and that the private interest of such a combination, so far as it is able to secure a monopoly of the commodity, may be opposed to the general interest. Observe that my objection to monopoly—whether resulting from combination or otherwise—is not that the monopolist may make too large a profit: that is a question of distribution with which I am not now concerned. My objection is that a monopolist may often increase his profit, or make an equal profit more easily, by giving a smaller supply at higher prices of the commodity in which he deals rather than a larger supply at lower prices, and so rendering less service to the community in return for his profit. Wherever, from technical or other reasons, the whole of any industry or trade in a certain district tends to fall under the condition of monopoly, I do not say that there ought to be governmental interference, but at any rate the chief economic objection to such interference is absent.

A familiar instance of this is the provision of lighting and water in towns. Experience has amply shown—what might have been inferred *à priori*—that in cases such as these it is impossible to obtain the ordinary advantages from competition. Competition invariably involves an uneconomical outlay on works, for which the consumers have ultimately to pay when the competing companies—necessarily few—have seen their way to combination.

And it is to be observed that the same progress of civilisation which tends to make competition more real and effective, when the circumstances of industry favour competition, also increase the facilities and tendencies to combination when the circumstances favour combination.

But again, *laisser-faire* may fail to furnish an adequate supply of some important utility for a reason opposite to that just considered, not because the possible producer has too much control over his product, but because he has too little. I mean that a particular employment of labour or capital may be most useful to the community, and yet the conditions of its employment may be such that the labourer or capitalist cannot remunerate himself in the ordinary way, by free exchange of his commodity, because he cannot appropriate his beneficial results sufficiently to sell them profitably. Contrast, for instance, the case of docks and lighthouses. In an enlightened community, the making of docks might be left to private industry, because the ships that use them could always be made to pay for them; but the remuneration for the service rendered by a lighthouse cannot be similarly secured. Or, to take a very different instance, contrast scientific discoveries and technical inventions. A technical invention may be patented; but, though a scientific discovery may be the source of many new inventions, you cannot remunerate that by a patent; it cannot be made a marketable article. In other cases, again, where it is quite possible to remunerate labour by selling its product, experience shows that the process of sale is uneconomical from the cost and waste of trouble involved. This, for instance, is why an advanced industrial community gets rid of tolls on roads and bridges.

It is under this last head that a portion at least of the expenditure of Government on education, and the provision of the means of knowledge for adults, may, I think, be defended in accordance with the general assumptions on which 'orthodox political economy' proceeds; so far as this outlay tends to increase the productive efficiency of the persons who profit by it to an extent that more than repays the outlay. For it will not be denied (1) that the poverty of large classes of the community, if left without aid, would practically prevent them from obtaining this increment of productive efficiency; and (2) that even when it is clearly worth paying for, from the point of view of the community, the business of providing it could not be remuneratively undertaken by private enterprise. So far, therefore, there is a *primâ facie* case for governmental interference on strictly economic grounds.

I do not, however, contend that this defence is applicable to the whole of the expenditure of the funds actually raised, by compulsory taxation, for educational purposes; still less that it is applicable to the whole of the expense that eager educational reformers are urging upon us. Nor do I mean to suggest that the economic reason just given is that which actually weighs most with such reformers. I should rather suppose that their strongest motive usually is a desire to enable the mass of the community to partake effectively in that culture, which—though not perhaps the most generally valued advantage which the rich obtain from their wealth— is at any rate the advantage to which the impartial philanthropist sincerely attaches most importance. Is this desire, then, one that may legitimately be gratified through the agency of Government? 'No,' say Mr. Spencer and his disciples; 'let the philanthropist diffuse knowledge at his own expense as much as he likes; to provide for its diffusion out of the taxes is a palpable infringement of the natural

rights of the taxpayers.' 'Yes,' say the semi-Socialists—
if I may so call them—taking the same ground of natural
right, 'the equalisation of opportunities by education, the
free communication of culture, are simple acts of reparative
justice which society owes to the classes that lie crushed at
the base of our great industrial pyramid.'

Now this whole discussion of natural rights is one from
which, as a mere empirical utilitarian, I should prefer to
stand aloof. But when it is asserted that the prevalent semi-
socialistic movement implies at once a revolt from orthodox political economy, and a rejection of Kant's and Mr.
Spencer's fundamental political principle, that the coercive
action of Government should simply aim at securing equal
freedom to all, I feel impelled to suggest a very different
interpretation of the movement. I think that it may be
more truly conceived as an attempt to realise natural justice
as taught by Mr. Spencer, under the established conditions
of society, with as much conformity as possible to the teachings of orthodox English[1] political economy. For what,
according to Mr. Spencer, is the foundation of the right of
property? It rests on the natural right of a man to the
free exercise of his faculties, and therefore to the results of
his labour; but this can clearly give no right to exclude
others from the use of the bounties of Nature: hence the
obvious inference is that the price which—as Ricardo and
his disciples teach—is increasingly paid, as society progresses, for the use of the "natural and original powers of
the soil," must belong, by natural right, to the human community as a whole; it can only be through usurpation that
it has fallen into the hands of private individuals. Mr.
Spencer himself, in his *Social Statics*, has drawn this
conclusion in the most emphatic terms. That "equity does
not admit property in land"; that "the right of mankind at
large to the earth's surface is still valid, all deeds, customs,
and laws notwithstanding"; that "the right of private

---

[1] I say "English" because Bastiat and other continental writers have partly,
I think, been led to reject the Ricardian theory of rent by their desire to avoid
the obvious inference that the payment of rent was opposed to natural justice.

possession of the soil is no right at all"; that "no amount of labour bestowed by an individual upon a part of the earth's surface can nullify the title of society to that part"; that, finally, "to deprive others of their rights to the use of the earth is a crime inferior only in wickedness to the crime of taking away their lives or personal liberties";—these conclusions are enforced by Mr. Spencer with an emphasis that makes Mr. Henry George appear a plagiarist. Perhaps it will be replied that this argument only affects land: that it doubtless leads us to confiscate land "with as little injury to the landed class as may be"—giving them, I suppose, the same sort of compensation that was given to slave-owners when we abolished slavery—but that it cannot justify taxation of capitalists. But a little reflection will show that this distinction between owners of land and owners of other property cannot be maintained. In the first place, on Mr. Spencer's principles, the rights of both classes to the actual things they now legally own are equally invalid. For, obviously, the original and indefeasible right of all men to the free exercise of their faculties on their material environment must—if valid at all—extend to the whole of the environment; property in the raw material of movables must be as much a usurpation as property in land. As Mr. Spencer says, "the reasoning used to prove that no amount of labour bestowed by an individual upon a part of the earth's surface can nullify the title of society to that part," might be similarly employed to show that no one can, "by the labour he expends in catching or gathering," supersede "the just claims of other men" to "the thing caught or gathered." If it be replied that technically this is true, but that substantially the value of what the capitalist owns is derived from labour, whereas the value of what the landlord owns is largely not so derived, the answer is that this can only affect the respective claims of the two classes to receive compensation when the rest of the community enforce their indefeasible rights to the free use of their material environment; and that, in fact, these different claims have now got inextricably mixed up by the complicated series of exchanges between land and movables that has taken place since the original appropriation of the former. To quote Mr. Spencer again, "most of our present landowners are men who have, either mediately or immediately, given for their estates equivalents of honestly-earned wealth"—at least as honestly earned as any other wealth—so that if they are to be expropriated in order to restore the free use of the land to the human race, the loss entailed on them must be equitably distributed among all other owners of wealth.

But is the expropriation of landlords a measure economically sound? We turn to the orthodox economists, who answer, almost unanimously,[1] that it is not; that, not to speak of the financial difficulty of arranging compensation, the business of owning and letting land is, on various grounds, not adapted for governmental management; and that a decidedly greater quantum of utility is likely to be obtained from the land, under the stimulus given by complete ownership, than could be obtained under a system of leasehold tenure. What then is to be done? The only way that is left of reconciling the Spencerian doctrine of natural right with the teachings of orthodox political economy, seems to be just that 'doctrine of ransom' which the semi-socialists have more or less explicitly put forward. Let the rich, landowners and capitalists alike, keep their property, but let them ransom the flaw in their titles by compensating the other human beings residing in their country for that free use of their material environment which has been withdrawn from them; only let this compensation be given in such a way as not to impair the mainsprings of energetic and self-helpful industry. We cannot restore to the poor their original share in the spontaneous bounties of Nature; but we can give them instead a fuller share than they could acquire unaided of the more communicable advantages of social progress, and a fairer start in the inevitable race for the less communicable advantages; and 'reparative justice' demands that we should give them this much.

[1] J. S. Mill is, so far as I know, the only important exception; and his orthodoxy on questions of this kind is somewhat dubious.

That it is not an easy matter to manage this compensation with due regard to the interests of all concerned, I readily grant; and also that the details of the legislation which this semi-socialistic movement has prompted, and is prompting, are often justly open to criticism, both from the point of view of Mr. Spencer and from that of orthodox economists; but, when these authorities combine to attack its general drift, it seems worth while to point out how deeply their combined doctrines are concerned in its parentage.

At this point the reader may perhaps wonder where I find the real indisputable opposition, which I began by admitting, between orthodox political economy and the prevalent movement in our legislation. The most obvious example of it is to be found in the kind of governmental interference, against which the request for *laisser-faire* was originally directed, and which is perhaps more appropriately called 'paternal' than 'socialistic': legislation which aims at regulating the business arrangements of any industrial class, not on account of any apprehended conflict between the private interests, properly understood, of the persons concerned, and the public interest, but on account of their supposed incapacity to take due care of their own business interests. The most noteworthy recent instance of this in England is the interference in contracts between (English) agricultural tenants and their landlords in respect of 'compensation for improvements'; since no attempt, so far as I know, was made by those who urged this interference to show that the properly understood interests of landlords and tenants combined would not lead them to arrange for such treatment of the land as was under their existing circumstances economically best.

A more important species of unorthodox legislation consists of measures that attempt to determine directly, by some method other than free competition, the share of the appropriated product of industry allotted to some particular industrial class. The old legal restrictions on interest, old and new popular demands for 'fair' wages, recent Irish legislation to secure 'fair' rents, all come under this head. Any such legislation is an attempt to introduce into a social order constructed on a competitive basis a fundamentally incompatible principle; the attempt in most cases fails from its inevitable incompleteness, and where it succeeds, its success inevitably removes or weakens the normal motives to industry and thrift. You can make it illegal for a man to pay more than a certain price for the use of money, but you cannot thus secure him the use of the money he wants at the legal rate; so that, if his wants are urgent, he will pay the usurer more than he would otherwise have done to compensate him for the risk of the unlawful loan. Similarly, you can make it illegal to employ a man under a certain rate of wages, but you cannot secure his employment at that rate, unless the community will undertake to provide for an indefinite number of claimants work remunerated at more than its market value; in which case its action will tend to remove, to a continually increasing extent, the ordinary motives to vigorous and efficient labour. So again, you can ensure that a tenant does not pay the full competition rent to his landlord, but—unless you prohibit the sale of the rights that you have thus given him in the produce of the land—you cannot ensure that his successor in title shall not pay the full competitive price for the use of the land in rent *plus* interest on the cost of the tenant-right; and, in any case, if you try by a 'fair rent' to secure to the tenant a share of produce on which he can 'live and thrive,' you inevitably deprive him of the ordinary motives — both attractive and deterrent—prompting to energetic self-help and self-improvement. I do not say dogmatically that no measures of this kind ought ever, under any circumstances, to be adopted, but merely that a heavy burden of proof is thrown on any one who advocates them, by the valid objections of orthodox political economy; and that, in the arguments used in support of recent legislation of this kind, this burden does not appear to me to have been adequately taken up.

IX

POLITICAL PROPHECY AND SOCIOLOGY

(*National Review*, December 1894)

" OF all the mistakes that men commit," says George Eliot, " prophecy is the most gratuitous." The epigram is effective, and convenient for quotation when one does not wish to commit oneself to a forecast of events. But, unless we take the word prophecy in a very special and narrow sense, it is surely an audacious inversion of the truth such as only genius could successfully venture on. It rather seems to me that among the countless mistaken affirmations which man makes—

> Sole judge of truth, through endless error hurl'd—

those which relate directly or indirectly to the future are the only ones which are *not* gratuitous. When we make positive statements as to unimportant details of past history —*e.g.*, as to the place at which, or the manner in which, the Battle of Hastings was fought—we incur a risk of error which may fairly be called gratuitous. And if this cannot be said of all our statements as to past events, this is only because and so far as our conception of such events may conceivably affect some historical generalisation by which political science—when it comes to be constructed—may furnish guidance for the future conduct of human beings. All rational action is based on belief of what is going to happen: all experts in all practical callings are always prophesying. The physician who orders a dose, the engineer who determines the structure of a bridge, no less than the statesman who proposes a tax, can only justify what they do by predicting the effects of their respective measures.

It may be said that these predictions are of proximate events, and that gratuitous error comes in when we try to prophesy far ahead, beyond the needs of practice. But it is surely very difficult to draw the line. Man is an animal of large discourse; in an early stage of civilisation he begins to take an interest in his posterity and in the welfare of his tribe; with advancing civilisation his interests extend, and the further they extend the more remote becomes the future by his conception of which his acts and feelings are influenced. It is perhaps gratuitous to trouble ourselves about the ultimate refrigeration of the solar system,— though I believe that the prospect of it seriously depresses some highly educated persons,—but no one can say that the probable exhaustion of our coal mines in the course of a century or two is not a matter of practical concern to Englishmen.

These reflections are, I fear, too obvious to be interesting; but it is somewhat less of a platitude to remark how much the importance of prophecy has increased, for the present generation, through the increasing prevalence of the 'historical method' of dealing with political and social questions. So long as unhistorical ideals are dominant— so long as men believe in the construction of a social order based on eternal and immutable principles of natural justice, which determine the only legitimate form of government and define the only legitimate sphere of its operations— any prophecy of what is coming can only affect their view of what ought to be done in a secondary and subordinate way. The plan of their work is laid down independently of all forecasts of wind and weather: it will be prudent, no doubt, to take account of any interruptions which these intrusive forces may cause, but they cannot modify the architectural design on which the social edifice is to be constructed. But the spread of the historical method, with its accompanying conviction of the relativity of all political construction to the changing condition and circumstances of society, inevitably destroys the belief in a polity eternally and immutably just: and in many sanguine minds it tends to substitute for this a belief in progress, which fuses the notion of what ought to be and what will be into one dominant conception of a 'good time coming'—believed to be good because it is coming, quite as much as it is believed to be coming because it is good. And even minds less sanguine, less confident that the process of human history is a continual progress from worse to better, are naturally led by the same line of thought to accept unresistingly a future which they cannot find altogether satisfactory to their desires and aspirations. For no sensible person wishes to row against the stream, unless he has a very decided conviction that the stream is going the wrong way; and even then, if the stream is in the long run irresistible, the duty of putting off the evil day is dreary and unattractive. If we are certainly going to "shoot Niagara," what matters it whether the catastrophe comes a little sooner or a little later? Let us drop the oars, enjoy the scenery, shoot, and have it over.

In this way what Matthew Arnold called the "policy of the jumping cat" comes to be invested by the historical method with a certain melancholy dignity; it presents itself as an inevitable result of a wide vision of truth, a refined adaptation of highly cultivated individuals to their social environment. When this attitude of mind is widely prevalent among educated persons generally, innovators whose social and political ideals are really in their inception quite unhistorical, are naturally led to adopt the historical method as an instrument of persuasion. In order to induce the world to accept any change that they desire, they endeavour to show that the whole course of history has been preparing the way for it—whether 'it' is the reconciliation of Science and Religion, or the complete realisation of Democracy, or the fuller perfection of Individualism, or the final triumph of Collectivism. The vast aggregate of past events—many of them half-known and more half-understood—which makes up what we call history, affords a malleable material for the application of this procedure: by judicious selection and well-arranged emphasis, by ignoring inconvenient facts and filling the gaps of knowledge with convenient conjectures—it is astonishing how easy it is plausibly to represent any desired result as the last inevitable outcome of the operation of the laws of social development; the last term of a series of which the formula is known to the properly instructed historian.

Prophesying of this kind is not by any means " gratuitous"; but it may be dangerous: it is certainly liable to fill the mind of the confiding reader with a vain illusion of knowledge. The object, accordingly, of my present paper is not to stop such prophesying—which it would be futile to attempt,—nor to argue that one prophet is as likely to be right as another—which would be a paradox opposed to common experience,—but to endeavour to make clear the limitations within which the guidance offered by such forecasts may reasonably be accepted.

I will begin by remarking that prophecies are not always put forward, even by the most highly educated prophets, as based on a scientific grasp of the laws of social evolution. Indeed, in the most impressive book of a prophetic nature which has appeared in England for many years—I mean Pearson's *National Life and Character* [1]—the prophecies are not announced with any such pretensions; they always rest on a simply empirical basis, and only distinguish themselves from the common run of such forecasts by the remarkably wide and full knowledge of relevant historical facts which the writer shows, and the masterly skill with which the facts are selected and grouped. His predictions are almost always interesting, and sometimes, I think, reach a degree of probability sufficient to give them a real practical value. At the same time, in spite of Mr. Pearson's masterly handling, or perhaps all the more on account of it, I know no book which brings home to one more forcibly the

[1] Published 1893 (Macmillan and Co.). I must take this opportunity of expressing my deep sense of the loss which the scientific study of politics has sustained through the recent premature death of this remarkable writer.

imperfection of all such empirical forecasts. Such predictions may be classed under two heads, in respect of the general procedure employed in them: they either proceed on the assumption that what is will continue to be, or that what has happened will happen again. Each procedure is, under proper conditions and limitations, quite legitimate when we are only aiming at a probable conclusion; but each has its own imperfections, which, though they are tolerably obvious, I may briefly analyse and illustrate from the work just mentioned.

I do not wish to exaggerate these imperfections. The assumption that what is will continue to be, is, even in its crudest form, one which the most enlightened persons continually make with practical success in their political forecasts: for under ordinary circumstances the amount of change that takes place in the structure even of a modern political society, and the functioning of its organs, is not great in proportion to what remains unchanged within the periods to which such forecasts usually relate. And, of course, as our statistical knowledge increases, through the greater amount of labour and the improved methods applied to the ascertainment of present social facts, the degree of precision with which we can predict these facts in the proximate future will proportionately grow. Thus we can predict pretty confidently about how many children will be born next year, about how many of them will go to school, about how much they will know when they leave school, about how many will marry, about how many will be tried for murder, and about how many will be convicted. Still, we do not, of course, assume that any of these numerical proportions will remain unchanged. The best knowledge of history, even if confined to current history, prevents us from accepting the proposition that what has been will be, in its crudest form, in which it excludes change. It is in the more refined form of the expectation that a process of change in a certain direction, which we can trace in past history up to our own time, will continue in the future in the same direction, that this assumption is liable to be too easily accepted by educated persons. I think that Mr. Pearson relied on it somewhat too much. After giving some striking instances of false and true prophecies, he concludes that "the power of divination among men seems rather to concern itself with general laws," and that we are "fairly successful in ascertaining a general law of progress." Accordingly, he proceeds to forecast confidently certain important changes in English national character, which, though he does not precisely date them, must, according to his reasoning, require a considerable time.

Now, firstly, I think that the mere ascertainment of the direction in which society generally has been moving within a certain period, especially in respect of important features of national character, is more difficult than is often supposed; owing to the great complexity of the whole social movement of thought and feeling and the very imperfect knowledge of it that even the most instructed student of social facts can possess. But grant that the direction in which our social world has moved up to the present time has been correctly ascertained, still, until we have grasped the law of the whole course of development we can have no certainty that the movement is not going to change. And I think that here we may conveniently bring the other form of the empirical prophecy—the assumption that what has happened will happen again—to show the extent of the liability to error involved in the assumption that we can infer, empirically, the movement of change in the future from its movement in the past.

Mr. Pearson found that in the last twenty years—I do not think that the experience on which he based his forecast goes farther back—the functions of Government have shown a tendency to expand (especially in the colony of Victoria): he also found that the influence of religion has shown a tendency to diminish, especially the belief in a future life, which our age tends to regard as "nothing more than a fanciful and unimportant probability": and, assuming these tendencies to continue, he predicted certain depressing effects on national life and character. Now, the tendency to Socialism is undeniable; and I am not prepared to deny that a drift to secularism is traceable in what may be in a wide sense called the educated classes; and I should quite agree with Mr. Pearson, that if both tendencies together continue operating long enough they are likely to affect our national character very seriously. But I hesitate to infer confidently that this effect will be produced, when I reflect how short a time it is since a more fully developed Individualism seemed to thoughtful minds " in the van of progress," and how impossible it would practically have been to prophesy on empirical grounds any one of the revivals of religious sentiment that have taken place during the history of Christianity.

As for the first point, we have only to look at our most eminent living philosopher, Herbert Spencer, who stands before us as an impressive survival of the drift of thought in the first half of the nineteenth century. He formed, before 1850, the opinion that a completed Individualism was the ultimate goal of human progress; and to this opinion he remains true in 1894, regarding the Socialistic drift of the last twenty years as a lamentable temporary divergence from the true and main movement of political thought and fact. It seems at least not improbable that some of the ardent youths who are now expecting the salvation of society through the triumph of Collectivism, may, before they reach old age, find themselves similarly contemplating the receding tide of public opinion.

As to the second point, let us consider the greatest change that West-European Christianity has seen—the Reformation. Is it not a historical commonplace that the tendency towards a practically secular view of human life has rarely been more marked than it was in the educated class—including the leading clergy of the most civilised country in Europe—in the age that preceded Luther? As Clough aptly says, in an ironical passage,—Luther made a sad mistake: he did not see how Leo X. and Co. were quietly clearing away worn-out superstitions;

> He must forsooth make a fuss and distend his huge Wittenberg lungs, and
> Bring back theology once yet again in a flood upon Europe.

Why should not another Luther, adapted to modern intellectual and social conditions, have a similar effect now?

I do not use these instances to predict either a new Reformation or a reaction to the Individualistic ideal; indeed, I regard prophecies, based on analogous historic cases—except when they are very carefully selected from comparatively recent history—as generally more untrustworthy than prophecies based on observation of current drift and tendency. For such analogies are always very imperfect. The history of civilised man is a process of change, usually, no doubt, gradual, but still sufficiently rapid to establish profound differences between any two stages separated by a considerable interval of time; so that even where a new phase shows an impressive resemblance in certain characteristics to some antecedent phase, this analogy can hardly ever be sufficient to justify a confident prediction.

Let us take, for example, an analogy that has been extensively used in political discussions. From the time of Montesquieu and Rousseau, down to the time of Sir Henry Maine, a leading place has been given in such discussions to the consideration of democracy, as known to us from Greek and Roman history. It has been apparently assumed that a study of this previous experience is likely to throw important light on the process of change now going on in West-European States. Now, I am far from thinking that such a study is not highly interesting and suggestive; since an instructive parallel may certainly be traced between the successive stages in the more rapid development of the City-States of ancient Greece and Italy, and the successive stages in the slower development of the Country-States of modern Europe. But before we allow ourselves to draw any practical inferences from this analogy, it is obviously necessary to take full account of the important differences between Græco-Roman political conditions and those of

West-European States—the difference between direct and representative Democracy; the change in the conditions and estimation of industry; the difference due to slavery, which excluded absolutely from political rights a large portion of the manual-labour class in the most democratic of ancient communities; the difference in religious organisation, and the yet profounder differences in the nature of the influence exercised by religion on the life of individuals. One who duly considers these differences may, doubtless, still find a knowledge of the phenomena of Greek democracy useful in the way of suggestion and warning; but he will hardly venture to use this knowledge as the basis of a prophecy, unless he holds himself to have grasped the fundamental laws of the whole process of political and social development.

This leads us back to the question which I first raised. Can we ascertain from past history the fundamental laws of social evolution as a whole? I have tried to show that only a positive answer to this question can justify us in confidently forecasting the future of society for any considerable way ahead. Can we give such an answer? To put it otherwise, Is the 'social dynamics' of which we have heard so much for half a century, a science really established and constructed, and not merely adumbrated?— I do not, of course, mean completely constructed, but constructed sufficiently for prevision. Fortunately there is a simple criterion of the effective establishment of a science —laid down by the original and powerful thinker who must certainly be regarded as the founder of the science of society, if there is such a science—the test of Consensus of experts and Continuity of scientific work; and, if we accept Comte's criterion, it is easy to show that the social science is not yet effectively constructed—at least so far as the department of 'social dynamics' is concerned— since it is certain that every writer on the subject starts *de novo* and builds on his own foundation.

As evidence of this I may refer to a vigorously-written and stimulating book of which, as I understand, several thousand copies have been sold, and which has much impressed the reviewers—I mean Mr. Benjamin Kidd's treatise on *Social Evolution*.

Mr. Kidd begins by "confessing"—with the frankness with which each successive sociologist has hitherto confessed the deficiencies of his predecessors—that " there is no science of human society properly so-called ": " From Herbert Spencer in England,"—who, in Mr. Kidd's view, has thrown but " little practical light on the social problems of our time " — " to Schäffle in Germany, . . . we have every possible and perplexing variety of opinion." In short, " science has obviously no clear perception of the nature of the social evolution we are undergoing"; and "has made no serious attempt to explain the phenomenon of our Western civilisation." This he considers to be, at least in part, the fault of "the historian," who usually is depressingly reluctant to generalise and obstinately refuses to predict. " The historian takes us through events of the past, through the rise and decline of great civilisations, . . . through a social development which is evidently progressing in some definite direction, and sets us down at last with our faces to the future with scarcely a hint as to any law underlying it at all, or indication as to where our own civilisation is tending." It is thus left for the biologist—or rather the amateur equipped with the latest and most controverted results of biological speculation—to rush in where the historian fears to tread, and tell us what history really means, and what it is all coming to.

Now, personally I have some sympathy with the complaint here brought against historians; I often find myself wishing that of the great volume of energy that is now being thrown into the study of history, a somewhat larger portion was devoted to the comparison and systematisation of facts already known, and somewhat less to the ascertainment of new facts. But probably everyone who has done anything which may by a stretch be called research in any departments of history will be able also to sympathise with the reluctance of the professional historian to perform the task which Mr. Kidd demands of him. For such a student is likely to have gone through an experience of the following kind. At the first stage of his knowledge,—*i.e.* when he has studied his subject in one or more of the general histories of the period, it yields to his mind an ample crop of impressive generalisations; he seems to know not only what happened but why it happened, and is ready to formulate sociological laws in abundance. Then when he has begun to feel more or less at home among the original authorities, he finds his confidence in this formulation diminish; he notices facts which his formulæ do not satisfactorily explain, and inevitable gaps in his knowledge which make his first insight into causes appear superficial. This process goes on; and ultimately the generalisations to which he still clings appear so reduced in number, so far from certain, so loaded with qualifications and reserves, so inadequate to the full complexity of the facts, that he feels inclined to postpone offering them for the enlightenment of mankind. Now, if some such process as this is a common experience of professional students of history, and if they thus come habitually to distrust and severely to control their own tendency to generalise, much more are they likely to distrust the generalisations of the professional sociologist, whose knowledge is apt to be distinguished rather by range than by depth or accuracy. If I am right in thus characterising the general attitude of the historian towards the sociologist, I fear it is likely to be confirmed rather than modified by a study of the remarkable chapters in which Mr. Kidd sketches the development of western civilisation.

The historian will here learn, for example, that in Rome occupations connected with agriculture " were regarded as unworthy of freemen," and that " the freemen of Rome could hardly be said to work; they fought and lived on the produce of the fighting "; and he will wonder what manual of Roman history Mr. Kidd has been using, whether it left out the familiar story of Cincinnatus, whether it mentioned Cato, what account it gave of the struggle between patricians and plebeians, of the Licinio-Sextian laws, and of the colonisation system of Rome. Again, he will learn that in *all* the

Greek city States " the ruling classes had a single feature in common—their military origin . . . they represented the party which had imposed its rule by force on the rest of the community"; and he will perhaps envy the boldness of conjecture which has illuminated the history of (*e.g.*) Attica for the special benefit of Mr. Kidd. Passing to mediæval history, he will find that " amongst all the Western peoples there has been a slow but sure restriction of the absolute power possessed under military rule by the hand of the State"; and will vainly try to divine what account of the feudal system has fallen under Mr. Kidd's notice. His perplexity will be at its height when he finds that in spite of this absolute power of the military head of the State, Western Europe has become in the twelfth century a vast theocracy in which the "church is omnipotent," one result of which is that " all the attainments of the Greek and Roman genius are buried out of sight ": and he will ask himself—to take one point among many—whether Mr. Kidd has really never heard of the throng of students from all parts of Europe to hear the teaching of Jurisprudence at Bologna in the twelfth century, or whether he is under the impression that Irnerius and his successors lectured exclusively on the Canon Law !

I might add similar statements with regard to more modern times; but I have said enough to explain why I think that the historian, after reading Mr. Kidd, will be more than ever inclined to draw a sharp line between his own methods and those of the would-be sociologist; and will hardly take much interest in any prediction of the future founded on such knowledge of the past as the specimens above quoted exemplify. It may be replied, perhaps, by the admirers of Mr. Kidd, that this only shows the historian's pedantic habit of laying stress on details; and that the main argument of Mr. Kidd's historical chapters—the demonstration of the importance of Christianity in the growth of West-European civilisation—remains unaffected. Let us turn, then, to his main argument.

According to Mr. Kidd the central feature of human history is the struggle of man, " moved by a profound social instinct" to keep his reason under by the aid of religion, and thus prevent the suspension of progress which the unchecked exercise of reason would inevitably cause. When Christianity was born, religion in the Roman dominion was practically dead, and consequently Roman civilisation had commenced to die; but with Christianity came a "fierce ebullition of life" of which the "amorphous vigour" "was so great that several centuries have to pass away" before we can see what "it was destined to build up." At length in the twelfth century A.D. reason is effectually subdued; and in the "European Theocracy of the fourteenth century" the "ultra-rational sanction" of the "altruistic ideal"—which it was the distinctive characteristic of Christianity to exalt —has attained "a strength and influence never before known." Then in the sixteenth century the "immense body of altruistic feeling" generated by Christianity is "liberated into the practical life of the peoples affected by" the Reformation: so that henceforward the evolutionist notes the greater development of altruistic sentiments in Protestant nations.

There is much that is true in this historic survey and much that is new; the difficulty is to find anything that is both. The fundamental importance of the Christian Church, in the long process of building up the West-European State-system, is a truth not left for Mr. Kidd to enforce: but I conceive that the movement towards Theocracy in the Middle Ages is essentially connected with the success of the Church in dominating the political disorder caused by Teutonic invasions and conquests. In the fresh life of civilisation ultimately exhibited in this system of States, the influence of Christianity is doubtless an indispensable factor; but the fresh material furnished by the Teutonic invaders would appear to be no less essential. Mr. Kidd, however, seems to treat the barbarian irruptions and their consequences as a 'negligeable quantity'; but on this view he was surely bound to show that Christianity had the vitalising effect that he attributes to it in the older political society in which it had its origin: and it is difficult to imagine how he would try to show this, with regard to either of the two portions of the Roman Empire, whose fates, in the fifth century A.D., begin to diverge so widely. The extent and the causes of the process of social decline, discernible in the Western Empire before the Teutonic conquests, is doubtless somewhat obscure; still it seems clear that Christianity, if it did not contribute to it, did little or nothing to arrest it: the process appears to go on in the fourth and fifth centuries, unaffected by the establishment of Christianity as the dominant religion. But the Eastern or greater half of the Empire is perhaps more important for our argument; partly because Christianity had its origin and earliest development here, but chiefly because this part of the Empire continued to exist as an independent political community during the centuries in which the Western Church was developing in a theocratic direction. Now, Mr. Lecky is one of Mr. Kidd's authorities; but I will not ask him exactly to accept that historian's view, that of the " Byzantine Empire the universal verdict of history is that it constitutes, with scarcely an exception, the most thoroughly base and despicable form that civilisation has yet assumed." This "universal verdict" is doubtless far too sweeping and unqualified: still, when all has been done that can be done to restore the lost character of the Byzantine Empire, its staunchest champion will hardly refer to its history as evidence of the vitalising and *altruising* effect of religion.

But even as regards Western Europe in the Middle Ages Mr. Kidd's claims seem extravagant. He tells us that the "ultra-rational sanction" of religion had attained, in "the European Theocracy of the fourteenth century, a strength and influence never before known." Let us recall one or two salient facts in the history of this century. It begins with the conflict between Philip the Fair of France and Boniface the Eighth when the king, with the general support of the laity of his kingdom, defies the Pope's authority, and publicly burns his bull "Ausculta Fili." Then after an intervening Pope's reign has been cut short, through his imprudence (as Villani suggests) in eating figs untasted, with Clement the Fifth begins the "Babylonish captivity" of the Papal Court at Avignon; in consequence of which, as Bishop Creighton says, "the luxury, vice and iniquity of Avignon became proverbial throughout Europe." Then, when the seventy years of this captivity have terminated, there follows the great schism that lasts on into the fifteenth century. Let us imagine a thinker of the fourth century B.C.—say Plato or Aristotle, acquainted only with the "narrow and egotistical morality" of Greece—resuscitated and made to read Mr. Kidd; and then introduced to the pair of rival popes who begin the schism, in the pages of the cautious and impartial ecclesiastical historian whom I have just mentioned. He will read, among other things, of the bargain by which in 1380 Urban the Fifth agreed to invest Charles of Durazzo with the crown of Naples, on condition of his confirming the grants of "all the richest part of the Neapolitan kingdom," which his Holiness has made to his nephew Butillo;—a profligate ruffian for whom his affectionate uncle pleads the excuse of youth, when subsequently, being forty years old, he breaks into a nunnery and violates a sister of noble birth. Then he might turn to contemplate Urban's rival, Robert of Geneva, stamping out sedition at Cesena as Papal Legate (in the year before he became Clement the Seventh), with a barbarity that revolted even the hardened captain that commanded the papal mercenaries. "For three days and three nights the carnage raged inside the devoted city; . . . five thousand perished in the slaughter, and the name of Cesena would have been destroyed if the barbarous general, Hawkwood, had not been better than his orders, saved a thousand women, and allowed some of the men to escape." This exploit, the historian adds, "seems to have stood Robert in good stead, as convincing his electors of the promptitude and decision which he possessed in emergencies."[1] I think our resuscitated philosopher, however willing to acknowledge the moral deficiencies of his own age and country, will hardly be

[1] See Creighton, *History of the Papacy during the Reformation*, vol. i. ch. i. p. 65.

much impressed by these evidences of the strength and influence of the "ultra-rational sanction" in developing altruism in mediæval Europe.

Let me not be misunderstood; I do not deny that, in spite of the facts just mentioned—and many others of the same kind—there is still an important element of truth in Mr. Kidd's arguments; but the truth, as he presents it, is distorted by exaggerations and omissions not only into error, but into absurdity. And there is similar exaggeration in what he says of the superior altruism of Protestant nations since the Reformation. England, no doubt, took the lead in abolishing the slave-trade and slavery; but we have also to remember the prominent part that it took, after the Reformation, in developing the slave-trade and negro slavery; moreover, in tracing the wave of philanthropic sentiment that swells gradually through the eighteenth century and prepares the way for the movement of Clarkson and Wilberforce, we must not forget the important contribution made to this tide of feeling by the free-thinking writers of Catholic France. Certainly I know nothing written on slavery in English before 1750 that stings and penetrates like the irony of Montesquieu.[1]

As for the general moral superiority of the Anglo-Saxon in his dealings with inferior races—I think that any Anglo-Saxon who will study with strict impartiality the "wretched details of ferocity and treachery which have marked the conduct of civilised men in their relations

[1] I will quote a few sentences from the chapter to which I refer (*Esprit des Lois*, Book xv. chap. v.) : "Si j'avais à soutenir le droit que nous avons eu de rendre les nègres esclaves, voici ce que je dirais :

" Les peuples d'Europe ayant exterminé ceux de l'Amérique, ils ont dû mettre en esclavage ceux de l'Afrique, pour s'en servir à defricher tant de terres.

" Le sucre serait trop cher, si l'on ne faisait travailler la plante qui le produit par des esclaves.

" Ceux dont il s'agit sont noirs depuis les pieds jusqu'à la tête ; et ils ont le nez si écrasé qu'il est presqu'impossible de les plaindre . . .

" Il est impossible que nous supposions que ces gens-là soient des hommes ; parce que, si nous les supposions des hommes, on commencerait à croire que nous ne sommes pas nous-mêmes chrétiens.

" De petits esprits exagèrent trop l'injustice que l'on fait aux Africains : car, si elle était telle qu'ils le disent, ne serait-il pas venu dans la tête des princes d'Europe, qui font entre eux tant de conventions inutiles, d'en faire une générale en faveur de la miséricorde et de la pitié ?"

with savages,"[1] is not likely to rise from the study thanking heaven that he is not a Frenchman or a Spaniard; but rather with a humble hope that the page of history recording these details is now turned for West-European nations generally, and that the future historian of the Europeanisation of Africa will have a different tale to tell.

But this is a subject which my limits do not allow me to discuss: and I have perhaps said enough to explain why I think that Mr. Kidd has left the science of society where he found it—unconstructed, so far as the laws of social development are concerned. It is permissible to hope that progress is being made towards its construction: and doubtless the study of biology would be a valuable preparation for any thinker who may attempt to further its progress. But I think that the biologist who is to succeed in this attempt will have to know a little more history than Mr. Kidd: and in any case some time must be expected to elapse before it will afford a solid basis for confident prophesying. It must be remembered that Sociology labours under many difficulties which we do not find in Biology. For instance, the organisms with which the latter deals are well-defined and mostly quite separate organisms, which normally pass through a tolerably uniform series of stages from infancy to death, the nature and duration of which only vary within narrow limits; while, though they are subject to diseases of which the incidence is not similarly uniform, we can at any rate usually distinguish their normal from their morbid conditions with approximate accuracy. Neither of these statements are true of the organisms which sociology studies. Mr. Kidd, indeed, thinks otherwise; in speaking of Rome under the Empire before Christianity, he says that " we have only to watch the progress of those well-marked and well-known symptoms of decay and dissolution which life at a certain stage everywhere presents." And here, I admit, he might shelter himself behind historical authority more respectable than any he could find for some

---

[1] This is the language of Merivale, *Colonisation and Colonies*, Lect. xviii.; and Merivale is not a writer who indulges in heated rhetoric.

of his statements before quoted. Still, I think, that in all such phrases an essentially vague analogy is strained to produce a false semblance of definite knowledge : since there is really no adequate reason for supposing that the Roman Empire could not continue to exist for an indefinite time if there had been no barbarians to invade it. And it is to be observed that though States, in a certain sense, come to an end through conquest, they are not thereby disintegrated, as the living organisms with which Biology deals are disintegrated by death natural or violent; the change they go through is always far less, and varies indefinitely in nature and extent. So again, in the case of the social organism there is no well-defined distinction between conditions properly morbid and beneficial processes of change. For example, Comte ultimately came to think that the whole condition of Western Europe between the Mediæval predominance of the Catholic Church and the proximate establishment of the Positive Religion must be regarded as a morbid and abnormal condition; and, though this is an extreme case, it sufficiently shows how unsettled our common conceptions of normal and morbid are, in their relation to social phenomena. Now, I suppose, that if biologists were hopelessly disagreed as to whether a given animal was healthy or diseased, and if they had no reason to think that it would ever die unless it was eaten by another animal, their power of prophesying its future would be confined within very narrow limits; and I conceive that this parallel accurately describes the present condition of the social science.

I conclude, then, that in the present state of our knowledge it is for most practical purposes wise to " take short views " of the life of civilised society : not quite so short as those of the ordinary politician,—who can hardly be described as an "animal of large discourse" except in the modern popular sense of the term : but certainly short compared with those of the aspiring constructors of social dynamics, from Auguste Comte downwards. Not that we are to discard as useless either historical enquiries, or the systematic ascertainment of present movements of change : such studies will point out dangers against which we should be on our guard, and cheer us with hopes which it is legitimate to indulge. But these fears and hopes may prove dangerously misleading, if they beguile us into imagining ourselves able to forecast scientifically the future stages of social development. Scientific prevision of this kind will perhaps be ultimately attained, as the slow fruit of long years of labour yet to come;—but even that is one of the things which it would be rash confidently to predict.

[In reprinting this essay one or two sentences have been omitted as repeating too closely what has already been said in the essay on the *Scope and Method of Economic Science.*—ED.]

X

THE ECONOMIC LESSONS OF SOCIALISM

(*The Economic Journal*, September 1895)

By "Socialism" I mean the practical doctrine, that it is desirable to abolish private property completely or to a great extent, with a view to increasing the ordinary remuneration of labour, and thus increasing happiness by producing a greater equality of incomes. By Political Economy I mean the theory of the natural and right mode—or the natural and the right modes—of arranging the production, distribution, and exchange of wealth in political or governed societies of human beings. My paper is concerned with the relations between the two.

The present unmistakable drift towards Socialism in Western Europe is a fact of great interest, and a reasonable source of alarm to some, and perhaps of hope to others, from the political and economic changes to which it tends. But I am not now concerned with it in this aspect;—in which probably most educated persons are now as well acquainted as they desire to be with the arguments on both sides. I propose to treat Socialism from a special point of view, somewhat less familiar.

Socialism as a political ideal is very ancient; but as a practical ideal for the modern state, it was born about the same time as modern political economy—Morellet's *Code de la Nature* was even a year or two earlier than Quesney's *Tableau Économique*. And though it was for a generation quite dreamy and feeble—politically a negligeable quantity

—it became formidable before the end of the century in the conspiracy of Babeuf (1795); when the desire for "égalité réelle," " égalité de fait"—instead of mere "equality before the law"—became a demand and a menace. Since this time, for a hundred years, the life of Socialism has run side by side with that of Political Economy. It is obvious that two systems or modes of thought, so close in their subject-matter—for the aim of both, so far as Political Economy has a practical aim, is to establish the production and distribution of wealth on a right basis—can hardly have lived side by side for a century without exercising an important influence on each other. I propose to examine this influence from the point of view of Political Economy, *i.e.* to inquire not what Socialism has learnt from Political Economy, but what Political Economy has learnt from Socialism. I take this point of view, partly because I am writing for Political Economists rather than for Socialists,— partly because, of the two, Political Economy has the more manifest and palpable continuity of life and progressive development during the century in question, in spite of the differences of its schools. Socialism, on the other hand, appears to die out and be born again : its leading ideas are indeed few and comparatively simple, but they seem to undergo a kind of transmigration from system to system, rather than continuous development.

And this transmigration carries the ideas that are at the root of Socialism not only from sect to sect, but from country to country. In fact the century with which we are concerned divides itself naturally into two approximately equal parts : in the first half of which Socialism is mainly French or English; while in the second half it is preponderantly German. I find that German writers—and some English writers who have learnt from them—are apt to distinguish the two periods differently : they call the Socialism of the first half of the century " unscientific," and that of the second half " scientific." There is some justification for this ; but, on the whole, the antithesis appears to me misleading. It is a natural tendency of Teutons, justly proud of the primacy that they have attained in the pursuit of truth, to assume that even the fallacies and utopias produced by the Teutonic intellect are superior in quality to the similar products of other nationalities. I submit that the superiority is overrated, in the present case; and that, at any rate, it does not amount to a distinction in kind. All modern Socialism has been based on *some* theory of the effects on the production of wealth that would follow from the total or partial abolition of private property, and none, I conceive, has been based on a *sound* theory. So far as I know, no positive contribution of importance has been made to Economic Science by any Socialist writer throughout the century: the lessons of Socialism to Economic Science have been mainly in the way of criticism—criticism partly direct and purposed, partly indirect and unintentional; by drawing extravagant inferences from accepted economic premises it has suggested shortcomings in these premises by an undesigned *reductio ad absurdum*. In this latter way, especially, the instruction derived from the German Socialists has been obtained from fallacious reasoning of a more elaborate kind, and showing a greater grasp of economic method. On the other hand, the earlier Socialism, though indefinitely more fantastic and obviously 'cranky' than the later, seems to me also more original, in the best sense of the word: Saint-Simon, in particular—though it was perhaps not without reason that his disciple and collaborator Auguste Comte, spoke of him as a "demoralised mountebank" (*jongleur dépravé*)—has certainly more claim to be called a man of genius than Karl Marx. And the leading ideas with which the later Socialism operates are all found in the earlier, though in somewhat vaguer forms. That the liberty which seemed to the eighteenth century a completely satisfying ideal really leads, in industry and commerce, to anarchy and conflict and the "exploitation" of the many by the few: that the problem for the nineteenth century is therefore social and industrial organisation, based upon a scientific study of society, and having for its end the amelioration moral, physical, and intellectual of the condition of the poor masses : that history, scientifically grasped, shows this end to be only attainable by a comprehensive association of labour, and by taking the instruments of industry—land and capital—out of private ownership and placing them under the control of associated labour,—so that every member of society, labouring according to his capacity, may receive the due reward of his labour, and no one may enjoy the "impious privilege" of living on the labour of others;—all this was emphatically declared by Saint-Simon and his disciples. That, again, the industrial reorganisation of society has been rendered at once more imperative and more practicable by the great development of machinery, the gain of which now goes to the few at the expense of the many: that labour, being the source of all wealth, is the only true measure and standard of value, and that therefore a currency based on labour is the proper medium in the reorganised system of exchange which society needs;—these were cardinal points in Owen's preaching and practical efforts. Put these ideas together and compare them with doctrines of later German Socialism, which piques itself on being scientific, and acknowledges no connexion with Saint-Simon or Owen: it will be found that there is, after all, little fundamentally new in the later scheme; only the older ideas have gained in precision, articulation, and coherence, by being brought into closer relation to the reasonings of Political Economy.

Let us begin, then, by considering the lessons learnt by Political Economy from the earlier Socialism, before we pass to the later. In order to make these clear, we must recall the original view of the nature and aims of Political Economy. It was, as the meaning of the word suggests, a part of the Art of Public Finance: its object was to make the people as rich as possible, in order that the funds required by Government might be obtained as amply and as easily as possible. And these two objects, "enriching the people" and "enriching the sovereign," are retained in Adam Smith's definition of the study; though by this time the first object has come to be conceived as independent of, and prior to, the second. "Political Economy," he says, "proposes two distinct objects: first, to provide a plentiful revenue or subsistence for the people, or, more properly, to enable them to provide such a revenue or subsistence for themselves; and secondly, to supply the state or commonwealth with a revenue sufficient for the public service." But in the view of Adam Smith—as in that of the Physiocrats his predecessors—the first object was best attained by what he calls "the obvious and simple system of natural liberty"; the true answer to the question, "how to make the nation as rich as possible," was "by letting each member of it make himself rich in his own way"—only protecting him against invasion of property and breach of contract. In order to establish this conclusion, the new school of Political Economy had to trace the processes by which wealth was or would be produced, distributed, and exchanged, apart from governmental interference: and it is with this task that the greater part of Adam Smith's book is occupied.

Thus it came about that Political Economy, as taught by the disciples and successors of Adam Smith, was a body of doctrine consisting of two distinct parts: one part being an analysis of the process by which wealth was, or tended to be, produced, divided, and exchanged, apart from governmental interference; the other being a demonstration that this process led to the best attainable result. It is obvious that these two pieces of reasoning have no necessary logical connexion; it is also to be observed that while in the former the subject of the distribution of wealth among different classes of producers tended to occupy an increasingly prominent place, the original aim of Political Economy so far dominated the latter as to leave the question of distribution rather in the background there. The original aim, as we saw, was to answer the question 'how to make the people as rich as possible,' not 'how to secure to individuals their proper share of wealth';—the sovereign and his finance minister having naturally a keener interest in the former question. Hence, when the new school succeeded in obtaining acceptance for their new answer—'*laissez-faire*'—to the old question, it was primarily as a solution of the problem of National Production—not Distribution—that it was accepted. No doubt the more enthusiastic adherents of the new doctrine were prepared to prove that *laisser-faire* led to the best possible results in distribution as well as in production; and that in an economic world properly let alone every individual would actually earn what he deserved. But I think that the leading English economists from Adam Smith downward kept clear of this extreme optimism; and in resisting governmental interference to raise wages were mostly content to argue that such interference, by hampering the *production* of wealth, would in the long run do more harm than good to the class that it was designed to benefit.

The first effect, then, of the collision with Socialism, and of the Socialistic criticism of the actual distribution of incomes, was to bring Political Economy to a clearer consciousness of the essential difference, from a scientific point of view, between the two parts of its teaching. It was thus led to treat the strictly scientific part—the analysis of the processes of social industry, considered as let alone by Government, and the ascertainment of their laws—as its primary business; and to maintain its traditional justification of the results of these processes in a more limited and guarded way. At any rate this change took place in English Political Economy, to which, for the sake of simplicity, I shall confine my attention in the present paper. It was admitted by Senior, as early as 1827, that a broad distinction had to be drawn between the "theoretical" and the "practical branch of the science," and that the conclusions of the latter must be regarded as "more uncertain." Ultimately the difference between the two branches seemed to the same writer to be even more marked; and he confined the term "Science of Political Economy" to the theoretical part, relegating the practical part to the Art of Government—an art, he is careful to point out, which aims at objects to which the possession of wealth is only a subordinate means. A similar view is taken by J. S. Mill, who —in express verbal contradiction of Adam Smith—declared that "Political Economy does *not* itself instruct how to make a nation rich": it was also adopted by Cairnes, and became in short the accepted view of English economists. Along with this, among the practical problems to which the Science of Political Economy was now conceived as furnishing data, the problem of ameliorating distribution was more distinctly recognised as important. Thus Senior makes the noteworthy statement that "diffusion of wealth" such that "all the necessaries and some of the conveniences of life may be secured to the labouring class, *alone entitles a people to be called rich*."[1] J. S. Mill went much further: indeed, in his case we have the remarkable phenomenon that the author of the book which became, for nearly a generation, by far the most popular and influential text-book of Political Economy in England, was actually—at any rate when he revised the third and later editions—completely Socialistic in his ideal of ultimate social improvement. "I look forward," he tells us, in his *Autobiography*, " to a time when the rule that they who do not work shall not eat will be applied not to paupers only, but impartially to all; and when the division of the produce of labour, instead of depending, in so great a degree as it now does, on the accident of birth, *will be made by concert on an acknowledged principle of justice.*"[1] Having this ideal, he "regarded all existing institutions and social arrangements as merely provisional, and welcomed with the greatest pleasure and interest all Socialistic experiments by select individuals." In short, the study planted by Adam Smith and watered by Ricardo had, in the third quarter of the nineteenth century, imbibed a full measure of the spirit of Saint-Simon and Owen,—and that in England, the home of what the Germans call "Manchesterthum."

I do not mean to suggest that those who learnt Political Economy from Mill's book during this period went so far as their teacher in the adoption of Socialistic aims. This,

[1] The italics are mine.

no doubt, was far from being the case. Indeed—if I may judge from my own experience—I should say that we were as much surprised as the 'general reader' to learn from Mill's *Autobiography* that our master, the author of the much-admired treatise "On Liberty," had been all the while looking forward to a time when the division of the produce of labour should be "made by concert." But though Mill had concealed from us the extent of his Socialism, we were all, I think, conscious of having received from him a certain impulse in the Socialistic direction : we had at any rate ceased to regard the science of Political Economy as opposing a hard and fast barrier against the Socialistic conception of the ideal goal of economic progress.

In the region, then, of practical ideals and ultimate aims the lesson learnt from Socialism had been very important : still the main part of the analysis and reasoning which constituted what was now called the Science of Political Economy remained *prima facie* unaffected by the interpenetration of ideas that I have described. The old division of those who share the produce of industry into landlords, capitalists, and labourers, receiving respectively rent, profit, and wages, was substantially retained ; and the improvements introduced by Senior and Mill into the definitions of rent, profit, and wages, and into the theory of the determination of their amounts, appeared to relate to points of subordinate importance. But on looking closer a marked change in tone, partly attributable to the influence of Socialism, is clearly discernible in Mill's treatment of the landlord. Adam Smith, indeed, had pointed out that the landlord's rent "costs him neither labour nor care," and is "not at all proportional to what the landlord may have laid out on the improvement of the land": and Ricardo, distinguishing rent proper, as the price paid for the use of the "original and indestructible qualities of the soil," from the interest on the capital laid out in agricultural improvements, had represented the former as inevitably growing continually larger with the "natural advance of society"; and had thus fixed on the landlords the invidious character of a useless class levying an ever-increasing tribute on the useful classes. But it was left for Mill to emphasise the claim of society to the 'unearned increment' of value thus continually generated by the industrial process ; and though 'land-nationalisation' is not one of the practical measures definitely advocated by Mill in his treatise, it looms, if I may so say, on the horizon.

Still, the share of produce which falls to the landlord as such is, after all, small compared with that which falls to the owners and employers of capital; and here the economists of the early Victorian period, no less than their predecessors, maintained a view of the laws determining the capitalist's share which seemed to offer a firm barrier against Socialistic ideas. Senior and Mill recognised that a portion of the gross profit of the employer of capital must be regarded as remuneration for his labour, "wages of superintendence"; but the main part of the capitalist's share—after allowing insurance for risk—was explained by Senior, and by Mill after him, to be "remuneration for the abstinence" exercised by the capitalist in employing his wealth productively instead of consuming it. On this view, the Socialist contention, that labour, being the source of all wealth, ought to be remunerated with the whole of its produce, was met by a simple and apparently cogent argument :—' Labour requires capital to be productive, and capital is due to abstinence : unless the possessor of wealth is remunerated for abstaining, abstinence and therefore capital will cease or be much diminished. Hence if associated labour were to refuse to remunerate capital it would—ultimately if not at once—diminish instead of increasing the individual labourer's share: for the loss of the aid afforded by capital to labour would diminish the total produce by an amount far exceeding the share now allotted to capital.'

This was, I think, the current argument of persons who had read Political Economy, in the third quarter of the century ; and it may be found even later in organs of opinion whose age and dignity tend to keep them somewhat in the rear of the movement of thought.[1] But it involved, as I am about to show, an elementary confusion of ideas; and I believe that the clearing away of this confusion has been due to the collision of orthodox Political Economy with the later—the German—phase of Socialism, in which Marx is the most influential teacher. I do not mean to suggest that this elimination of confusion was due to the superior clearness of Marx's economic insight; on the contrary, Marx's elaborate argument to show that the labourers naturally and properly should divide up the whole produce of labour among themselves appears to me to involve a still more fundamental muddle—which the English reader, I think, need hardly spend time in examining, as the more able and influential among English Socialists are now careful to give it a wide berth. But here, as sometimes happens in controversy, the collision of two muddles ultimately brought the truth out clear and unmistakable; and the truth was substantially on the Socialists' side.

The fallacy in the argument above summarised was due to a confusion between the need of capital—in the form of instruments, etc.—as an aid to labour in production, and the demand of the private owners of capital, based on this need, for a share of the product. As things are, the labourer's share of consumable commodities is less than it would be if his labour could be equally effective without instruments, because he has to devote a part of it to the making of instruments; and it is further less than it would otherwise be, because he has to devote another part of it to the making of the commodities on which the owner of capital spends that part of his interest which he does not save. The two diminutions are separate and distinct, though the political economist, used to individualistic conditions, naturally thinks of them together; and it is only the former that depends on conditions of production which Socialism could not alter. A Socialistic State would have to exercise abstinence, but it would not have to be paid for exercising it; the

---

[1] See *e.g.* the *Edinburgh Review*, July 1878, p. 174.

associated labourers would have to devote labour no less than now to the making of instruments: but—assuming the labour unchanged in quality and efficiency—they might divide what the private capitalist now consumes (so far as it is not remuneration for the skilled labour of the capitalist employer) without any further abstinence.

The clearing away of this fallacy seemed likely to affect rather seriously the individualist position in the controversy with Socialism. So much stress had been laid on the indispensability of the saving of the private owner of wealth and on the inexorable necessity of remunerating his abstinence with interest, that the admission that this latter necessity would not exist in a Socialistic State seemed at first serious. But need, controversial as well as physical, is the mother of discovery; and in this case it served to open the eyes of economists to important shortcomings in the traditional view of the function of capital and the law of its increase. In Mill's chapter on the "Law of the Increase of Capital," attention is entirely concentrated on saving: we are told that "since all capital is the product of saving, the increase of capital must depend on two things: the amount of the fund from which saving can be made, and the strength of the dispositions prompting to it":—and these, in fact, are the only topics dealt with in the chapter to which I refer (I. xi.). Now no doubt if we ask how the mass of instruments aiding labour that England possesses—the factories and machines, ships, steam-engines, railroads and their rolling stock, etc.,—came to be accumulated, one part of the answer is that persons were found sufficiently supplied with wealth not required for immediate consumption to be able to pay for the production of these articles, and disposed to spend their money in this way in view of the prospective interest or profit. But this answer is obviously incomplete: it is through saving that capital is there to be employed, but it is through invention that there is a field of employment for it: Watt and Stephenson are at least as important factors in the causation of our railway system as the good people who were willing to put their money in railways. Of course this aspect of the matter was not ignored by Mill: but it is certainly left too much in the background in his discussion of the laws of production; and the fuller light thrown on it in more recent treatises is partly, I think, due to the influence exercised by the controversy with Socialism. It should be added that in considering invention as a part-cause of the increased efficiency which labour derives from the aid of capital, we must not limit the notion to technical inventions; we must include all expedients for saving labour or augmenting its utility, not only by improved instruments, but by improved processes, in the organisation of business and trade no less than in manufacture.

This leads me to another shortcoming in the older view of the capitalist's function, to which attention was directed by the controversial crisis above described,—the inadequate recognition by the older writers of the importance of business ability. A reader of Ricardo would be inclined to suppose that any owner of capital would be likely to earn average profits on his capital,—unless he suffered from a want of average intellect: and Mill's phrase above quoted—" wages of superintendence "—suggests that the skilled labour required from an employer of capital in business is on a par with that required from a superior clerk. And no doubt in certain businesses at certain quiet times this may be true: but where change is active—*i.e.* in a continually increasing part of modern business—a much higher quality both of skill and energy is needed for success. And the higher profit which the skill and energy obtains is not merely got out of the unsuccessful competitors: it is, speaking broadly, obtained by an economic service to society: the successful man of business has through acumen, promptitude, and resource, commonly been able to provide a given utility to the consumer more economically than it would have been provided without his efforts.

This completer analysis of the process of accumulating and employing capital, bringing into prominence inventive and industrial skill, is, I conceive, the latest important lesson for which Political Economy has been in some measure indebted to the controversy with Socialism. Perhaps the next lesson of importance will come through experiment rather than reasoning. This leads me to my last remark.

My readers may think that, in what I have said, I have spoken too exclusively of the lessons learnt from reasoning, criticism, and controversy, and not said enough of experiment. I should have much liked to be able to say more of the instruction derived from Socialistic experiment. But the truth is that there is very little to say: the reason being that while the earlier Socialists were much disposed to experiment, their experiments were mostly such palpable failures that their only effect was to harden the orthodox economist in his prejudices as well as his sound conclusions. It is true that the success of the artisans' co-operative stores —and, in a much more limited degree, of attempts at co-operative production—may be partly set to the account of Socialism; as, without the impulse given by Owen to the co-operative movement, the venture of the Rochdale Pioneers would probably never have been made. But the successes of these co-operative stores, though they have taught us something worth knowing, have not taught the lesson that Socialists have desired to teach: they have not demonstrated the great capitalist or great employer to be superfluous, but only that competition does not tend to the most economical supply of the services of the ordinarily humble and struggling retail tradesmen of the poor.

The tendency of the later school has been to discourage all voluntary essays in Socialism: on the pretext that no instructive experience can be gained except through the action of the State. From a scientific point of view this attitude is to be regretted, but I can quite understand that it is politic in those who aim at producing an immediate and far-reaching movement in a Socialistic direction: since a study of the broad results of previous experiments of the kind certainly does not tend to encourage such a movement. At any rate it seems at present that if we are to derive important economic instruction from Socialistic experimentation, the *corpus vile* will have to be a West-European nation. One nation will probably be found sufficient: and I trust that we shall all agree to yield the post of honour to Germany, in this branch of the pursuit of knowledge.

XI

THE RELATION OF ETHICS TO SOCIOLOGY

A PAPER READ BEFORE THE LONDON SCHOOL OF ETHICS
AND SOCIAL PHILOSOPHY

(*International Journal of Ethics*, October 1899)

IN selecting the subject of my lecture this evening I was influenced by the title of the body to whose invitation I responded—the London School of Ethics and Social Philosophy. For I take this title to imply that the studies of the school are not concerned only with ethics in the narrow sense :— *i.e.* with the inquiry into the principles and method of determining what is right and wrong in human action, the content of the moral law, and the proper object of rational choice and avoidance. This is, indeed, a vast, comprehensive, and difficult subject, even if we pursue it, so far as possible, as a separate and independent inquiry ; still, I take it to be the aim of your school not to confine the work of your students to the theory of what ought to be— of the ideal relations of human beings living in society ; but rather to combine with this the scientific study of the actual relations of men regarded as members of societies, as they have been, are, and will be. For it is only by a combination of the two studies that we can hope to attain that wider view which belongs to philosophy as distinguished from science ; from which we endeavour to contemplate the whole of human thought — whether concerned with ideas or empirical facts — as one harmonious system. It is as a contribution to social philosophy thus understood that I offer the observations that follow on the relation of ethics to sociology.

But at the outset I find myself in some perplexity. In order to examine closely the relation between the two studies, we ought to be able to bring the general character and outline of each in turn clearly before our minds. Now, I may assume that my audience can do this in the case of ethics; or, at least—as the range of the subject is somewhat vaguely and variously conceived—the brief description that I just now gave will suffice to indicate to you the body of systematic thought that I have in my mind when I use the term. But it is not so clear that I can assume this with regard to sociology; since, though the educated world has heard of sociology for about three-quarters of a century, it can hardly be said, in England at least, to have yet attained the rank of an established science,—at any rate, if academic recognition can be taken as a criterion of the establishment of a science. There is, so far as I know, no chair of sociology in any English university; it is not formally included in any academic curriculum; there is no elementary manual of English manufacture by which a student may learn to pass an examination in sociology with the least possible trouble. It is otherwise in the United States, where sociology has already got both professorial chairs and handbooks. Perhaps in intellectual as well as industrial matters the Anglo-Saxons across the Atlantic are more apt than we are to seize and effectively apply new ideas. Still, the leading English philosophers of the latter half of the nineteenth century, J. S. Mill and Herbert Spencer, have both devoted an important part of their energies to the exposition of the subject,—which, indeed, occupies three out of the ten volumes of Spencer's great system of synthetic philosophy. And, largely under their influence, in spite of the cold shade of official neglect in which it still lingers, the ideas of sociology have more and more tended to penetrate and pervade current ethical discussion. Take, as an instance of this, the following statement made some years ago by a writer of repute:—

A man's first and last duty is to see and do those things which the social organism of which he is a member calls upon him to do.

"The social organism" is essentially a sociological conception; and if we admit this statement in its full breadth, we implicitly admit the claim—which the young science has in fact been making since its birth from the brain of Auguste Comte—to dominate the older subject of ethics and even to reduce it to a department of itself.

This claim I propose to examine in the present lecture; but, for the reasons I have just indicated, it seems best that before proceeding to examine it I should briefly sketch the aims and method of sociology as presented by the leading writers whom I have named.

Sociology, as conceived by Comte and Spencer, may be briefly described as an attempt to make the study of human history scientific by applying to it conceptions derived from biology, with such modifications as their new application requires. We have, however, for this purpose to include, along with history in the ordinary sense, a large part of what is commonly known as anthropology,—that is, the comparative study of the contemporary social conditions, and recent social changes so far as ascertainable, of those parts of the human race that have not arrived at a sufficiently advanced stage of civilisation to have a history in the ordinary sense.

To begin, we may definitely conceive the objects which sociology studies as a number of groups of human beings which at the outset I shall consider to be each an independent political or governed society, though this view must be taken subject to important modifications later on. Each such society may be to a great extent properly regarded—and I shall begin by regarding it—as having an organic life of its own, distinct from the lives of the individuals composing it. It is in this view that I call it an 'organism,' meaning by the term first that such a group is not a mere aggregate of individuals, but an aggregate of which the members have definite relations that, though themselves subject to change, remain comparatively constant while the individuals change; and that these relations bind the individuals together into mutually dependent parts of a larger whole, performing mutually dependent functions. The society has thus a structure which so far resembles the structure of a living animal that its existence depends on its functioning; it cannot cease to function and retain its structure, as a machine can. I further mean to imply that such a society goes through processes of growth and change which are at any rate largely caused—as the changes of a plant or animal—by interaction with its environment, physical and social; and especially changes by which it adapts or adjusts itself to its environment,—*i.e.* tends to preserve itself amid changes in environing conditions even, if need be, by the occasional sacrifice of the lives of individual members. With this definite meaning, finding in such societies these characteristics, we may agree to call them organisms in spite of their unlikeness in other important respects to the organisms which biology studies.

Then, following Spencer and combining the results of history and archæology with the study of less advanced societies now existing, somewhat as the biologist combines the results of geology with those of zoology and botany, we may note how the prevalent type of social organism, like the prevalent types of animals or plants, tends, as evolution goes on, to grow in mass both by multiplication of units within each group and by union of groups. We may note further how along with increase of mass goes development of social structure, by which the differentiation of its mutually dependent parts becomes continually more complex; until from the simplicity of a little tribe of hunters, with hardly any division of functions except what is connected with sex, we arrive ultimately at the complexity of a modern industrial society, with its vast diversity of occupations.

Spencer proceeds to draw an instructive parallel between the sociological and the biological differentiation of organs. He bids us observe in each case—

(1) A "sustaining system," alimentary in the animal and industrial in the society,

(2) A "distributing system," carrying about nutriment in the animal and commodities in the society, and

(3) A "regulating and expending system." By this last notion he represents an analogy between the apparatus of nerves and muscles in an animal which carries on conflict with other animals and the governments and armies of political society; taking the governmental system as ultimately developed to correspond to the brain and nervous centres, the supreme deliberative assembly being analogous to the cerebrum.

So much for the resemblances between the social organism and the animal or plant. As we should expect, they belong primarily to the physical life of human societies; but when we turn to note the differences, we shall be led gradually to contemplate their intellectual life.

We may begin by observing that a political society has not, like an animal, a normal period of life and a normal series of vital changes from infancy to senility and death. Indeed, the political societies historically known to us do not ordinarily die unless they are assailed and structurally destroyed by other societies; and when death, in a certain sense, thus befalls any such society, it does not entail the death of the human beings composing it. Some of them, no doubt, perish in the collision, but the bulk of them are absorbed alive by the conquering society. Even in peace an important mingling of units from different societies goes on, as is most conspicuously illustrated at the present time by the comparatively new societies formed in America. They are largely made neither by "multiplication of units" nor by "union of groups," but by composition of units from a number of groups.

But it is still more important to observe that the social organism to which an individual is found to belong, through the social relations binding him to other men, becomes very different in its range as we pass from one set of relations to another. There is nothing corresponding to this in the case of an animal. Each animal has its own sustaining system, its own distributing system, and its own regulating and expending system, quite unconnected with the corresponding systems of other animals. The alimentary organs of one animal do not provide, nor its blood-vessels convey, nutriment to the organs of other societies, nor does its brain co-operate in directing their movements, except indirectly by producing external movements of its own organs. The case is quite otherwise with the organic life of societies. The channels of communication by which commodities are carried run, as we know, not only within States, but across States, almost ignoring their boundaries; and the same is true of the process of differentiation which localises particular branches of industry in situations specially favourable to it, and thus tends to bind the inhabitants of the districts in question into one economic whole. We all know that England forms part of an economic system extending far beyond the limits of the British empire.

But again a very similar set of cross-divisions, lines of separation that cut across the boundaries of States, is found in what we cannot but regard as an important part of the regulative apparatus of social organisms: I mean the ecclesiastical systems. We all know how, throughout the civilised world, members of the same States are divided from one another, and members of different States are united, by communities formed for the purpose of religious instruction and worship. No fact is more striking in the history of regulating social agencies than the manner in which religions claiming to be world-religions—Buddhism, Christianity, Mohammedanism—have arisen and spread and overleaped all the lines of separation of political societies; binding their converts, through the most powerful ties of common beliefs and common worship, into organisms quite different from States, though they come to have an elaborately differentiated quasi-political organisation. Now, in studying these ecclesiastical organisms from the outside, we might of course dwell on the social differences and relations between priests or monks and laymen, and the organisation of ecclesiastical government. But it would be a very shallow insight that did not penetrate further, and recognise as the most essential social relation which binds human beings together on this side of their life community of thought and sentiment—a common stock of ideas and convictions about the universe, its ground and end, and human destiny. Hence, when the sociologist studies these ecclesiastical bodies, it is to the laws of change and growth of this intellectual and emotional context, this common body of ideas and sentiments, that his deepest attention should be directed.

And this is true also of the political regulation of social man. Mr. Spencer, as we saw, compares the brain of an animal with the supreme deliberative assembly of a nation. But surely the political brain of England is not limited to the six hundred and seventy respectable gentlemen who chiefly make our laws : it is to be found wherever political thought is going on which will take effect in determining the action of the English Government. And if so, the history of political ideas shows that no modern nation has a brain strictly and entirely its own. If we insist on keeping the analogy, we have for the main movements of political thought to trace the operation and development of at least a West-European brain ; whose range of influence in modern times has not only extended to European colonies in other parts of the globe, but has even included a people so alien in its origin and previous history as the Japanese.

And, finally, what I have said of religious and political ideas is equally true of moral ideas and sentiments. Indeed, throughout the history of European civilisation morality has had an intimate connexion both with religion and with polity. Still, the study of the development of morality and its conditions and laws of growth and change may be pursued, no less than the study of religious or political thought, as a partially independent branch of sociological inquiry ; and when we so pursue it we soon find that the aggregate of human beings bound together spiritually by sharing a common moral life is not to be identified with any one of the political societies which we began by regarding as social organisms. And the same may be said in modern times of the possession of a common body of scientific knowledge; indeed, science is less modified by national differences than morality; and European science has united the educated portion of the Japanese people more completely with our educated world than European political ideas. Thus, in contemplating the continual enlargement of these spiritual bonds of social union we are irresistibly led—as the founder of sociology, Comte, was led—to an ideal future, when the whole population of the globe will form, from an intellectual point of view, a single social organism. There is a striking passage, remarkable in a writer who claims to expound a purely positive method, in which Comte tells us that Sociology, reading the future into the past, "represents the whole human race, past, present, and future, as constituting a vast and eternal social unit, where different organs, individual and national, concur in their various modes and degrees in the evolution of humanity."

To sum up, as we pass from one aspect to another of the many-sided social life of man, we are led gradually from the conception of an indefinite number of social organisms, subject, like plants or animals, to the struggle for existence as a main factor in their development,—a conception which physical analogies and the contemplation of the earlier stages of human history combine to press on us,—to the idea of a single social organism, which a study of later civilised history, especially in its spiritual aspect, renders no less inevitable.

I turn now to examine the relation of sociology to ethics, and especially the claim of the former study to absorb the latter and reduce it to a subordinate department of itself. I may perhaps say that I come to the examination of this claim in an impartial spirit. Speaking as a professor of ethics, I do not consider myself as holding a brief for the independence of my subject. It is for the true good of any department of knowledge or inquiry to understand as thoroughly as may be its relation to other sciences and studies, to see clearly what elements of its reasonings it has to take from them, and what in its turn it may claim to give them; and the value of this insight becomes greater in proportion as the steady growth of human knowledge, the steady extension of the range of human inquiry, brings with it a continually more urgent need for a clear and rational division of intellectual labour. If, therefore, the relation of ethics to sociology is truly one of subordination, it is important that students of ethics should fully recognise this truth and render due obedience to the superior authority.

Of course, in order that this authority, however ideally unquestionable, should be actually unquestioned, sociology must have become an established science, and be not merely struggling towards this position. And if I were speaking as an advocate of the claims of ethics to actual independence, I should have much to say on this topic; and my brief would be stuffed with quotations from very recent treatises on sociology, whose authors—to quote a well-known epigram—show themselves most emphatically " conscious of one another's shortcomings." But this advocate's work is not now my affair. I wish to assume for the purposes of my present discussion that the struggle of sociology to become an established science, a struggle carried on now for three-quarters of a century, has been crowned with the success which I hope will ultimately crown it. I will assume that it has attained as much consensus as to principles, method, and conclusions, and as much continuity of development, as the physical sciences dealing with organic life, and as much power of prevision as Comte hoped for it;—for he was not sanguine enough to suppose that sociology could ever predict with the exactness and minuteness of astronomy, and foretell the stages of a political revolution as astronomy foretells the stages of a solar eclipse. Let us suppose this consummation attained, and consider how far this scientific prevision of social effects will so far determine ethical reasonings as to reduce ethics to a subordinate department of sociology.

I think it must be admitted that this effect will be produced to a considerable extent, upon any view of ethics except the ultra-intuitional, in respect of the deduction of

s

particular rules of morality from fundamental principles.
For all schools, except that which takes the immediate
judgments of conscience as infallible guides in all questions
of conduct, admit that the application of moral principles
to practice must be largely governed by foresight of consequences, and must therefore admit that rules of social
behaviour will properly be determined in detail by the
scientific prevision of social consequences so far as such
prevision is available. We may compare, as a parallel case,
the relation of the moral duty or virtue of temperance to
human physiology, including pathology; the ethical maxim
that the bodily appetites ought to be strictly obedient to
the regulation of reason must receive its practical application
from a forecast of consequences; and this, with the development of physiological knowledge, must change from a merely
empirical to a more or less scientific forecast. We commonly recognise that the diet scientifically known to be
promotive of health and efficiency is the truly temperate
diet; and the most ascetic moralist has to admit that self-
denial, no less than self-indulgence, must be limited and
guided by medical prevision. Similarly we must admit that
our social affections and sentiments will have to yield to the
control and obey the guidance of sociological previson when
sociology has become a really established science.

Indeed, some effect of this kind has already been produced on current ethical notions and habits by the branch
of sociology which has been separated from the general
science of society, and received a development in advance of
the rest under the name of political economy. For instance,
under the influence of the economic forecast—deductively
and inductively established—of the bad consequences of
indiscriminate almsgiving, the old and eminent virtue of
charity, in its narrower signification, has materially changed
its practical content for the modern educated man, while
retaining its principle and motive unchanged. Its application to conduct has become more complex and exacting;
it is recognised as demanding thought and care, besides
the mere altruistic preference of the satisfaction of others'

desires to the satisfaction of our own, and as imposing restraints on sympathetic impulses as well as on self-regarding ones.

A similar effect of economic forecast on ethical conceptions and accompanying sentiments is traceable in the case of justice; but with the difference that in this case we have marked ethical divergences resulting from divergences in the economic or sociological prevision of consequences. Suppose we take the principle that desert ought to be requited as expressing the abstract essence of distributive justice. Its practical application cannot but be different, on the one hand, for the individualist who holds that any important relaxation in the competitive struggle for existence must result in the arrest and decline of human improvement, through the equalising of the prospects of survival of the unfit along with the fit; and, on the other hand, for the socialist who forecasts a more rapid and effective improvement under the stimulus of altruistic affection, sympathy, and public spirit, when these nobler impulses are no longer starved and depressed by the egoistic habits and sentiments that necessarily result from the present competitive struggle. The former will tend to interpret the requital of desert to mean securing to each man the precise social value of his services; the latter will tend to interpret it to mean securing him what he requires for the most efficient performance of his social function. Of course, as sociological prevision extends in range and increases in exactness, we must suppose fundamental divergences of this kind to diminish and a more decisive effect to be produced.

I have said enough to show the import of my admission, as a representative of ethics, that if we suppose sociology an established science, we must suppose its forecast of social consequences to exercise a fundamentally important effect on the practical application of general ethical principles or maxims, and on the deduction of subordinate rules of conduct from these.

I now turn to the more important and more disputable element of the claim of sociology to absorb and subordinate ethics,—*i.e.* the claim not merely to modify the practical application of ethical principles, but to determine these very principles themselves.

Here, first, I quite admit that the connexion of sociology, supposing it an established science, with the subject-matter of ethics must necessarily be so intimate and so comprehensive, that its claim to dominate and subordinate ethics is natural and almost inevitable; and we cannot be surprised that it should appear irresistible to students of sociology who have never made a systematic attempt to purge their moral notions of the confusions of popular thought. For, as we have seen, sociology undoubtedly comprehends in its subject-matter the study of morality as a social fact, and this study must include morality as a whole, the principles accepted in any age and country, no less than the accepted and current application of the principles to particular concrete problems of conduct. It is a part of the business of sociology—at least as important, from a purely sociological point of view, as any other part—to ascertain first the facts, and then, as far as possible, the laws of the development of moral opinions and sentiments, as one element in the development of human society as a whole: to show how it has influenced and been influenced by other elements in the whole social evolution: to trace it back, if possible, to its origin: and—always supposing sociology to have arrived at the stage of scientific prediction—to foretell its future conditions.

It is natural to infer that a sociology supposed able to accomplish all this—and I am willing, for the sake of argument, to make the supposition—would reduce ethics to a subordinate department of itself. I do not, however, think that this inference is logically sound. Indeed, I think that in most cases it arises from a confusion of thought that a little reflection ought to dispel.

To show this, let us suppose ethics and sociology as independent and established systems of thought, and then try to imagine a conflict between them, a conflict such as sometimes takes place between established sciences,—*e.g.* there was one some time ago between physicists and geologists as to the time of duration of the earth.

We shall find that we cannot really suppose such a conflict possible. No ethical proposition can possibly contradict a sociological proposition, since they cannot relate to the same subject-matter,—that is, so long as ethics is understood in the limited sense that I have defined [see p. 249], and so long as sociology keeps strictly within the bounds of its domain as a positive science. Sociology thus conceived is strictly incapable of answering any ethical question, and ethics thus understood is strictly incapable of answering any sociological question,—for ethics is only concerned with what ought to be, and sociology, even when it deals with ethical judgments, is only concerned with what is, has been, and will be judged, and not at all with the question whether it is, has been, or will be truly judged. So far as any sociologist expresses any opinion on the latter point, he assumes a knowledge which the method of his science, regarded as a study of empirical fact, is quite incompetent to supply.

I do not think that this is likely to be disputed, so far as sociology is concerned with the mere ascertainment of particular facts, past and present; but it may be disputed in respect of the general truths which sociology as a science must be supposed to have established. And I admit that if we examine this dispute with care we shall find, not indeed a possible conflict between ethics and sociology, but a possible coincidence so close as, if actually accepted, to justify the view that sociology is destined to absorb ethics.

But here, again, I must point out that the dispute sometimes arises from mere confusion of thought. It is rightly seen that the aim of sociology is not merely to ascertain, but to explain, the variations and changes in social morality, and that this explanation must lie in reducing to general laws the diversity of moral opinions prevalent in different ages and countries; and it is vaguely thought that these general laws, at any rate when brought to a sufficiently high degree of generality, must coincide—if they do not clash—

with ethical principles. But not only is there no *primâ facie* reason why they should coincide, but *primâ facie* every reason why they should not. For the sociological laws must explain, and be manifested in, the erroneous moral judgments that have been prevalent in human society no less than in true moral judgments; they must explain the prevalent opinion of certain groups of primitive men that successful thieving is honourable and virtuous, or that the revenge of a blood-relation is the holiest duty that man can perform, no less than the opposite moral opinions now prevalent in Europe.

There is, however, a subtler form of the same view which cannot be so decisively put on one side. It may be urged that the subject-matter of sociology, no less than the subject-matter of animal or vegetable biology, is a kind of organic life; and that as the varied structures and functions of animal or vegetable organisms can only be understood if we regard them as adapted or adjusted to the preservation either of the individual organism or its type, so sociology requires the same conception of adaptation to the end of social preservation in its explanation of social facts. Accordingly, morality, prevalent moral opinions and sentiments, being an important complex of relations among the members of a society, must be brought under the same general conception; so that the most comprehensive and fundamental sociological law, explaining the development of morality, will consist in just this statement of Preservation of the Social Organism as the end to which morality is normally and broadly a means,—though in any particular society at any particular time details of positive morality may not be perfectly adapted to this end. If this is so, it may be said, the moralist must adopt this sociological end as his ultimate ethical end, since otherwise he would be setting up an ideal opposed to the irresistible drift of the whole process of life in the world, which would be obviously futile.[1]

---

[1] Some writers would substitute "welfare" or "health" for "preservation" in this reasoning. But unless "welfare" or "health" is interpreted to mean merely preservation in a condition favourable to future preservation, in which case simple preservation is still the ultimate end, the terms seem to me to introduce an ethical conception which cannot be arrived at by any strictly sociological method.

Now, supposing a *consensus* of sociologists to declare that the preservation of the social organism is the one all-comprehensive end, by continual adjustment to which the actual evolution of morality may be simply and completely explained; and supposing a *consensus* of moralists to accept this sociological end as the ultimate good to the attainment of which all human action should be directed, then, I admit, it would be broadly true to say that ethics was absorbed by sociology. For on these hypotheses there would, firstly, be a complete coincidence between the sociological and the ethical end; and, secondly, as I have already explained, the working out of the rules conducive to the end must, so far as social morality is concerned, consist in an application of sociological knowledge. Ethics would not, indeed, even so, be exactly a branch of the science, but it would be an art based on the science and having as its fundamental principle the highest generalisation of the science, modified so as to take on an ethical import.

It would still, I think, be *formally* important to insist that this fusion of studies can only be rationally effected by the judgment that identifies the sociological and the ethical ends; and that this judgment is not one to which the moralist can be cogently driven by any sociological arguments. For the argument that if he declines to accept it he places himself in opposition to the process of nature is only forcible if we introduce a theological significance into our notion of nature, attributing to it design and authority; and this introduction of theology carries the sociologist beyond the limits of his special science. But, though it would be formally important to insist on this, the fusion would still be complete on the two hypotheses, sociological and ethical, above stated.

But neither of these hypotheses can be accepted as more than partially true.

Take the ethical question first—can we regard the *mere preservation* of the life of a human being, or of any number of human beings combined in a society, as an ultimate and paramount end and standard of right action, apart from any consideration of the quality of the life preserved? I appeal confidently on this point—it is the only appeal possible—to the deliberate judgment of thoughtful persons, when the question is clearly set before it. Doubtless a fundamentally important part of the function of morality consists in maintaining habits and sentiments preservative of individual and social life; but this is because, as Aristotle said, in order to live well we must live. It does not follow that life is simply the ultimate end; since if all life were as little desirable as some portions of it have been in the experience of most of us, we should judge anything tending to its preservation as unmitigatedly bad. It is not life simply, but good or desirable life, that is the ethical end; and though—as all students of your school will know—there is still much controversy as to the precise content of the notion " good " in this application, it is a controversy which ethics has got to work through, and in settling which it cannot derive any material aid from sociology.

But, again, the sociological hypothesis seems to me equally unacceptable when put forward as a complete explanation of the facts to which it relates.

The view that morality has been developed under the influence of the struggle for existence among social organisms as a part of the complex adaptation of such organisms to the conditions of their struggling existence is, I think, a probable conjecture as regards the earlier stages of its development in prehistoric times. It is reasonable to suppose that the observance of duties to fellow-tribesmen within a primitive tribe tended to the survival of the tribe in the struggle for tribal existence, by increasing the internal coherence of the tribe and the effective co-operation of its members. But it is not reasonable to accept this as the main explanation of the evolution of morality even in primitive ages, because it is certainly not a cause that has had any great effect on the important changes in moral beliefs that have taken place in historic times. Take one of the greatest of such changes—that resulting in the conversion of the Greco-Roman civilised world to Christianity.

Not only would it be obviously absurd to attribute this change to the struggle for existence among civilised societies; there is not even any adequate evidence that it had a preservative effect on the political society in which the conversion took place. I should conjecture that before Constantine its operation was the other way, considering the passive alienation of primitive Christians from the secular society in which they lived, over which they believed a swift and sudden destruction to be impending. And, though this split between religion and the State was healed by Constantine, it is difficult, even after this, to see any tendency in Christianity to preserve the Roman empire, or even arrest its decline and fall. The Christian empire seems simply to continue the process tending towards surrender to the barbarians outside.

In short, the sociological hypothesis that I am now considering—so far as it is offered as a complete explanation of moral evolution—seems to me due to the onesidedness of view which I before noted as a source of sociological error: the concentration of attention on the physical side of social life and its primitive conditions, unduly ignoring its spiritual side and the later stages of its development. And this is true, not of morality only, but of the development of knowledge, of art,—indeed of all the chief elements of that ideal good which we most deeply value in what we call the progress of civilisation. We cannot say of the most signal contributions to this progress that they are always decisively preservative of the particular nation in which they are made; if we are to view them as adjustments of means to a social end, it can be no lesser or more limited end than the welfare of humanity at large.

I now turn to consider an objection that may be taken against the whole line of thought that I have adopted. I may be asked, 'Why insist on this artificial separation between the subjects of ethics and sociology? Why not allow the development of both to be influenced by the natural play of thought between the two? Why attempt the impossible task of keeping different portions of our thought on human relations in separate water-tight compartments?'

To objections of this kind my answer is,—First, that I fully recognise the propriety of the demand that our ethical and our sociological thought should be brought into clear and consistent relations: indeed, I regard the harmonising of different sciences and studies as the special task of philosophy. I think, however, that the impulse to put together different lines of thought requires methodical restraint, because one of the most fruitful sources of error in philosophy has been over-hasty synthesis and combination without sufficient previous analysis of the elements combined. But, secondly, in order to avoid this error, I by no means wish to prevent altogether mutual influence, interpenetration of ideas, between the two studies I am now considering. I only urge that it should be carefully watched and criticised, in order that it may not be the source of confusion, which is especially dangerous in the condition of controversy and conflict of opinion on fundamental points from which neither sociology nor ethics has as yet successfully emerged. To illustrate this, let me consider first the current influence on ethics of sociological conceptions. I will take the fundamental conception of the social organism.

Although as a utilitarian I cannot regard mere preservation of the social organism as the ultimate end and supreme standard of right action, I recognise the value of the conception in making our general view of duty, whether framed on utilitarian or any other principles, fuller and truer. In any case it is important for an individual that he should not conceive himself merely as a member of an aggregate, capable of benefiting or injuring by his actions other individuals as such, but also as a member of a body formed of individual human beings bound into a whole by complex mutual relations; a whole of which the parts, whether individuals or groups, have functions diverse and mutually dependent. Adopting this conception, he will, whatever view he takes of the ultimate ethical end, judge actions largely by their effect in promoting or impeding the coherent and harmonious co-operation of different organs of society, and in strengthening or weakening habits and sentiments that tend to the efficient performance of social functions.

All this is highly important. But some writers seem drawn by the interest of the novel conception to regard it as supplying a complete determinant of duty. That is, it seems to be supposed that adequate guidance to particular duties is given in all cases by the facts of social relations. 'A man,' it is said, 'finds himself as a member of a society in certain relations to other human beings. He is son, brother, husband and father, neighbour, citizen. These relations are all facts, and his duties lie in fulfilling the claims that are essential parts of these relations.' Now, no doubt the claims or conscious expectations connected with these relations, and the common recognition of these claims by other members of the society than those primarily concerned are important social facts. But it can hardly be maintained that it is an absolute duty to fulfil all such expectations, as they are to a certain extent vague, varying, liable to conflict with each other, sometimes unreasonable, sometimes sanctioned by custom, but by custom "more honoured in the breach than in the observance." In short, so far as these claims are actual facts they are not indisputably valid, and do not form a harmonious system, and the study of them as facts does not give a criterion of their validity and a means of eliminating conflict. In considering which of the demands made on us by our fellow-men have to be satisfied and which repudiated, and, when two conflict, which is to be postponed, we require a system of principles of right conduct which the study of social facts as such cannot alone give, but which it is the business of ethics to give.

On the other hand, just as this wide and quasi-architectonic use of sociological conception in ethics leads to a mistaken attempt to get the ideal out of the actual, so the converse influence of ethics on sociology leads to equally mistaken attempts to get the ideal into the actual,—*i.e.* to predict a future state of society in harmony with ethical ideas without any adequate support in scientific induction from the known facts of past social evolution.

In criticising this 'evolutionary optimism,' as we may call it, I ought to explain that I am not opposing optimism as a philosophical doctrine. I am not myself an optimist; but I have a great respect for the belief that, in spite of appearances to the contrary, the world now in process of evolution, is ultimately destined to reveal itself as perfectly free from evil and the best possible world. What I would urge is that, in the present state of our knowledge, this belief should be kept as a theological doctrine, or, if you like, a philosophical postulate, and that it should not be allowed to mix itself with the process of scientific inference to the future from the past.

The sociologist who brings his optimism into his sociological reasonings must, I think, find the tendency almost irresistible to give a one-sided prominence to those facts in the past history of society which make for a favourable view of its future progress, and to ignore those facts which make for the opposite conclusion. It is only in this way that I can account for Mr. Spencer's belief, regarded by him as a strictly scientific inference from a survey of historical facts, that the evolution of human society will ultimately bring about a condition of social relations in which the voluntary actions of normal human beings will produce "pleasure unalloyed by pain anywhere." And, similarly, I think that his hypothetical conclusion that "there needs but a continuance of absolute peace externally, and a vigorous insistence on non-aggression internally, to insure the moulding of men into a form naturally characterised by all the virtues," has not really been reached by a strictly sociological method; but that the sociological reasoning which has led him to it has been influenced and modified throughout by an individualistic ideal formed prior to systematic sociological study.

I seem to find this confusing effect of 'evolutionary optimism' in an even more extreme though vaguer form in a good deal of popular discourse about progress. The believer in 'a good time coming' often seems inclined to believe that what is coming is good because it is coming, no less than that what is good is coming because it is good. Now, granting the latter proposition to be well founded, it does not in any way imply the former; granting that man is destined to unalloyed bliss, still his road to this bright goal may be in parts very devious and distressful; and some of the most distressful turns that would otherwise be found in it may be avoidable evils, but only avoidable by vigorous resistance to present tendencies of change. This seems obvious enough: but it is an obvious truth which is liable to be missed because the opposite error is not explicitly propounded, but lurks in a vague acquiescence in the drift of events.

[In reprinting this essay one or two sentences have been omitted as repeating too closely what has already been said in the essay on the *Scope and Method of Economic Science*: but mere repetition of phrases (like the epigram in the last paragraph about 'a good time coming,' which appears also on p. 218) it seemed needless to remove.—ED.]

XII

THE THEORY OF CLASSICAL EDUCATION

(From *Essays on a Liberal Education*, edited by F. W. Farrar.
Macmillan and Co., 1867.)

IT is my wish to examine, as closely and completely as I am able to do within the limits of an essay, the theory of classical education: meaning thereby the body of reasons, which, taken together, may be supposed to persuade the intelligence of the country, that the present course of instruction in the Greek and Latin languages and literature is the best thing that can be applied in the minds of English boys, in the year 1867 A.D.,—or at least better than anything that it has been proposed to substitute for it. Such a theory is somewhat difficult to extricate and expound in the case of this as of other institutions established long ago, in obedience to an impulse that has ceased to operate, under intellectual and social conditions which have since been profoundly modified. It is always, I think, a shallow view of history which represents such institutions as existing by *vis inertiæ* alone; *vis inertiæ* is a blind and irrational force, which we have to calculate and allow for in explaining to ourselves why institutions exist but it is powerless (especially in an age like our own), unless combined with a respectable array of more rational forces. These forces are found in the convictions of intelligent and open-minded men who work the system, that it is supplying actual needs of the present age, is doing good work which the existing society wants done. But since it has never been incumbent upon any set of men, as a distinct and inevitable duty, to set forth what these needs and this work are; since it is evident to the most superficial inquirer that the system was originally established— or grew up—to meet very different needs, and to do very different work, its real *raison d'être* as an existing institution has to be elicited in the irregular, and, to a speculative mind, unsatisfactory way of volunteer conservative advocacy. The reasoning of advocates is generally apt to be vague, sweeping, rhetorical: but the arguments constructed to support what exists are perhaps the worst, as they are constructed under less pressure, with less felt need of intellectual exertion, and are inevitably addressed to the more docile and less critical portion of the public. A good reason, no doubt, is none the worse for being made to order; still it is natural to regard such reasons with suspicion, and the suspicion is often justified by closer examination. For, whatever be the cause, the arguments for classical education are often stated, even by able men, in a manner hardly worthy of their ability. They seem often so trivial and shallow, so partial and fragmentary, so vague and sweeping; they seem to suggest such narrow views of culture, such imperfect acquaintance with the intellectual development of mankind, so slight an effort to comprehend all the conditions of the infinitely important problem with which they deal. At the same time, the advantage that experience gives can hardly be too highly estimated. The result of handing over education to the most comprehensive theorist, with whatever gifts of lucid expression, would be, I doubt not, disastrous. The history of education is the battle-ground and burial-ground of impracticable theories: and one who studies it is soon taught to abate his constructive self-confidence, and to endeavour humbly to learn the lessons and harmonise the results of experience. But a teacher's experience must be measured not by the length of time that he has been engaged in his work, but by the amount of analytical faculty and intellectual labour that he has applied to the materials with which it has furnished him; by the way in which he has availed himself of the opportunities of observation and experiment which he, beyond all other men, has possessed. It not unfrequently happens—and perhaps it is not surprising—that even successful schoolmasters, immersed in the business of their profession, are found to have learned the theory of what they are doing casually and long ago from other men, and to have let it remain in their minds in undigested fragments, not really brought to the test of, and therefore not modified by, experience. When such men become advocates, we soon detect their incapacity to give us any real instruction. Of course, many of a very different stamp have written in defence of classical education, and probably in the works and pamphlets that now exist on the subject, amounting to a considerable literature, all possible arguments have been brought forward. Still the wish that forms itself in the mind on the perusal of these works is, that the period of advocacy should if possible now close, and that not one or two, but a number of intelligent educators should take the arguments provided for them, revolve them carefully, and by close, sober, accurate observation, obtain their exact value; and then express this in carefully guarded and limited statements. The very mistakes and contradictions of such observers would elicit truth, and we should soon feel a legitimate confidence, which we can hardly feel now, that our systematic treatment of youthful intellect, if not absolutely the best conceivable, was at least approximately the best attainable.

In beginning to treat of classical education, it is perhaps desirable to make a protest against the notion which seems to prevail in some quarters, that the course of instruction which now bears that name is an organic whole, from which it is impossible to cut off any part, without converting the rest into something of very inferior value. A boy is considered to have been made a complete classical scholar when he has been taught to translate elegantly and correctly from Latin and Greek into English prose; to compose correct and elegant Latin and Greek prose, and Latin and Greek verse. Classical study, the result of which does not include all these accomplishments, is supposed to be deficient in thoroughness.

Now there seems no adequate reason why Latin and Greek should be regarded as a sort of linguistic Siamese twins, which nature has joined together, and which would wither if separated. No doubt, the study of the one is a good preparation for the study of the other; but it has no special need of it for its own completeness. The qualities of the two languages, and the reasons for which it is desirable to study them, are in many respects very different: and it is only by a palpable looseness of thought that they can be joined together in discussion as frequently as they are. When, for instance, Dr. Woolley[1] says these two languages are the "master-keys that unlock the noblest tongues of Europe," he forgets how little Greek has to do with any of these tongues, except in forming their scientific terminology. When again the "severe regularity" of both languages is eulogised, it is forgotten how strong the tendency is in Greek to deviate from the normal type of the sentence, and to frame constructions which are not difficult to understand, but which can be brought under no grammatical rules. Moreover, the assumption is often made that, because there are strong arguments to prove that the thorough learning of *one* dead language is a valuable element of education, and that this language ought to be *either* Greek or Latin, therefore there is justification for teaching both Greek and Latin —I will not say thoroughly, but so as to engross the lion's share of time and trouble.

Again, it seems undeniable that a person may learn to read even a dead and difficult language with correctness and ease combined, without ever attempting to compose elegantly or even idiomatically in it; without, in fact, writing more than a sufficient number of exercises to fix thoroughly in his mind the more important part of the grammar. Many students of Sanskrit, Hebrew, and other languages do not do as much as this, and yet obtain a sufficiently firm grasp, for their purposes, of the languages they study. The fact

---

[1] Late Principal of the University of Sydney.

T

seems to be, that if the sole end in learning a language be to read it easily, with correct apprehension of its meaning, the only means absolutely necessary is to read a great deal, and take care that the meaning is correctly apprehended. But perhaps the most singular assumption is, that it is an essential part of the study of Greek and Latin to cultivate the faculty of writing what ought to be poetry in these tongues. No one of the large and increasing body of students, who concentrate their energies upon other ancient languages: no one of the professors, who elucidate with the most subtle and delicate apprehension the most obscure and difficult poems in these languages — ever dreams of trying to develop such a faculty, except as the merest pastime. The composition of verses, and of elegant prose, may, or may not, be a desirable element of education; but these exercises must be defended independently on their own merits, not as forming an essential part of instruction in Greek and Latin.

In the discussions on classical education, we find debated, and decided generally, though not always, in the same way, a preliminary question of great importance— namely, whether education ought to be natural or artificial. I use these as the most convenient words, but they require some explanation. By a "natural" education is meant, that which teaches a boy things in which, for any reason whatever, he will be likely to take an interest in after life. It may be, that for commercial or professional reasons only, he will be forced to take an interest in certain subjects; in that case his education must at some time, and to some extent, begin to be commercial or professional, and not liberal. One can hardly be content that any human being should be trained entirely for his *métier*, and have no share of what may be called a liberal education,—for every human being will have at least so much leisure, as to make it important for himself and for others, that he should be taught to use it rightly. But taking the term in its ordinary sense, and applying it to those who are able to defer the period of professional study till at least the close of boyhood, a liberal education has for its object to impart the highest culture, to lead youths to the most full, vigorous, and harmonious exercise, according to the best ideal attainable, of their active, cognitive, and æsthetic faculties. What this ideal, this culture may be, is not easy to determine; but when we have determined it, and analysed it into its component parts, a natural education is evidently that which gives the rudiments of these parts in whatever order is found the best; which familiarises a boy with the same facts that it will be afterwards important for him to know; makes him imbibe the same ideas that are afterwards to form the furniture of his mind; imparts to him the same accomplishments and dexterities that he will afterwards desire to possess. An artificial education is one which, in order that a man may ultimately know one thing, teaches him another, which gives the rudiments of some learning or accomplishment, that the man in the maturity of his culture will be content to forget. This is the extreme case, but in proportion as the system of education approximates to this, in proportion as the subjects in which the boy is instructed occupy a small share of the thoughts of the cultivated man, so far that system may be called artificial, rather than natural. Now I think it must be allowed that, however much, historically and actually, the *onus probandi* may rest on those who oppose an artificial system of education, and wish to substitute a more natural one, yet, logically, the position of the combatants is reversed, and the *onus probandi* rests on those who maintain the artificial system. If a boy is to be taught things which, it is distinctly understood, are to be forgotten, the good that they do him during the time that they remain in his mind ought to be very clearly demonstrated. In order to escape the severity of this demonstration, the advocates of classical education are sometimes inclined to make an obviously unfair assumption. They assume that "training the mind" is a process essentially incompatible with "imparting useful knowledge." And no doubt the attack on classical education has frequently been of so vulgar and ignorant a character, that this assumption might be, if not fairly, at least safely, made. The clamour has been, 'useful knowledge at any rate, and let the training of the mind take care of itself.' Against assailants of this sort the defence of classics was, and deserved to be, victorious. But the question is now posed in a suitable form. It is now urged that the process of teaching useful knowledge affords as valuable a training in method as any other kind of teaching. However difficult it may be to appraise exactly two different kinds of training, this task distinctly devolves on those who would teach knowledge that they admit to be useless.

But in the case of classics the uselessness is by no means admitted. Though I think it may be fairly said that classical education is supported chiefly as an artificial system, it is supported partly as a natural system. Though many of its advocates would urge that it ought to be maintained for the training alone, even though the knowledge imparted were all to be forgotten, the majority urge also that this knowledge is in various ways of permanent value. In estimating the utility of the results of classical study, we naturally range these results under two heads: the knowledge of language gained, and the acquaintance with literature. The latter is the more splendid result, that which affords more scope to the eloquence of advocates, and is more impressive to the outside world; but the former is the more certain and universal acquisition, and the one upon which most stress is laid by educators. Whatever else is denied, the bitterest reformer cannot deny that boys do acquire some knowledge of two dead languages. We may therefore fitly commence our examination by inquiring what this knowledge is worth.

In the first place, although the classicists are, on the whole, the staunchest supporters of a liberal as opposed to a professional education, they also point out that a knowledge of Greek and Latin is useful professionally. This line of argument has been taken by able and accomplished men;[1]

[1] I may mention Sir W. Hamilton (*Edinburgh Review*, October 1836. See his *Discussions on Philosophy*, etc.), and the Rev. W. G. Clark (*Cambridge Essays*, 1855).

but I am not sure that it has, on the whole, been of service to the cause. The professional advantages are found to be unequally distributed among the different professions; and in some cases there is an almost comical discrepancy between the labour expended and the utility acquired. A clergyman has to interpret the Greek Testament, and therefore it is important that he should be able to read it in the original. It might, perhaps, from a professional point of view, be better that he should be familiarised a little less with the Attic, and a little more with the Hellenistic dialect; but still Greek is, after all, Greek.[1] When, however, this point is strongly pressed, we cannot avoid contrasting the great anxiety shown that a clergyman should know Greek, with the complacent indifference with which his total ignorance of Hebrew is usually contemplated.

We may admit, again, that a lawyer—even an English lawyer—ought to be able to read Roman law in the original. It is not clear that he is likely to advance himself in his profession by the study, but it is for the benefit of society that he should engage in it. He ought, therefore, to be acquainted with Latin grammar, and a certain portion of the Latin vocabulary. As to doctors, can we gravely urge that they ought to understand the language in which their prescriptions are written, and that they find it instructive to read Galen and Hippocrates in Greek?[2] To men of science, it is pointed out that their ever-increasing technical terminology is systematically formed from Greek and Latin words. This is true; and it is also true that a man of science might obtain a perfect grasp of this terminology by means of a list of words that he would learn in a day, and the use of a dictionary that he might acquire in a week. It may be further remarked,

[1] Some writers seem to extend the necessity of learning Greek, for the purposes of religion, much more indefinitely. "No religious nation," says Mr. Thring, "can give up Greek." I do not suppose that Mr. Thring means more than that it is desirable that there should be, besides the clergy, a body of learned persons studying Greek (and Hebrew), so as to keep the study safe from any professional narrowness. In this I should heartily agree. But it is a very aristocratic view of religion that makes it depend in any degree on a knowledge of Greek.
[2] See *Cambridge Essays*, 1855.

that though a clergyman might conceivably dispense with
Latin, a learned clergyman, one from whom original
research in the field of ecclesiastical tradition is expected,
cannot dispense with it; and generally every antiquarian
student, every one who inquires into the early history of
any European nation, or of any department of modern
science, will require to read Latin with ease. Science has
at length broken its connexion with what was so long the
learned language of Europe; but it is still the key to what,
in contradistinction to science, is usually called erudition.
To sum up: Greek is of use (we may say indispensable) to
clergymen: Latin to lawyers and learned men. The
other infinitesimal fragments of utility may be disregarded
for our present purpose; and finally, in all these cases, it is
only the power of reading that is of use, and not that of
writing the language.

Much more importance is claimed for the knowledge of
the classical languages as an element of a truly liberal
culture: as the best introduction to the study of Philology,
as including the best instruction in the universal principles
of Grammar, and as indispensable to a real knowledge of
English and of other modern languages. It seems rather
important to attach as clear and precise ideas as we can to
the words "Philology" and "Grammar": as the looseness
with which they are sometimes used creates an inevitable confusion of thought. Grammar is sometimes regarded as either
an introduction to, or an extension of, Logic. It is called
"the logic of common speech."[1] Now it would appear that
Grammar, in this sense, includes only a small portion of
what is taught as the grammar of any particular languages.
It teaches some of the facts and laws of thought and
expression which Logic also teaches (both studies being
united by a common root), and also certain other facts and
laws, which the theory of syllogistic reasoning is not obliged
to notice, but which are equally universal, and—if I may
use the term without provoking a controversy — equally
necessary. Such are—the distinctions of substantives and

---

[1] Report of the Public Schools Commission, published in 1864.

adjectives, of transitive and intransitive verbs, the existence and classification of the relations expressed by the other parts of speech, the distinctions of tenses and voices, of principal and subordinate, declarative and conditional sentences, etc. It is clearly impracticable to separate this part of any particular grammar from the rest : because it is difficult to say what is, and what is not, universal : since each man is biassed in favour of the distinctions which his mother tongue brings into prominence ; and since there are many distinctions, which, when they are once pointed out, we not only see to be true, but cannot conceive how we could ever have overlooked. The most philosophical branch of Philology is that which busies itself with such real but not indispensable (what we may call potentially universal) distinctions of thought : collecting them when they lie scattered in the grammar of particular languages, and clearly defining, arranging, and comparing them. This seems a study both extremely interesting in itself, and intimately connected with—we may even say a branch of —mental philosophy. And, no doubt, in learning Latin or Greek many such distinctions are taught to an English boy, of which the closest observation of his mother tongue would leave him ignorant. But it cannot be denied that nine-tenths of his time is occupied in storing up facts which in no sense belong to universal grammar : in learning, not new shades and distinctions of thought, but simply special ways of expressing old shades and distinctions, facts which are so patent in his own language, that Latin instruction is an extremely tedious and circuitous process of teaching him to observe them. In learning the usage of a new language we always find some things which seem to us convenient and rational, and which we should like if possible to incorporate into our own : but the greater part of what we learn appears accidental and arbitrary, while a good deal we regard as provokingly useless and troublesome. There is probably always a scientific explanation of this last, as the result of ages of growth, but there is often no philosophical explanation of it as belonging to a present instrument of thought. When, therefore, we are told that "the principles of universal grammar which are necessary as the foundation of all philosophical acquaintance with every language, carry the young scholar forward till his mind is deeply imbued with the literature,"[1] etc., we see what large deductions must be made from this statement. A boy does no doubt learn principles of universal grammar which he will always desire to retain: but he learns them along with a large assortment of formulæ which, when he has once ceased to study Latin, he will be willing as soon as possible to forget.

By Philology is generally understood the study of language historically, of its changes, its laws of growth and development. It deals chiefly with the vocabulary and accidence of languages, as distinguished from the philosophical study of Grammar, of which I have spoken, that deals chiefly with the syntax. It is a study to which the thorough learning of either Latin or Greek forms an excellent introduction; but Latin from its relation to English possesses peculiar advantages in this respect; and these advantages would be much increased if French were learnt along with Latin, and every opportunity taken of pointing out the mutual relations of the three languages, Latin, French, and English. No cultivated man can fail to feel the interest and charm of Philology, or would wish to say a word in its disparagement. Its materials are abundant, its processes productive, the aid it affords to History and Anthropology most valuable. Still it must be classed among the sciences that are studied from "pure curiosity"[2] alone; and however noble an impulse we feel this to be, however true it is that any great increase of its force marks a step in human progress, yet such studies must be ranked, in importance to society, below sciences like Physics, Chemistry, Astronomy, animal and vegetable Physiology, which (besides the gratification they afford to curiosity) have had, and promise still to have, the greatest influence on the material welfare of the human race. And if we cannot

[1] Dr. Moberly.
[2] I use the word in the more elevated signification which the corresponding term in French bears.

(as we certainly cannot) include all the sciences in the curriculum of general education, it seems (from this point of view) that those studied from pure curiosity are precisely those that ought to be left to students of special bias and faculty, every care being taken to yield to this bias and foster this faculty. If then it appear desirable on other grounds that boys should learn Latin (or Greek), the fact that they will be thereby initiated into the study of Philology is a real additional advantage; but taken by itself it does not constitute a very strong reason for learning either language.

We are told, however, in the strongest and most unqualified terms, that we cannot understand our own language without a knowledge of Latin and Greek: and this in two ways—both in respect of its grammar, and in respect of its vocabulary. This claims to be so cogent a proof of the direct utility of these ancient languages, that it deserves our most serious consideration. We shall find, I think, that it has been urged by the advocates of classics with more than usual exaggeration. The limit of extravagance seems to be reached in the following utterance of Professor Pillans (which is quoted with approbation in the Report of the Public Schools Commission): "It (English) is, besides, so uncompounded in its structure, so patchwork-like in its composition, so broken down into particles, so scanty in its inflections, and so simple in its fundamental rules of construction, that it is *next to impossible to have a true grammatical notion of it, or to form any correct ideas of grammar and philology at all*, without being able to compare and contrast it with another language, and that other of a character essentially different." Why the rules of a language should be hard to teach because they are simple, because the character of the language is analytical and not synthetical, because in it the relations of words and sentences are expressed almost entirely by particles, without the aid of inflection: why in such a language it should be "impossible" to convey "correct ideas," not only of the facts and principles of universal grammar (which are

ex vi termini[1] common to all languages), but also of the
formulæ in which its special usage is summed up, is not
attempted to be shown. That a person who had learnt
English grammar only would have a very limited idea of
grammar is undeniable, but it is obvious that his idea might
be correct as far as it went. The learning of the rules of Latin
usage, would, no doubt, sharpen our perception of the rules of
English usage ; and this indirect utility (which belongs rather
to the second part of our subject) I do not wish to undervalue.
And it may be advantageous to excite a boy's interest in the
laws of language first, by making him feel that, without the
observation of these laws, he cannot obtain the results that
are demanded from him. But to assert that Grammar could
not be taught analytically, instead of synthetically, seems
contrary to common sense and experience alike.[2]

When we take the vocabulary, as well as the grammar,
of English into our view, we find still more startling statements as to the difficulty of mastering our mother tongue.
Mr. Thring tells us that "it is scarcely possible to speak
the English language with accuracy or precision, without a
knowledge of Latin and Greek." "It is not possible to
have a masterly freedom in the use of words, or a critical
judgment capable of supporting its decision by proof without
such knowledge." These are the words of a vigorous
writer, and their substance I find stated, though less
extravagantly, by several others. They seem to me well to
illustrate the ignorance of the real nature of language, and
the laws of its apprehension, in which our long tutelage to
Latin and Greek has left us.

[1] As the word universal is generally used, I have indicated another application of it, in the signification, as I have expressed it, of "potentially universal."

[2] Some persons have a vague idea that it is not worth while trying to teach English and some other modern languages systematically, because they are "hybrid" ; as if a language could be "hybrid" in its grammar, however mixed in its vocabulary, and as if Latin was not hybrid, in the same sense, though not to the same extent, as English. Others cannot divest themselves of the notion that familiar phenomena must be simple, and seem almost irritated when shown how varied and complex are the rules of using their vernacular. For instance, a French writer complains "l'on raffine la grammaire française : on questionne un enfant . . . sur des distinctions subtiles auxquelles Pascal et Bossuet n'ont jamais songé" : as if Virgil ever thought of a tertiary predicate, or Thucydides of the peculiar usage of ὅπως μή.

The fact is, that the study of Latin (for Greek, except in respect of scientific terminology, has much less to do with the question, and would hardly have been placed on a par with Latin here, but for the hasty and random way in which the stock arguments on this subject are continually repeated) cannot tell us what the English language is—it can only help us to understand how it has come to be what it is. In order to learn to speak English with accuracy and precision, we have but one rule to follow,—to pay strict attention to usage. The authority of usage, the usage of cultivated persons, is in all disputed points paramount. The history of language is the history of continual change, and just as in learning Latin and Greek (or any other language), the tiro finds a knowledge of derivation frequently puzzling and misleading, the usage of words having often strayed from their original signification by long routes that can be only conjecturally traced : so in the case of words that we have derived from the Latin, the meaning of the Latin term has often been so modified, that it would be the merest pedantry to pay attention to it. No doubt we are all liable to make mistakes in our own language, especially in the case of terms which we meet with so rarely that the natural process by which we learn the rest of our mother tongue cannot completely operate. And as these words are often derived from the Latin, a Latin scholar has a certain additional protection against such mistakes: he will naturally fall into them rather less than another man who pays no particular attention to the subject. But he is liable to fall into a different set of errors if he ever attempts, as pedants have attempted, to make his knowledge of Latin override English usage. Mr. Thring regrets the loss of the original meaning in the case of words like "edify" and "tribulation"; and no doubt the historic interest in the derivation of these words is very great, and the non-classical reader has every reason to be grateful to books like those of Archbishop Trench, that open this new field of interest to him. But for a man in search of accuracy and precision, seriously to try and shackle himself by attention to these lost significations—to refuse, for instance, to use the word "tribulation" except when the idea of "threshing" seemed suitable, would be pedantic frivolity. To the masters of English style, natural instinct and unconscious tact as to the living force of language is the chief and primary guide; while English dictionaries and English classics are the only corrective and court of appeal in case this tact breaks down. In short, the application of Latin to the historical interpretation of English is a branch of Philology—a most entertaining and instructive branch—which I should be glad to place within the reach of every one, but which must be regarded, like the rest of Philology, as an intellectual luxury. When we are threatened, that, without a knowledge of Latin and Greek, our language would be to us "a strange collection of inexpressive symbols,"[1] we are at first alarmed; but on reflection, we perceive that our verbal signs would become "inexpressive," in the sense that they would only express the things signified; and the menace does not seem so terrible. We reflect also, that the historical study of language is of very modern growth, and that Greek and Latin must have been "strange collections of inexpressive symbols" to the writers of the master-pieces and models which we are invited to cherish.[2]

Some exception to what I have said ought to be made in the case of scientific nomenclature; because, as this is the one part of our language of which the growth is deliberate, and determined by the learned—not natural, and determined by the mass of the nation—it has a living and

[1] *Edinburgh Review*, cxx.
[2] Mr. Joseph Payne, in a pamphlet remarkable for sobriety of statement, breadth of view, and close observation of the educational process, brings forward a somewhat different argument to show the advantage a Latin scholar has in reading English. He quotes several uses of English words derived from the Latin, in our older authors (such as 'civil,' 'resentment,' 'prevent'), which a classical scholar understands at a glance, but which puzzle or mislead a man uneducated in classics. But these uses ought to be found in dictionaries, and noticed by commentators. Every man reading older authors in his vernacular ought to know that a part of their vocabulary is archaic, and ought to be on the watch for the archaic terms. I cannot think that the trouble is very considerable of acquiring as complete an acquaintance with these archaisms as is necessary for literary purposes. A knowledge of Latin would only save a part of this trouble; much more would be done by the direct teaching of English literature which I advocate in this essay.

progressive connexion with Latin and Greek which no other part of the language has. But even here it is necessary to make distinctions. It seems too sweeping to say that "no man can expound any subject-matter with scientific precision unless he is acquainted with the *etymologies* of the terms he employs."[1] The newer terms of scientific phraseology have been formed generally in a systematic way, upon fixed principles, and we may assume that, for the future, all additional technical terms will be so formed. Therefore, though it is not absolutely indispensable to the scientific student to possess the key to this phraseology (as he can learn the meaning of each word from its usage and place in the system to which it belongs), it will save him a great deal of useless trouble if he does possess it. But in the case of many of the older terms of science, formed irregularly or on false principles, a knowledge of the derivation will be useless or misleading. They have often great interest for the historical student : to the scientific man, the sooner they become mere counters the better. I have already indicated with what ease men of science might learn all the Greek and Latin words necessary to give them the required key. Instruction in such words ought to form a distinct part of the direct teaching of English, to which all these arguments for learning Latin and Greek seem to point as an educational desideratum.

I have said that Latin was important chiefly with a view to the historical study of our own language, and not in order to obtain a complete grasp of it, as a living instrument of thought. It ought to be added, that though Latin forms one element in this historical study, it forms *only* one element, and that the other elements—and, indeed, we may say the study itself—have been surprisingly neglected in our educational system. Hardly in our Universities does any one dream of learning Early English, and though we teach some French and German in our schools, we teach them merely colloquially and practically, without any reference to their historical development or their linguistic

[1] *Cambridge Essays*, 1855.

relations. This neglect (which some efforts have been made to repair during late years) will be commented upon more in detail elsewhere in this volume.[1] I have referred to the point here chiefly because it affords an example how the arguments for learning classics, being "made to order," are found, as far as they are worth anything, to prove more than they were intended to prove, and to support, not the existing course of instruction, but something of which that would form only one part.

In the eyes of many persons, however, the most important of the direct utilities supposed to be conveyed by a classical education is still that for which a classical education was originally instituted—acquaintance with the Greek and Latin literatures. In the first place, just as the ancient languages were called a master-key to unlock all modern European tongues, so the ancient writings are said to be indispensable to the understanding of all the best modern books. "If," says Dr. Donaldson, "the old classical literature were swept away, the moderns would in many cases become unintelligible, and in all lose most of their characteristic charms." A moment's reflection will show this to be a most strange and palpable exaggeration. For instance, Milton is the most learned of our poets: nay, as a poet he is generally said to be obtrusively learned—learned to a fault. Yet how grotesque an absurdity it seems to assert that *Paradise Lost* would "lose most of its characteristic charm" to a reader who did not understand the classical allusions and similes. The real state of the case seems analogous to that which we have just discussed. A knowledge of classics is indispensable, not to the general reader, but to the historical student of modern authors: without it he can enter into their ideas and feelings, but not the antecedents which determined those ideas and feelings. He cannot reproduce the intellectual *milieu* in which they lived; he can understand what they said, but not how they came to say it. But for the general reader, who has no wish to go so deep, classical knowledge does not do much more than save some

[1] [The volume in which this essay originally appeared.—ED.]

trouble of referring to dictionaries and histories, and some ignorance of quotations which is rather conventionally than really inconvenient. Many allusions to the classics explain themselves; many others are explained by the context; and the number of those that remain incomprehensible to a person who has read histories of Greece and Rome, and knows as much about the classics as he must inevitably pick up from a good course of English literature, is not very considerable. We may grant that "literature can only be studied *thoroughly* by going to its source."[1] But the conception conveyed in this word *thoroughly* assumes an exalted standard of reading, which, if carried out consistently, would involve an overwhelming encyclopedic study of literature. For the modern authors whom the stream of fame has floated down to us, and whom we do read, contain numerous allusions to preceding and contemporary authors whom we do not think of reading, and require, in order to be *thoroughly* understood, numerous illustrations from preceding and contemporary history which we have no leisure to procure. We content ourselves with the fragmentary lights of a casual commentator. I do not see that it would be so dreadful if classical allusions were apprehended by the general reader in the same twilight manner. It may be very desirable that we should read everything more accurately and thoroughly; but let us have one weight and one balance. The historical study of literature, for the completeness of which I allow classics to be indispensable, is a most interesting and improving pursuit, and one which I hope will gain votaries yearly. But, after all, the branch of this study which seems to have the greatest utility, if the space we can allot to it is limited, is surely that which explains to us (as far as is possible) the intellectual life of our own age; which teaches us the antecedents of the ideas and feelings among which, and in which, we shall live and move. Such a course, at this moment of history, would naturally contain a much larger modern than ancient element: it would be felt in framing it more imperatively

[1] Dr. Temple.

necessary to represent French, German, and English thought of recent centuries, than to introduce us to any of the older influences that combined to determine our immediate intellectual antecedents.

But the intrinsic value of Latin and Greek literatures seems to many to outweigh all other considerations. It is true that these literatures are no longer supposed to contain all knowledge; even their claim to give the best teaching in mental, ethical, and political philosophy, the last relic of their old prestige, is rapidly passing away : still they undeniably convey, with great vividness, a knowledge of what the Greeks and Romans were, how they felt, thought, spoke, and acted; and some persons of great eminence consider it of the highest importance that Greek and Roman life in all its phases should be kept continually before the mind of the modern world.[1] Persons of very opposite views agree in inculcating this. Clerical advocates tell us that to feel the real force of Christianity, we must acquaint ourselves with the vices of the ancient world, and learn how impotent, ethically speaking, the unassisted human intellect is ; while enthusiasts of a different stamp point to the narrow rigidity, the withering pettiness, the complacent humdrum of our modern life, and urge that ancient literature teaches just that passionate love of country, love of freedom, love of knowledge, love of beauty, for which they pant. I do not wish to undervalue either kind of instruction, but I cannot say that I see the absolute want of either : I cannot but think that if we were debarred from Latin and Greek, a careful teaching of modern history and a careful selection of modern literature would supply our youth with all the stimulus, example, and warning that they require. Further, even if it be granted that we cannot dispense with the lessons of the ancient world, it is easy to exaggerate the disadvantages of learning them through the medium of modern languages. We must remember how many excellent translations we have of ancient authors, some of which

[1] This has been urged by Mr. Mill with his usual impressiveness, and is illustrated in a beautiful essay of Villemain's, called *Demosthènes et le Général Foy*.

take rank as English classics; and how much of our very highest historical ability has been devoted to this period of history. Of course, every student who takes up the period as a speciality, will desire to know the languages thoroughly well, in order to have an opinion of value upon disputed points; and even the general reader always feels the additional vividness, and, therefore, the additional pleasure and stimulus and improvement, that a knowledge of the original gives. But it would be absurd to say that an Englishman (particularly if he can read French and German) has any difficulty in accurately and thoroughly informing himself what sort of people the Greeks and Romans were. And it might, I think, be truly asserted, however paradoxically, that even under our classical system, the greater part of the vivid impressions that most boys receive of the ancient world are derived from English works; from Pope's *Homer*, Macaulay's *Lays*, the English *Plutarch* (if they have the good fortune to get hold of that delightful book), and afterwards from Arnold, Grote, and Merivale.

But the æsthetic importance of ancient literature is even more insisted on than the value of its moral teaching. If we do not teach a boy Latin and Greek, it is said, we cut him off from the highest literary enjoyment, and we prevent him from developing his taste by studying the best models. It would avail little to call in question (had I space and inclination to do so) the surpassing excellence of ancient literature. For my present purpose, I must regard this point as decided by an overwhelming majority of persons of culture. But it will not be denied that in the English, French, and German languages[1] there is a sufficiency of good literature to fill the leisure of a person engaged in any active calling, a sufficiency of works calculated to give a high kind of enjoyment, and to cultivate, very adequately, the literary taste. And if such a person was ever visited by a painful hankering after the time-honoured volumes

[1] I only omit Italian because it is rarely taught at schools, and I am not prepared to recommend that it should be more generally taught.

that were sealed to him, he might console himself by taking
note how often his contemporaries who had enjoyed a complete classical education, were in the habit of taking down
these masterpieces from their shelves. For I cannot help
thinking that classical literature, in spite of its enormous
prestige, has very little attraction for the mass even of
cultivated persons at the present day. I wish statistics
could be obtained of the amount of Latin and Greek read in
any year (except for professional purposes), even by those
who have gone through a complete classical curriculum.
From the information that I have been able privately to
obtain, I incline to think that such statistics, when compared with the fervent admiration with which we all still
speak of the classics, upon every opportunity, would be found
rather startling. I am willing to admit that those who
have a genuine preference for the classics are persons of the
purest, severest, and most elevated literary taste; and I
cannot conceive that these relics will ever cease to be
reverently studied by those who aspire to be artists in
language. But this by no means proves that they ought
to occupy the place they do in the training of our youth.
"It is admitted," says a *Quarterly* reviewer (summing up
very fairly the Report of the Public Schools Commission),
"that education must be literary, and that of literary
education, classical learning must be the backbone."
Whether I should agree with this or not, depends upon
the sense in which "backbone" is interpreted: at present
classical learning forms, so to say, the whole skeleton; and
the result is, that, to a very large number of boys, what is
supposed to be a purely literary education, what is attacked
as being exclusively a literary education, is, paradoxical as
it may sound, hardly a training in literature at all. For
surely it is essential to the idea of such training that it
should have some stimulating power; that it should inspire a
fondness for reading, educe the capacity for enjoying eloquence
and poetry, communicate an interest in ideas; and not merely
guide and chasten such taste and interest if they already
exist. The instruments of literary training ought to be

not only absolutely admirable, but relatively attractive. If we wish to educate persons to enjoy any kind of art, I do not say that we are not to put before them things hard to appreciate, but we must certainly put before them also things that they will find easy to appreciate. I feel sure that if the schoolmaster is ever to be, as I think he ought to be, a missionary of culture,—if he is to develop, to any extent, the æsthetic faculties of other boys than those who have been brought up in literary homes, and have acquired, before they come into his hands, a taste for English classics, —he must make the study of modern literature a substantive and important part of his training. It may be said that some part of ancient literature, especially Greek, is ever young and fresh; and no doubt, in most good schools, some boys are made to feel this, and their path becomes flowery in consequence. But the majority want, to stimulate their literary interest, something that can be read with more ease, in larger portions: something, moreover, that has a visible connexion with the life of their age, which exercises so powerful a control over their imaginations. I do not know that, if difficulties of language were put aside, some ancient historians, such as Herodotus, might not be more attractive to boys from their freshness and *naïveté*, than any modern ones. But just when the difficulties of language are beginning to be got over, boys cease to relish this *naïveté*. They want something that speaks to their opening minds and hearts, and gives them ideas. And this they are seldom able to find to a great extent in the ancient works they read. This is true, I know, of some at least among the minority who study classics at school and college with all the stimulus of uniform success; much more is it true of the majority who fail or are but indifferently successful. If such boys get imbued with literary culture at all, it is not owing to the classical system; it is due to home influence, to fortunate school friendships, to the extra-professional care of some zealous schoolmaster. In this way they are taught to enjoy reading that instructs and refines, and escape the fate of the mass, who temper small compulsory sips of Virgil, Sophocles, Tacitus, and Thucydides, with large voluntary draughts of James, Ainsworth, Lever, and the translated Dumas.[1]

I wish this occasional and irregular training to be made as general and systematic as possible ; and I feel sure that whatever classical teaching was retained would become more efficacious by the introduction of the new element; and this not merely because every new mental stimulus that can be applied to a boy is immediately felt over the whole range of his work, but because the boy would gain a special motive for learning Latin and Greek, which he had hitherto been without, and the want of which had made his studies (to use the words of a *Quarterly* reviewer) " a prolonged nightmare." He might not at once begin to enjoy the classics : his progress might be still so slow, and his attention so much concentrated on the form of his authors, as to allow him but a feeble interest in their substance. But he would be cheered by the hope of this interest becoming daily stronger : he might distinctly look forward to the time when Sophocles would be as dear to him as Shakespeare, when Cicero and Tacitus would stir him like Burke and Macaulay. Again, some modern literature has a direct power of revealing to us the charm of ancient literature, of enabling us to see and feel in the older masterpieces what the *élite* of each generation could see and feel for themselves when the language was once understood, but what for the mass requires an interpreter. Some, for instance, would perhaps be ashamed to confess how shallow an appreciation they had of Greek art till they read Goethe and Schiller, Lessing and Schlegel. No doubt there are boys who find out the beauties for themselves, just as there are some to whom it would be a feast to be turned into a room full of fragments of antique sculpture. But our system is framed for the mass, and I feel convinced that the mass require, to appreciate both the one and the other, a careful preparation, the most important part of which would be

---

[1] I must be pardoned for using the names familiar to my generation. I have no doubt there are other favourites now.

supplied by a proper introduction into education of the element I am advocating.[1]

Further, I am disposed to think that the literary education of even the best boys is liable to suffer from the narrowness of the existing system. In the first place, there is a great danger in the predominance that classics are made to gain over their minds, by the indiscriminate eulogy and unreserved exaltation of the ancient authors *en masse*,[2] which they frequently hear. They are told, dogmatically, that these authors " are perfect standards of criticism in everything that belongs to mere perfect form," that " the laws that regulate external beauty can only be thoroughly known through them," that "they utterly condemn all false ornament, all tinsel, all ungraceful and unshapely work"; and the more docile of them are apt to believe these dogmas to a degree that warps and oppresses the natural development of their critical faculties. The truth is, that the best classical models only exemplify certain kinds of perfection of form, that several writers that boys read exemplify no particular perfection at all, and that some illustrate excellently well the precise imperfections that the enthusiast I have quoted enumerates.[3] How can it be said, for instance, that there is no " false ornament " in Æschylus, no " tinsel " in Ovid, no " ungracefulness " in Thucydides, no " unshapely work " in Lucretius ? In what sense can we speak of finding " perfect form " and " perfect standards of criticism " in such inartificial writers as Herodotus (charming as he is) or Xenophon ? There is perhaps no modern thinker, with equal sensitiveness to beauty of expression, who (in those

[1] The *Quarterly Review*, a journal that does not often clamour for rash and premature reforms, says (vol. cxvii. p. 418) :—

" Much more is it a thing to wonder at and be ashamed of, that, with such a literature as ours, the English lesson is still a desideratum in nearly all our great places of education, and that the future gentry of the country are left to pick up their mother tongue from the periodical works of fiction which are the bane of our youth, and the dread of every conscientious schoolmaster."

We may add that the question whether native literature is to be systematically taught, has long been decided in the affirmative both in France and in Germany.

[2] I allow that there are some exceptions to this statement ; for instance, one of the most exquisite artists in language, Euripides, has been perhaps unduly depreciated. Still I think I have fairly described the general tendency.

[3] Mr. Thring.

works of his which have been preserved to us) has so neglected and despised form as Aristotle. Any artist in words may learn much from Cicero, and much from Tacitus; but the profuse verbosity of the one, and the perpetual mannerism of the other, have left the marks of their misdirection on English literature. I am simply repeating what are now the commonplaces of cultivated criticism, which can no longer be charged, on the whole, with being servile towards antiquity; but education is less emancipated, and as long as these sweeping statements of the perfectness of ancient literature are reiterated, a demand for careful limitation seems necessary.

But secondly, it can hardly be said that the artistic training which might be given by means of ancient literature (which I should be sorry to seem to undervalue) is given under our present educational system. A few attain to it self-taught: and even these are liable to all the errors and extravagances of such self-education. But what effort is made to teach literary criticism to the great majority in our schools (or even in our universities)? Are they encouraged to judge as wholes the works that they so minutely analyse? to attain to any synthetical apprehension of their excellence? The point on which the wisest admirers of ancient art lay most stress is the completely organic structure of its products and the instinct for complex and finely articulated harmony that is felt to have guided the production. But in so far as schoolboys (with a few exceptions) are taught to feel the beauty of these products at all, it is the beauty of parts, and even of minute parts, that they are taught to feel. And, from the mode in which these beauties are studied for purposes of composition it is not only a partial, but generally a perverted appreciation that is attained. In the effort to prepare his mind for composition, a boy is led to contemplate his authors under conditions as unfavourable to the development of pure taste and sound criticism as can possibly be conceived. He is led to break the diction of great masters into fragments for the purpose of mechanical ornamentation, generally clumsy and often grotesque. His memory (as an advocate exultingly phrases it) is "stored with precious things": that is, it is stored with long words, sounding epithets, imposing circumlocutions, salient extravagances and mannerisms: so that his admiration is directed to a great extent to what is *bizarre*, fantastic, involved, over-decorated in the admirable models he studies: and even of what is really good he is apt to spoil his delicacy of apprehension, by the habit of imitating and introducing it unseasonably. I am aware how much careful training may do to correct these vicious tendencies: but they are likely to exist in overwhelming force as long as the imitative instinct is so prematurely developed as it is now, and applied to a material over which so imperfect a command has been gained.

This forms a convenient transition to another part of my subject: the examination in detail of the existing instruction in Latin and Greek, regarded primarily as a species of mental gymnastics, a method of developing the intellectual faculties: without reference to the permanent utility of the knowledge conveyed. When, however, the methods of classical instruction are spoken of as a "fine training," the word "training" may be used in two senses, which it is necessary carefully to distinguish. Sometimes, merely a rhetorical training is intended; the boy, it is said, is taught not only a special dexterity in the use of particular languages (his own included), but a complete grasp of language in general: he learns to dominate the instrument of thought instead of being dominated by it: "his mind is enabled to conceive form as an object of thought distinct from the subject-matter, and *vice versâ*, and hence generally to judge of the application of the one to the other in literature, with a degree of accuracy which is never attained except by those thus trained."[1] Sometimes, again, it is claimed that classics supply a complete general training to the mind: that, in the words of M. Cournot:[2] "Rien ne se prête mieux que l'étude grammaticale et littéraire d'une langue au développement graduel et méthodique de toutes

[1] Rev. W. G. Clark. [2] *De l'Instruction publique.*

les facultés intellectuelles de l'enfance et de l'adolescence. Cette étude exerce la mémoire, la sagacité, le goût, le jugement sous toutes les formes, logiques ou non logiques, c'est-à-dire, soumises ou non à des classifications, à des déductions et à des règles précises. Elle forme l'homme toute entier." It will be convenient to take the narrower of these pretensions first : and examine whether composition in the ancient languages, and translation from them into our own, appear to form a complete course of instruction in the art of speech.

I think that few who have considered the subject can deny, that translation from a Latin or Greek author into English prose, under the guidance of a competent teacher, is a very vigorous and efficacious training in the use of our language, and gives very considerable insight into the nature of speech, and its relation to thought and fact. Our only doubt will be, whether the training and insight is not, by itself, one-sided; whether we do not require something else as a supplement, to give us a complete view and a complete grasp of language. "The art," says Dr. Moberly, " of throwing English with facility into sentence-moulds made in another language . . . what is this but to learn to have the choicest, most varied, words and sentence-frames of our language constantly at command, so that, whatever varieties of thought and meaning present themselves to a man's mind, he will never be at a loss for expressions to convey them with an accuracy at once forcible and subtle to the mind of his hearers." This is no over-statement : but it leaves out of sight the dilemma in which even the matured scholar, and therefore infinitely more the tiro, is perpetually placed between exact English and elegant English, between the set of words that represents the precise meaning of the original (and is endurable in the vernacular), and the nearest English phrase that can be called tasteful. A schoolmaster must inevitably sacrifice accuracy or style, and he, as a rule, wisely determines to sacrifice style for the time. But if style is sacrificed here, it becomes desirable to cultivate it carefully in another part of the education. The result of laboriously forcing our language into " moulds " unnatural to it, will not be to give us an easy flow of it in natural moulds. Even when the process is carried further, as in the case of the more advanced students, and style is gradually more and more regarded, still the translator's dexterity remains a special dexterity, and does not amount to the whole art of composition. Translation is continually straining and stretching our faculty of language in many ways, and necessarily imparts to it a high degree of a certain kind of vigour ; but the precise power that will be of most use to us for the purposes of life it does not, by itself, give, and it even causes us to form habits adverse to the ultimate acquirement of that power. Teaching the art of Rhetoric by means of translation only, is like teaching a man to climb trees in order that he may be an elegant dancer.[1]

I have allowed the efficacy of translation in teaching English expression ; it must also be said that it develops very sufficiently the sense of one kind of excellence of form in all the more intelligent and appreciative minds : I mean of minute excellence, the beauty of single words and phrases. It does this simply because it enforces a close and reverent examination of masterpieces. We are apt to neglect many excellences in writings that we read with ease, simply because we read them with ease ; and as we are forced in these times to read much hastily, we find some trouble in forming a habit of reading worthy things as they deserve. The best training for such a habit is to read fine compositions in some foreign language. But it must be remarked that it is only at a certain stage in a youth's

[1] The conclusions of a thorough-going advocate of classical education in Germany are as follows : "Das Uebersetzen der antiken Meisterwerke ist eine Schule für die Gewandtheit und Gediegenheit des Ausdrucks, wie es keine zweite gibt. Die Verirrung aber, zu der diese Uebungen verkehrt betrieben führen könnten, die steife Nachbildung des griechischen und römischen Sprachgeistes, mit Verletzung des Deutschen, diese Verirrung wird verhütet durch das Lesen unserer deutschen Klassiker. . . . Um den Schüler zur richtigen Ordnung der Gedanken anzuleiten, werden zu den Uebersetzungen aus dem alten Versuche in eignen deutschen Ausarbeitungen hinzutreten müssen."— Raümer, *Geschichte der Pädagogik*. And this seems to me a well-balanced view of the question.

progress that Latin and Greek begins to give this training. In many cases the boy (and even the undergraduate) never becomes able to extract and feed on the beauties of his authors. A mind exhausted with linguistic struggles is not in a state to receive delicate literary impressions: instead of being penetrated with the subtle and simple graces of form, it is filled to the brim with thoughts of gender, quantity, tertiary predicates, uses of the subjunctive mood.

The training in æsthetic perception is thus by no means general, and it is, as I have before pointed out, very incomplete. But such as it is, it seems to me to be conveyed much more satisfactorily in the process of translation, than in that which is generally supposed to teach it, composition in Greek and Latin. We are told that a boy "cannot have appreciated the delicacy, taste, or the feeling of his models in literature, if he have not in some degree learned, from his own clumsy efforts and occasional better successes, at how almost immeasurable distance they stand from the rude rough things which otherwise he might be led to compare with them." I have spoken of the false and distorted view of literary excellence that this gives. A thoughtful boy feels the hardship of being made to imitate persons who have so unfair an advantage over him as the writers in a language now dead. An ambitious boy often loses all delicacy and truth of taste in the effort to assimilate all "useful" words and phrases which, however bad in taste they may be, will at least decorate and set off his own "rude rough things." The assertion that masterpieces cannot be appreciated without an effort to imitate them seems to me contrary to common sense, to our experience in our own language, to our universal practice in studying foreign literatures, and to the analogy of other arts.[1] And the imitation that is encouraged at schools in the process of verse-writing is the very worst sort of imitation; it is

---

[1] There is some reason for urging that a connoisseur in painting should have handled the pencil and the brush. But this is surely not in order to improve his taste, but to teach him closeness and correctness of observation, without which, in so directly imitative an art, a sense of beautiful effect may be misleading.

something which, if it were proposed in respect of any other models than these, we should at once reject as intolerably absurd.

There is much more to be said for the exercise of writing elegant Latin prose, though I am not sure that it is not prematurely attempted in our present system of education. I do not think, as I have before said, that even this accomplishment is at all essential to the most accurate and complete knowledge of the Latin language. It cannot be too much insisted, that the faculty of reading a language and that of composing in it are almost entirely distinct, and have to be acquired separately. A development of the latter faculty tends, no doubt, to improve the former to a certain degree; but it is a very roundabout way of improving it; if our object is to learn to read and translate, the time would be much better spent in reading and translating. I quite admit that by simply reading, without much sustained effort to translate, a language so remote from our own in its idiom as the Latin, a habit of loose apprehension is formed, and not only the refinements of expression are lost, but many mistakes are made in the substantial signification of sentences. But I should urge that written translation carefully looked over is, as a remedy for lax habits of reading, very far superior to any amount of composition.[1] Perhaps also too much has been made of the rhetorical utility of writing Latin prose: and too little of the logical training given to maturer students by the process of translation from English into Latin. The close and prolonged meditation over familiar words and expressions, which the effort to reproduce their full substance in an alien and difficult tongue entails, imparts a very delicate discrimination of the exact import of these current phrases. Moreover, the effort to write so extremely synthetical a language as the Latin is very beneficial to an Englishman, as teaching him much

[1] I have previously noticed the only function for which composition seems to me preferable to any other exercise—that of fixing firmly in the mind the grammar and the commoner rules of usage, which we require to have firmly fixed before we can read with ease and security. It does not seem to me indispensable even for this function; but it is probably a distinct abridgment of labour.

about the real connexions of thought, the logical interdependence of sentences, which the analytical tendencies of his own language prevent his noticing. With reference to the rhetorical utility of this exercise, I will quote some remarks of Dr. Moberly, with which I partly agree, but which seem to me much too unqualified. "It is a very great part of the benefit to be derived from writing Latin prose, that a boy learns thence to write prose in any language. . . . He is taught what constitutes a sentence; how much meaning he may put into a sentence; how many clauses a sentence will bear. . . . One of the most common faults in composing English is that of stringing clauses upon clauses, without heeding the necessary rules of periodic structure. . . . I do not wish to recommend the building up of elaborate sentences after the manner of the writers of the seventeenth century, but I wish to observe that the slipshod style of modern English, with its loose clauses and involved parentheses, would be greatly corrected by a careful course of original composition in Latin. . . . Loose ungoverned clauses, dissimilar nominatives, and verbs hung together by unmeaning 'ands,' no less than mixed metaphors and impossible figures, will not go into Latin. 'Try it in Latin,' might often suggest to a young writer the absurdity of what may seem to be rather fine in English. . . . The boy (who can write Latin) has obtained a master-secret which he can apply to many a difficult lock besides." There runs through all this the erroneous idea, which is pointed in the last sentence, that Latin style forms a kind of skeleton-key, or universal touchstone, for all other styles. No doubt by teaching any style thoroughly, we also teach, to a certain extent, how to penetrate the mysteries of any new style. But each language requires its own art of rhetoric; the "rules of periodic structure" are special for each: the questions, "What constitutes a sentence?" etc., are answered as differently as possible in different languages. In some important points (mentioned by Dr. Moberly) practice in Latin forms a specially useful corrective to faults in English —it is like showing blemishes by a magnifying-glass: some things that are bad in English are clearly seen to be inadmissible in Latin. But precisely the same is true of French. Either language, properly used, may be made to improve our style in our own; any language (and not least these two), if carelessly used, may spoil it. It is indispensable that practice in writing the vernacular should proceed *pari passu* with the practice in an alien tongue, and receive as careful attention.

Again, Latin is a language in which the rhythmical effects are broad, palpable, easy to apprehend. This is also true of English, and (however hopeless it is in our broken utterance to emulate the continuous music of the more synthetical language) we might educate the ear very thoroughly by a careful study of our own masters of eloquence. Still, writing Latin, at a stage when elegance can be made a prominent object, seems well adapted to assist this education; and of course we attain a larger view of melody in general, by the study of literary models so widely different from our own.

Hardly any of the reasons that I have enumerated can be urged in favour of writing Greek prose. Useful as the Greek language is to teach subtlety and delicacy of thought, it is so much more lax in its laws of expression and structure than the Latin, that it has very little of the corrective effect of this latter upon English composition. Besides, one or two most charming and impressive Greek writers are exceedingly bad models. It will sound a paradox to mention Plato. Still, a style which is an intentional imitation (often an exaggeration) of the flexible and irregular movement of conversational utterances, can hardly be a good pattern for ordinary prose. Thucydides, again, with all the wonderful weight and pregnancy of his words, is the product of what few will deny to have been a thoroughly vicious school of rhetoric; and I think the unqualified admiration with which docile boys are, by many educators, led to regard his writing, frequently tends to injure or perplex the natural development of their taste. Besides, we are naturally very little sensible to the rhythm of Greek prose (which may perhaps be accounted for by our manner of reading it). It is hard for a boy even to pretend to himself that he appreciates the melody of even Demosthenes.

But, if it were granted that Greek composition supplied as valuable a training as Latin, there would be very little to be said for adding the one accomplishment to the other. We thereby burden the memory with much additional material, while we give the logical and rhetorical faculties but little additional training. It is becoming more and more evidently important in classical education to save time, without lowering the standard of excellence in the work required. One easy method of doing this is to reduce the number of the kinds of composition cultivated.

On the whole, we are led to the conclusion that all these processes form a one-sided and incomplete training in the use of English, and require to be supplemented by some careful and independent teaching of English composition. It seems equally true that, in order to insure that complete view of the relation of language to thought, which, if we spend so much time in linguistic studies, we may fairly expect to insure, we can hardly dispense with some direct teaching of English. The immediate task set before a boy in all the processes of classical education is to ascertain exactly the equivalence of two languages, not the relation of either to thought and fact. It is impossible that he should not indirectly gain much insight into this relation; but it is not impossible that in the case of many scattered words and phrases, he may learn to fit one language to another without expressing a really clear idea in either. Moreover, he reads at a time such small portions of the ancient authors, that there is very little opportunity for teaching him to grasp a long and elaborate argument as a whole; for training him quickly to apprehend the bearing not only of sentence on sentence, but of paragraph on paragraph. Again, just as it was urged that the appreciation of English literature, though it might perhaps be left to nature in the case of boys brought up by intellectual parents in a literary atmosphere, requires to be directly taught to boys without these advantages: so it may be said that the same boys are in danger of never learning a considerable portion of the English vocabulary. I do not exactly mean technical terms, but the half-technical, the philosophical, language which thoughtful men habitually use in dealing with abstract subjects. Of some of these terms such a boy may pick up a loose and vague comprehension from ordinary conversation, novels, and newspapers; but he will generally retain sufficient ignorance of them to make the perusal of all difficult and profound works more weary and distasteful than their subject-matter alone would make them. If English authors were read in schools so carefully that a boy was kept continually ready to explain words, paraphrase sentences, and summarise arguments; if the prose authors chosen gradually became, as the boy's mind opened, more difficult and more philosophical in their diction; if, at the same time, in the teaching of natural science, a great part of the technical phraseology (from which the main stream of the language is being continually enriched) was thoroughly explained to him,—then we might feel that, by direct and indirect teaching together, we had imparted a complete grasp of what is probably the completest instrument of thought in the world.[1] I have admitted that, in the first stage in the analysis of language (assuming that we are right to begin it as early as we do now) the intervention of a foreign language may be valuable, in order that each step in knowledge may be felt as an increase of power. But I think that the last and crowning stage of this analysis, where the learner's view of the relation of language to thought is to be made as complete and profound as possible, being abstract and difficult, and involving a considerable

[1] Mr. Johnson, of Eton, in his interesting evidence before the Public Schools Commission (see *Report*, vol iii. p. 159), expresses the opinion that, in the process of more careful cultivation of French, the English language might be (as he phrases it) "used up," and all its terms explained; whereas it is impossible to use it up in translation from Greek and Latin. This suggestion seems to me valuable and important, but I should still rely more on the direct teaching I speak of, though there is no reason why the two should not be combined.

strain on the reflective faculty, is generally best taught in the most familiar language, and therefore in the vernacular.

I hope that I have shown my anxiety not to underrate the power over language developed by learning a foreign tongue, and especially one very alien in its laws and structure to our own. But I do not think it has been ever shown that this mode of development of our faculty of speech is absolutely necessary, or even, with reference to the place which language occupies in our life, obviously desirable. The normal function of language is not to represent another language, but to express and communicate facts. Scientific men are justly told by the classicists that all their discoveries would be useless without language; and the answer that the most inarticulate discoverers have generally found means to communicate their message to mankind, though a natural rejoinder, is not complete for our present purpose, for this inarticulateness is precisely the sort of evil which education ought to remedy. To describe a fact or series of facts methodically, accurately, perspicuously, comes by nature to some people, just as eloquence does; but it requires to be taught carefully to others. Only it is hard to see why the study of language, in this sense, should be separated at all from the study of subjects; why, as "things" cannot be taught without "words," the use of words should not be learnt *pari passu* with the knowledge of things. Indeed, it must be so learned to some extent. The only question is, whether care and attention shall be bestowed on the process; whether the scientific teacher shall be content that his pupil should make it evident to him that his mind has grasped ideas, or whether he shall insist on those ideas being adequately expressed. If he does this latter, he will give gradually a training in language sufficient, not only for the ordinary uses in life, but even for the purposes of most professional students. The delicate perception of subtle distinctions which a good classical education superadds is an intellectual luxury that ought not to be despised, but may easily be overvalued.

We have now to consider whether, in the acquisition of linguistic and literary knowledge, and linguistic and literary dexterity, by the various processes that we have been considering, there is really given to all the mental faculties a most complete and harmonious training;—and, if not, where the training appears defective and one-sided, and what the natural supplement is. There can be no doubt, I think, that the training, as far as it goes, is strong and effective, and there is no doubt, too, that it is much more varied than its depreciators are willing to allow. Indeed, it is curious that so many men of science fail to perceive that the study of language up to a certain point is very analogous in its effect on the mind to the study of any of the natural history sciences. In either case, the memory has to be loaded with a mass of facts, which must remain to the student arbitrary and accidental facts, affording no scope to the faculties of judgment and generalisation. This is the weak point of either study, regarded as an exercise of the reason, and makes it desirable that the initiation into either should take place early in life. But, as in natural science, so in language, there is a large amount of material that not only exercises the memory, but enforces constant attention and perpetual close comparison: rules and generalisations have to be borne in mind, as well as isolated facts; habits of accuracy and quickness in applying them are rapidly developed, and the important faculty of judgment is perpetually educed, trained, and stimulated. And the remark I quoted from a French writer is most just, that the judgment is exercised "in all its forms, both logical and non-logical." In applying each newly learnt rule, it acts at first deliberately, by an express process of reasoning, afterwards instinctively, by an implicit process. I think, however, the common statement, that in learning a language the mind is exercised in induction, requires much qualification. The mind of the matured, the professional scholar, is so exercised, because he stands on a level with the authors of his grammars and dictionaries, and from time to time observes new rules of usage which they have not noted. But the boy, or youth,

x

learning his lesson with ample grammar and dictionaries, is not, or is very rarely, called upon to perform any such process. For each doubtful case that comes before him his books and memory combined soon furnish him with an abundance, a plethora of formulæ :[1] he has only to choose the right one. In making this choice, besides close attention and delicate discrimination, an unconscious tact, a trained instinct, combines to guide him, and, by applying a mental magnifying-glass to this tact or instinct, we may discover in it rudimentary inductive processes ; but we might find the same in the mental operations of every skilled artisan, and it is perhaps misleading to dignify them by the name. Besides this training of the cognitive faculties, the creative are also, as we have seen, developed. In composition, the boy applies the same rules, by the aid of which he has analysed complex products of speech, to form similar products for himself; and as in the former case he acted under the guidance of a gradually developing scientific tact, so in this he works under the influence of a slowly educed æsthetic instinct. He is taught to make an effort to be an artist in a material hard to manipulate, and the benefit of this training will, it is presumed, abide with him in whatever material he has afterwards to work.

If, then, say the advocates of classics, we offer a study of literature which at the same time combines scientific and artistic training, why is not the completeness of our system admitted, and why are we asked to introduce any new element except for the vulgar reason that it would be more useful ? Simply because each element of the training is not (at any rate taken alone) the best thing of its kind or the thing we most want. We may allow that the education is many-sided : still, if it is defective on each side, this many-sidedness will not count much in its favour. And the very fact that the same instrument is made to serve various educational purposes, which seems at first sight a very plausible

[1] If a boy could be more debarred from grammars and dictionaries, there would naturally be more induction in the process of learning the language. But the efforts that have been made in this direction (though deserving of all attention) do not seem as yet to have been conspicuously successful.

argument in its favour, is really, for the majority of boys, a serious disadvantage. In the actual process of education one or other of the purposes is continually sacrificed. Some boys with strong taste for literature and natural power of expression pass with moderate success through their classical work by means of their literary tact alone, and get, after the first rudiments of grammar are acquired, very little training in close observation or accurate reasoning. But with the greater number (especially of boys who do not go to the University) the case is reversed. The mind, exhausted with the labours of language, imbibes miserably little of the lessons of literature. And here I may observe that some educational reformers have committed a most disastrous error—an error that might have been fatal, if anything could be fatal, to their cause, in allowing the notion to become current, that there is a sort of antagonism between science and literature, that they are presented as alternative instruments of education, between which a choice has to be made. It is so evident that if one or other must be abandoned, if we must inevitably remain either comparatively ignorant of the external world, or comparatively ignorant of the products of the human mind, all but a few exceptional natures must choose that study which best fits them for communion with their fellow-men. But I absolutely deny this incompatibility : nor do I think it would ever have occurred to any one except for the strange illusion that in the age in which we live classics must *necessarily* be the " substratum," " basis," " backbone " (or whatever analogous metaphor is used) of a literary education : and that therefore we must leave on one side every other form of literature with the view of imparting as much classics as possible. The consequence is that half the undergraduates at our Universities, and a larger proportion of the boys at all (except perhaps one or two) of our public schools, if they have received a literary education at all, have got it for themselves : the fragments of Greek and Latin that they have struggled through have not given it them. If so many of our most expensively educated youth regard athletic sports as the one conceivable mode of enjoying leisure : if so many professional persons confine their extra-professional reading to the newspapers and novels : if the middle-class Englishman (as he is continually told) is narrow, unrefined, conventional, ignorant of what is really good and really evil in human life; if (as an uncompromising writer [1] says) " he is the tool of bigotry, the echo of stereotyped opinions, the victim of class prejudices, the great stumbling-block in the way of a general diffusion of higher cultivation in this country "—it is not because these persons have had a literary education, which their "invincible brutality" has rendered inefficacious : it is because the education has not been (to them) literary : their minds have been simply put through various unmeaning linguistic exercises. It is not surprising that simple-minded people have thought that since a complete study of Latin and Greek was felt by some [2] of those who had successfully pursued it to have been (along with the other reading that they had spontaneously absorbed) a fine literary education, therefore half as much Latin and Greek ought to produce about half as much of the same kind of effect; and that when they see the education on the whole to be a failure, instead of demanding more literature as well as more science, they cry for less literature. But the time seems to have come for us to discern and repair this natural mistake. Let us demand instead that all boys, whatever be their special bent and destination, be really taught literature : so that as far as is possible, they may learn to enjoy intelligently poetry and eloquence : that their interest in history may be awakened, stimulated, guided : that their views and sympathies may be enlarged and expanded by apprehending noble, subtle, and profound thoughts, refined and lofty feelings : that some comprehension of the varied development of human nature may ever after abide with them, the source and essence of a truly humanising culture. Thus in the prosecution of

---

[1] Dr. Donaldson.
[2] I say advisedly "some." Many successfully trained scholars feel very differently with regard to their training.

their special study or function, while their energy will be even stimulated, their views and aims will be more intelligent, more central; and therefore their work, if less absorbing, not less effective.

If this be done, it is a subordinate question what particular languages we learn. We must allow all weight to the advantages which a dead and difficult language has, as an instrument of training, over a modern and easy one.[1] But we must remember that it is a point of capital importance that instruction in any language should be carried to the point at which it really throws open a literature : while it is not a point of capital importance that any particular literature should be so thrown open.

The defects of the usual exercises in Greek and Latin composition, as an artistic training, have been incidentally noticed ; and the disadvantages of verse composition in particular are pointed out elsewhere in this volume.[2] We must not forget, however, that the place which these exercises fill in education must be filled in some way or other ; the boy must be taught to exercise his productive faculty, and to exercise it in a regulated, methodical manner. In the later stage of education, when discursive thought on general and abstract themes may properly be demanded, essays and careful answers to comprehensive questions seem to constitute the best mode of developing this faculty, as attention may thus be paid to style and substance at the same time. In the earlier stages we require easier exercises

[1] I think there would be a great advantage in combining a difficult with an easy language. The more facile conquest a boy would make over one, might encourage him in his harder struggle. Of course, for this, or any other valuable result to be attained, the easy language must be studied with as much attention and respect as the hard one. This is one of the numerous reasons for selecting French and Latin as the languages to be taught in early education. Another reason for teaching them together is their relation to each other and to English. (See Professor M. Müller's evidence before the Public Schools Commission, vol. iv. p. 396.) This eminent scholar there illustrates the way in which the rudiments of Comparative Philology might be taught by comparing words in the three languages, and ventures to assert that "an hour a-week so spent, would save ten hours in teaching French and Latin."

[2] [The volume in which this essay originally appeared. The essay referred to in the text is that *On Greek and Latin Verse Composition as a General Branch of Education*, by the Rev. F. W. Farrar.—ED.]

in English prose, such as narratives and descriptions, drawn from experience or imagination, or freely compiled from authors read; the teaching of physical science would give occasion to descriptions of a different kind; the history lesson would suggest orations and declamations at appropriate points, so that rhythm and melody might be naturally taught. It is a doubtful point whether all boys should be exercised in producing poetry; it is hardly doubtful that they should be exercised, if at all, in a material less difficult than Latin or Greek is, up to a very advanced stage of its acquisition. Perhaps translations into English poetry of fine passages in foreign authors might be occasionally required from all; and original poetry, encouraged only by prizes. If, too, it is once admitted that production of the kind that develops the æsthetic faculty is to be encouraged, if the boy is to be stimulated to produce beautiful things, there seems no adequate reason why the brain alone should be exercised in such production; the training of the hand and eye which drawing affords is probably desirable for all boys up to a certain point; while after this point, boys who are absolutely unproductive in language, may develop their sense of beauty in pictorial art.

Then remains the training of the cognitive faculties which the process of mastering the classical languages supplies. We have seen that this training is in many respects very efficacious, and that it (unlike many supposed utilities of classics) is really given, to some extent, to most boys.[1] As I have said, it appears to me very similar to that which would be supplied by one or more of the physical sciences, carefully selected, limited, and arranged for educational purposes. It is clear that this latter study develops memory (both in extent and accuracy), close attention, delicate discrimination, judgment, both instinctive and deliberate, the faculty of rapidly applying the right general formula to the solution of any particular problem.

[1] If the pernicious influence of Bohn's Library could be entirely excluded, this might be stated more strongly. But it must never be forgotten, in discussing this question, that the training afforded by classics read with translations is very different from that afforded by classics read without them.

I am not in a position to institute a close comparison of the efficacy of the two kinds of study in educating those faculties of the mind which both in common call into exercise.[1] But the study of language seems to have certain distinct advantages. In the first place, the materials here supplied to the student are ready to hand in inexhaustible abundance and diversity. Any page of any ancient author forms for the young student a string of problems sufficiently complex and diverse to exercise his memory and judgment in a great variety of ways. Again, from the exclusion of the distractions of the external senses, from the simplicity and definiteness of the classification which the student has to apply, from the distinctness and obviousness of the points that he is called on to observe, it seems probable that this study calls forth (especially in young boys) a more concentrated exercise of the faculties it does develop than any other could easily do. If *both* the classical languages were to cease to be taught in early education, valuable machinery would, I think, be lost, for which it would be somewhat difficult to provide a perfect substitute.

But the very exclusions and limitations that make the study of language a better gymnastic than physical science, make it, on the other hand, so obviously inferior as a preparation for the business of life, that its present position in education seems, on this ground alone, absolutely untenable. The proof of this I cannot attempt adequately to develop; but it seems appropriate to indicate the more obvious reasons, as they are still ignored by many intelligent persons. One point the advocates of the classical system sometimes admit by saying "that it does not develop the faculties of external observation"; and the more open-minded of them would desire that these faculties should be somehow or other exercised, without interfering with the

[1] It is much to be wished that some competent person, equally acquainted with languages and science, and with equal experience in teaching the rudiments of both, would carefully make such a comparison. At present, the best exponents of the effect of either study generally speak of the other with comparative ignorance. It is, perhaps, an indirect testimony to the advantages of scientific education, that this ignorance is more frequently combined with contemptuous dogmatism in the case of the classical advocate.

"more important part of education." But this is a most inadequate view of the question. It is not enough that the intelligence should be trained at one time and in one way, and the senses exercised separately; we require that the intelligence should be taught to exercise the important functions of which we have spoken in combination with the senses; and we require this, because this is the normal mode of the action of the intelligence in human life. It is not enough that we should learn to see things as they are, important as this is: we must also train the memory to record accurately, and the imagination to represent faithfully, the facts observed: we must learn to exercise the judgment and apply general formulæ to particular phenomena, not only when these phenomena are broadly and clearly marked out (as they are when we come armed with complete grammars and dictionaries to the interpretation of foreign speech), but also when they are obscure, hard to detect, "embedded in matter," mixed up with a mass of other phenomena, unimportant for our purpose, which we have to learn to neglect. The materials on which our intelligence has ordinarily to act, even when we are thinking, and not observing, are ideas of the external world, mixed products of our mind and senses: and it must never be forgotten that the training of the eye and hand given by the various branches of physical science, the development of our sense of form, colour, weight, etc., is not merely a training of these external organs, but of our imaginative and conceptive faculties also, and will inevitably make our thinking more clear and effective. Similarly, the training in classification which most immediately fits us for life is that which the natural history sciences afford. In learning them the student is taught not only how to apply a classification ready made, but also, to some extent, how to make a classification. He is taught to deal with a system where the classes merge by fine gradations into one another, and where the boundaries are often hard to mark; a system that is progressive, and therefore in some points rudimentary, shifting, liable to continual modification; along with the immense value of a carefully framed technical phraseology he is also taught the inevitable inadequacy of such a phraseology to represent the variety of nature ; and these are just the lessons that he requires to bear in mind in applying method and arrangement to any part of the business of life.[1] And finally, above all, the study of language does not in the least tend to impart the most valuable and important of all the habits that we combine under the conception of scientific training : the habit, as is generally said, " of reasoning from effects to causes, and from causes to effects " ; it might be more distinctly defined as the habit of correctly combining in imagination absent phenomena (whether antecedent or consequent) with phenomena present in perception. Physics and Chemistry are the most natural and efficacious way of teaching boys from some part of any of the invariable series of nature to infer and supply the rest ; their place could not be adequately occupied by History and Literature, if ever so philosophically taught ; as History and Literature are taught at present, this training is simply absent from the classical curriculum.

Again, the advantage that the minds of the educated might obtain from a sufficient variety of exercise is lost under the present exclusive system. This absence of variety is indeed sometimes claimed as a gain ; we are solemnly warned of the paramount necessity of studying one thing well. And certainly the encyclopædic courses of study which some theorists have sketched out have given practical men an easy victory over them : it is so easy to show that this encyclopædic instruction would impart a great deal of verbal, but very little real, knowledge. But " est quadam prodire tenus, si non datur ultra." No doubt the studies of boyhood must be carefully limited and selected ; but they may be representative of the diversity of

[1] Cuvier, speaking of his own study, says :—"Every discussion which supposes a classification of facts, every research which requires a distribution of matters, is performed after the same manner ; and he who has cultivated this science merely for amusement, is surprised at the facilities it affords for disentangling all kinds of affairs."
I do not think a student of languages could honestly claim an analogous advantage for his own pursuit.

the intellectual world in which men live. A boy must not be overwhelmed in a mass of details: he ought to be forced by all possible educational artifices to apprehend facts and not to repeat words; but in order that he may attain a thoroughly cultivated judgment according to the standard of our age, his education must be many-sided, he must be initiated into a variety of methods.[1] And it may be observed that under the present system neither the advantages of concentration, nor the advantages of variety, are gained. A boy, in passing from Greek to Latin, has not sufficient change to give any relief to his faculties, but he has sufficient to prevent him from making as rapid progress in either language as he would make if he studied either alone. The transition from the study of language to the study of external nature would give so much relief, that it would be possible for a boy to spend more time in his studies on the whole, without danger of injurious fatigue. A still more important advantage of variety of studies is its certain effect in diminishing the number of boys who take no interest in their school-work: a net is spread that catches more; and it is generally found that if a boy becomes interested, and therefore successful, in one part of his work, a stimulus is felt throughout the whole range of his intellectual efforts.

In general the advocates of classical education, while they rightly insist that educational studies should be capable of disciplining the mind, forget that it is equally desirable that they should be capable of stimulating it. The extreme ascetics among them even deny this. Thus Mr. Clark[2] says, "it is a strong recommendation to any subject to affirm that it is dry and distasteful." I cannot

[1] When people talk of "training the memory, judgment," etc., they often ignore the difference between a general and special development of these faculties. There is great danger lest, if trained to a pitch in one material only, they will not work very well in any other material. The mind acquires, as Mr. Faraday says, a certain bent and tendency, a desire and willingness to accept ideas of a certain kind, while it becomes slow and languid in dealing with ideas of a different kind. Mr. Faraday's evidence of the inferiority of educated men to children in apprehending scientific ideas, is very interesting and impressive. (See *Report of Public Schools Commission*, vol. iv. p. 377.)

[2] *Cambridge Essays*, 1855.

help thinking that there is some confusion here between "dry" and "hard." No doubt the faculties both of mind and body must be kept a sufficient time in strong tension in order to grow to their full strength: but we find in the development of the body that this tension can be longest and most healthily maintained by means of exercises that are sought with avidity.[1] Those who have argued that the pursuit of knowledge might be made agreeable to boys, have been somewhat misunderstood by the apologists of existing institutions. They never meant that it could be made pleasant to him as gingerbread is pleasant, but as a football match in the rain, or any other form of violent exercise under difficulties. The "gaudia" of the pursuit of knowledge are necessarily "severa": but there seems to be no reason why the relish for them should not be imparted as early as possible. The universality and intensity of the charms of science for boys have been sometimes stated, I admit, with almost comical exaggeration. But it will not be denied that the study of the external world does, on the whole, excite youthful curiosity much more than the study of language. The intellectual advantage of this ought to be set against whatever disciplinary superiority we may attribute to the latter instrument. On the moral advantage of substituting, as far as possible, the love of knowledge, as a nobler and purer motive, for emulation and the fear of punishment, I have not space to dilate: but it seems difficult to exaggerate the importance, though we may easily over-estimate the possibility, of developing this sentiment.

And the superior efficacy of natural science in evoking curiosity is not due entirely, though it is due partly, to the exercise it gives to the external senses as well as the brain. It is due also to the fact that education in physical science is (in the sense in which I have previously used the word) a *natural* education in the present age. The

[1] It is curious in contemplating English school life as a whole, to reflect how thoroughly we believe in natural exercises for the body and artificial exercises for the mind.

book which it opens to the student is not one which he will ever shut up and put by : it is not one that he could easily have ignored. In the age in which we live the external world forces itself in every way, directly and indirectly, upon our observation ; we cannot fail to pick up scraps of what is known about it : sciolism is inevitable to us, unless we avoid it by becoming more than sciolists. The boy's instinct feels this : so that, besides the obvious and primary advantages that a natural system of education has over an artificial one, there is this in addition : it not only teaches what the pupil will afterwards be more glad to know, but what he is at present more willing to learn. We may admit that a knowledge of the processes and results of physical science does not by itself constitute culture : we may admit that an appreciative acquaintance with literature, a grasp of the method as well as the facts of history, is a more important element, and should be more prominent in the thoughts of educators ; and yet feel that culture, without the former element, is now shallow and incomplete. Physical science is now so bound up with all the interests of mankind, from the lowest and most material to the loftiest and most profound : it is so engrossing in its infinite detail, so exciting in its progress and promise, so fascinating in the varied beauty of its revelations : that it draws to itself an ever-increasing amount of intellectual energy; so that the intellectual man who has been trained without it must feel at every turn his inability to comprehend thoroughly the present phase of the progress of humanity, and his limited sympathy with the thoughts and feelings, labours and aspirations, of his fellow-men. And if there be any who believe that the summit of a liberal education, the crown of the highest culture, is Philosophy—meaning by Philosophy the sustained effort, if it be no more than an effort, to frame a complete and reasoned synthesis of the facts of the universe, —on them it may be especially urged how poorly equipped a man comes to such a study, however competent he may be to interpret the thoughts of ancient thinkers, if he has not qualified himself to examine, comprehensively and closely, the wonderful scale of methods by which the human mind has achieved its various degrees of conquest over the world of sense. When the most fascinating of ancient philosophers taught, but the first step of this conquest had been attained. We are told that Plato wrote over the door of his school, " Let no one who is without geometry enter here." In all seriousness we may ask the thoughtful men, who believe that Philosophy can still be best learnt by the study of the Greek masters, to consider what the inscription over the door should be in the nineteenth century of the Christian era.

In conclusion, it seems desirable to sum up briefly the practical changes (whether of omission or supplement) which have been suggested from time to time by a detailed examination of the arguments for the existing system; and at the same time to add one suggestion which, if I do not over-estimate its practical value, will very much facilitate the introduction of such other changes as I desire. I think that a course of instruction in our own language and literature, and a course of instruction in natural science, ought to form recognised and substantive parts of our school system. I do not venture to estimate the amount of time that ought to be apportioned to these subjects, but I think that they ought to be taught to all, and taught with as much serious effort as anything else. I think also that, partly for reasons which I have indicated and partly with a view to practical advantages, more stress ought to be laid on the study of French. While advocating these new elements, I feel most strongly the great peril of overburdening the minds of youth, to their intellectual or physical detriment, or both. From Germany, where the system is now more comprehensive than ours, we hear complaints which show that this evil has arisen. I do not know which is its worst form, that the brains of boys should be perpetually overstrained, or that a number of things should be taught, all inadequately and superficially, so that verbal memory is substituted for real apprehension. A certain amount of time will be gained by the omission of

verses as a general branch of education (so that only the
few who have a special capacity for such exercises be
encouraged to pursue them). But I do not think the time
thus gained will suffice; especially as it is desirable that
the study of every language that is studied should be made
more complete than it is now. I have before hinted at
what appears to me the obvious remedy for the evil I dread
—namely, to exclude Greek from the regular curriculum,
at least in its earlier stage. The one thing to be set against
the many reasons that exist for choosing Latin (if a choice
between the two languages is, as I think, inevitable), is the
greater intrinsic interest of Greek literature. But I do not
think that, if this change were made, Greek literature would
be thrown really open to fewer boys. I think that if Latin
(along with French and English) was carefully taught up
to the age of sixteen (speaking roughly), a grasp of Greek,
sufficient for literary purposes, might be attained afterwards much more easily than is supposed; particularly if
at that period (when in the case of all schoolboys the
stringency of the general curriculum ought to be considerably
relaxed) a proper concentration of energy were insured in
the first assault on the rudiments of the language. It is
supposed that there is a saving of time in beginning the
elements of Greek early. I am inclined to think that very
much the reverse is the case, and that if several languages
have to be learnt, much time is gained by untying the
fagot and breaking them separately. There are two classes
for whom the present system of education is more or less
natural,—the clergy and persons with a literary bias, and
the prospect of sufficient leisure to indulge it amply. The
former ought to read Greek literature as a part of their
professional training, the latter as a part of a comprehensive
study of literary history. Boys with such prospects, and a
careful previous training of the kind I advocate, would, on
the average, feel, as they approached the last stage of their
school life, an interest in Greek strong enough to make
them take it in very rapidly. I believe there are one or two
living instances of eminent Greek scholars who have begun

to learn the language even later than the time I mention. The experience of students for the Indian Civil Service shows how quickly under a stimulus strong enough to produce the requisite concentration, languages may be acquired more remote from Greek and Latin than Greek is from Latin. The advantage that young children have over even young men in catching a spoken language has led some to infer that they have an equal superiority in learning to read a language that they do not hear spoken : an inference which, I think, is contrary to experience.

Of the benefit of such a change to all other boys now taught in our public and grammar schools, I need say no more than I have said already. Without such a change their interests (even if the recommendations of the Public School Commissioners be carried into effect generally) will still be sacrificed to the supposed interests of the future clergy and literary men—a great clear loss for a very illusory gain.

XIII

IDLE FELLOWSHIPS [1]

(*Contemporary Review*, April 1876)

THAT a real and—within certain limits—a final settlement of the question of University Organisation is seriously contemplated by Her Majesty's Government, is evident from the Bill that has just been introduced for Oxford, and the speeches of the minister introducing it. It is true that the weakness of merely permissive legislation has not been altogether avoided; and such weakness is peculiarly dangerous here, where the problem is to bring into effective co-operation the action of several distinct and nearly independent corporations. Still, if the new Commission is united and firm, it can easily provide that the Colleges, while allowed to determine the details of their own reform, shall yet be reconstructed in such a manner as to constitute them harmonious members of one coherent academic system. And the main lines of the reform, towards which public opinion in both Universities has long been steadily tending, have been laid down by Lord Salisbury with much clearness and decision. The " Idle Fellowship " is to become a thing

[1] [It is with some hesitation that this essay has been reprinted, as the circumstances under which it was written have changed, and the evils of which it complains have greatly diminished. It was written on the eve of the appointment of the University Commission, of which one result has been a great reduction in the number of prize fellowships; the value of those that remain has been greatly reduced by agricultural depression; and there is now less tendency than there was to give to mathematics and classics an advantage over other subjects in the distribution of fellowships. Still it cannot be said that prize fellowships and the waste of funds involved have altogether disappeared, or that the general educational considerations discussed in the essay are less true than they were, so that, on the whole, it has seemed well to republish it.—ED.]

of the past; academic endowments are to be restored to academic uses. How urgently the need of this restoration is felt, in Cambridge at least, is as yet hardly realised by the world outside. This University has for years been struggling and starving in the most pitiable manner, unable to provide decently for the most indispensable functions; while what are commonly talked and thought of as "her rich endowments" have been distributed among thriving schoolmasters, school-inspectors, rising journalists, barristers full of briefs, and barristers who never look for briefs. Many important branches of study are not represented at all within the limits of the University: several more are inadequately and precariously represented by college lecturers only. The Professorships that do exist, outside the sacred and fruitful precincts of theology, are supported by incomes varying in amount from a third to a fifth of the salary of a county court judge. The utmost economy is unable to provide Cambridge with a sufficiency even of the ugliest buildings required for scientific teaching and research in the present stage of the progress of knowledge. How these deficiencies are to be supplied, how the different grades of academic teachers and investigators are to be appointed and paid, how the co-operation of University and Colleges is to be organised on a stable and satisfactory basis, are questions requiring much further discussion and much skill and judgment to settle. It would be impertinent in a paper like the present to anticipate summarily the results of the seven years of labour appointed for the new Commission. The task that I have proposed to myself is the much humbler one of examining the actual results of the existing distribution of college endowments; in order that while its shortcomings and the positive evils that flow from it are traced to their proper sources, whatever good is really done by it may be as far as possible secured in the impending redistribution of the fund. For the sake of clearness and precision, I have thought it best to confine the discussion to Cambridge; though the greater part of it is obviously applicable to both Universities alike.

Y

There is no doubt that the Fellowship fund was originally designed for the maintenance of learned leisure: and a considerable part of the confusion of thought that exists on the subject of Fellowships arises from the difficulty of ascertaining how far the original, historical *raison d'être* of the institution has actual application and force at the present time; a difficulty which commonly arises in the case of old institutions of which the working has been subjected to a long gradual process of indefinite customary change, with or without an intermixture of abrupt legal changes. No one of course is so ignorant as to suppose that the majority of existing Fellows of Colleges are persons employing an unbroken leisure in the cultivation of learning. Still there is a vague idea current that resident Fellows at least are in some degree bound to devote themselves to the cultivation of learning; not legally bound, but morally, as a parish clergyman is morally bound to take care of the spiritual welfare of his parishioners, though his legal obligation extends only to the performance of certain religious services. All who hold with the present writer that this obligation ought to be made far more stringent and definite, and enforced by more substantial sanctions, cannot but rejoice that even a vague sense of it is still generally recognised. At the same time, it seems impossible consistently to maintain this sense of obligation together with that other view of a Fellowship which regards it as a legitimate assistance in the early struggles of a practical career. The duty cannot, without obvious absurdity, be made to depend on the mere choice of residence in Cambridge. If a Fellow who goes to London is employing his time legitimately in writing for newspapers and magazines, how can a Fellow living in Cambridge suffer the slightest moral condemnation for giving himself up to similar avocations? And if any kind of work is morally open to him, however remote from the original purpose of his Fellowship, how is it possible to blame him, *quâ* Fellow, if he prefers polite idleness to all kinds of work? And hence the obligation to learning has now almost faded from men's minds in spite of tradition, and is only felt by the few who cherish what Mr. Disraeli once called a historical conscience. Under the existing system, the broad common-sense even of academic persons cannot but regard a resident Fellow as a man who, having won the great prize of successful juvenile study, has since in the exercise of a perfectly legitimate choice preferred a limited income, unlimited leisure, and the innocent pleasures of college life to a struggle with the world. If he is advancing knowledge, he is doing so as an amateur, not as his recognised professional work; if, again, he is not advancing knowledge, the fact may be regretted, but can hardly be charged against him, under the existing conditions of tenure, as a dereliction of duty.

It is to be observed, however, that the resident Fellows who do not form part of the educational staff of the University or the Colleges are a comparatively small minority—so small, indeed, that not a few persons take a different view from that which we have just discussed; and conceive Fellowships to be intended, and actually to be operating, as part payment for the service of academic instruction. In a certain sense this view is not incompatible with the former; in fact, it must be a prominent feature in any scheme of University reform, that at least the higher part of academic education should be in the hands of persons who are also engaged in independent study and research; and that their income should consist in part of College Fellowships. If this principle were carried out, it would be almost indifferent whether the Fellowships were primarily regarded as salaries for investigators or for instructors, as the two functions would be normally combined. At present, however, it is only to a comparatively slight extent true that Fellowships are employed as salaries for teachers. In some Colleges, under the statutes approved by the former Commission, Fellowships are allowed to be retained by members of the educational staff of a College, after the time at which their tenure would under ordinary circumstances have terminated. Such Fellowships as are actually held on these terms may legitimately be regarded as endowments used for the payment of teachers; and the same view may be taken of a few other Fellowships held by University Professors as such; though since these latter are not regularly and systematically connected with Professorships, but only bestowed on particular Professors by the somewhat arbitrary and accidental selection of the Colleges, they produce the minimum of effect in the way of attracting able men to the posts. But these two classes taken together form a small minority even of those Fellowships which are held by resident academic teachers. In most cases the remuneration that the Fellow receives for his work as a teacher consists entirely in a salary paid over and above his Fellowship, from a fund provided by the fees of undergraduates (with some very trifling supplement from endowments). It is the actual and prospective amount of this salary—apart from his Fellowship—which the Fellow compares with the income that could be obtained in some other career, in considering whether or not it is his interest to take part in academic teaching.

At the same time it must undoubtedly be admitted that the services of the able and highly educated men who form the educational staff of Colleges are obtained at a cheaper rate than would be possible without Fellowships—even apart from the exceptional tenure above noticed, under which the Fellowship is definitely converted into a salary for teaching. In many Colleges certain allowances are regularly made to residents as such: and, even independently of these allowances, a Fellow who has no special ground for living elsewhere regards his College as his natural home; and if he resides there, the most natural thing for him to do, and the easiest way to make a little money, is to take part in teaching. And since his Fellowship alone—as long as it lasts—enables him to live there a life of dignified comfort, with little or no increase of income, it is natural that he should often be content with a comparatively scanty remuneration for the not very laborious work which it lies in his way to do. Still it must be observed that this method of organising academic instruction has serious and inevitable drawbacks. It is obviously inexpedient that the majority of academic teachers should be appointed by selection not from the whole range of the available educational talent in the country, on the ground of special fitness for their respective departments of the work, but from the small number of persons who constitute in each case the selecting body. The Fellows who become lecturers thus rather choose their work than are chosen for it; and it may often be said that they choose it rather negatively than positively. Partly the restriction of celibacy, and partly the very smallness of the salaries to which I have referred, have commonly prevented college tuition from being regarded as a regular profession. Hence a large proportion of those employed in it have taken it up as a stop-gap, to fill the interval between the completion of their education and their entrance on the main business of their life; and thus can hardly bring to it the intensity and concentration of energy which a vigorous man throws into whatever he has deliberately chosen as his life's work.

We may conclude then that the existing distribution of Fellowships, while it produces a few amateur students, and enables society to obtain, more cheaply than would otherwise be the case, the services of college tutors and lecturers, yet cannot be held to provide a satisfactory endowment either of learning and research, or of teaching; and still less of that complete academic career which consists in the combination of the two. It is necessary to make this plain, because the proposal to employ the funds of the Colleges in constituting such a career appears to excite surprise in the minds of many who have vaguely supposed that at least a great portion of them were already used for this purpose. Well-informed advocates of the existing system are, however, quite aware that—history and tradition notwithstanding—Fellowships are now normally bestowed not as payments for any present services to society, but as rewards to young men for the past trouble that they have taken in receiving a good education. They maintain such rewards to be desirable in the first place merely as prizes, to draw youths of talent to the Universities, and stimulate and sustain their industry when there; and secondly, as affording to such youths pecuniary support during the first years of their struggle with the world. This latter argument seems to be the one on which most stress is laid; and in so far as it is valid at all it seems to become of more importance in proportion as we conceive the distribution of the rest of our educational endowments to reach the ideal perfection which reformers contemplate. In the ladder which is to bear the child of talent upwards from the gutter, the College Fellowship presents itself as the last step; and it is not unnatural for academic reformers no less than conservatives to imagine that a serious hiatus would be left if this step were taken away. I think, however, that it will appear on careful consideration that this last round of the ladder is nearly if not quite superfluous; and that even if it ought to be constructed at all, it certainly is not the function of academic endowments to furnish it.

First, however, it is important to remove a certain ambiguity as to the nature of this step. The University does not at present provide a complete preparation for any profession (with the doubtful exception of the profession of education); and though it seems desirable that it should adapt its curriculum somewhat more than it at present does to the practical needs of its *alumni*, there will always be a certain part of the training necessary for any profession which can only be got by serving some kind of apprenticeship to persons who are actually engaged in it. Hence, even in the case of the ablest men, destined for practical careers, an interval must normally elapse after the taking of their degree, before their education is really completed; and there are the same grounds for supporting poor men of merit during this period out of educational endowments as there are for giving them exhibitions and scholarships at school and college. I do not now consider whether these grounds are adequate: I merely urge that if eleemosynary training is to be given at all, it should be given completely. It is a very different thing to continue paying them pensions for some years, when the pensioners have or ought to have already entered on the work of life, after the most complete training that society can provide. If we consider the matter in the abstract, apart from the historic names and associations which lend, as it were, a picturesque and time-honoured naturalness to the present composition and state of collegiate corporations, it must surely appear very doubtful whether such an expenditure of money—not merely of academic funds, but of any funds whatever—is at all desirable in the interests of society; however agreeable it may be for the young men themselves, who are thus temporarily placed in comfortable circumstances. We can hardly conceive such a distribution of funds coming into existence, except through that slow historic perversion of endowments from their original uses which has actually occurred in the case of our colleges.

It is urged, as I have said, that young men of talent require the support of these pensions, on account of the difficulty they find in earning a livelihood during the early part of their professional career. But this argument, if it is intended to cover the whole case, affords a curious illustration of the fallacy of generalising from a few striking instances. Most university men have heard of one or two prosperous barristers who would not have been able to go to the bar without their Fellowships; and they have probably never asked themselves how large a proportion of College Fellows have actually adopted careers which in the absence of this peculiar institution would have been closed to them. And yet the argument is eminently one of which the force cannot be ascertained without some quantitative estimate of the results to which it refers. In order to obtain such an estimate, careful statistics [1] have been obtained of the careers of the Fellows of Colleges elected in Cambridge from 1857

---

[1] These statistics have been collected by the Rev. H. A. Morgan, Fellow and Tutor [now, 1904, Master] of Jesus College, who has kindly permitted me to use them.

to 1868 inclusive—more than 300 in all. It appears that rather more than a fourth of these Fellows have adopted an academic career; most of these are now resident in Cambridge, either as holders of college offices or as private tutors, while a few others have obtained professorships elsewhere; about another fourth have become schoolmasters; others again have obtained employment not strictly educational but connected with education, as inspectors of schools or clerks in the Privy Council Office, or are serving the State as astronomers or geologists. To these cases, which amount to more than half of the whole, the argument just mentioned is obviously inapplicable, because in the competition for these posts the academic distinction for which a Fellowship is given is itself an amply sufficient advantage. The men who are made Fellows are precisely those for whom, however the University were organised, an academic career affording from the outset a sufficient income would be at once open; they are the men for whose assistance the headmasters of our chief public schools compete; in any decent administration of the public service they are naturally selected for all posts for which academic attainments are required. Thus they are sure of obtaining from the first a better income than their less distinguished contemporaries who still manage to live by their employment; and there is a peculiar and palpable absurdity in supporting them further by a pension of £300 a year from academic endowments. A few other Fellows, again, join the ever-increasing profession of journalism and magazine-writing—a highly honourable and useful function, but one which no one would wish to support artificially by Fellowships. A few others have been received into houses of business or solicitors' offices; for them, too, no extraneous source of livelihood seems to be necessary, when once they have entered upon their work. No doubt this entrance cannot be effected without either capital or connexion; but to suggest that the college revenues should furnish the former would surely be regarded as a *reductio ad absurdum* of the principle that we are considering. About sixteen per cent of the Fellowships are occupied by parochial clergy,[1] whether as holders of college livings or otherwise. The case of these is somewhat different, as it may be plausibly urged that the incomes of curates (at least) are too small, and that it is an advantage to supplement them from any source. Still even here it seems a rather paradoxical method of remedying the deficiency, to select a few of the more talented of the younger clergy for pensions of about twice the amount of a curate's average salary. Probably no one at the present day would maintain that it is desirable to draw young men of ability into the service of the Church by giving them this large pecuniary advantage over their colleagues; since the gain to religion of the intellect thus purchased must appear to be very doubtful. The relation of the Church to the Universities is, however, a burning question, which I hardly like to mix up with the present discussion; but perhaps it will be agreed, on dispassionate consideration, that the University owes to the Church the maintenance, by endowment or otherwise, of theological education and learning in as good a condition as possible, rather than a small contribution of money to the incomes of the parochial clergy, however this contribution may be distributed.

There remain the professions of the Bar and Medicine, in which this difficulty of obtaining employment during the early years of the professional career certainly exists, even for men of talent, completely trained and industrious. And if we are considering the actual results obtained by sinecure Fellowships, we may almost neglect Medicine, as not more than one or two per cent of the Fellows of Colleges in Cambridge enter upon this profession. The Fellows, then, who are actually supported in careers from which they would otherwise have been excluded, turn out to be almost entirely barristers. An argument for sinecure Fellowships which finds its only solid basis in the special circumstances of a single profession—entered by not more than sixteen per cent of the Fellows of Colleges, as far as our statistics go—

---

[1] Clerical posts in the University and Colleges rest, of course, on a different footing, and would always receive, as they do at present, their full share of academic endowments.

must be admitted to be in an unstable condition. But we must observe that even of this number only a small fraction represents the real gain of society in the way of additional legal talent through the institution of Fellowships. We have to subtract first the not inconsiderable quota of those whose " call to the bar " does not imply a real vocation for the legal profession; and, secondly, we have to subtract the genuine barristers who would equally have become such if they had been thrown on their own resources or those of their parents, and who, it may be remarked, would perhaps have thrown themselves into their work with more energy and decision if they had had no Fellowships; for it is in many cases a doubtful boon to remove from a young man the stimulus supplied by straitened means or the sense of dependence upon others. But even if we confine our attention to the funds distributed among the small residuum of Fellows who go to the bar to become lawyers, and really do become lawyers, and would not have done so except for their Fellowships, it does not seem after all clear that these funds are wisely bestowed, if we consider the matter from the point of view of society, and not of the fortunate individuals who receive them. In fact, the very reason why they are needed seems also a ground for doubting whether their effect is on the whole beneficial. Why is it difficult to obtain employment at the Bar? Obviously because the profession is so attractive that it is crowded by a throng of able competitors competing eagerly for employment. Why, then, it may fairly be asked, should we spend money in artificially swelling the crowd and increasing the keenness of competition? It will perhaps be answered that, though there may be at present no lack, or even a superfluity, of competitors quite adequate to the ordinary work of advocacy, there is certainly no superabundance of men possessing at once legal attainments and the general intellectual grasp which ought to be combined in the lawyers who reach the highest posts in the judiciary and become the legal advisers of the Crown. A few thousand a year, it may be urged, is a small price to pay for the advantage of having the best ability of the whole nation to choose from in selecting Attorney-Generals, Chancellors, and Chief Justices. That there is some force in this I would not deny: in fact, it seems to me that we have here the one solid grain of argument in all the plausible talk about "supporting young men in their careers." But granting it to be desirable that one or two pensions tenable for a few years should be given away annually to young lawyers of exceptional ability and scanty means, it hardly falls within the province of the University to distribute these pensions. The corporations charged with the supervision of the Bar, who have funds, and lately at least have shown a laudable desire to spend them in promoting the best interests of the legal profession, appear the proper bodies to make this distribution. They are better able than the Universities to say from time to time how far they are needed, and they ought to be better able to secure in the recipients of the pension the special talents and knowledge which it is desirable they should possess. Again, if distributed by them, such pensions need not be exactly sinecures. They could easily be given on condition of performing some light educational duties, so arranged as not to hamper the pensioner in the competition for professional employment, while at the same time they might be an inducement to him to resign his pension when his time began to be fully occupied in ordinary legal work.[1]

But whatever may be the best way of providing for the interests of the Bar, it seems clear that the allotment of £300 a year apiece to all the successful competitors in University examinations, of whom about sixteen per cent go to the Bar, is not a good adaptation of means to this end. And we have seen that in the case of the great majority of Fellows no similar need exists for giving this eleemosynary support after their education is completed. I pass, therefore, to consider the other argument by which these gifts are defended —that, namely, which points to the attractive and stimulative influence which they exercise as prizes for study. This argument, I am aware, appears strong to many; but I must

[1] Similarly, a somewhat ampler remuneration of medical teaching might surely do all that is necessary for the support of talented young physicians.

confess that twenty years' experience of University life has gradually led me to regard it far more unfavourably than the one just discussed. Considered as a means of support after education has been completed, the prize-fellowship has (as we have just seen) a partial justification, though within a very limited range. In a small number of cases it does meet a definite need, and there is at least a probability of its producing a certain amount of gain to the community; and even in the great majority of cases, where there is no such need, we have little ground for attributing to the institution any positively bad effects. There is no reason to believe that the pension drawn from academic endowments by (*e.g.*) a young schoolmaster at Eton or Harrow is spent in any worse way than any other portion of the superfluous wealth of the community. But as a prize by which students may be attracted to the University, and sustained in their industry when there, the Fellowship operates in a manner which must, I think, be pronounced positively pernicious. It places the University in a radically false relation to the community, and seriously impairs its performance of its proper function as a centre of intellectual life. In saying this I do not wish to propose any impracticably high standard as to the spirit in which study ought to be carried on by undergraduates generally; but all will admit that the highest ideal of such study requires that knowledge should be cultivated for its own sake, and that it should be the aim of academic teachers to maintain this ideal as far as possible—that the University should be, as it were, a shrine in which the noble ardour of disinterested curiosity is kept ever burning, and communicated in each generation of students to all who are in any degree capable of receiving it. No one who knows the German universities can doubt that, whatever their defects may be, they do perform satisfactorily this invaluable service to the community: and probably no one who really knows Cambridge would deny that, speaking broadly, she fails in this respect. And the blame of this failure cannot, I think, be fairly thrown, as it sometimes is, on the exclusively practical character of the English people; when we consider the amount of disinterested study that is being carried on all over England, sometimes under the greatest possible disadvantages and by persons who have to earn a livelihood in some laborious trade or profession. It would be more apparently reasonable to throw the blame on the teaching body of the University, and I am not prepared to repudiate the charge altogether. But I would urge those who are disposed to censure us harshly for this failure to reflect how difficult it is to resist the strong perpetual pressure exercised, on the minds of teachers and pupils alike, by this fatal possession of large pecuniary prizes for successful study as tested by examinations. It is almost inevitable that the pursuit of knowledge should be gradually turned into a training for an intellectual wrestling-match. The possibility of gaining such large immediate rewards by examinations naturally concentrates the student's attention on the attainment of the particular kind of knowledge and skill by which this success may best be won. And thus the proper relation of instruction and examination is inverted. Examination, instead of being merely the means of testing the thoroughness with which a subject has been taught and learnt, becomes the end to which teaching and learning are directed, and the standard to which reference is naturally made in determining both the matter to be learnt and the method of learning it. The student feels himself under the necessity of limiting his reading to those subjects and parts of subjects on which questions are likely to be set; he has to check himself from pursuing any interesting inquiry too far, for fear it should occupy an amount of time disproportioned to the amount of 'marks' he may hope to gain by it in examination. His object is not so much to know truth as to be able to write it out rapidly in fragments of a certain size. This species of intellectual discipline has doubtless some advantages; but it must be allowed that, regarded as a means of conveying either actual present knowledge, or the habits of thought and feeling which will lead to the acquisition of knowledge in the future, it is open to very serious objections. There is no kind of study which does not suffer to some extent from being pursued in this frame of mind; at the same time, some subjects are much more liable to deterioration from this cause than others, as the difference between the rational and—if I may coin a word—the *examinational* manner of studying a subject varies very much in different cases. Thus we are led to notice another bad result of the undue influence at present exercised by examinations, which is strongly felt by those who have charge of education at Cambridge — viz. that they are seriously hampered in choosing subjects and framing courses of study by the necessity of adapting them to *examinational* reading and teaching. They cannot merely consider, even in the case of the most intelligent pupils, what would be the most desirable subject of study if the student were supposed to be simply seeking for knowledge or intellectual training: they must assume that their pupils will, speaking generally, read with a view to examinations, and therefore must choose subjects which admit of being examined in satisfactorily.

In saying this I am anxious not to exaggerate either the existing defect or the extent to which it might be expected to be removed by a change in the distribution of endowments. No doubt even now there are many disinterested students at our Universities and not a few teachers, who earnestly foster the impulse towards study for its own sake; but I think any one who knows Cambridge will admit that students and teachers of this class have to set themselves against the general tendency of the system. Again, it must be admitted that the influence of examinations does not depend entirely on the Fellowships: the immediate pleasure of success in an intellectual competition, and the various professional and social advantages that may be expected from it, would in themselves exercise a powerful attractive force on the minds of students generally. Still it is due to the large pecuniary prizes that this influence becomes an almost irresistible control. How can one persuade a poor man not to concentrate his energies on success in a given competition, when the possession of £300 a year for a long term of years may depend upon it? And it is only this overwhelming influence that depresses and demoralises; for up to a certain point the guidance and stimulus of examinations is highly beneficial. But though a good servant, the examination is a bad master; and the prize-fellowships inevitably make it master.

It may be urged that the number of students in whom disinterested curiosity could be made to operate effectively as the sole or chief motive for study form but a small minority of the whole contingent that the country annually sends to Cambridge. It must be remembered, however, that this minority is likely to be found chiefly—though not entirely—among the more gifted and well-trained students: that is, it coincides to a great extent with the equally small class that is directly affected by the competition for Fellowships. But the influence of the tone and spirit in which study is carried on by the intellectual *élite* of any place of education extends, in varying degrees of intensity, far beyond the limits of the class itself. It depends not a little on the system which is brought to bear on these whether the whole generation of students [1] shall receive whatever measure of truly academic culture they are capable of receiving, or whether they shall in after-life look back upon the University (apart from its social advantages) as an institution for giving them a certain amount of intellectual drill. And even if we confine our attention to the *alumni* of the most exclusively practical turn of mind, we shall find that their interests suffer considerably under the present system. For the desire of obtaining a Fellowship is not only not the best possible motive by which to stimulate and direct youthful study: it is out of several alternatives almost the worst. Under its influence the "practical" youth is often led to devote the precious years of his University life to a course of reading which is equally out of relation to his intellectual tastes and needs, and to his professional prospects: he studies in a thoroughly utilitarian spirit what he yet regards

---

[1] I use this term advisedly, as my remarks do not apply to the "residuum" of undergraduates who are in no sense students: which would probably be uninfluenced by any system.

as useless for all purposes, except that of obtaining academic prizes. No doubt the education may turn out to be of more use to him than he anticipates: still it may easily happen that it is not the course of training which his teachers and advisers, any more than himself, would have selected, except for the one decisive consideration that it offers him the only or the surest road to a Fellowship. It may be said that the blame of this rests upon the University, or rather on the corporations of the Colleges, who ought to distribute their Fellowships with more judgment. But the truth is that to all the other forces of academic conservatism, already sufficiently strong, the system of prize-fellowships inevitably adds golden weights, which operate independently of the deliberate choice of any College authorities. Of late years the University of Cambridge has consistently shown the greatest possible liberality and impartiality in offering her *alumni* a free choice among the different branches of learning and science. She has yielded to every proposal that has been supported by names of any weight for the establishment of a new ramification of the curriculum, with new examination, board of studies, selected books, class-list of honours, etc.—in short, with all the apparatus with which the University can commend a department of study to the attention of undergraduates. In this way there are now no less than seven courses of study thus distinguished and recommended, and ranged by the side of the older classical and mathematical courses on a footing of apparent equality. And many at least of the Colleges are sincerely desirous of being equally comprehensive and impartial in the distribution of their rewards; but, as was just said, the present Fellowship system encloses both the electors and the candidates for Fellowships in a sort of vicious circle of old customs, which it requires exceptional independence and enterprise on either side to break through. The College wishes to elect the ablest of the youth that it has trained, whatever course of study they may have adopted: a youth of talent, very likely, would prefer on other grounds to enter for one of the new Triposes; but he is led to choose one of the older lines of study, because he rightly thinks he is more sure of obtaining a Fellowship by distinction in these; and he is more sure of this because the College rightly thinks that the competition in these older lines is more keen, and that there is consequently more security that the men who attain distinction in them will be men of real ability. Each of these opinions is justified, as long as its counterpart is maintained: and accordingly each tends to maintain its counterpart. There is no logical emergence from this circle; and so, generally speaking, it can only be broken down on either side when the undergraduate is prepared to run some risk for the sake of a favourite study, and the College is prepared to accept a somewhat less complete guarantee of ability.

If then we may conclude that it is inexpedient to employ, as a stimulus to the study of undergraduates, a system of pecuniary prizes so large that they inevitably become the end and goal of such study, and determine its nature and direction, it still remains to be considered whether—as is sometimes urged—these prizes are necessary to attract young men to the University. It would need a good deal more evidence than I have ever seen adduced to render this probable; and if it were proved, it would only be more clear that the relations between the University and the country are in need of radical alteration. What parents ought to seek from the University for their sons is knowledge and intellectual training, and not money. Let them be as watchful and exacting as they please in their demands for the former commodity: it is surely desirable that their vigilance, and the efforts of the University, should be as little as possible distracted by the distribution of the latter. I am not now speaking of the case where the one gift is necessary to place the student in a condition to receive the other. Let it be conceded that academic education is a benefit, the communication of which, in certain cases, may be made nearly or quite eleemosynary. Let the endowments be used as liberally as possible in providing support for poor youths of real talent during the whole period of education. This species of alms certainly does not demoralise the recipient; and it seems a gain to the community that he should receive it. But I can hardly acquiesce in regarding academic education as a serious burden, which must be offered along with heavy bribes, if it is to be accepted by able men. If this view be really prevalent, I should hold that there must be something wrong either in the education itself, or in the estimate generally set upon it; and it seems clear that the continuance of the system of bribes is not calculated to remedy either defect.

But I cannot believe that Cambridge would to any important extent diminish the range of its influence, if the prize-fellowships were abolished. I doubt whether even now these rewards occupy a very prominent place in the deliberations of parents who are considering the wisdom of sending their sons to the University. That they have some weight is, of course, undeniable; comparatively few parents could afford to disregard two or three thousand pounds; especially when our educational system tends so much to foster the belief that the most valuable gift that Cambridge has to bestow is money. But if we conceive a reconstructed University, concentrating its attention on its proper function of acquiring the best knowledge on all subjects and imparting it in the best manner, and relying for attraction solely on its excellent performance of this function, I see no reason to believe that its work would not be rated at its true value by the country generally. We are justified, I think, in inferring this from the experience of neighbouring countries on the same level of civilisation as ourselves, who have never felt the need and never entertained the idea of alluring their youth to literary or scientific culture by thus directly connecting it with cash. We might infer it even without looking outside England, from the abundant zeal manifested throughout the country in the case of education generally, and especially of the most advanced portion of it: one evidence of which is furnished by the recent remarkable success of the Cambridge scheme of University extension. And all experience combines to show that the faith of Englishmen in the efficacy of their educational institutions is hardy enough to stand very rude shocks, and generally errs by excess rather than defect. To suppose that even a temporary decrease in the numbers of Cambridge would result from the restoration of her endowments to learning and research seems a most groundless alarm.

XIV

A LECTURE AGAINST LECTURING

(*New Review*, May 1890)

I HAVE for many years held the opinion that the traditional method of academic teaching needs a radical alteration. I have hitherto kept this opinion private, because I found that it was not shared by most of the persons whose experience gave them adequate means of forming a judgment; but as my own experience and reflection have continually strengthened it, I think it now desirable to publish it—giving due warning to the reader that it is a heresy. My object is primarily to obtain sympathy: there may possibly be others who have long been secretly cherishing similar views; and perhaps, if we could communicate and combine, we might at any rate call the attention of persons interested in education to the gravity of the question, and stimulate some kind of movement in the direction of the required change. But I also partly wish to obtain advice: since—except in a very limited part of the whole subject—I seem to see more clearly the general direction in which improvement is needed than the precise nature of the changes of method that should be recommended.

In speaking of "method" I mean simply the way in which instruction is imparted; I am not concerned with the questions (1) where University teaching should be carried on, or (2) what subjects should be selected for study, or (3) how the student's industry should be stimulated and tested. These appear to be the points in which, in England, most University reformers are interested : they are either for having academic centres in large cities, instead of small provincial towns like Oxford and Cambridge ; or they are for modern languages and experimental science as against classics ; or they are opposed to the tyranny of competitive examinations, and the degrading influence of pecuniary bribes to learning. All these are most interesting topics, on which there is much to be said on both sides. But the change that I am now to advocate relates to a much more simple and fundamental question : viz., how, when we have located our teacher, and selected his subjects, and collected a class of intelligent and industrous youth—with or without the stimulus of prospective gain and glory—the instruction should be imparted which the class may be presumed to be fairly eager to acquire.

The answer—or at least the main answer—to this question appears to be thought by most persons so simple as hardly to require a moment's consideration. All that seems to them necessary is that the teacher and the class should be brought together in a room at a certain hour on certain days in the week—varying usually from two to six —and that the teacher should expound his subject in a series of lectures, varying from forty-five to sixty minutes in length. This is the traditional, time-honoured, almost universal practice of University professors, ordinary or extraordinary, in the countries that share European civilisation : it is supported by an overwhelming consensus of opinion and practice, and most persons with whom I have spoken on the subject hardly seem able to conceive it as either needing or admitting fundamental alteration. I do not mean that what I have just described is universally held to constitute the whole of a professor's educational function. In England, at any rate, it is generally thought that academic teaching, to be effective, must include some kind of exercises written by the student and looked over by the teacher, and some kind of oral communication between the two, in the way of question and answer. In Germany, however, the instrument of academic instruction is—in most departments of study, and so far as the majority of students are concerned—simply the lecture; and even in England it is commonly thought to be the main if not the sole educational business of a professor to expound his subject in a course of lectures.

It is this opinion that appears to me radically erroneous. I regard the ordinary expository lecture—in most subjects, and so far as the most intelligent class of students are concerned—as an antiquated survival: a relic of the times before the printing-press was invented; maintained partly by the mere conservatism of habit and the prestige of ancient tradition, partly by the difficulty—which I quite admit—of finding the right substitute for it.

This, then, is the heresy that I have to defend; but before defending it I wish carefully to limit it, in order not to present too broad a front to an orthodox opponent; and I therefore wish to except from condemnation various classes of lectures on various grounds. Thus, I except lectures of which the method is dialectic and not simply expository; and lectures on science or art, in which the exhibition of experiments or specimens forms an essential part of the plan of instruction; and again, lectures on art or literature, so far as they aim at emotional and æsthetic, not purely intellectual, effects; and lectures on any subject whatever that are intended to stimulate interest rather than to convey information. For all these purposes I conceive that the use of lectures will increase rather than diminish as civilisation progresses. Further, I have only in view the *élite* of academic students: the intelligent and industrious youth, who have been trained from childhood in the habit of deriving ideas from books, and are able and willing to apply prolonged labour and concentrated attention to the methodical perusal of books under the direction of their teachers. My remarks have no reference to that large part of the community that has never had the opportunity of acquiring a thorough mastery of the art of reading books; nor do they refer to the class of—so-called—academic students who require the discipline of schoolboys. It may be necessary to drive these latter into lecture-rooms in order to increase the chance of their obtaining the required instruction somehow. I say "increase the chance" because it is by no means certain that young people of this turn of mind will actually drink of the fountain of knowledge, even if they are led to it daily between 10 A.M. and 1 P.M. But the compulsion may, no doubt, increase the chance of their imbibing knowledge, since it is difficult to find amusement during a lecture which will distract one's attention completely from the lecturer; although I have known instances in which the difficulty has been successfully overcome by patient ingenuity.

Leaving, then, out of account exhibitory lectures, dialectic lectures, disciplinary lectures, as well as lectures primarily designed to produce an effect on the emotions, let us confine our attention to the ordinary expository lecture, in which the lecturer's function is merely to impart instruction by reading or saying a series of words that might be written and printed. My view is that this species of lecture, when addressed to students who have duly learnt, and are willing to use, the art of reading books, is, in most cases, an unsuitable and uneconomical employment of the time of the teacher and the class. In giving the arguments for this view I shall first assume that an adequate exposition of the lecturer's subject either is already obtainable in print, or might be provided in this form by the lecturer himself, if it were considered to be his professional duty to provide it. This being granted, it seems to me obvious that the class of students whom I have in view had better obtain the required instruction by reading the print. The student who reads has two capital advantages over the student who listens: he can vary the pace at will, and he can turn back and compare passages; and, according to my experience as a student, these advantages altogether outweigh the counter-advantage of the additional intelligibility which discourse acquires from the inflections of the human voice and the variations of the speaker's emphasis. For in learning anything it seems to me fundamentally important to be able to take in rapidly what is easy or familiar, and pause to reflect as long as one likes on what is novel or difficult. No doubt a competent lecturer will always try to vary the length of his treatment and the fulness of his illustrations in different parts of his subject, according to his conception of their comparative difficulty. But no lecturer can be sufficiently acquainted with the nature and causes of the transient hesitations and perplexities which beset the intellectual progress of any individual mind; and even if his sympathetic insight were ever so keen and subtle, the diversities in previous knowledge and faculty of apprehension which are commonly found among the members of an actual class render it impossible for him to adapt his exposition closely to the intellectual needs of any individual. Besides, the one thing that the lecturer cannot allow is the pause for reflection : he must go on talking.

Nor, again, can a lecturer give anything that corresponds to the advantage of comparison of passages. It is fundamentally important that anyone systematically studying a new subject should keep as clear as possible in his mind the relation of what he is now reading or hearing to what he has read or heard before. But it must continually happen that this relation becomes temporarily obscured : the student feels that he is assumed to remember distinctly something that he only remembers vaguely, and perhaps finds what is now said difficult to reconcile with what has been said before. It is very desirable that this vagueness and difficulty should be at once removed by a reference to the half-remembered statements and arguments; this he who reads can do, but he who listens has to listen on with a perplexed and dubious mind.

It may, perhaps, be said that the listener can perform this process after the lecture is over; he can read over his notes and compare them with books or with the notes of other lectures. This I admit; but then, if a lecture is treated in this way—as something to be taken down at the time and understood afterwards—the advantages of oral exposition are largely lost : the process is nearly reduced to one of mere dictation. For the most intelligent pupil feels that if he does not get down on paper the whole substance of the lecture, he may possibly omit some statement of vital importance for the work of reflection and comparison which he has to postpone.

I remember well the occasion on which the view that I am now expressing first presented itself to me in a clear form, nearly thirty years ago. It was the first time that I attended a lecture—by an eminent professor—in a German university. I went at the hour announced; the small lecture-room gradually filled, becoming even fuller than was quite agreeable in the heats of July; and I waited in expectant curiosity. The eminent man came in, according to custom, punctually at the quarter; he carried in his hand a manuscript yellow with age; he did not seem to look at his audience, but fixing his eyes on his manuscript he began to read it aloud with slow monotonous utterance. I glanced round the room; every pupil that I could see was bending over his notebook, writing as hard as he could. The unfamiliar surroundings and the unfamiliar language stimulated my imagination, and I fancied myself back in a world more than four centuries old, in which it had not yet occurred to Coster or Gutenberg that it would be a convenience to use movable types for the multiplication of copies of MS. I have since listened to many other lectures in German university lecture-rooms, some of which have been admirably delivered; still, the effect of this first experience has never been entirely effaced.

And it is to be observed that so far as the task of a lecturer's class is reduced to a process of multiplication of copies it is a task that might be performed through the medium of a printing-press, not only more economically, but more accurately. It is one more disadvantage of expository lectures as compared with books that they are often not taken down quite correctly. Some important words are misheard, as is very natural when what is written down is imperfectly understood at the time; and the work of subsequent comprehension is thereby needlessly and perhaps seriously confused. I once heard of a man who spent six hours in endeavouring to understand the notes of a lecture that had occupied a single hour! It is true that the lecturer was a bad lecturer, in form and style, but he was not phenomenally bad, nor was the pupil exceptionally unintelligent. Again, I was once told in an Oxford common-room of the sad fortune of a student of philosophy, who had succeeded in reproducing with tolerable fidelity the doctrines of a Transcendentalist metaphysician whose lectures he had been attending, until, in his very last answer, he had occasion to refer several times to the "universal I" which constitutes the centre of the Transcendentalist world. Unluckily he always designated this all-important entity as "universal eye,"—an unauthorised variation which blasted his fair prospects of success. I admit it to be doubtful whether this gentleman would have fathomed the mysteries of Transcendentalism if they had been presented to his eye—I mean his individual eye—instead of his ear; but he would certainly have had a better chance of comprehending them.[1]

My opponents will perhaps reply that all my argument is based on the unwarrantable assumption that what the lecturer has to say—or an adequate substitute for it—is obtainable in print. But, they will say, if the lecturer is worth his salt this will not be the case; he will always have something to say which is not in print and which will yet be important for the student to know, and it will be worth the latter's while to go through some trouble to get this. I do not deny that this is to some extent true; an active-minded man, however many books and papers he may have printed, is likely always to have something to say on a subject on which his thoughts are strenuously at work, which may convey the truth as he sees it more exactly or more comprehensibly than he has yet managed to express it in print. I admit, therefore, that there must

---

[1] I do not vouch for the literal truth of this story—as truth is sometimes mingled with fiction in Oxford—but I have myself had experiences somewhat similar, though less striking.

always be *some* place left for the expository lecture. All I contend is, that the need for it might be very much reduced, and ought to be reduced, by giving every possible encouragement to the teacher to disseminate his doctrine through the medium of the press. My complaint against the existing system is that it has the precisely opposite effect. It gives the utmost inducement to a teacher to keep the most indispensable part of his teaching unpublished. For since law or custom requires him to deliver a certain number of lectures on a given subject, when he has once published a systematic treatise on this subject he finds himself in a dilemma resembling that presented by the Omar of tradition to the Alexandrian Library. What he says in his lecture is either in his book or it is not; if it is there, it is superfluous to say it over again; if it is not there, he cannot regard it as very important unless his views have changed, or some new discovery has been made since he wrote his book. It is easy for him to avoid this dilemma by not printing; and thus—always assuming that what he has to say is of real value—the students elsewhere who cannot go to his lectures are deprived of useful instruction, and the students who do attend them have to receive it in an inconvenient form, in order that the professor may be enabled to fulfil with *éclat* the traditional conception of his functions.

I do not wish to degrade the tone of this discussion by laying stress on sordid pecuniary considerations; but I must mention that I have heard of a professor whose class diminished very markedly after his systematic treatise was published; and it seems obvious that, where there is an active competition among teachers, a man who is conscious of having attracted an audience rather by his matter than by his manner may reasonably fear and avoid this result. And it is surely a serious economic drawback in the organisation of any kind of labour that the labourer has a strong interest in diminishing, or hampering with inconvenient conditions, the utility that he is appointed to render to society.

My conclusion, then, is that it ought to be regarded as the primary duty of an academic teacher, in relation to the class of students for whom advanced teaching is mainly provided, to supply the best possible instruments of self-instruction in the form of printed books or papers. These ought to be partly his own work, if he is worthy of his position; but the extent to which this ought to be the case will vary with circumstances. To the study of this printed matter his oral teaching ought to be frankly and completely subordinate and supplementary.

In saying this I am anxious not to undervalue oral teaching, or to overlook the counterbalancing advantages which the listener's position has as compared with the reader's. I quite admit that oral delivery must be very bad if the inflections of voice and variations of emphasis do not materially add to the intelligibility of the sentences uttered. Also it may be fairly urged that the line which I have tried to draw, between lectures designed to arouse interest and lectures designed to give information, is only partially tenable; since a good lecture will stimulate while informing, more than the same discourse would do if printed, through the effect of personal presence and utterance in stirring intellectual sympathy. I should be disposed to admit this as a general rule, though I think that there are important exceptions. For instance, having heard J. S. Mill speak, I rather doubt whether, if he had delivered his *Liberty* in oral discourses from a professorial chair, their effect would have been as stimulating as the perusal of the book actually was. Still, on the whole, I allow the advantages claimed for oral teaching in both the respects that I have just mentioned; but I venture to think that both the gain in facilitating comprehension and the stimulus through intellectual sympathy would be more effectually secured if the lecture were used as I desire it to be, as frankly secondary and supplementary to the perusal of printed matter. For in this case the lecturer would be free to devote the larger part of his time and labour to the work of explaining over again whatever parts of the subject his hearers had been unable adequately to learn from the printed matter which he had placed in their hands.

The precise nature of the supplementary explanations which would thus constitute the main material of ordinary lectures would differ importantly with different subjects, and probably also with different teachers and different classes. The general principle would have to be applied in somewhat diverse ways to linguistic studies, historical studies, mathematics, and moral sciences; and I feel that it would be presumptuous in me to make detailed suggestions with regard to any subject except moral sciences or philosophy, to which my own practical experience has long been almost entirely confined.

In moral sciences, in their present state of uncertainty and controversy, the student must expect—even after the most careful selection of books for his perusal—to find much that will perplex him in all the earlier stages of his progress. Indeed, I may say that if he does not find this, he is either above or beneath our present consideration; he either does not need oral teaching or is not likely to derive much profit from it. Assuming him to be intelligent enough to feel difficulties, and as yet without the grasp of method necessary for solving them, the chief service that the oral teacher can render is to assist in their solution: first by mildly but firmly pressing the pupil to state his difficulties as clearly as possible; and secondly, by giving his own mind to the task of comprehending and answering them. I think that both parts of this indispensable process are liable to be performed without adequate care. Especially I have found it hard to convince my pupils of the importance, for progress in philosophy, of stating perplexities clearly and precisely. The art that has to be learnt in order to achieve this result has been called the art of "concentrating fog." In the earlier stages of philosophical study, fog is sure to arise from time to time, in the perusal even of the best attainable books; from the obscurity of some statements, or their inconsistency with other statements of the same or other writers, or with the reader's previous beliefs. An intellectual fog, like a physical fog, is very pervasive, and liable rapidly to envelop large portions of a subject even when its original source really lies in a very limited and not very important difficulty. The great thing, therefore, is to concentrate it; and the most effective way of concentrating it is for the student to force himself to state the difficulty on paper. Sometimes, in the mere process of writing it down, the difficulty will disappear like the morning mist, one does not know how; but when this result does not follow, the difficulty has at any rate been brought into the very best condition for being removed by a teacher. And the step gained by such removal of a difficulty, so prepared, is hardly ever lost again.

But though this precise and definite statement of difficulties is always to be recommended, to require it always would be impracticable: the worst confusions and misunderstandings are those of which one is only dimly conscious, in the vague form of a lack of perfect comprehension. A teacher, therefore, while urging precise statement as an ideal to be aimed at, should give ungrudging welcome even to vague and tentative statements of difficulties: he should count it a gain if a pupil will merely tell him that he does not quite understand page 5 of chapter iv., or the second paragraph of page 156. Even if the teacher cannot guess the exact point of the difficulty he will at any rate know on what parts of the subject he should direct his faculty of elucidation. Having thus received all available information as to the intellectual needs of his class, the teacher will be in a position to make his lecture effectively supplementary to the reading of printed matter, by giving a second exposition on the subject, specially framed to fill up the gaps of apprehension left by the first. He must not flatter himself that this second exposition will completely attain his end, but he may hope that the difficulties which remain will not be too extensive to be adequately dealt with in conversation with the students individually after the lecture is over.

This, then, is the practical conclusion to which experience has led me: that in the teaching of philosophy provision should be regularly made for explaining any important argument, if necessary, three times over—first, in books and printed papers which the student is to read in his own room; secondly, in a supplementary lecture, framed in view of written statements of difficulties received from the students; and thirdly, if necessary, in subsequent informal conversation. These three times ought, I think, normally to suffice to make clear to students who are really fit to study the subject anything which the lecturer really understands. A cynic may say that the practical question for a professor of philosophy is more often how to explain what he only half understands to a class of which at least half had better be studying something else. There may be some truth in this; but from the investigation of the new practical problem presented by these conditions the indulgent reader will permit me to recoil.

XV

THE PURSUIT OF CULTURE AS AN IDEAL

[The following paper is part of a lecture delivered in 1897 to the students of the University College of Wales, Aberystwith. The portion omitted here —which discusses more fully the nature of culture and Matthew Arnold's definitions of it—also formed part of a paper read about the same time to the London School of Ethics and Social Philosophy, which has already been published under the title "The Pursuit of Culture," in a collection of essays by Henry Sidgwick, entitled *Practical Ethics* (Swan Sonnenschein, 1897). We the more readily omit this portion here, as the subject is also dealt with in the essay on *The Prophet of Culture*, printed above.—ED.]

WHEN I selected "The Pursuit of Culture" as the subject of my address this evening, it was my desire to choose a topic falling within the range of my habitual thought, which should at the same time have an interest, not for students of moral philosophy alone, but for academic students generally. On the one hand, culture is recognised as a fundamentally important part of the human good that it is the business of practical morality to promote; and the recognition of this has grown during the last generation with the enlargement of our conception of the future of human life to be lived on this earth. The problem of making that life a better thing has become more and more clearly the dominant problem for morality; and in the doubtless imperfect conception we form of this betterment, mental culture—which, according to usage, I shall simply call culture—has an increasingly prominent place. When thoughtful persons ask themselves what social end is served by the luxurious expenditure of the wealthy, the most persuasive answer is that this expenditure is largely indispensable to the promotion of culture. Again, when the same persons ask themselves what of the goods that the rich enjoy, it is really important for human happiness to diffuse among the poorer classes—at any rate after the elementary needs of physical existence are satisfied—the answer again is 'culture.' When, finally, we ask, 'How, then, is this element of human well-being to be adequately promoted and diffused?' an obvious and familiar answer is, 'By founding schools and universities, and keeping them in a condition of full efficiency.' It seems, therefore, to concern us all deeply to obtain as clear a conception as possible of the ideal aim, which we find thus presented from so many different points of view.

. . . .

Since the most essential function of the mind is to think and know, a man of cultivated mind must be concerned for knowledge: but it is not knowledge merely that gives culture. A man may be learned and yet lack culture: for he may be a pedant, and the characteristic of a pedant is that he has knowledge without culture. So again, a load of facts retained in the memory, or a mass of reasonings got up merely for examination—these are not, they do not give culture. It is the love of knowledge, the ardour of scientific curiosity, driving us continually to absorb new facts and ideas, to make them our own and fit them into the living and growing system of our thought; and the trained faculty of doing this, the alert and supple intelligence exercised and continually developed in doing this—it is in these that culture essentially lies. But how to acquire this habit of mind, and to acquire along with it the refinement of sensibility, the trained and developed taste for all manifestations of beauty which no less belongs to culture — this is the practical problem for all who pursue this ideal good: and in a special manner and degree for academic students.

. . . .

And for academic students there is one question of deep interest—Is the specialist a man of culture, even so far as the knowledge-element of culture is concerned? And the

2 A

answer, I think, must be No, so far as he is a mere specialist—so far as his intellectual interests and sympathies are confined within the limits of his specialty. If the root of true culture is in him, he will resist and react against this limiting and cramping of his thought—which yet, as I have said, the progress of science renders in some degree inevitable; and there is nothing that can strengthen and stimulate him more to this noble conflict than the habit of taking delight in the best literature.

It is this intellectual function of literature—to maintain, in spite of the increasing specialisation inevitably forced on us by the growth of knowledge, our intellectual interests and sympathies in due breadth and versatility, while at the same time gratifying and exercising our sense of beauty—it is this that partly justifies the one-sidedness of modern education in respect of the fine arts. This one-sidedness—the fact that we make so little systematic effort, in school and college, to educate the taste and judgment in music, painting, sculpture, architecture—has sometimes been criticised by those who feel strongly the importance for human life of adequately developing the sense of beauty. I am not sure that the criticism can be completely answered; and possibly the twentieth century will set itself to remedy this defect. But there are other considerations, besides the one I have mentioned, which must always give a special prominence to literature in æsthetic education.

First, literature alone of the arts shows us the highest excellence in a kind of productive activity in which we all take some part. We do not only, as the *bourgeois* of comedy puts it, talk prose all our life without knowing it, but when eager to communicate experiences, ideas, and feelings, we talk or write as impressive prose as we can; thus the *technique* of the great artists in words is only a glorified form of a skill that we all seek, and in some humble degree learn to exercise. Perhaps if, in the infancy of civilisation, picture-writing had not passed into hieroglyphics and been lost in the dull symbolism of alphabets, we should now be in the same position in respect to painting; but, as it is, literature is unique in this relation to life. Secondly, literature is the only art in which the greatest works can be at little cost completely presented to the minds of all students everywhere. The products of the genius of Sophocles or Dante are within the reach of the scantiest purse, if only its owner has learnt Greek or Italian; but more or less costly travel is required to bring us similarly face to face with the masterpieces of Greek sculpture or Italian painting. And, finally, literature is, if I may so say, the most *altruistic* of the fine arts. I mean it is an important part of its function to develop the sensibility for other forms of beauty besides its own. I wonder how many of my generation have learnt to love not only the beauties of nature more, but also painting, sculpture, architecture, through the literary genius of John Ruskin.

But here I come upon a fundamental question, which some of you may think I ought to have raised long ago. I have assumed that it is a main aim of a liberal education to impart culture, but it may not unreasonably be asked —Can culture be really taught? We can doubtless acquire knowledge through teaching, but can we acquire the love of knowledge, the ardour for seeing things as they are, which I have assumed to be an essential element of culture? So, again, the *technique* of the fine arts may in some measure be taught; but can we really learn taste for fine works of art, susceptibility to things of beauty? It is rather like the old question of the age of Socrates—Can virtue be taught? And the same answer applies, I believe, in both cases. Virtue can be taught by a teacher who loves virtue, and so can culture, but not otherwise; since, as Goethe sings:—" Speech that is to stir the heart must from the heart have sprung." [1] Experience shows that the love of knowledge and beauty can be communicated through intellectual sympathy: there is a beneficent contagion in the possession of it; but it must be admitted that its acquisition cannot be secured by any formal system of lessons. No

---

[1] [Perhaps *Faust*, i. 191—Doch werdet Ihr nie Herz zu Herzen schaffen,
Wenn es euch nicht von Herzen geht.]

recipe for it can be enclosed in a syllabus, nor can it be tested by the best regulated examinations.

And it has further to be observed that school methods of studying a great writer—with dictionary or glossary, and grammar, and learned notes, and inevitably snail-like progress—are somewhat antagonistic to the realisation of the culture-value of the study. I remember once, when a reformer was advocating the study of native literature in English schools, a friend of mine—himself a lover of books —implored him to abandon the idea. He said—'You will destroy the public schoolboy's last chance of literary culture if you make him hate Shakespeare as he now hates a Greek play.' The paradox, I need hardly say, is not even a half truth; still, there is some truth in it, at least as regards languages other than the vernacular. In many —perhaps most—cases, Sophocles and Virgil will only become instruments of culture after they have ceased to be consciously and prominently instruments for learning foreign grammar and idioms. How to deal with this situation is a difficult question, which it is fortunately not my business now to answer: but from the point of view of culture there is one condition to lay down, and one consolation to offer.

The condition is laid down on behalf of that large and increasing class of students, who are led by the bent of their tastes and faculties, or the requirements of their chosen profession, to make science, not literature, the main object of their academic study; and here I would take science in the widest sense, to include not only mathematical and physical sciences, but moral and political sciences, and history as providing data for the latter. I think it fundamentally important for this class of students that any teaching of languages which is applied to them— whatever language may be chosen—should be carried to the point at which they can read with ease when they leave school; and that it is indefinitely better that they should reach this point in any *one* of the great culture-languages of Europe than that they should be carried half-way to it in two. Unless this is the case, if they are still liable, while reading, to be perplexed in every page by difficulties of grammar, idiom, and vocabulary, they will not be able to use the language at the University—and still less, generally speaking, in after life—either as a means of gaining knowledge (other than philological) or as a source of literary enjoyment. In this case, their chief gain from learning the language will be in the way of intellectual gymnastic—the training in special kinds of observation, discrimination and inference, and in the accurate expression of shades of thought. I do not undervalue this educational gain; but I think the main part of it may be obtained from the study of any one language other than the vernacular, if properly taught; and surely it is a sad pity that this should be the sole gain from the labour of years spent upon a great historic tongue.

I am aware that the condition I am laying down is practically hard to realise in the case of languages so difficult as Latin or Greek; and, therefore, I hasten on to my consolation. It is that for the essential needs of literary culture—for learning to grasp great and subtle thoughts, to share fine emotions, to taste with fulness and delicacy the beautiful expression of both, to follow with ready and versatile sympathy the varied manifestations of man's spiritual life—any one of the great national literatures of which I have spoken, properly studied, would suffice; the travel into other literatures is a luxury, not indispensable, however justly valued. Take English: suppose a man acquainted with the best works of the best writers, from Chaucer to the present time; able to learn what they have to teach, to feel with due discrimination their special beauties and at the same time their limitations, to understand their aims and antecedents and judge their achievements—so far as this can be done without knowing of other literatures more than he can now know through good English translations; suppose him to have the knowledge of history that this would involve, and at the same time to be duly trained by and instructed in science;—surely the pedant who would dispute such a man's claim to culture would only show his own ignorance of that gift. I do not of course say that a lover of literature ought to be content with this: I only offer this indisputable truth as a consolation to anyone who finds his working time absorbed in scientific or professional study before he has got sufficient hold of Latin or Greek or French or German to read it in hours of relaxation. In the house of culture there are many mansions; and to exhaust the lessons and the delights that English literature by itself can offer would take considerably more than the leisure that most busy lives can afford for reading what is not in the newspapers.

One word more before I sit down. So far I have spoken of culture as something to be communicated by teachers or acquired by solitary study. But when men of my age look back on their University life, and ask themselves from what sources they learnt such culture as they did learn, I think that most would give a high place—and some the chief place—to a third educational factor, the converse with fellow-students. Even if we did not learn most from this source, what we so learnt was learnt with most ease and delight; and especially the value of this converse in broadening intellectual interests, and keeping alive the flame of eager desire to know truth and feel beauty, is difficult to over-estimate. Indeed, this always appears to me one great reason why we have Universities at all, as at present organised.

Forty-five years ago a fine intellect, continually engaged in swimming against the stream—John Henry Newman—set before the world an ideal of University education, in which all students, whatever else they learnt, should give the first place to the royal and ruling study of philosophy—universal knowledge of things mundane and divine, sought as its own end, in disregard of all sordid utilities. In defending this ideal, he referred contemptuously to some bygone Edinburgh reviewers who "wish one student of a University to dedicate himself to chemistry, and another to mathematics." "Now," says Newman, "if half-a-dozen systems of education are to go on on the same spot, unity of place is but an accident, and I do not see what is the use of a University at all." We all know how the development of all sciences and studies, and especially the expansion of our ideas of the preparation required for different professions and callings, have inevitably driven English University education to develop in the direction opposed to Newman's view. This has more or less been the case everywhere; but—to my regret I confess—it has been most prominently, the case in the University from which I come. Certainly a Cambridge man must admit that he is bound to find an answer to Newman's question : " What is the use of a University if all that it means is that half-a-dozen "—I might say a dozen—"systems of education are to go on in the same place ? " Why, at any rate, it may be asked, when we are making a new University, should we not—instead of the present local colleges—have a great school of science in one place, a great school of history in another, and so on ?

I was interested to find that Newman had supplied an answer himself in the discourse preceding the one from which I have quoted. " When," he says, " a multitude of young persons, keen, open-hearted, sympathetic, and observant as young persons are, come together and freely mix with each other, they are sure to learn from one another, even if there be no one to teach them ; the conversation of all is a series of lectures to each, and they gain for themselves new ideas and views and fresh matter of thought day by day." That is so, no doubt ; and that is an important part of the reason why " unity of place " is more than an " accident " for the students of diverse courses ; it tends to produce a general breadth of intellectual sympathies and interests among the students which could not otherwise be obtained. I do not mean that this is the sole answer to Newman's question ; for the teachers similarly learn from each other, and of course the separation of studies is nowhere so complete as his caricature supposes. Still this informal mutual education of students will always be an important factor in the work of the University; and it is one on which the thoughts of any academic teacher, conscious of the limitations and defects of his own labours in the service of culture, will always gladly dwell.

This, then, is my last word to the younger part of my audience: that it rests largely with themselves, and with the use they make not only of hours of work but of hours of leisure, to determine whether they will make the gifts of culture their own. And the burden that this lays on them is not a heavy one; it is not—as so many moral precepts necessarily are—an injunction to endure and refrain. It is simply a direction to live, in the fullest manner, those higher modes of mental and social life from which our finest human pleasures most directly and spontaneously spring.

SUPPLEMENT

ALEXIS DE TOCQUEVILLE[1]

(*Macmillan's Magazine*, November 1861)

IN the cluster of great writers who were swept from the world in the fatal year 1859, Alexis de Tocqueville holds a distinguished place. Perhaps there is no foreign author of this century whose works have been received in England with so universal an echo of applause and assent. His first and only complete work—the *Democracy in America*—was, from the nature of its subject, one which especially excited English interest and appealed to English judgment: and the unique and strongly defined position which he occupies, as a political thinker, in France, gives him at once a peculiar value as a teacher for us, and a peculiar claim on our sympathy. He himself ever manifested a more than stranger's interest for England, where, as his correspondence will show, he had many friends: his admiration for our institutions and character was no mere theoretic enthusiasm, but was founded on a close acquaintance and a temperate appreciation of our merits and faults alike : and he attached so much importance to the estimate formed in England of his writings, that in one letter he speaks of her as "almost a second fatherland intellectually." It was only a fit testimony to these close relations, that English voices should join in the tribute of regret paid by his countrymen to his memory.

The recent publication, by M. Gustave de Beaumont, of his friend's remains, has been the signal for some utterances of English feeling. M. de Beaumont's collection has been received, both in France and in England, with an eagerness fully merited. In the case of a man who wrote so little and so carefully as Tocque-

---

[1] *Memoir, Letters, and Remains of Alexis de Tocqueville.* Translated from the French by the translator of *Napoleon's Correspondence with King Joseph*, with large additions. Two vols. Macmillan and Co., Cambridge and London.

ville, the few fragments left behind unpublished are of peculiar value; while the letters that M. de Beaumont has given to the world seem to have been selected and arranged with skill and good taste ; and the short memoir which forms a prelude to the collection is gracefully written, and shows an enlightened appreciation of Tocqueville's character, as well literary as personal.

The faults of the work are chiefly those of omission. In the first place, I think M. de Beaumont's refusal to publish anything that has not received the author's last touches, displays an excessive scrupulousness, an exaggerated sensitiveness for his friend's fame. It is tantalising to learn how large and how valuable a portion of the fruits of Tocqueville's studies is kept from us for this reason. When we read those letters of Tocqueville, in which we are admitted, as it were, into his literary workshop; when we see the eager determination with which he ensures his originality, the laborious patience with which he gathers his ideas one by one in their native soil;—we feel that thoughts so slowly and carefully obtained ought not lightly to be withheld from the world, because they have not been completely arranged and polished. M. de Beaumont himself notices how he "observed much and noted little"; how rarely he found himself mistaken in those original notes ; how rarely he did more than develop them; how frequently they were incorporated verbatim into the substance of the ultimate work. We cannot but regret that these cogent reasons did not induce his editor to modify his rigid resolution.

Nor is the brief memoir prefixed to the collection quite satisfactory. The sketch is flowing and interesting ; the indications of character good as far as they go; the criticisms of Tocqueville's writings just and appropriate. But M. de Beaumont does not show us the man himself at all; he envelops him in a veil of vague phrases and general expressions of praise, which leave no idea behind. He tells us, for instance, that "the striking features of Tocqueville's political life are firmness combined with moderation, and moral greatness combined with ambition." Is not this worthy of Sir Archibald Alison ?

There is another omission, for which, however, no blame is due to M. de Beaumont. The political life of Tocqueville, which began in 1840, and died at the death of French liberty, could necessarily only be sketched with the faintest touches. To have gone into detail with reference to the earlier part would have been, as M. de Beaumont says, to revive antagonisms now buried in a common mourning; while a more definite and obvious restraint compels the curtailing of the more recent letters. This forced imperfection in the picture is strongly felt. For, whether in public life or not, Tocqueville was eminently a politician. His patriotism was no intermittent enthusiasm, no latent fire—it was the guiding principle of his whole life. His sole profession was to devote the rare powers of thought that nature had bestowed on him to his country's service.

Fortunately this omission has been to a great extent supplied in the English translation, recently published, of M. de Beaumont's book. This translation is enriched with several new fragments of correspondence, and some valuable extracts from the journal of Mr. Senior, one of Tocqueville's numerous English friends. Besides filling up the blank we have mentioned, these additions serve another important end; they give us the *talk* of Tocqueville to compare with his writings. Both are marked by exactly the same traits; the same eager activity of mind; the same energetic originality; that rich fertility in epigrams, which is not uncommon among the countrymen of Voltaire, but which in Tocqueville was kept in perfect restraint, so that the pointed phrase always served to make some truth more clear and impressive. Indeed he might himself have adopted a boast of Voltaire's that he quotes, "Madame, je n'ai jamais fait une phrase de ma vie"; so free and natural are his most piquant sayings. That rare faculty of illustration, that fixes in the memory so many isolated passages in his writings, shows even more exuberantly in his conversation; while the rapidity with which his clear and ready mind seized every new fact, to systematise and generalise, contrasts well with the patient soberness of judgment that kept sifting and examining his first conclusions, till it evolved that calm and lucid exposition of causes and effects which his books contain.

The difficulties of translation, in respect of the letters, have been well overcome by the English translator. It is always a bold undertaking to translate French memoirs or correspondence, as the French language is so peculiarly adapted by nature to this kind of composition. And Tocqueville's style is one that brings into play all the resources of his native tongue. The more we examine any of his most careless effusions, the more we are struck with the exactness and subtlety of his expressions: we feel the difficulty of altering any of them without spoiling the sense. It must have cost more trouble than appears on the surface to preserve so much of their character in an English dress.

I have said enough to show my admiration for these letters. Indeed they seem to me to bear comparison in most respects with any similar collection, ancient or modern. They bear testimony to the truth of the old saying, "that politeness is but the best expression of true feeling." The warm affection that breathes in them shows beautifully through the dress of delicate compliment, varied by most genial humour, in which it is clothed. M. de Beaumont observes on "the immense space that friendship occupied in his life." The same fact will strike every reader of the letters. Tocqueville's heart and mind shared the same restless activity. He could not, therefore, be happy without a wide field of personal relations. It was as impossible for him to rest satisfied with that abstract philanthropy, which, absorbed in plans for the general good, neglects individual ties, as it was to assent to the "modern realism" (as he called it), which ignores all individual rights in behalf of the general utility of society. His hatred of this tendency seems to spring from a one-sided experience, and one may feel it exaggerated; but he calls it himself one of his "central opinions," and it was curiously in harmony with many others of his ways of feeling and thinking. Another thing that strikes one in the correspondence is the perfection with which he adapts both matter and style, apparently without effort, to suit correspondents of the most various opinions, and the most various degrees of intellectual culture. A comparison of the two first series of letters in the book, those to his two oldest friends, Louis de Kergorlay and Alexis Stoffels, will afford an excellent example of this. At the same time this happy versatility never involves the sacrifice of the smallest tittle of his individual convictions. A sensitive hatred of insincerity is one of the most marked features of his character. "You know," he writes to M. de Corcelle, "that I set a particular value on your friendship. . . . I have always found that you believed what you said, and felt what you expressed. This alone would have been enough to distinguish you from others." The same sentiment recurs in more than one of his letters. He expresses his general feeling on the point in a letter to Madame Swetchine, —warmly, but with his usual avoidance of exaggeration. "I am not one of those," he writes, "who think all men false and treacherous. Many people are sincere in important affairs and on great occasions, but scarcely any are so in the trifles of every day. Scarcely any exhibit their true feelings, but merely those which they think useful or popular; scarcely any, in ordinary conversation, seek and express their real opinions, instead of searching for what will sound ingenious or clever. This is the kind of sincerity which is rare—particularly, I must say, among women and in drawing-rooms, where even kindness has its artifices." Sincerity, such as he here longs for, was not merely a principle with Tocqueville: it was a necessity. Without it, correspondence would have lost its whole charm for him. There are two or three letters in which he endeavours to smooth away, if possible, the dissent which some opinion of his has evoked. Here we see the eager desire for sympathy combined with the resolution not to modify or disguise his sentiments in the smallest point. In compositions of all kinds, description as well as dissertation, this love of truth is paramount with him. He complains that "people say the ruins of Pæstum stand in the midst of a desert; whereas their site is nothing more than a miserable, badly-cultivated country, decaying like the temples themselves! Men always insist on adorning truth instead of describing it. Even M. de Chateaubriand has painted the real wilderness in false colours." His own *Fortnight in the Wilderness* will interest even those who are sated with pictures of wild life. The fire and vivacity, the susceptible imagination and the keen observation, may be met with elsewhere; but hardly ever controlled by a reason so sober and truthful, or enlightened by such breadth of view.

When, however, in analysing the picture of character which Tocqueville's letters leave upon my mind, I try to seize the ground-colour that gives the tone to the whole, it seems to me to consist in a child-like elevation of feeling. In one passage of the memoir, M. de Beaumont observes that "intellectual superiority would hardly be worth having if the moral feelings and the character were to remain at the ordinary level." This outburst of naïf enthusiasm strikes one as almost comic, in the mouth of an elderly politician; but it suits Tocqueville exactly. The lofty moral ideal, which in the case of so many men shines clearly in youth, and then gradually fades away before the commonplaces of practical life, exercised over Tocqueville a perpetual and harmonious influence. This seems to have been partly due to the delicate balance that he always preserved between reason and feeling. Neither enthusiasm, passion, nor vanity, of all which he had his fair share, ever hindered him from seeing things exactly as they were; and this striking soberness of judgment protected his youthful enthusiasm, and prevented it from being too rudely shaken by a contact with the realities of the world. Consequently, his letters indicate remarkably little development of character, considering the period over which they extend; and what little they do show is very calm and equable.

Nor is there any exaggerated mock-maturity in his youthful wisdom, or forced vivacity in the outbursts of his later years. We see, indeed, that his unbounded ambition—that Promethean fire which is needed to impel the most finely compounded characters into proper action—was calmed gradually into a quieter and more hidden feeling; yet even this ambition had never made him over-estimate the success towards which it strove. He writes at the age of thirty to his most intimate friend: "As I advance in life, I see it more and more from the point of view which I used to fancy belonged to the enthusiasm of early youth, as a thing of very mediocre worth, valuable only as far as one can employ it in doing one's duty in serving men, and in taking one's fit place among them." And, fifteen years later, he writes to M. de Beaumont: "I consoled myself by thinking that, if I had to live this quarter of a century over again, I should not on the whole act very differently. I should try to avoid many trifling errors, and many undoubted follies; but as to the bulk of my ideas, sentiments, and even actions, I should make no change. I also remarked how little alteration there was in my views of men in general during all these years. Much is said about the dreams of youth, and the awaking of mature age. I have not noticed this in myself. I was from the first struck by the vices and weaknesses of mankind; and, as to the good qualities which I then attributed to them, I must say that I still find them much the same." It is truly refreshing to us whose ears are filled with the painful cynicism of premature experience, to find that even now, to some favoured souls, is granted the privilege of perpetual youth.

If any lack of interest should be felt in these letters, it will be, I think, from a cause which is not altogether a defect. There are no shadows, in one sense, in the picture. It is all clear sunshine in Tocqueville's life, both inner and outer. The perfect healthiness of his nature excludes the charm that is sometimes derived from an element of morbidity. But one may also say with truth, that there is a want of depth. Perhaps the most interesting element in the lives of great thinkers is their imperfect utterance of deep truths only half-grasped; their consciousness of enveloping mystery and darkness, into which the light that shines from them throws only dim suggestive rays. We find nothing of this in Tocqueville. "Shallow" and "superficial" are the last epithets that could be applied; and yet we cannot call him profound, either in character or intellect. Earnest as he was in the search after truth, he was destitute of one power, necessary in the pursuit of the highest truth; he could not endure to doubt. M. de Beaumont extracts from his early notes this remarkable passage: "If I were desired to classify human miseries I should do so in this order:—(1) Sickness, (2) Death, (3) Doubt." In respect, therefore, of the deepest interests of humanity he was content to be guided. He was devoutly attached to Romanism; but rather from the felt necessity of having a religion, than from a deliberate conviction in favour of the particular creed. He had acutely observed some of the more particular mutual influences of religions and forms of government; but his remarks on the more general relations of religion to humanity seem to me to constitute the weakest part of his writings. To metaphysics he had a dislike which he frequently shows. He sends M. de Corcelle a copy of Aristotle, with the remark that it is "much too Greek to suit him"; and in the second part of his *Democracy in America* we can detect, here and there, that his acquaintance with philosophy is somewhat superficial. It is no contradiction to this, that Tocqueville displays considerable skill in psychological analysis. He shows the same superiority in everything that depends only or chiefly on individual observation and reflection. His insight was always both keen and wide, his analysis both ingenious and sound; but systematic abstract thought was not to his taste, and he never pursued it with his full energy. We may sum up much by saying that Tocqueville applied to the study of politics a mind that, both in its merits and in its defects, was of the scientific rather than the philosophic kind. We notice in him many traits peculiar to students of physics. Thus, he early chose and always adhered to a special and definite subject of study; his method was purely inductive; he always went straight to the original documents, which formed, as it were, the matter whose laws he was investigating; he wrote down only the results of long and laborious observation; and these results were again rigorously winnowed before they saw the light. "For one book he published," says M. de Beaumont, "he wrote ten." And this is corroborated by the glimpses into his laboratory that his letters from time to time allow. Thus at the outset of his preparation for his last work he says: "I investigate, I experimentalise: I try to grasp the facts more closely than has yet been attempted, and to wring out of them the general truths which they contain." And again, three years later: "I make the utmost efforts to ascertain, from contemporary evidence, what really happened; and often spend great labour in discovering what was ready to my hand. When I have gathered in this toilsome harvest, I retire, as it were, into myself: I examine with extreme care, collate and connect the notions which I have acquired, and simply give the result." As an example of his conscientious labour, I may mention that he learnt the German language at the age of fifty, read several German books, and travelled in Germany for some months, for the sake of obtaining information which he compressed into a few paragraphs of his *Ancien Régime*. While taxing thus the resources of his observation to the utmost, he depended upon it too entirely; his avoidance of other writers on his own subject caused him, as he allows, great waste of power; his treatment of economical questions strikes one often as too empirical and tentative; political economy, when he first wrote, had not taken rank as a true science, and his was not the mind to labour at systematising and correcting a mass of alien generalisations. But, while this diminishes occasionally the intrinsic value of his speculations, it adds to the harmonious freshness of his writings; and, his observation being unerring, his most hasty generalisations are always partially true.

The writings of Tocqueville mark an era in the study of political science. Hitherto writers on this subject have laboured under defects of two different kinds. Their science was only struggling into birth, and their own insight was rarely clear from the mists of partiality. For a long time, it is true, the study of man will lag far behind the study of nature, but Tocqueville's books indicate a transition to a better phase. The pioneers in the van of all sciences will be men rather of a strong imagination than a sober reason; they have need of the former to fight the various obstacles that an unknown country presents. Consequently, their view will be wide and indefinite; their assertions confused, yet violent; they will not be content to trace the development of a few principles out of many, but they will make their own poverty the measure of Nature's variety, and group all the facts they meet with round the few principles they have strongly grasped. Such men are necessary to make the first move in any science, but they must pass away and give place to others. The early Greek physicists, the founders of science, bear, of course, this character. In the study of external nature we have now attained to a learned modesty which smiles at their ignorant rashness; but in the more difficult study of man we are still taught by thinkers who, for hastiness of generalisation and audacity of assertion, may be compared to the well-known Greek philosopher, who held that "all things were made of water."

But what has most hampered political thinkers in all ages is the little free play that has been allowed to their intellects, by passion, prejudice, and interest. These have warped unconsciously the speculations of the nobler souls, and consciously those of the ignobler. Not that the slavery has been complete; but the extraneous influence has fixed in the field of inquiry impassable limits and unassailable posts. Where men have overcome the promptings of selfishness, they have been unable to throw off early beliefs, cramped by the narrowness of a caste: or they have fallen into the equally fatal bondage of a violent reaction from these beliefs. In the latter case, however, where the restraints have been merely negative, where the reason of men has been free to choose anything *except* certain received opinions, the philosophy of politics has always made greater progress. This was the case with the French philosophers who preceded '89. The natural wildness of awakening speculation was enhanced by their negative position, their sweeping antagonism to an effete system. This extravagance, however, will always be gradually corrected, either by the bitter teachings of experience, or less painfully by the progress of science, and the bloodless contests of the pen. The first half-discoverer of a truth is apt to shout out arrogantly his half-discovery; his successor, to equal enthusiasm, joins greater modesty of assertion. Not that the cast-off chimeras fall immediately to the ground; but they are taken up by men of inferior intellect, and with smaller following. In freedom, however, from the defects I have noticed, Tocqueville has outstripped his age, and his works will long remain models both in style and matter. They are not made to strike or startle, but they powerfully absorb the attention and convince the reason. Their excellence often conceals their originality; the perfect arrangement of facts makes the conclusions drawn from them appear to lie on the surface; the ideas are so carefully explained, defined, and disentangled, the arguments are strained so clear, that we are cheated into the belief that we should have thought the same ourselves if we had happened to develop our views on the subject. Thus conviction steals in unawares, and it is only by carefully comparing our views before and after perusal that we find how much we have gained.

Tocqueville may be considered from another point of view as an embodiment of the spirit of the age. As civilisation progresses, unless patriotism decays, the votaries of political science will increase very rapidly in number. Not only will the men think who are thinkers by nature, but the men of action will be forced into the study of first principles. As the barriers between castes are effaced, and national prejudices fade before increasing mutual communication, every honest and sincere patriot will find it more and more impossible to submit, in any degree whatsoever, to political leading-strings. If he is without independence of mind, he will become a disciple; if he possesses it, he will study widely and impartially for himself. In any case he will not be the partisan he would in another age have been. The bent of Tocqueville's mind was eminently practical and patriotic: he did not enter into study so much for the sake of abstract truth as for the sake of his country. He was an aristocrat by birth and sentiment, whose education and experience had enabled him to get rid of aristocratic prejudices without contracting opposite ones. His impressible mind had early conceived a strong enthusiasm for liberty; and his common sense accepted social equality as inevitable. His unique position is due to his clear discrimination between the two—liberty and equality; between the motives for which they are sought, and the results that follow their attainment. He was one of the first to tear the sophism that the tyranny of the majority is freedom, and the sophism that popular election of an omnipotent government constitutes the government of the people. But this article is not the place for an analysis of Tocqueville's writings, and without such an analysis I could not do justice to his opinions on this subject—for the investigation of the mutual relations of liberty and equality occupied the whole of his literary life; it forms the guiding thread of both his books.

Before the time comes for writing the history of the period of Tocqueville's public life, we may hope that a more copious selection from his correspondence will be vouchsafed to the world. The additions, however, in the English collection are of considerable value, especially in following Tocqueville through the troubled years 1848-52. At first sight it seems surprising that Tocqueville did not make more impression as an active politician. It is not, of course, his mere literary pre-eminence that would cause this surprise; but practicality, as I have shown, is one of his chief characteristics as a thinker. Clearness, soberness, and shrewdness, together with breadth and originality of views, form a perfect combination for a statesman. He was, however, always in circumstances unfavourable to the display of his talents; and he had not the egotistic force of character which overcomes unfavourable circumstances. At the outset of his political career, in an interesting correspondence with Count Molé, he displays an exaggerated moral sensitiveness; and his very ambition was of the kind that hampers rather than sustains a man. He was not content that his motives should be elevated and his conduct pure; he desired to excel in purity and elevation. To this overstrained purism we must attribute his remaining in opposition during the years 1840-48. It is true that his disagreement with the Duchatel-Guizot policy was sufficient to justify parliamentary opposition in ordinary times; but a patriot so sober and enlightened as Tocqueville might have discerned the necessity of sacrificing minor differences at that crisis, in the general cause of order and constitutional government. As it was, he attached himself to a composite party, with many of whose heterogeneous elements he must have had far less sympathy than with the ministry. Thus his oratory, far more adapted to exposition than attack, found no scope; his moderation kept him unnoticed among men more bold, more captious, or more unscrupulous than himself: altogether he gained respect rather than influence, and came to be considered rather as a useful adviser than a capable leader.

The Revolution of 1848 came. Tocqueville had predicted a similar event a month before, but he was not deceived as to its factitious nature. The more we examine this "sham Revolution," the more perfect an instance it appears of the irony of history. Never were causes more disproportionate to effects. It was the mere sound of the names "French" and "Revolution" combined that shook the thrones of Europe; the resemblance between the different movements of the year is thoroughly superficial. The cry for social reform at Paris is echoed by a cry for national union at Berlin, a cry for national independence at Pesth and Milan; and this Parisian cry for social reform was steadily repudiated by France. "The nation," says Tocqueville, in a letter to Mr. Grote, "did not wish for a revolution, much less for a republic." And he argues "That the whole of the year 1848 has been one long and painful effort on the part of the nation to recover what it was robbed of by the surprise of February." He shows that it was only by a decision and rapidity of action worthy of a better cause that the house of Orleans contrived to lose the throne. The monarchy yielded to an *émeute* far less formidable than that which the feeble and ephemeral Provisional Government quelled in June. Tocqueville describes, from his own experience, how an hour's delay might have saved it.

With a heavy heart, but with undiminished zeal, Tocqueville addressed himself to the task of supporting the Republic. Grieved and disgusted as he was with the Revolution and the follies of the Provisional Government, he saw in the Republic the last chance of constitutional freedom. He was not slow in estimating how fatal a wound the frenzy of a day had inflicted on the country. The revolution, executed in the name of the

masses, had stirred among those masses only a feeling of dull
distrust and languid fear, hardly chequered by a little vague hope
and curiosity. Had the Provisional Government had any real
work to do, any desired social improvement to effect, it might
have regained public confidence. But, as it was unable at all to
counterbalance the necessary evils of a revolution, while it showed
marked incompetence in the ordinary business of administration,
affairs grew daily worse. The peasant proprietors of France,
to whom appeal had to be made, have the ordinary characteristics of their class. They are well-meaning and intelligent, but
selfish and narrow: very shrewd on all matters within their
ken, very ignorant upon all without: entirely absorbed in their
individual struggle for prosperity, and desiring peace, order,
stability, above all other goods. They had never appreciated the
advantages of government by parties; before the close of 1848
they were decidedly prejudiced against it, and longing to repose
on one strong arm. Such were the men to whom universal
suffrage confided the fate of France.

It is melancholy to follow, under Tocqueville's guidance, the
details of the long death-struggle of French freedom. He had
the pain of seeing clearly the present and future evils, while
totally unable to heal the one or prevent the other. Even had
he possessed more influence, his peculiar talents were hardly
fitted for such troublous times; he would always have shrunk
from the slightest violation of forms, though hampered by one
of the worst constitutions ever framed, and face to face with an
unscrupulous foe. In truth, the struggle was most unequal. On
the one side were the *débris* of old parties, disunited by long
habit, disorganised by the entire change in their position, stunned
by the rapid succession of political shocks, confused by the working of their new constitution, vacillating between the desire to
deal fairly with their President and the desire to protect themselves from his attacks, distrustful of each other and distrusted
by the nation. To the uncertain and inconsequent action of this
heterogeneous body, Louis Napoleon opposed an egotism pure
and simple, a calm and complete self-confidence, chequered by no
doubts and hampered by no scruples. The constitution brought
him into continual collisions with the Assembly, in which he had
all the advantage given by singleness of will and purpose. The
patience and dissimulation which his exile had sufficiently taught
him were all he required for the development. He had but to
profess the profoundest unselfishness, and seize every opportunity
for self-aggrandisement: he could thus, while gradually con-
solidating his own power, and bringing the Assembly into con-

tempt, contrive always to be or appear in the right. Perhaps the greatest blot in his selfish policy was the dismissal in October 1849 of the ministry in which Tocqueville held a portfolio. The step was necessary for his ends; but it was impossible to find a plausible excuse for it. The ministry had passed successfully through a period of great difficulty; and, as Tocqueville says, there was actually a danger of constitutional government again becoming popular. Imperialist writers tell us that "the elected one responded to the national wish that he should have more freedom of action"—a reason at once felicitous and frank.

At length Tocqueville's worst expectations were realised by the 2nd of December. He was at his post in the National Assembly on that day; and from a letter he wrote to *The Times* soon after (republished in the English edition), supplemented by his conversations, we get a vivid idea of those memorable scenes. The noble indignation he expresses in the letter at that signal outrage to law and liberty was shared by many; but there were few who mourned its effects so deeply and so long. He complains affectingly in his later letters of the state of moral isolation in which he finds himself: that his contemporaries have ceased to care for what he still loves passionately: that they solace themselves for its loss with tranquillity and material comfort, while he is destitute even of sympathy in his sadness—sympathy, which was to him almost a necessity of life. It moved him especially to see the coldness with which England, the nurse of liberty, looked on the enslavement of France: the arrogant contempt of his countrymen, as though unworthy to be free, or even happier as slaves: the selfish indifference at the tyranny, followed in a year or two by blind approval and applause of the tyrant. "Et tu, Brute," is the tone of several of Tocqueville's later letters to England.

Reduced to political inaction, Tocqueville adopted the only method left him of serving his country. He chose a period of the past, fraught with instruction for the present, and devoted to its study all the powers of his ripened intellect. The result of this work, the volume on *L'Ancien Régime*, is but a fragment; yet it shows a decided improvement on his former book, both in style and matter, and is equally likely to have an enduring reputation. From the midst of this work he was snatched away by a sudden illness, in the spring of 1859. He left behind him, besides his writings, an example bright in itself, and especially valuable to the present generation—the example of one who combined the merits of the man of thought and the man of action;

of one who, possessing all the graces and refinements of modern civilisation, its enlarged knowledge, its enlightened moderation, its universal tolerant philanthropy, yet fashioned his life according to an ideal with mediæval constancy and singleness of purpose, and displayed a passionate patriotism and an ardent love of freedom worthy of a hero of antiquity.

NOTE ON BENTHAM'S *DEONTOLOGY*

A footnote to page 168, end of first paragraph.

[In the preface to the third edition of his *Outlines of the History of Ethics*, published in 1892, Professor Sidgwick says: "I have . . . changed my opinion on a point of some importance in the history of Utilitarianism : I am now disposed to accept the posthumously published *Deontology* of Bentham, as giving a generally trustworthy account of his view as to the relation of Virtue to the virtuous agent's Happiness." And on p. 244 of the same work he says: "In the *Deontology* . . . it is distinctly assumed that, in actual human life as empirically known, the conduct most conducive to general happiness *always* coincides with that which conduces most to the happiness of the agent; and that 'vice may be defined as a miscalculation of chances' from a purely mundane point of view. And it seems probable that this must be accepted as Bentham's real doctrine, in his later days; since he certainly held that the 'constantly proper end of action on the part of every individual at the moment of action is his real greatest happiness from that moment to the end of life,' without retracting his unqualified acceptance of the 'greatest happiness of the greatest number' as a 'plain but true standard for whatever is right and wrong in the field of morals' (see Bentham's *Works*, vol. x. (*Life*), pp. 560, 561, and 79); and the assumption just mentioned is required to reconcile these two convictions, if the empirical basis on which his whole reasoning proceeds is maintained."—ED.]

THE END